FRONTIER CAPITALIST

The Life of John Evans

FRONTIER CAPITALIST

The Life of John Evans

by

HARRY E. KELSEY, Jr.

Published by the

State Historical Society of Colorado

and the Pruett Publishing Company

Library of Congress Catalogue Card Number 68-55240

Copyright © 1969 by Harry Edwards Kelsey, Jr.

Printed in the United States of America

For my father and mother

Contents

Illustrations

Preface

Born on the Ohio frontier just after the War of 1812, John Evans spent most of his adult life in the emerging communities of the West. Combining a religious commitment to the betterment of society with an ambition to succeed in public life, Evans very early became active in the fields of education, medicine, and speculative investment. He was already a rich man before he came West as governor of the fledgling Territory of Colorado. Nearly fifty years old but possessed of boundless energy, he turned his talents to railroad building and politics. By the time of his death in 1897, John Evans was recognized by his fellow citizens as one of the leading men in Colorado. Yet those who write history have not been sympathetic to him.

Many historians still cling with a death grip to the classic stereotype of the nineteenth century American capitalist—a ruthless, hardbitten entrepreneur, manipulating church and state, men and money to advance his schemes for wealth. John Evans has frequently been interpreted in this light, for his activities have usually been recounted from the viewpoint of those on the opposite side of the fence in business and politics. A careful examination of the record seems to justify a more favorable view of his endeavors and accomplishments.

A strong humanitarian bent inherited from his parents led the restless Ohio farm boy to choose a career in medicine. At the age of twenty, with little formal education, John Evans began medical training and earned an M.D. from one of the best schools in the country, the College of Medicine at Cincinnati. He then married and moved to Indiana, was converted to Methodism, and with a few colleagues and coreligionists began to insist on state support of an institution to care for the insane. Public recognition of his work in this field brought him an appointment to the faculty of Rush Medical College in Chicago, where he earned a substantial reputation as a physician and an educator.

A few small investments in Chicago real estate soon began to pay handsome dividends, and by the time he was forty, Evans was no longer dependent on his medical practice or his college salary for a livelihood. His interests then turned to other fields. He was one of the principal founders of Northwestern University, and he worked effectively in raising the standards of public education in Chicago. After holding minor political offices in Illinois, Evans was able to secure appointment as governor of Colorado Territory.

His impressive performance as a territorial chief executive was overshadowed by criticism of his handling of Indian relations, and he was forced to resign the governorship after three years in office. He remained active as one of the leaders of the Colorado statehood movement, however, and continued to be an important figure in the Colorado Republican Party for the rest of his life.

The undeveloped territory was a challenge to Evans' business instincts. He organized and successfully built three major railroads in the state, including one that eventually linked Colorado with the Gulf of Mexico. Other profitable investments helped establish his position as one of the wealthiest and most influential men in the region.

Still interested in religion and education, he helped to found the University of Denver and was very active in Methodist church affairs. A continuing interest in civic improvement made John Evans an early leader on the Denver Board of Trade, the movement for better streets and parks, the United Charities of Denver, and other similar activities.

His death in 1897 was an occasion for statewide mourning. His body lay in state in the rotunda of the Capitol, and most of Colorado's social, political, and religious leaders attended the funeral.

A special acknowledgment is due to the many people who helped me gather material for this book. Dolores C. Renze, state archivist of Colorado, and her former deputy, George Warren, gave me complete access to the John Evans Collection while it was housed in the Colorado State Archives. Mrs. Alys Freeze and her staff in the Denver Public Library Western History Department provided a great deal of assistance in tracking down obscure sources. Miss Lucile Fry, former librarian of the University of Colorado Western Historical Collections, also rendered invaluable aid. Mrs. Laura A. Ekstrom, formerly of the State Historical Society of Colorado, was particularly helpful in locating photographs and newspaper references.

Dr. Robert D. Clark, then dean of the College of Liberal Arts of the University of Oregon, allowed me the use of his notes on Bishop Matthew Simpson and answered a number of questions regarding the relationship between Evans and Simpson. Miss Florence Stewart, archivist emeritus at Northwestern University, located much significant material on the Evanston period. Mrs. Ruth Cibulka Gilbert of the Chicago Historical Society helped clarify many of Evans' business activities in Chicago. Miss Caroline Dunn, librarian of the Indiana Historical Society, supplied many suggestions for the documentation of Evans' role in Indiana politics. Mr. Willard Heiss, director of Indiana Quaker Records, first called my attention to the uncatalogued David Evans Papers. Mr. and Mrs. W. B. Wetherill, librarians of the Nebraska Methodist Historical Society, assisted me in locating references to Oreapolis, Nebraska, in Methodist records; and Donald Danker, former state historian of Nebraska, guided me to other material related to the Oreapolis venture. Dr. Harold H. Dunham of the University of Denver read the manuscript and corrected many intemperate judgments.

Probably the greatest debt is owed to the late Edgar C. McMechen, who began organizing the John Evans Collection of the State Historical Society of Colorado, and who wrote the first extensive biography of Evans. Through interviews with friends and members of the family, McMechen was able to gain insights into the character of John Evans to a degree that is not now possible. His *Life of Governor Evans* was an invaluable source of information in compiling this biography.

Harry Kelsey

LANSING, MICHIGAN

xiv

1

"Arise and Flee"

His name was Zachariah Dicks, and he was said to have the gift of prophecy. He came to the Quaker settlement on Bush River in South Carolina at the opening of the nineteenth century and warned the prosperous farmers that they courted disaster by tolerating slavery. American Negroes, he said, would soon turn on those who kept them in bondage.[1]

"Arise and flee," shouted the Quaker prophet, "for this land should be overthrown and wasted, and blood should flow as a mighty river, and a wail should be heard therein." He warned the good people that "the cry of the downtrodden" had "come up before the Lord," who would soon "manifest his mighty power for their deliverance."[2]

"Disgusted with slavery,"[3] a number of settlers from the Bush River Monthly Meeting had moved to the Little Miami River in southern Ohio a few years earlier, in 1799,[4] and now a general exodus to Ohio began.[5] Good Carolina farm land, valued at ten to twenty dollars an acre, often went begging at six.[6] But land was cheap in Ohio, and the God-fearing Quakers took whatever price they could get. By 1808 hardly a Friend could be found on Bush River.[7] Among the first to leave was the family of Benjamin and Hannah Evans.[8]

Benjamin Evans had moved from Pennsylvania[9] to the

Quaker settlement on Bush River. He learned the trade of toolmaker and opened a shop in Newberry where he and his brother Owen manufactured screw-augers and shipped them to Charleston for distribution. Some say the brothers invented the device, but the record is not clear. Other Newberry craftsmen learned the technique, and Newberry remained a center of auger-making for years after the Evans brothers left.[10]

In 1790, when he was thirty years old, Benjamin married a Quaker girl, Hannah Smith. The Society would not tolerate mixed marriages, so Benjamin Evans left the Episcopal church to join the Society of Friends.[11] A son, Thomas, was born the next year, followed by David in 1793. A daughter and two more sons were born in the next decade.[12] Although Benjamin's business prospered,[13] he sold out in 1803 and took his family to a new Quaker settlement at Waynesville, Ohio.[14]

Some ten years later, on a visit to Middletown, in Butler County, Ohio, young David Evans met an attractive Quaker girl named Rachel Burnet. Brownsville, Pennsylvania, was Rachel's original home, but in 1803, after the death of her parents, Rachel moved to Ohio and made her home with her Grandmother Vail.[15] In the spring of 1813, when David Evans was nineteen and Rachel Burnet eighteen, he courted the girl and finally proposed marriage.[16] The simple Quaker marriage ceremony followed on June 2, 1813, in the Friends' White Brick Meeting House in Waynesville, the first wedding in the new structure.[17] The young couple began their married life in a new log cabin[18] located on a small farm about two miles from that of Benjamin Evans, and two miles from Waynesville.[19] In this cabin, on March 9, 1814, their first child was born. He was a boy, and they named him John.[20]

David very quickly became dissatisfied with the meager income from his farm, and he began to work in his father's auger shop, continuing to farm on the side. Soon David opened a general store in Waynesville, but he still continued his tool-making and farming interests, at least for a time.[21] In

The Friends White Brick Meeting House,
built in 1811, is still in use.

*In 1837 young John's father David Evans
moved the family to this house
in Waynesville, Ohio.*

1815, with Rachel expecting a second child, the family built and moved to a larger cabin on their farm. A second son, Joel, was born there on January 23, 1816. David Evans' combined farming and business interests evidently prospered, and in 1817, by the time a third child was due, the Evans family was building a new brick house on the farm.[22] Two more sons—Evan, July 1, 1820; and Owen, August 17, 1821 —were born in the new house. Nevertheless, these were sad years for the Evans family; Evan died in October, shortly after Owen's birth; and Owen died in January, 1823.[23] Six other children, more resistant to infant maladies, were born in the brick farmhouse, and the family home became too small. Since David's store and other business interests in Waynesville required more and more of his time, he constructed a new house in town, and the family moved there in 1837.[24]

David Evans invested heavily in real estate, particularly in land surrounding his Warren County farm. According to one family story, David's ambition was to purchase "all the land that joins us."[25] Among the local farmers David's business acumen was highly regarded, and in later years he spent a good part of his time as a guardian of minor children and as an executor or administrator of estates.[26]

By the 1830's Waynesville was a booming frontier community, with several distilleries, a "brick mill" belonging to John's uncle Jason Evans,[27] the David Evans general store, the Evans auger-making shop, and the Cook and Evans flour mill in which Jason was a partner.[28] The town boasted two resident physicians.[29]

Sober-minded Friends sniffed the distillery fumes and declared it was no wonder the town had more than its share of "drunken loafers."[30] Rachel Evans, so one story goes, often stationed herself in front of the town saloon, singing hymns and waiting to follow a wobbly customer home, where the poor man's family looked on while she proceeded to "pray fervently for his redemption."[31]

The Evans children attended school in a log building at one

corner of their father's farm, perhaps in one of the log cabins in which the family first lived. In all likelihood the other children in the neighborhood also came. John later recalled that he had only "one or two different teachers" at this school, which probably meant an attendance of three or four years.[32]

A nearby Quaker school probably paralleled the one on the Evans farm. The West Branch School was opened January 13, 1806, with the local minister, William Neall, as teacher. Parents of the children subscribed to a fund for the teacher's salary of eighteen dollars, payable "in cash, corn or pork at the market price." In return, Neall agreed to hold school for three months—which was about the average length of a school year at that time—and to teach the children "to reade, Rite and Sipher to the best of his knowledge." As added recompense, Neall received board for himself and keep for his horse while school was in session.[33]

Most of the schools in the area were held in vacant log cabins or in meetinghouses. Both the seats and the writing tables were of rough-sawn lumber. A dim light filtered through oiled paper pasted over the transverse windows. All classes met in the same room. About half of the school day was spent in recitation by separate grades, and the other half was taken up by reading or spelling exercises in which the entire student body participated. Although the quality of instruction was not usually high, at least one teacher in the West Branch school was able to write Latin selections for the older students to copy.[34]

Itinerant lecturers helped to supplement the brief period of formal education. C. P. Bronson, who was one of the most popular speakers of the region, so charmed the young people with his system of elocution that they organized a "Bronsonian Society."[35] First called the Franklin Society, it was then reorganized as the Waynesville Literary Club. Bronson gave lectures and demonstrations of his system, and in addition published a chart with woodcut illustrations of appropriate

*"Scorn," as illustrated
in Bronson's elocution booklet.*

gestures, stances, and facial expressions. In Waynesville, at least, these charts found a ready market at fifty cents per copy.[36] John Evans and his close friend and cousin, Benjamin, frequently took long walks in the woods to find the necessary privacy for memorizing their "pieces of Bronsonizing."[37] But the club seems to have depended as much on John Evans as on C. P. Bronson, since the Waynesville Literary Club expired as soon as John left for college.[38]

For recreation, in good weather, the boys liked to wander through the woods, swim, and perhaps hunt or fish.[39] Almost any diversion was a welcome relief from the hard work John and his brothers were required to do on the farm, in the store, or in the auger-making shop. None of the work appealed to John, and more than a half century later he told an interviewer: "As a boy, as near as I can recollect, I was lazy."[40]

Bored and restless, in August, 1834, John prevailed on his father to send him to an "Academy" at Richmond, Indiana.[41] The school was not his first choice, but his family belonged

7

to the Hicksite Branch of the Society of Friends,[42] and attending the Hicksite school in Richmond was the only clear alternative.

Two frame buildings, each sixty feet long and forty feet wide, near the corner of Ft. Wayne Avenue and Franklin Street,[43] housed the primary department as well as the advanced students. Enrollment was small, for each department fit comfortably into a single room. In a letter to his cousin Benjamin, John wrote that there were "eight young men" in the advanced division. He spoke of these older students as "large schollars, mathematicians, grammarians, &c." Studies included "Algebra, Euclid, Geography, and Dictionary,"[44] and constituted a sort of college preparatory course.

After classes were over, Richmond had its diversions for the students. A local "belle," John told a friend, "comes nearest taking my attention of any person I have met with." A girl of many charms, she was pleasant and comely and possessed a maidenly "*virtue*."[45] As might be expected, a rival had already appeared on the scene. Surely, John thought, she was "worthy of a better husband,"[46] perhaps himself. Mail delivery was a chancy thing in the thirties, and experience proved conclusively that intimate thoughts were better unexpressed. "If I understood Latin," John observed, "I could write more about this, but I do not and am lost thereby."[47]

Both cousin Benjamin and brother Joel, who also worked in the store, were invited to join young Evans at Richmond. Joel probably did not, but it is possible that Benjamin did, since he was able to qualify for a leading medical school a year later, in November, 1835.[48]

David Evans did not share his son's enthusiasm for higher education, and he resisted the young man's requests for financial aid. When the Richmond school term was finished, John reluctantly returned home to work again on his father's farm.[49] The future in Waynesville seemed unattractive, and he was determined to continue his schooling.

2

"Tu et Ego Erimus Medici"

Doctors Isaac and Elias Fisher, father and son, shared a prosperous medical practice in Waynesville. Impressed by the professional dedication of the Fishers, both John and Ben Evans decided to attend medical school and become practicing physicians.[1-2] Although Benjamin encountered no serious opposition, John and his father argued bitterly through an otherwise dull Waynesville summer. Then, just when everything seemed hopeless, a compromise was reached. John and his cousin Noah Haines would attend Gwynedd Boarding School in Montgomery County, Pennsylvania, where distant relatives could watch their progress.[3] If his father thought John had abandoned his intention to become a doctor, he was destined for quick disillusionment. The son obviously considered Gwynedd nothing but a temporary delay on the road to medical school.[4]

On the first of November, 1835, after a few days of hasty preparation, the two young men left Waynesville for the trip to Gwynedd.[5] Cousin Benjamin Evans, who had decided to attend the highly-regarded Transylvania University medical school at Lexington, Kentucky, accompanied them part of the way. David Evans and his employee, John Suber, went with them as far as Cincinnati, about a day's journey from Waynes-

*Located on the Ohio River,
Cincinnati was a thriving community in 1836.*

ville.[6] A short distance from Cincinnati, Benjamin Evans left the group where the road to Lexington turned off. Except for the fact that John Suber disappeared with ten or fifteen dollars, the trip was uneventful. After a night in Cincinnati, John and Noah paid the eight-dollar fare and boarded the steamboat *Clinton*, bound for Wheeling, Virginia. As luck would have it, the boat grounded on a sand bar before reaching Wheeling, forcing the two to change their plans.

A mail coach took them to Frederick, at that time the western terminus of the Baltimore and Ohio Railroad.[7] Never having been farther from home than Richmond, Indiana, young Evans found the trip through the November countryside delightful, "the most transcendant scenery I ever saw, or in fact ever heard described." Everything was new and strange.

> Near Cumberland up Wills Creek bottom the mountains are very grand, rocks to an amazing height, interspersed with green cedars, and just before we came to Fredericktown we had the reverse of the above, that was, a beautiful fertile valley to a great extent bordered on each side by a high mountain, and the valley extended to the Potomac river. This served to cheer our then drooping spirits, for we slept little in the stage on account of the jolts and fear of upsetting. We next got on a railroad car and travelled until midnight to Baltimore, and though it was night and cold, I stood on the outside to look at the country a great part of the time.[8]

Baltimore prices seemed outrageous. A night's lodging was fifty cents, but the next day's boat trip across Chesapeake Bay made it seem worthwhile. To a boy from the Ohio frontier, it was "the largest water I have ever seen."[9] A train took them overland to the Delaware River. "When we came to frenchtown at the head of the bay we got into some great waggons they called rail-road carrs and we went fast enough for a while 16 miles in 50 minutes the fastest travelling I ever done on land yes or any how else."[10]

Another boat brought them to Philadelphia, where they stayed for several days. Well-dressed citizens and carefully-

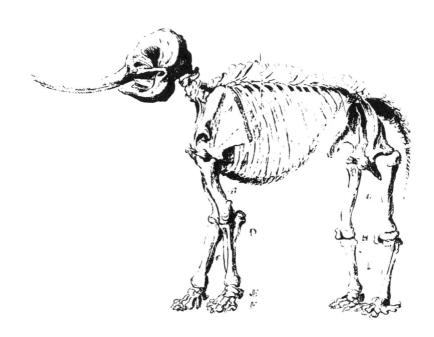

John Evans was much impressed with the "mammoths skeliton" at Peale's Museum.

tended public parks gave Philadelphia a cosmopolitan air. "The prettiest walks art can contrive were open for our rambles."[11] Peale's Museum took half a day, with its "mammoths skeliton" and other "natural curiosities." Evans left there with reluctance, for it "would take more days than one" to do justice to the place.[12]

Other enticements put his Quaker principles to the test. A play at the Chestnut Street Theater was reputed to be "the best on the continent." The first performance seemed to call for a second, and on the next evening, Evans and Haines "were again found listening to the pure excellent eloquence of the stage."[13] There were "comic songs, farces &c," as well as a few "pretty girls flirting around so as to show their legs high up."[14] This was strong medicine for Ohio farm boys.

Cousin Benjamin, with daring exploits of his own to report, pretended shocked amazement. "A pretty Quaker indeed! Go to a theater *two times*! . . . I am almost at a stand whether to send word to *David*."[15] To which a chastened John Evans replied: "Say nothing about it, I do not expect to go anymore. It spoils any body's studies."[16]

The return to the classroom was intellectually stimulating. Evans found at Gwynedd that he "would rather read philosophy than eat peach pie." Geometry was a revelation,[17] but Benjamin's enthusiastic letters from Transylvania University strengthened his resolve to make medicine his career. The distance between Gwynedd and Waynesville made parental opposition seem less important than it had before.[18]

Early in December, John wrote his father that he was still determined to become a doctor.[19] His letter and a series of replies were lost or delayed in the mail, so that father and son had a cold and bitter exchange before the matter ended. His own innate good nature and a gently reproving note from his mother finally restored John's sense of propriety.[20] He wrote again to David begging not to be sent "back into the old store to loll on the counter." He wanted desperately to be a doctor, but he told his father: "Thy word is sovereign and I hope to be dutiful."[21] Finally the matter was settled. John could study medicine, but at his own expense. David would lend the money, but with no special consideration.[22]

Gwynedd Boarding School proved to be a great disappointment to Evans and Haines. The enrollment was very small— only seven students, including Evans and Haines. The Quaker headmaster was a man of little learning. The course of instruction was limited, and the quality of his teaching was not high.[23] Gwynedd was a disillusioning experience, and it seems to have shaken young Evans' faith in the Quaker religion. To cousin Ben he confessed: "I am almost no Quaker."[24]

13

On New Year's Day, 1836, Evans and Haines left Gwynedd, giving as their excuse to the headmaster the fact that Gwynedd did not offer Latin.[25] They enrolled in Clermont Academy, a school about two miles from the Philadelphia city limits on the road to Frankfort.[26] Clermont had about sixty or sixty-five students and four faculty members, under the direction of Professor Samuel Griscom. The courses offered included mathematics, Latin, Greek, German, Spanish, French, chemistry, and music. There were about two thousand volumes in the library, and the scientific laboratory housed the "air pump, electrifying machines and such things as appertain to them." This equipment had "not cost less than a thousand dollars at a rough guess." Tuition was forty dollars per quarter, and each teacher received a five- or ten-dollar share of the fee.[27] Evans and Haines shared a room on the third floor of Mrs. Rickey's boarding house[28] and paid twenty dollars each month for room and board.[29]

With expenses mounting, Evans and Haines bought some of the paper money issued by the Miami Exporting Company, paying $10.00 in cash for $150 in banknotes.[30] The company had a solid reputation in Ohio, and the money was traded regularly there at par.[31] The only question was whether or not the bills were genuine. "If it is good it will help us," Evans wrote to Benjamin. "If not we are sucked; so goes speculation."[32]

Philadelphia girls had a certain charm that Evans found hard to resist. "I have fallen in love with several girls," he wrote once, and "hope some of them will fall in with me."[33] On another occasion he said: "I have a notion to swear myself bachelor for life." The thought was sobering. "No ther is Mary—and Miss Jane Eliza &c."[34] He also kept in touch with the girls back home. One father, disturbed by the idea of a doctor son-in-law, intercepted the letters and forbade further correspondence. Nothing daunted, Evans sent his next note to her brother-in-law for personal delivery.[35]

14

Another young lady was the object of much attention until Evans discovered she had been married once and was just recently a widow.[36] Greatly embarrassed by the whole affair, Evans wrote his cousin to "say no more about that love scrape."[37] But it was not that simple. Ben offered one of his old girl friends in trade. "The minute you become acquainted with her you will forget Miss L or I suppose I must say Mrs. L."[38]

Moved perhaps by the anti-Catholic propaganda that flooded Ohio in the thirties,[39] John visited a Catholic church in Philadelphia to see what the fuss was all about. He found the service "a most splendid sight," and the music was excellent. "There is the crucifix before which they all bow and the priest says Mass in Latin bowing to the image placed on a cross. He has a shield on his back with a gold cross on it everything gold in crosses."[40] But the ceremony was strange, "more like mockery than worship." It was "nearly as much of a sight as the theatre," but since Catholics practiced "idol worship," a good Christian could hardly take it seriously.[41]

In spite of the distractions, Evans enjoyed the challenge of his new studies, particularly Latin and chemistry,[42] both of which were prerequisites for medical school. In addition, he and fifteen other Ohio men at Clermont organized a debating society. As the most accomplished speaker, Evans was elected president of the group, and he served as judge at the semi-weekly debates.[43]

A Philadelphia friend took him to visit classes at the University of Pennsylvania Medical School. Here he saw for the first time a human body being dissected in an anatomy class. Here also he attended at least one chemistry lecture delivered by Professor Robert Hare and heard Professor W. E. Horner, the dean of this highly-regarded institution, lecture on anatomy.[44] Another Philadelphia acquaintance, Dr. I. F. Wright, took Evans to the anatomy classes at Jefferson Medical College. Thus Evans was able to get a close look at medical education in two of the best schools in the country, and he came away more determined than ever to become a doctor.[45]

Since the regular school term lasted only about three months, John was ready to return home on the first of April. With cousin Ben he had discussed the possibility of attending the spring course in anatomy at Transylvania University, but the two ultimately decided to spend the summer under the preceptorship of Doctors Isaac and Elias Fisher in Waynesville.[46] Doubtful about the arrangement with the Fishers,[47] Ben came home in early March and worked out a more satisfactory agreement. The physicians were to set aside a private reading room for their students, make substantial additions to their medical library, and give frequent examinations, a point which was of great concern to Ben. They promised to obtain a cadaver for dissection, but with the proviso that the work had to be finished before warm weather arrived.[48]

Ben's fear of being "a menial at Fishers" was well founded, if the experience of other medical students is any guide. Under the preceptorship system, the student's status varied from that of "indentured servant to medical technician." He mixed powders and rolled pills, and learned "to cup, bleed and do bedside nursing." He was expected to care for the doctor's horse, buggy, and harness, and he often performed other domestic duties. For this reason, the student usually paid no fee, or only a very small one, for his training, room, and board. On the other hand, if he lived outside the preceptor's home, his duties were usually limited to clinical work and care of the doctor's horse. In this case he often paid a fee ranging to a hundred dollars per year. The preceptor furnished books and equipment; and students were required, before beginning their training, to have an adequate knowledge of Latin, mathematics, English grammar, and natural history.[49] After a period of about three years, the student received a certificate from his preceptor and could then practice on his own, although some local medical societies required him to pass an examination before practicing. Those who wanted a degree from a medical school would attend a course of lectures at the school for a term or two, but in the meantime they were allowed to practice and call themselves doctor.[50]

John's parents had become "pretty well reconciled" to his idea of a medical career. A Waynesville neighbor had said rudely that if his son were studying medicine, he would "change his will and disinherit him." To this Mrs. Evans retorted that if her oldest son wanted to be a doctor, it was probably a fine idea.[51] She urged her son to study for the summer under the Fishers and to board at home.[52] The arrangement was a fortunate one. John and Ben became even closer friends of the Fishers, and in John's final term at medical school the doctors gave him considerable financial assistance.[53]

With a mind that automatically reduced a problem to its simplest terms, and an enthusiasm for public debate, John's interest in medicine was matched by an interest in politics. During the fall of 1836 he apparently campaigned for some sort of judicial post but failed to win it.[54] His efforts in behalf of presidential candidate William Henry Harrison were more successful.[55] His Whig tendencies were rooted in an opposition to the monetary policies of the Democrats. As one of his friends remarked later, "their currency is so very hard [it] won't work at all."[56]

During the course of the election campaign John had decided to return with cousin Ben to attend Transylvania University. Dr. Isaac Fisher, who did not have a medical degree, decided to accompany them.[57] Just how John intended to pay his expenses is not clear, but on October 22, 1836, he borrowed a hundred dollars from Robert Head, promising to pay it back within ninety days at ten per cent interest.[58]

The three young men left for Lexington at the end of October, again going by way of Cincinnati. Stopping to see the new medical school at Cincinnati College, they decided to enroll there, rather than at Transylvania University. What prompted the change is unclear, but relatives and friends were taken by surprise.[59] Elias Fisher called it a bad choice, for he considered the new college inferior to Transylvania University.[60]

Established first in 1819 and closed during the depression of 1825, Cincinnati College was reopened in 1834, and a medical department was established in 1835.[61] Dr. Daniel Drake, the enterprising director of the new medical school, had gathered a distinguished faculty. One author has described the period of Drake's leadership—1835 to 1839—as "the most brilliant four years . . . of medical history in the West up to that time."[62] Another called Drake the "Father of Western Medicine."[63] The faculty was said to be composed of "the brainiest, most brilliant and famous medical teachers of the day."[64] Drake had served on the faculty of Jefferson Medical College in Philadelphia[65] and had taken a leading role in the founding of both Cincinnati College and the Medical College of Ohio. While teaching at the latter institution, he had a serious disagreement with the administration and left to organize the medical department of Cincinnati College.[66]

The faculty of Cincinnati College in the fall of 1836 included Joseph Nash McDowell, Drake's brother-in-law, and a former instructor at both Jefferson Medical College and Transylvania University. The chair of surgery was held by Willard Parker, a Harvard graduate who would later hold the chair of surgery in the College of Physicians and Surgeons of New York. Obstetrics and the diseases of women and children were taught by Landon C. Rives, who had graduated with honors from the University of Pennsylvania in 1821. Drake himself held a professorship in the theory and practice of medicine.[67]

The term of study—a standard in medical schools of the period—was four months, November through February. To be eligible for the degree Doctor of Medicine the student was

The first building of Cincinnati College,
where John and Benjamin Evans studied medicine for a time.

required to attend two terms, the last of which must be at Cincinnati College, and to pass a comprehensive examination. Under an alternate plan, a student who had practiced for four years could receive the degree after attendance for one year and successful completion of the examination. Degree candidates were also expected to write an acceptable thesis.[68]

Since the Commercial Hospital was controlled by the Medical College of Ohio and was therefore not available to students of Cincinnati College, Drake opened Cincinnati Hospital in a building across the street from his new medical school.[69] Candidates for graduation had to attend classes in surgery and theory and practice of medicine at the hospital for three hours each week.[70] If the hospital training seems shockingly brief, it can be contrasted with the later statement of a Civil War doctor, who said: "In two years of college I did not once receive bedside instruction or enter the ward of a hospital."[71]

Total cost for a term at the college was one hundred twenty-five dollars, including the five-dollar library fee, which was optional. The cost also included fifteen-dollar "tickets" for attendance at each class, a five-dollar matriculation fee, a five-dollar hospital ticket, and a ten-dollar anatomical fee. Faculty members had organized the Cincinnati Medical Society, and all students were invited to attend the weekly meetings, at no charge.[72]

Added to the tuition and fees was the cost of room and board, about three dollars per week.[73] Although the expenses were not particularly great, banking practices worked a hardship on some students, who found their state banknotes accepted only at a heavy discount, except in payment for the college fees. In an 1837 announcement with obvious political overtones the Cincinnati College faculty said: "As we have no national circulating medium, the Faculty consider it proper to give notice, that they will receive from students, at par, the current bank bills of the different states in which they respectively reside."[74]

The three Waynesville students attended Cincinnati College for the full term. Benjamin Evans and Isaac Fisher planned to graduate at the end of the term and were therefore required to stay for examinations and graduation ceremonies. John, however, had another year to complete, so he was able to leave Cincinnati at the end of February.[75]

If the period of required formal schooling was brief, the oral examination was a real trial. Several candidates, including a very popular student named Hand, failed the examination of February 28, 1837. Hand's friends signed a petition that he be given a rehearing, and many who passed the oral threatened to refuse their diplomas if Hand did not graduate with them. As a result, Hand was retested and allowed to graduate, but the faculty extracted a secret promise that he would return to attend lectures during the ensuing summer and winter sessions.[76]

The thesis apparently did not present a great challenge to any of the candidates. There is no indication that research was carried out in any other place than the thousand-volume library,[77] and research was apparently confined to the last term of residence. Benjamin Evans and Isaac Fisher passed their examinations without difficulty. Their theses were accepted, and both graduated on March 3, 1837.[78]

John Evans spent the next few months in Waynesville, probably working with the Fishers. With graduation in sight, he began courting Hannah Canby, daughter of the prominent Ohio physician, Joseph Canby. Hannah was born in Lebanon, Ohio, on June 9, 1813.[79] Her mother's sister, also named Hannah, had married John's uncle, Thomas Evans. Since Thomas' son Benjamin was John's closest friend, it was natural that John should meet Hannah when she visited the Thomas Evans home in Waynesville.[80]

Before spring had ended John wrote to Hannah Canby, asking the important question: "Were I to offer myself to you as a candidate for your affection,—as a suitor, might I entertain any hope of success?" The girl was probably in town when he wrote, but such delicate negotiations were handled best through an intermediary who perhaps had more experience in the art.[81] Her answer, apparently, was yes.

Odd things were happening to medicine in Waynesville. Still without a medical degree, John Evans opened an ill-paying practice at Frederick, a small settlement in Montgomery County near Union, Ohio,[82] and also near Hannah Canby's home. Elias Fisher suddenly left for Illinois, to look at business conditions,[83] and Isaac Fisher, who had just received his degree in medicine, sold his practice to enter the ministry.[84] Still, the Doctors Fisher and Evans remained close friends.

Benjamin Evans evidently did not practice at all after his graduation. Shortly before John left for Frederick,[85] Ben fell ill from an "acute inflammation" of the lungs, then epidemic in Waynesville.[86] The young physician's condition suddenly grew serious. He died the evening of July 26, 1837, and was buried the next afternoon.[87] Although Frederick was not a great distance from Waynesville, heavy rains made the dirt roads impassable, and John was not notified until the funeral was over.[88]

Ben's death was a terrible shock to John Evans, and for a long time he was unable to face the thought of going to Waynesville to view the grave of his departed friend.[89] Finally, in early October, he went home and visited the grave with his brother Seth.[90] Later he wrote to Benjamin's sister that he "rather envied than lamented" him.[91]

But the visit broke the spell of gloom, and when Evans returned to Frederick, he spent the remainder of the month "doctoring the people with might and main."[92] After another short stay at home he left again for Cincinnati to spend his second and final term at Cincinnati College. He was more than a week late for the fall term,[93] which began officially on Saturday night, October 29, 1837.[94] Dr. James C. Cross, dean of the Transylvania University medical school, had urged Evans to transfer and offered to accept the credits Evans had earned at Cincinnati College.[95] Several months spent in private practice at Frederick had increased his self-confidence, so he felt it was not necessary to appear before the late-registration deadline of November 20.[96] With a firm offer from Transylvania there was no reason to hurry to Cincinnati. Once at the school, however, John devoted himself completely to his studies, telling Hannah that he was "about as devoted a student as we have in the college."[97] Class work went well, and Evans began to consider teaching in a medical school "someday."

William Holmes McGuffey, gaining fame for his new *Eclectic Readers*, was at that time president of Cincinnati College.[98] His lectures on the "Physiology of the Mind" were a highlight of the new term.[99] According to the report which John relayed to Hannah, Professor McGuffey castigated popular fiction for its failure to give an accurate portrayal of human nature. He criticized the theater for "exhausting the sensibility of the heart," as Evans expressed it.[100]

The school year was a hard one for John Evans financially. His few months' practice in Frederick had done little more than pay expenses,[101] and in February, 1838, John wrote to both Isaac and Elias Fisher asking additional money for graduation expenses. Isaac was unable to help, but Elias sent forty dollars.[102] This paid for "books and board"[103] and helped to meet the new twenty-dollar graduation fee.[104] Examinations were a breeze. He finished a thesis on brain tumors, gave it the title "Medullary Sarcoma," and it was accepted without question. On graduation day, March 3, 1838, he became officially a Doctor of Medicine.[105]

3

"Some Chance for Distinction"

Frederick, Ohio, could not support a doctor, as past experience had shown, and Evans had to look for a new practice. Forced to borrow money for graduation expenses, now he "had to scratch" to make ends meet.[1] His father refused to help,[2] and no other Ohio locations seemed promising.

There was room for a small practice in West Milton, five miles out of Frederick, but this seemed little better than Frederick itself.[3] During a trip to Illinois the previous summer, Elias Fisher had noted the shortage of qualified doctors in that state.[4] Fisher talked about his young protégé in Illinois, and soon after he returned to Waynesville, Evans had an offer from a Dr. Stickel of Hennepin, Illinois, to share an established practice in "the snake country." Stickel's glowing letters sounded attractive—a partnership in his drugstore and medical practice, with an equal division of the profits. Evans determined to give it a try.[5]

But Hannah Canby was not anxious to begin married life so far from her father's comfortable home. They quarreled, and though she gave a reluctant approval, she apparently had no intention of spending her life in the wilds of Illinois.[6] The wedding would be in Ohio in the fall, which left only a few months for the trip to Illinois. To seal the bargain, Hannah offered her ring to John. Brooding over her coolness toward his Illinois plans, he thoughtlessly refused the gift. They were still at odds when he left the Canby home. No sooner had he gone, however, than both were struck by pangs of remorse, and their letters of self-reproach crossed in the mail.[7]

Worried and uncertain, John remained in Waynesville for several days, urging Isaac Fisher to go with him to Illinois. On a brief trip to Cincinnati with Fisher he had his picture painted in miniature for Hannah. When he sent the picture, he asked for a lock of her hair in return and mentioned that he would be glad now to have the ring. The refusal "was done very unthoughtedly," he said, but the ring was apparently not forthcoming.[8] Country post offices being what they are, he had his cousin Margaret address and mail the letter, so the Waynesville postmaster would think she was sending her own picture to Hannah.[9]

A poet of local repute, with more enthusiasm than talent, Evans frequently included copies of his latest work in letters to his friends. Some of his poems eventually appeared in the local paper.[10] Accompanying the miniature painting was one such literary effort, a stanza of which follows:

> Oft when you see this little toy
> Pray leave imagination free
> That nothing trivial may decoy
> Your vision from beholding me.[11]

Evans delayed his departure until May 11 so that he might attend the wedding of his cousin Susan Cook and his old friend Samuel Hill. Hill's home was Richmond, Indiana, and Evans seems to have met him while attending school there in 1834.[12] He had acted as go-between with Susan for Hill. The result was predictable: "She said you had not requested her to write and had referred her to me—therefore she would trust to me to answer your billetdoux by telling you to come over and attend to it for yourself."[13] The wedding a year and a half later is evidence that Hill did just that. At the wedding dinner, John was "boss of the carving knife and waiter." The celebration lasted for another day, but Evans performed his social duties and left for Illinois soon after the wedding dinner. With his new black mare Fanny, he was able to travel fifty miles on the first day and spent the night in Richmond, Indiana.[14]

A friend from Frederick, Dr. McReynolds, was to meet him there, but McReynolds was not in Richmond. A letter told Evans that he did not wish to go to Illinois. Rather than continue the trip alone, Evans then decided to wait for the arrival of the wedding party, which was to travel along the same route on the following day. He rode with Susan and Samuel to Indianapolis, and from there went alone to Hennepin, Illinois. The entire trip took ten days. In a letter home Evans said that with a few exceptions—loneliness, a sunburned nose, and presumably saddlesores—the trip was quite enjoyable.[15]

Hennepin was a disappointment to the fledgling physician. The people were uncommonly healthy, and as he told Hannah, "unless there should be more sickness in the country, practice must be scarce."[16] He suffered "most severely" from homesickness for the first week or so and on several occasions almost decided to return to Ohio and try again in Frederick or Milton.[17]

The discouragingly robust Hennepin citizenry caused Evans to decline the partnership with Dr. Stickel. Instead they agreed that Evans would spend a good part of his day in the drugstore and receive in payment ten dollars a month, room, board, food and shelter for his horse, and "half the proceeds of our joint practice."[18]

As luck would have it, the editor of the Hennepin *Journal* was an old friend of Dr. Canby. Evans was thus able to write articles for the paper, and several of these were published in the issues of June 2 and June 9, including one on railroads.[19] Unfortunately, none of these issues are now extant.

The Fourth of July was celebrated "gloriously" in Hennepin. There was a speech, a dinner, toasts—most of them composed by Evans—and a ball in the evening.[20] There was also a girl. She was from New York, and as he later told Hannah, was "a very intelligent lady." Dancing was wicked, and they did not dance, he was careful to point out, but as a result of his attention he "was obliged to conduct her home a whole days ride." Of course, he told the girl that he "was engaged to be married to a buckeye," and she said that she "wished she could" meet Hannah. It was an odd story for a young man to write to his fiancee. Perhaps the editor's friendship with Dr. Canby made Evans fearful that the tale would get back to Hannah, so he assured her that "all was light and gay."[21]

On the twentieth or twenty-first of July, the situation in Hennepin having proven completely unsatisfactory, Evans moved to Indian Creek, located about fifteen miles north of Ottawa and about forty-five miles northeast of Hennepin.[22]

By this time Hannah had expressed her complete willingness to move to Illinois, but John was becoming disillusioned with the state and was half-inclined to move back to Ohio and settle in West Milton. At any rate he planned to be back in Ohio sometime in November and a final decision could be made at that time.[23]

Evans' practice seems to have improved in Indian Creek. In the first four days he collected eight dollars in fees.[24] This prosperity was short-lived, however, and before long he came down with one of those mysterious frontier maladies that left him weak and feverish for months. In November, almost well again, he returned to Ohio, full of ideas about a prosperous future in the growing settlement to the west.[25]

But for now West Milton was as far from home as Hannah would go. It was near enough to Frederick that some of his former patients would be able to come to West Milton. He established a practice there, and in December, 1838, he and Hannah Canby were married in Bellefontaine, Ohio.[26]

No official record of the wedding has ever been found,[27] but it was not a Quaker ceremony. Dr. Canby had left the Society of Friends and become a Swedenborgian,[28] and the wedding perhaps took place in his church.[29] John had referred to the wedding ceremony of Susan Cook and Samuel Hill as "the good old Quaker order of marrying," but he was not a devout Quaker, and more than once he said that the ceremony could stand "a few modifications."[30]

On November 30, 1837, after having attended the marriage of his brother Joel to Susan Sharp in a civil ceremony in Cincinnati,[31] John was moved to write that the Quaker law forbidding marriage outside the Society "ought to be done away [with], for the good reason that it looks to me like an attempt to rule with a rod of iron the affections which are too tender for the austeer government." Young people, he said, were often forced into an unhappy marriage with another Quaker:

> Thus I believe that young persons with limits prescribed within which their affections shall play, often live out a cold and dreary life of celibacy, or what is worse, join in wedlock without feeling the emotion of love to warm the heart, thus profaning the hallowed bonds of matrimony.[32]

The sturdy citizens of West Milton, Ohio, seldom found occasion to seek the professional services of the young physician. Before the winter was out Evans was forced to ask for a loan from his cousin Lydia Cooper just to meet living expenses.[33] Before long he remembered a small town in Indiana that he had passed through on the trip back from Illinois.[34] Attica, Indiana, had a large contingent of former Waynesville citizens, and Isaac Fisher promised to open a joint practice with Evans.[35] With little reluctance he abandoned his meager practice in West Milton and moved to Attica in July, 1839. Hannah remained in Ohio, and by September she was staying in Waynesville, waiting for John to take her out to their new home.[36]

Attica proved to be just the place he had been seeking. Business was good, and medical fees were high. Within two months Dr. Evans had "done upwards of five hundred dollars worth of practice at a very moderate rate of charging for this country."[37] While he probably did not collect this amount in cash, his financial prospects were greatly improved.

He rented a two-room house, with "an old shell of a kitchen" that could be used for storage, and he spent a considerable sum in furnishing it. A carpenter was hired to build "a commodious clothes-press" with shelves and two drawers on one side, and also "a safe with a drawer over two doors like a sideboard." In addition, Evans purchased a cabinet with glass doors for Hannah's dishes, "one high post and one low post bedstead," and a stand to place beside one of the beds. To please Hannah he also bought a rocking chair and "a set of fancy windsor chairs." He preferred rush-bottom chairs for himself and bought three of these to complete the furnishings. He apparently thought of everything. Tomatoes were cheap that year, so he had a small lot canned for their use. Evans even considered buying a carriage, although the one he had in mind was finally sold to someone else.[38]

His sudden prosperity brought a number of business offers. A man named Dunkin wanted him as a partner in a drugstore. This project, however, was dependent on a loan from Hannah's brother Richard, and the project was apparently abandoned. A printer wanted Evans to be his partner in a newspaper—perhaps even editor. It was a tempting offer, but Evans finally concluded that a newspaper would interfere too much with his medical practice.[39]

Two children were born to John and Hannah, Joseph Canby Evans in 1839 and David Evans in 1841.[40] John's medical practice continued to grow, and in 1840 the young family built a new home in Attica. A year later Evans erected a modest office building on Main Street that remains in use more than a century later.[41]

Although business was good, money was scarce. Evans and Fisher had received a large stock of corn in payment for medical bills, and in the spring of 1842 they decided to take it down the Wabash River to the Mississippi and sell wherever a good market could be found.[42] Meanwhile, Hannah and the children would visit her home in Quincy, Ohio.[43]

Evans and Fisher had a flatboat built to carry their corn;[44] they planned to break up the vessel and sell the lumber at the end of the trip. But the venture was risky, physically and economically. Riding on the crest of the spring flood, the flatboat was easy prey for snags and sandbars. Moreover, the early arrivals at New Orleans were the only ones who received top prices from grain dealers. Latecomers were victims of the seasonal "Wabash Glut" that set prices tumbling each spring and fall.[45] In 1842, as Evans reported, there were "immense quantities of corn on the river."[46]

Stopping at markets along the river, the doctors had their first encounter with slavery and were appalled. John wrote to his wife about one case involving a drunken overseer, who suspected one of his slaves of having stolen a turkey and had the man whipped so fiercely that his "back was one entire scab." The turkey was later found "running at large," but the overseer showed little remorse. Even while admitting that the Negro was so intelligent he could do sums faster in his head than the overseer could on paper, the man seemed only to regret that he had temporarily lost the services of a good worker.[47]

His Quaker conscience affronted, Evans wrote bitterly: "Slavery can only be maintained by the most inhuman barbarity." Evans saw "clustering around the institution of slavery wickedness in all its forms." The planter class was able to "revel in luxury" only by "tasking under the lash their fellow beings."[48]

Although several hundred bushels of corn were sold at plantations along the way, demand was low, and the partners decided to go on down the river. New Orleans prices were nearly as low, but they did sell their remaining three hundred bushels and doubtless the boat as well.[49]

It is not entirely clear whether Evans maintained any religious affiliation after his move to Indiana. There was no Quaker meeting in Attica, and John had not been an active member of the Society for some time. The only Friends group to which he might have belonged was the Hovey Creek Monthly Meeting; their records show that he was not a member, and the records of the Miami Monthly Meeting indicate that he was not granted a certificate of transfer to any other group. Hannah, on the other hand, had evidently been a devout Quaker prior to her marriage,[50] but she also failed to remain active in the Society.

Under these circumstances, it is not surprising that when Hannah and John heard the moving sermons of young Matthew Simpson, they were immediately attracted to the Methodist faith. Simpson had been president of Indiana Asbury University since that school opened in 1839. He made it one of his main tasks to refute the charge of Presbyterian Samuel Bigger (soon to be elected governor of Indiana) that the Methodists did not have enough learned members to staff a university.[51] Evans and his partner Isaac Fisher heard Simpson's locally-famous address on education in an unfinished mill[52] when Simpson came to Attica in 1841.[53]

Simpson, he said, was "the first man that ever made my head swim in talking."[54] Evans was so impressed that he traveled four miles the next evening to hear Simpson preach on the topic "Lord Show Me Thy Glory."[55] A few months later John and Hannah were invited "to go into the Love Feast of the quarterly meeting." Impressed by the testimony of church members, both John and Hannah joined the Methodist Church.[56]

One author has suggested that it was natural for Quakers in this period to be attracted to Methodism. In his opinion,

American Quakers had begun veering toward "that quietism which had characterized English Friends" since the early eighteenth century. "Methodism," he said,

was a return toward the forms of primitive Quakerism. With them, as with the Methodists a century later, religion took the form of excessive emotion. The convicted sinner shook from head to foot; there were many groans and sighs and tears. . . . The early Methodists were simply leading their hearers back to the good old days of the past.[57]

Other strong religious currents helped shape events. An anti-Masonic spirit was still current in Indiana in the 1840's, and the North Indiana Conference of the Methodist Church in its 1844 meeting passed a resolution recommending that preachers refrain from joining either the Masons or the Odd Fellows.[58] Stubbornly independent, Evans joined the Masonic order and received the degree of Master Mason in Attica Lodge Number 18 on July 6, 1844. After moving to Indianapolis he became the first Worshipful Master of Marion Lodge on May 28, 1847, when that lodge received its charter. Evans had acted as Worshipful Master since July 6, 1846, while the lodge was being organized. He later became the first member to be initiated into the Knights Templar in Roper Commandery Number 1 in Indianapolis, May 17, 1848.[59]

In later years Evans seems to have acquired an appreciation of his own place in the history of the West, and the record after 1860 is quite complete. Information concerning Evans' personal life during this early period is sparse, even though these were the years that shaped his political and financial future. Nonetheless, several facts stand out. Evans was friendly and well liked. Determined to succeed, he enjoyed the challenge of speculative investment. He acquired a reputation as a businessman, after he had made a number of successful investments in real estate with his own money and with sums borrowed from members of the family.[60] An avid "joiner," he was beginning to be recognized as an important civic figure. Thus in several ways, by the latter 1840's, the young doctor had begun to assume a leading role in community affairs.

4

Politics in the Amen Corner

Almost immediately after the move to Attica, Indiana, the young doctors, John Evans and Isaac Fisher, took the lead in a move to establish a state hospital for the care of the insane. The complete lack of facilities for the care of mentally disturbed persons and the resultant pitiable plight in which both the demented and their families found themselves was obvious to the two young men.[1] As physicians, they would naturally treat a number of such cases in the ordinary course of their work.[2]

Establishment of the hospital was an uphill battle, for the state's finances were very precarious, and both the governor and the legislature seemed to regard the problem as a relatively minor one. As it turned out, a dispute between the Presbyterians and the Methodists helped significantly to change the political complexion of the state government, and once this change was accomplished, a new source of revenue was devised to fund the project. In this way, state care for the insane in Indiana became closely involved with a move by the Methodists to secure political recognition.

In December, 1841, Evans and Fisher sent a memorial to the state legislature, asking that a hospital be built to care for the insane.[3] Since there was no committee on state institutions in either house, the document was due to be referred to the Committee on Education. For this reason, the memorial was introduced in the House, where the Committee on Education was headed by Dr. James Ritchey, a physician who was sympathetic to the proposal.[4] The committee not only made a favorable report, but Dr. Ritchey, the chairman, became one of the most ardent proponents of the idea. Ritchey recommended immediate action by the House, but nothing more was done on the bill during the session.[5]

Evans continued to press for approval of the plan that he and Fisher had developed. During the ensuing year John and Hannah Evans, together with the Fishers, Dr. and Mrs. Caleb V. Jones, Representative Edward O. Hannegan and his wife, and Mr. and Mrs. William Crumpton, all of Fountain County, combined in an informal association to promote the establishment of state institutions to care for the deaf, the mute, the blind, and the insane.[6] Evans and Fisher maintained an extensive correspondence with heads of institutions in other states, and Evans particularly, growing in political stature in Attica, was able to exert enough influence to keep the issue alive.[7] With earlier experience in writing for newspapers, he now turned his journalistic talents to the subject of an institution for the insane, and the Wabash *Express* published at least one of his articles in the fall of 1841.[8]

By this time Evans and Fisher had gained the ear of Governor Samuel Bigger. In a message to the legislature on December 7, 1841, the governor reminded the lawmakers that the first state legislature had set aside a plot of ground in the city of Indianapolis as a site for a lunatic asylum. He also recalled the failure of successive legislatures to build such an institution and pointed to the example of some of the neighboring states that already provided such care for their own people. Nonetheless, Bigger refused to make a forthright recommendation, saying that the legislature must decide whether anything should be done.[9]

Governor Bigger's comments were sent to the Senate Committee on Education. This group expressed sympathy for the plight of the insane in the state, but said the state was too poor to do anything about it.[10]

Disgusted by the governor's halfhearted support, Evans again appealed to the legislature. On January 5, 1842, Representative Edward Hannegan introduced Evans' petition, and again the matter was referred to the Committee on Education.[11] This time the committee chairman, Dr. Ritchey, minced no words in his report. He condemned the state's extravagant expenditures on internal improvements, which had brought about the existing financial crisis and, after listing examples of the treatment then provided for the mentally afflicted in their own homes, concluded that the state must begin to care for them.[12]

The result was a resolution, passed by both houses, and signed by the governor on January 31, 1842. The chief executive was directed to correspond with superintendents of insane asylums in other states and obtain plans and other information to present to the next General Assembly.[13] In spite of his approval of the measure, the governor apparently did nothing during 1842 to carry the resolution into effect. Nor was the matter mentioned in his message of December, 1842.[14]

Stung by the governor's failure to act, Evans and Fisher, on December 27, 1842, presented a third memorial to the legislature regarding state care for the insane. Since financing seemed to be the main stumbling block, they suggested that proceeds from public land sales be used to pay for the erection of an institution for the insane. The proposal was rejected by the legislators on the ground that the financial condition of the state would not allow them to consider such an appropriation.[15]

Apparently this stand did not mean the legislature was opposed to the construction of an insane asylum, for on February 13, 1843, the House of Representatives adopted a resolution criticizing Governor Bigger for his failure to present the report they had requested in January, 1842. The House resolution demanded that he prepare the report and said that any further delay would be criminal.[16]

The governor then employed I. P. Smith, an architect from New Albany, Indiana, to draw plans for a building. Smith visited the Ohio Lunatic Asylum and completed a set of plans based on the design of that institution. The governor sent these plans to the legislature in the following session.[17]

In the meantime, however, Governor Bigger's political enemies were girding for battle. The Presbyterians had gained control both of the faculty and of the board of trustees of the recently-opened state university at Bloomington and were running it as a Presbyterian institution. Methodists, who outnumbered Presbyterians in the state four to one, objected; in 1834, the Indiana Conference of the Methodist Church had petitioned the legislature to resume the power of appointment to the hitherto self-perpetuating university board. Samuel Bigger, an ardent Presbyterian and at that time a member of the legislature, led the successful fight to table the proposal,[18] and the Methodists never forgot it. When their own university was opened at Greencastle in 1839, Matthew Simpson, president of the school, quickly assumed leadership in the field of Methodist political action.

Gubernatorial candidate Bigger led the Whig ticket to victory in 1840 and soon gave the Methodists additional reasons for opposing him. The New School Presbyterian College secured an $8,000 loan from the state, and in 1842 college trustees found themselves unable to make the interest payment. When the state agreed to suspend interest payments until December 31, 1846, the Presbyterian governor became the target of renewed Methodist criticism.[19]

During the 1842-43 session of the legislature, a statewide educational convention was to be held to discuss the future of the common schools and the disposition of the money in the state "sinking fund." On the day before the convention opened

Henry Ward Beecher, pastor of the Second Presbyterian Church in Indianapolis, and two prominent Presbyterian bankers appointed themselves to the principal offices in the convention and invited Governor Bigger to serve as chairman.[20] The Presbyterian governor told the assembled delegates that there was "not a Methodist in America with sufficient learning to fill a professor's chair."[21] President Simpson now had an issue to unite Methodists in a campaign to defeat the governor in 1843.

Evans, for his part, had become convinced that Bigger did not intend to support the plan for an insane asylum. Therefore, in spite of the fact that Evans himself was a Whig, he and his group in Fountain County worked for the nomination of Dr. Caleb V. Jones for the state Senate on the Democratic ticket.[22]

Just how Evans viewed the squabble between the churches is not known, but, when the Whigs nominated Samuel Bigger for re-election in 1843 and the Democrats nominated Methodist James Whitcomb, the religious lines were pretty clearly drawn. Both Presbyterians and Methodists had traditionally gravitated toward the Whig Party, and Indiana Democrats were now making a definite bid to change the pattern.[23] The Democratic *Indiana State Sentinel* reported that Whig attacks against Whitcomb were based solely on religious grounds. The *Sentinel* continued to repeat this charge in the face of vigorous Whig denials. One exasperated Whig, recognizing Simpson's role in the opposition to Bigger, threatened that if the Methodists deserted the party, the Whigs would "blow their college and church to Hell."[24]

Held in August, 1843, the election resulted in a Whitcomb victory by a margin of 2,000 votes out of a total of 110,000.[25] In Fountain County, Caleb Jones, who had been backed by Evans, won a decisive victory. In addition, all the members of the House from Fountain, Warren, Vermillion, and Park Counties were pledged to support the plan for an insane asylum.[26]

It is difficult to gauge the importance of the religious issue in the 1843 election. Even the tariff seems to have exerted some influence; Democrats charged that factory workers, with an average annual income of $500 and a high protective tariff prospered at the expense of farm workers, with an average annual income of $213 and no tariff protection.[27] Locofocos also attracted a number of Methodists away from the Whig ranks. Even more important, according to the *Indiana State Journal*, was the fact that a good many Whigs seem to have stayed home, since Governor Bigger's successful opponent received 6,000 fewer votes than Bigger had garnered in the previous election.[28]

For Methodist Church leaders an easy explanation was at hand. E. R. Ames, then secretary of the Missionary Society of the Methodist Episcopal Church, said: "It was the Amen corner of the Methodist church that defeated Governor Bigger, and I had a hand in the work."[29]

Evans moved his family to Indianapolis for the 1843-44 session so he could shepherd his proposal through the legislature.[30] The departing governor told the legislators on December 5, 1843, that he had collected information from other states and that the architect's plans would be ready shortly.[31] The lawmakers were in no mood for delay, however, and the governor's plan, so long awaited, was not even considered.[32]

Evans' memorial urging the establishment of an institution to care for the insane was introduced in the Senate and again referred to the Committee on Education. The committee reported that no funds were available to support such a project. Caleb Jones, however, would not accept the report, and he and Dr. Ritchey led a fight to have the memorial sent back to the committee for further study.[33]

On Christmas Day, 1843, in a public meeting of the House Committee on Education, Evans made a new proposal.[34] He had prepared a workable scheme for financing construction work. Since 1839, when the financial strictures of the Panic of 1837 had begun to be felt in Indiana, the state had embarked upon a program of issuing its own scrip and accepting this in payment of taxes. In spite of the fact that the scrip bore six per cent interest, it quickly depreciated and was discounted in Cincinnati at a rate of fifty per cent or more.[35] Evans now proposed a property tax of one cent on each hundred dollars of valuation. He pointed out to the legislators that few could object to such a tax since the use of scrip would give the taxpayer a fifty per cent discount.[36] Caleb Jones was instrumental in persuading the Senate committee to consider the new plan.[37] A bill embodying Evans' proposal was finally approved, becoming law on January 15, 1844.[38]

Little further action could be taken until the new tax law brought funds to the state treasury. In the meantime, Governor Whitcomb corresponded with county sheriffs throughout the state and compiled figures on the number of insane persons confined in the local jails.[39] Finally, on January 13, 1845, after $12,000 had been collected from the new levy of 1844,[40] the legislature passed an act creating a three-man Board of Commissioners to select and purchase a suitable site for the asylum. The members of this first board were Dr. John Evans, Dr. Livingston Dunlap, and a layman, James Blake.[41]

At their first meeting in Dr. Dunlap's office in Indianapolis, two weeks later,[42] the commissioners quickly agreed that they could not "act understandingly without more information on the subject." They therefore accepted Evans' offer to travel through the East, tour the major institutions, and report on current practices and recent developments in the care of the insane.[43]

Evans decided to make this trip at his own expense, "relying on the liberality of the legislature for remuneration," rather than suffer another year's delay waiting for an appropriation.[44] The legislature apparently reimbursed him as he had supposed they would, for he made no comment to the contrary in any of his subsequent references to the subject of the state hospital.[45]

Among the major institutions which he visited were the Ohio Lunatic Asylum, the Pennsylvania Hospital for the Insane, the Bloomingdale Asylum, the McLean Asylum, the Massachusetts State Lunatic Hospital, the Hartford Retreat for the Insane, and the New York State Lunatic Asylum. In addition, he stopped at several other institutions dedicated wholly or partially to the care of the insane. Although there were minor differences in operation, he found all the specialists at these institutions in agreement on major points.[46]

A "healthy site" with good water in ample supply was a basic requirement. According to the "miasmatic" theories then current, diseases were transmitted by contaminated air from swamps and "putrescent matter."[47] A "healthy site," then, was one that was elevated and could be drained properly. Water for drinking and washing would be obtained from wells, but a running stream of water was deemed necessary to carry off waste from the sewers.[48]

Evans recommended locating the institution near the state capital. Here it would be under the eye of newspapers and those "who diffuse information and give caste to public opinion." Its presence would serve as a constant reminder to the legislators that they must continue to appropriate money for the proper care of the inmates. A location near a large town would also make it easier to purchase goods and find skilled workmen.[49]

Evans' report suggested a location outside the city limits. Here it would be possible to establish a farm to produce food and provide healthful employment for some of the patients. A rural area would presumably be sufficiently isolated to discourage the idly curious visitor.[50]

He recommended a scenic location that would lend itself to flower gardens and wooded parks. "In short," he said,

a hospital for the insane should be so situated, that it may be made to assume the appearance of, and actually to be, a delightful retreat from the turmoils and perplexities of the busy world—freed from its cares, anxieties, and disappointments; where the insane may enjoy the comforts of life and the kindness of friends at a home of contentment.[51]

By comparing the population of Indiana with that of Ohio, Evans concluded that space for a hundred and fifty patients would suffice.[52] He felt that the building and its appointments need not be expensive, since even wealthy people in the state were not used to opulent surroundings. Furthermore, he thought "most paupers would be rendered unhappy by such accommodations as would be necessary for effecting the greatest amount of good to patients accustomed to affluence and luxury."[53] This did not mean that patients were simply to be housed in great wards. On the contrary, he recommended that patients be segregated according to their affliction, and suggested that at least half should have private rooms.[54]

Following the submission of Evans' report, the commissioners purchased from Nathaniel Bolton the Mount Jackson Tavern and adjoining 160-acre farm two miles west of Indianapolis on the macadamized National Road.[55] The site, costing $5,300, seemed to meet all the requirements specified by Evans in his report.[56]

An architect, John Elder, was retained to design a building based on Evans' report and the plans which had been given him at other institutions. The architect planned a building to meet the needs of the next few decades, but the commissioners decided to erect only part of the structure. The main building and two small wings would accommodate nearly 150 patients, and this was considered ample for the time being.[57]

The commission report recommended that the state sell the four-acre tract in the town of Indianapolis that had originally been set aside for a hospital. The report also urged the appointment of a physician with experience in the treatment of the insane to supervise the erection of the building.[58]

The legislature agreed to all the proposals, including the Evans building plan,[59] and on January 31, 1846, John Evans was appointed to fill the position of superintendent, after resigning his place on the commission. Since the law required Evans to supervise the actual work of construction and this would require his "whole time . . . during at least the larger portion of the year," his salary was a generous $800 a year.[60]

In late 1845, just prior to his appointment as superintendent, Evans began teaching in Chicago's Rush Medical College.[61] The regular school year was only sixteen weeks,[62] and Evans believed the teaching position would not conflict with his work at the Hospital for the Insane. In a letter to one of his colleagues on the Rush faculty Evans said that hospital construction would have to be suspended during the winter months. Then, he said, he would "be at liberty to pursue my practice all the time."[63]

Accordingly, Evans established a medical practice when he moved to Indianapolis in the summer of 1846 to assume his duties as superintendent,[64] but the job with the Insane Hospital was more demanding than he had expected. Although the commissioners seemed satisfied with his performance,[65] Evans asked them to accept his resignation. When they refused,[66] he suggested that an architect be retained to supervise construction work and that his own duties be restricted to advising the architect on medical points. To this the commissioners agreed.[67]

As a result, Joseph Willis, an Indianapolis architect, was appointed to supervise the work of construction.[68] Since Evans expected that the assistance of Willis would materially lessen the duties which he was required to perform, he asked the board to reduce his salary to $600 per year.[69] No sooner had this been done than it was found advisable to have both Evans and Willis personally supervise the bricklaying. The board agreed that their salaries should now be increased, but delayed action pending approval by the legislature.[70]

In the summer of 1847 Evans notified the board that he did not intend to remain as superintendent after the institution was

John Evans was instrumental in the establishment of the Indiana Hospital for the Insane.

sufficiently completed to receive patients.[71] Therefore, in July, 1848, with the construction work substantially finished, Evans resigned his post. Dr. R. J. Patterson, of the Ohio Lunatic Asylum, was appointed to take his place, and Evans was re-appointed to the Board of Commissioners. As Dr. Patterson would be employed full time supervising the treatment of patients, his salary was set at $1,200 per year. A young graduate of Rush Medical College, Dr. John Nutt, was employed as Assistant Physician at a salary of $400.[72]

Even while he was urging the establishment of an institution to care for the insane, Evans began to receive recognition for his leadership in that field.[73] His printed address of December 25, 1843, attracted such widespread attention that the Indiana General Assembly authorized a second printing.[74]

In the fall of 1846, while superintending construction of the hospital at Indianapolis, Evans wrote in a medical journal that general practitioners should treat less advanced cases themselves, since most of the mentally ill would respond to *"the laws of humanity and kindness."* He believed that there were very few afflicted persons who could not "be made to feel those heaven-born influences that flow from the benevolent heart." No force of any sort should be used in their treatment except that which "is necessary for safety, and [for the] protection and comfort of the patient."[75]

Evans convinced the commissioners and the legislature that the institution should be called a "hospital for the insane" rather than a "lunatic asylum," since a hospital was regarded as "a curative establishment." He believed that it was not proper to confine the insane in jails, and he had determined not to rest until they were provided for.[76]

When Dorothea Dix inspected the jails and poorhouses in Indiana in 1847, she became particularly impressed with the work of Dr. Evans at Indianapolis. "To the present superintendent of this excellent work, Dr. Evans, the citizens of Indiana owe a debt of gratitude which few can estimate," she wrote to the *Indiana State Journal*, "because it is but few who have the opportunity of understanding the measure of his labors or the ability requisite for devising and carrying out such plans as are comprised in the Indiana State Hospital for the Insane."[77]

Since moving to Indiana in 1839, Evans had established a good medical practice and had begun to make some money from investments. He made himself an expert on the care of the insane and led a sucessful campaign for the construction of a state hospital for the insane. As lobbyist, commissioner, and superintendent he received a firsthand education in practical politics. Matthew Simpson showed him how to rally the voters in support of a cause, and Evans found that he often enjoyed the contest more than the fruits of victory. When the challenge was gone, he began to look for other areas of interest.

5

"The Great Institution of the Northwest"

Rush Medical College in Chicago had been chartered in 1837, but because of the financial crisis and subsequent hard times, it did not open until 1843.[1] The school was named in honor of Benjamin Rush, the famous surgeon who signed the Declaration of Independence. Dr. Daniel Brainard, founder of the school, hoped the Rush heirs might provide an endowment, but in this he was disappointed, for the Rush family apparently ignored the school altogether. Brainard himself came to dislike the name and referred to the school as the Medical College of Illinois or the Medical College of Chicago.[2]

Among the considerations that led doctors to accept faculty positions in this new college, those of financial gain and increased prestige seem to have been of prime importance.[3] The school term was of such short duration—sixteen weeks[4]—that it could hardly be expected to interfere with the private practice of the professors. In any case, they were required to lecture only once a day during the session. In addition to these light demands on their time, there was a special benefit—a medical journal was projected, and articles published therein would further add to the prestige and influence of the faculty members.[5] The other important consideration was, of course, the income obtained from tuition fees.[6]

During the first session twenty-two students were in attendance, and lectures were given by four professors in two small rooms above a saloon at Clark and Lake Streets.[7] At the end of the session, that is, in the summer of 1844, a regular college building was erected at the corner of Dearborn and Indiana Streets. This building, twice remodeled, continued in use until it was destroyed by the Great Fire in 1871.[8]

Rush Medical College,
as it looked when John Evans taught there.

John Evans made his first trip from Attica to Chicago some time before his appointment as Superintendent of the Hospital for the Insane at Indianapolis. He seems to have been impressed with the commercial possibilities of the city on Lake Michigan,[9] and, when he was offered a chair at Rush Medical College in 1845, he quickly accepted.[10]

His work in Indiana in behalf of the proposed insane hospital greatly enhanced Evans' reputation in the profession. When Dr. James V. Z. Blaney, a member of the original Rush Medical College faculty, published the first issue of the *Illinois Medical and Surgical Journal*, a review of the Christmas address which Evans had made to the Indiana Legislature in 1843 was included.[11] In December, 1844, Blaney published an article by Evans entitled "Treatment of the Fracture of the Clavicle,"[12] and in May, 1845, he included another Evans article, this one headed "Two Cases [of] Uterine Hydatids."[13] Since Blaney's journal was the official Rush publication, the space allotted to Evans amounted to an official recognition of his accomplishments by the college faculty.

Typical of many college students, John Evans in his last year at Cincinnati Medical College had dreamed of someday being able to "attain an office in some college." At that time it seemed unlikely that this would ever happen. As he told his cousin Margaret: "I hardly dare think of such a thing."[14] Now his own considerable prestige in the medical profession had brought the coveted offer.

When Evans joined the Rush faculty in 1845, Chicago had a population of about 12,000. The city had grown by fifty per cent over the previous year and had nearly tripled the 1840 figure of 4,470.[15] But while the professional opportunities in Chicago were obvious, the offer of the superintendency at the Indiana Hospital for the Insane was also attractive. He accepted this latter position at the conclusion of his first term at Rush and hoped to keep both jobs, at least for a time. Each position seemed promising, and he was unable to decide immediately whether to remain in Indiana or to move to Chicago.[16]

Brainard was a little reluctant to retain Evans after he accepted the appointment in Indianapolis. The young professor convinced him, however, that the superintendency would not interfere with his duties at Rush, at least not until the buildings at Indianapolis were finished.[17] Furthermore, Evans had received an offer from Dr. M. L. Knapp to publish a medical journal sponsored by "a La Porte Medical Society."[18] Knapp had been dropped from the Rush faculty after serving during the first term, and was now spending much of his time at the La Porte, Indiana, medical school circulating false tales critical of the Rush faculty.[19] Evans wrote of the publishing offer to Dr. John McLean, another member of the Rush faculty, thereby insuring the fact that Brainard would find out.[20] Brainard apparently did not relish the thought of having a man of Evans' ability on the side of Knapp, so he was even more inclined to keep Evans at Rush.

Another factor which doubtless convinced Brainard that Evans should be retained at Rush was the necessity of attracting qualified students. With his dynamic personality, Evans had exactly the sort of enthusiasm necessary for recruiting students, and his reputation would attract many whom he did not meet personally. His efforts were largely responsible for the growth of the Rush student body to more than a hundred students by 1849.[21]

As with many private non-denominational schools of the day, Rush was owned and controlled by the faculty.[22] Professors were expected to furnish their own scientific apparatus and specimens and to supply books at their own expense for the college library. In addition to such requirements, they were expected to travel in Illinois and nearby states at their own expense, recruiting students for the coming session.[23]

Requirements for graduation from Rush were similar to those at Cincinnati College. Students were expected to study for three years under a reputable physician, attend lectures for two terms, present an acceptable thesis on some medical topic, and pass an examination covering all of the subjects taught in the college. Only one term of study need have been at Rush, and it was also possible to substitute two years of medical practice for one of the required terms.[24]

Competition for students was keen, since there were several medical schools serving the area, and this fact made it very difficult to raise standards of medical education. Faced with demanding professors at one school, students frequently left for other institutions where a degree could be obtained more easily.[25] The faculty at Rush was concerned about the problem, but felt reluctant to act alone to raise standards. Consequently, progress in this area was slow.

When the American Medical Association held its third annual meeting at Boston in May, 1849, John Evans was selected by his Rush colleagues to be faculty representative. On the last day of the four-day meeting Evans outlined a new plan for selecting instructors in medical schools. He referred to teaching positions in medical schools as "places of profit and honor in our profession," and he suggested that vacancies be filled through public examinations.[26] In his opinion this course of action would "control the rapid multiplication of Medical Schools and improve the character of the teachers," because those less qualified would be reluctant to submit to "a public concours or trial."[27] He presented a resolution calling upon "trustees and others, exercising the office of appointing Professors in Medical Schools, . . . to adopt the system of *Concours,* or public trials," for the purpose of "calling out the talent of the profession and ascertaining the qualifications of applicants." This resolution was adopted by the convention, as Evans reported, "by a very large vote."[28]

Rush Medical College announced the adoption of this policy in January, 1850, when it became necessary to appoint a new instructor of anatomy. The applicant was to submit a written application accompanied by suitable recommendations. In addition he would be required to demonstrate before the faculty a dissection of "some region of the body" and to prepare casts or molds of various limbs and organs.[29] Although the plan seems not to have been followed consistently, the entire faculty was required to submit to a competitive examination when the school reopened in 1872, after having been destroyed in the Chicago fire of October, 1871.[30]

The convention evidently failed to approve a second resolution presented by Evans. This dealt with the preceptorship system, which still constituted a substantial part of the training for medical students. The convention had been considering a proposal by Dr. Nathan Smith Davis to raise the standards of medical education by requiring county committees to examine and approve applicants before they could be admitted to medical school. Evans thought that the real problem lay in the fact that many young men, upon completion of their study under a preceptor, failed to attend medical school and simply began to practice on their own. His resolution recommended that physicians refuse to act as preceptors for students who failed to meet the educational standards established by the association. The suggestion apparently was not adopted by the association, although it probably came closer to resolving the problem than the Davis idea.[31]

In spite of this difference of opinion, Evans was greatly impressed by Davis, who had taken the lead in organizing the American Medical Association. He invited Davis to accept the professorship of physiology and pathology at Rush.[32] Davis did so and brought to Rush his own widely circulated ideas for reforming medical education. Sensitive to the charge that his earlier plan to lengthen the medical school term would exclude farm boys who could attend only in the winter, Davis now proposed that medical education be free. Only those of obvious ability would be allowed to attend medical school.[33]

At the opening session in the fall of 1849 Davis announced that the faculty of Rush had adopted in principle his plan for free medical education. Students would receive three of their class tickets free, and the hope was that ultimately all would be free.[34] In taking this action the members of the faculty were not guided entirely by altruistic motives. They hoped to secure financial support from the state legislature. State support was justified on the ground that the physician's income was usually small and that the public would benefit from improved medical care.[35] Other medical schools complained that Rush was using the fee reduction as a device to attract additional students, and threatened to ask for a censuring resolution at the next meeting of the American Medical Association.[36] The Rush faculty refused to be influenced by such pressure tactics, and for at least the next two or three years the fees continued at the reduced rate.[37]

This rate had brought the annual tuition at Rush from $60 down to $35.[38] In spite of its lower income, the school was still able to pay Evans a salary of $500 in 1851, a sum which he considered to be quite ample.[39]

Continuing its experimental policy, the college admitted its first woman medical student, a Mrs. Brockway, in the 1850-51 session.[40] She apparently did not return for a second year, but Emily Blackwell, sister of Elizabeth Blackwell, the first woman medical school graduate in the United States, attended lectures in 1852. In the face of bitter criticism, particularly from the Illinois State Medical Society, the school declined to readmit her to finish her studies.[41]

During the 1846-47 session a Negro was admitted to studies at Rush. Critics called Rush a "Nigger School," and the young man apparently was not allowed to graduate. Evans thought the faculty was wrong in thus bowing to public pressure, since that level of criticism "can't do much harm."[42]

In 1847 a hospital was opened by members of the Rush faculty. With a good deal of community support they had been able to acquire an old warehouse on the northeast corner of Kinzie and Wolcott Streets and to convert it for medical use

under the name of "Tippecanoe Hall."[43] The venture seems to
have failed, and when a cholera epidemic struck the city in
July and August, 1849, it was necessary to build an emergency
hospital to care for the thousand or more cholera victims in
the city.[44]

By the time the second session of the Illinois legislature
convened late in 1849, a petition had been prepared asking for
a charter for a new hospital. Approved by the legislature October 29, 1849, the charter named Judge Mark Skinner, Judge
Hugh T. Dickey, and Dr. John Evans as trustees of the institution, which was to be called the Illinois General Hospital of
the Lake.[45]

Some difficulty was encountered in raising funds for equipment, so finally in September, 1850, Dr. Davis agreed to give
a series of public lectures "on the sanitary condition of the
city and the means for its improvement." Proceeds were to be
devoted to the purchase of furniture for the hospital.[46] Davis
had hardly begun his series when the Campbell Minstrels
arrived in town. Realizing the minstrel show would be tough
competition, Davis cancelled his remaining lectures, and the
minstrels, in turn, gave a benefit performance for the hospital.[47]

It was difficult to find a suitable building. At one time the
trustees proposed locating the hospital in Tippecanoe Hall.[48]
But by November, 1850, a suite of rooms was rented in the old
Lake House hotel, and the hospital began to receive patients
on November 23, 1850.[49] Dr. Brainard was appointed surgeon;
Dr. Davis and Dr. Levi D. Boone were chosen as physicians;
and Evans, who was also secretary of the board of trustees, was
named physician to treat female patients.[50]

At first the hospital tried to operate with students from Rush
acting as nurses, but this proved to be completely unsatisfactory. Dr. Brainard and Dr. Evans finally asked the bishop of
the Roman Catholic diocese to request the Sisters of Mercy in
the city to do the nursing. The bishop consented, but the sisters were reluctant to assume the new duties, because they had

*Lake House in Chicago is shown
in this photograph taken about 1860.*

no nursing experience. Finally, however, the bishop and the doctors answered all their objections, and the sisters assumed their new posts on February 22, 1851.[51]

Rates at the new institution were quite low. Patients whose bills were paid by the county were accommodated for $2.50 per week. Other patients could have private rooms for $2.50 to $4.50 per week.[52] Services of the medical staff were available to all hospital patients without charge, and in return, the college was allowed to use the hospital for its clinical courses.[53]

Davis is usually given credit for assuming the initiative in the organization of the first hospital in Chicago.[54] But this assumption overlooks the fact that Evans and the other members of the Rush faculty were instrumental in founding the short-lived 1847 hospital;[55] that an emergency hospital was provided after the cholera epidemic started in 1849;[56] that, following this step, Evans and the other faculty members doubtless insisted on the establishment of a permanent hospital; and that, significantly, Davis was not a trustee of the Illinois General Hospital of the Lake.

In the spring of 1850 Evans, Dr. W. B. Herrick, Dr. Levi D. Boone, Dr. Daniel Brainard, Dr. Davis, and a number of other Rush faculty members organized the Chicago Medical Society. On April 19, 1850, a constitution was adopted and officers were elected. Dr. Boone was chosen president and Evans was selected to represent the society at the meeting of the American Medical Association in Cincinnati in May, 1850.[57] Perhaps because he was not named to an office, Brainard refused to attend after the first meeting of the Society, and a number of others followed his example.[58] Consequently, with no quorum present, the meetings became what one author has called "pathological sociables."[59] Evans, Davis, and several others continued to attend regularly, but it was impossible to transact business. In 1852 the group was reorganized as the Cook County Medical Society and attendance improved.[60]

Although Evans was the delegate of the Chicago Medical

Society, several other members also attended the 1850 meeting of the American Medical Association. Dr. Brainard was elected to the office of third vice president, and Dr. Davis examined the connection between the cerebellum and "The Sexual Propensity, or Function of Generation." Evans introduced his new medical instrument, the obstetrical extractor, and "demonstrated upon the mannakin, the mode of its application in practice."[61]

Invented by Evans in 1848 while he was teaching at Rush,[62] the obstetrical extractor consisted of two identical jointed steel fingers, eleven inches long; a one-inch silk band, nine inches long; and four half-inch braided silk straps, eighteen inches long. These were connected in such a way that the device could be fastened about the baby's head during birth, and the silk band and straps would allow the pulling force to be distributed over a wide area.[63]

Evans considered the new instrument to be a great advance over forceps, because use of the latter involved possible injury to both mother and child. The simple instructions provided that, after use, the silk bands were to be rinsed in soapy water.[64] Although the era of antiseptic surgery had not arrived, Evans suggested that during puerperal fever epidemics the physician could, without undue expense, discard the silk bands after one use. Ordinarily they would be used over and over again.[65] The success of his device is illustrated by the fact that in 1855 an enterprising Rush College student began manufacturing obstetrical extractors and selling them as his own invention.[66]

In September, 1849, following the great cholera epidemic in Chicago, Evans published an article asserting that cholera was contagious and that quarantine regulations should be adopted.[67] This view of cholera was rejected by most members of the medical profession at the time. Their attitude could be attributed partly to the fact that many prominent physicians were also heavy investors in real estate and commercial ventures, and a quarantine might be expected to affect them adversely. Brainard, Boone, and Davis, for example, held that cholera was not contagious and that quarantine would be of no value in checking its spread.[68]

Among the more bizarre theories regarding the spread of cholera were the "electrical theory," which held that cholera spread when the amount of electricity in the air decreased;[69] and one called the "boundary theory," which held that cholera had an affinity for limestone districts and avoided areas of granite. Regarding the boundary theory, Evans wrote that cholera would probably avoid granite "until high and craggy mountains . . . become eligible sites for great commercial cities."[70]

Although his ideas on contagion were not popular at the time, Evans refused to abandon his efforts in this matter. In February, 1866, after he had quit the practice of medicine, he was in Washington as senator-elect, attempting to secure approval for the Colorado statehood bill. When he learned that an epidemic of Asiatic cholera threatened to strike the country, he urged Congress to enact a national quarantine law. Reprinting his "Observations on the Spread of Asiatic Cholera" that had appeared in the September, 1849, issue of *The North-Western Medical and Surgical Journal,* he added new comments relative to the current danger and distributed copies to members of Congress.[71] As a result of his efforts and those of other prominent medical men, and in spite of serious opposition, a joint resolution was approved on May 26, 1866, authorizing the Secretary of the Treasury to take whatever steps he might deem necessary to prevent the introduction of cholera into the United States.[72] The law expired in 1867, but the precedent was established which allowed permanent legislation to be adopted in 1893.[73]

In 1844 the Rush College faculty had begun to publish the *Illinois Medical and Surgical Journal,* under the editorial guidance of Dr. James V. Z. Blaney.[74] When Evans joined the faculty in the following year, it was decided to widen the scope of the publication. The name was changed to *The Illinois and Indiana Medical and Surgical Journal*, and an editorial staff, consisting of Drs. Blaney, Brainard, Herrick, and Evans, was appointed. The magazine began simultaneous publication in Chicago and Indianapolis, so that physicians in both areas would feel it was their own publication.[75]

Evans had a deep appreciation of the value of professional publication, and he constantly urged his colleagues to write for the journal. In a letter to Dr. John McLean he said:

> Dr., you must see that the character, usefulness and success of our school must depend upon the reputation of its teachers. Then it becomes important for us each not only to teach well and profoundly, but to write well and extensively. This, while it enriches our Journal, extends the reputation of the school.[76]

Evans wrote frequently for the journal, and when the chance came in 1848 to become part-owner of the publication in partnership with Dr. William B. Herrick, he seized the opportunity. In order to appeal to a wider audience, the name was changed to *The North-Western Medical and Surgical Journal*, and beginning with the first issue of April, 1848, publication was made bimonthly rather than monthly. The quality of the articles improved noticeably, and circulation zoomed.[77] Each issue usually held at least one signed article, book review, or editorial by Evans. Beginning with the issue of May, 1850, Evans was the sole editor of the journal,[78] and by March, 1851, he had acquired complete ownership of the magazine.[79]

Payment was not required in advance, and as a result there was a continuing problem in collecting for subscriptions. By March, 1852, some subscribers were three years in arrears.[80] The regular rates were two dollars per volume, if payment were made in full before the close of the current volume. After the volume was closed, the rate became three dollars. Evans finally offered to take two dollars per year as full payment if an account were paid by March 1, 1852. After that date, he

THE NORTH-WESTERN

MEDICAL AND SURGICAL

JOURNAL.

EDITED BY JOHN EVANS, M.D.,

PROFESSOR OF OBSTETRICS &C. IN RUSH MED. COL.; MEMBER OF THE AM. MED. ASSOCIATION;
ONE OF THE PHYSICIANS TO THE ILL. GEN. HOSPITAL; FORMERLY SUP'T OF THE
IND. HOSPITAL FOR THE INSANE, ETC., ETC.

VOLUME IV.---WHOLE SERIES VOLUME VIII.

CHICAGO AND INDIANAPOLIS:
PRINTED BY LANGDON & ROUNDS,
161 Lake street, Chicago.
1852.

promised, delinquent accounts would be "placed in the hands of an attorney for collection."[81] As he explained plaintively in an earlier issue, "we need the money to pay the printer."[82]

In spite of these difficulties the journal was a paying proposition. In 1851 Evans estimated that his income from the journal would be $1,000.[83] In 1852 he was able to trade the journal for five acres of land on Chicago's West Side.[84] He had speculated in Chicago real estate since 1847 and was beginning to make money at it.[85]

When he moved permanently to Chicago in 1848,[86] Evans opened a private practice in an office at 53 Clarke Street.[87] John Nutt, who had received his M.D. at Rush in 1848 and worked for Evans on the staff of the Indiana Hospital for the Insane,[88] married John's sister Ann, and by 1852 had joined Evans in practice in Chicago. They remained partners until 1857, when John gave up his practice and his teaching position at Rush.[89]

During his medical career in Chicago, Evans played a leading role in improving educational standards in medical schools and in promoting professional medical societies. He was one of the first to ask for public regulation of the profession,[90] and he insisted that doctors should be on the watch constantly for medical charlatans.[91] He led the successful fight for state care of the insane in Indiana, and after he left that state, he trained himself to become one of the leading obstetricians in Chicago. His campaign for a cholera quarantine was temporarily thwarted by other members of the medical profession, but his efforts to establish a hospital in Chicago were more immediately successful. By 1857, however, medicine seemed to offer few additional challenges, and his interest began to wander to other fields.

6

"A Stranger in a Strange Land"

Late in 1848, following his resignation from the position of superintendent of the Indiana Hospital for the Insane, Evans moved his family to Chicago.[1] Four children had been born to John and Hannah while they lived in Indiana, but three of them died during early childhood. Two little boys, Joseph Canby Evans and David Evans, succumbed in 1844, the same year in which Josephine was born. A third, John, died in 1848, probably just prior to the move to Chicago.[2]

Chicago was not a pleasant place to live, and Hannah did not like it.[3] No grading had been established for streets, and with little or no natural drainage they were constantly full of mud and filth. Buildings were erected with their front entrances at varying elevations, and the sidewalks changed levels accordingly.[4] An eastern reporter described it this way:

> With almost every block of buildings there is a change of grade, sometimes of one foot, sometimes of three feet, sometimes of five. These ascents or descents are made by steps or by short, steep inclined planes of boards, with or without cleats or cross-pieces, to prevent slipping, according to the fancy of the adjoining proprietor who erects them.[5]

The Chicago climate took its toll, and Hannah was stricken with tuberculosis,[6] but after a few months in Indiana in the summer of 1849 her health improved dramatically.[7] By the end of the summer of 1850 it seemed as though the disease had been arrested and Hannah was on the road to recovery.[8] The future looked promising.

Evans' real estate investments were earning substantial profits, and he always regarded his Chicago landholdings as the basis for his sizable fortune. "Over and above what was necessary to live," he remarked later, "that was the first money I had made."[9]

In these early real estate ventures Evans joined in a partnership with Dr. Daniel Brainard. One of their most successful investments was a three-story brick building, which they erected opposite the Sherman House. The partners had obtained a twenty-year lease on a corner lot extending 180 feet on Clark and 80 feet on Randolph. David Evans, after a trip to Chicago to inspect the site, agreed to lend the money to cover John's share of the project. Upon completion of the building Evans moved his office into the structure, and space was also occupied by the Chicago *Tribune* and the U.S. Post Office. Within a short time Evans bought out his partner's interest, and by 1852 the building was called the Evans Block.[10] Evans realized an average net income of $5,000 per year from this building during the term of the lease.[11]

Because of this increasing success with investments, the Evans family began to enjoy an improved standard of living. In the summer of 1850 they built a new home at 92 Washington Street, just a block or so away from his office on Clark and Randolph.[12] The lot on which the house was built cost $2,000, and the rather elaborate structure itself cost $1,700, exclusive of furnishings.[13] The cost of the house and lot was probably several times his yearly income in 1847 and about equal to his 1850 income.[14] By the time he was ready to move into the house in the fall, Hannah's health was improving, and they both looked forward to a life of comparative wealth and comfort.[15]

Perhaps it was the excitement of moving; possibly there had been too much exertion required in decorating and furnishing the house. In any case, no sooner had they moved into their new home than Hannah again fell ill. She was unable to eat and grew weaker by the hour. This new malady was apparently not the direct result of tuberculosis, for, as John reported, "she had no cough, no cold, none of the symptoms of consumption except the great emaciation . . . she has had for about two years."[16]

Hannah knew she was dying, but her main concern was for the welfare of her husband and her child. She calmly gave John instructions to place the girl under the care of his mother, at least for part of the time. She asked John and her friends "to prepare and meet her in heaven." Death offered a blessed relief from her lingering illness, and she told him "that she had no doubt at all of her acceptance with Christ."[17] When her death occurred, October 9, 1850, her body was taken back to Attica for burial beside her three children.[18]

Her death was a crushing blow to John, and for months he struggled to find a new meaning to life. In January he wrote to his father: "I am almost a stranger in a strange land."[19] The early years of their married life had been difficult, and he said:

> Just as I was preparing for the enjoyment of life, and to return to her the reward of a faithful and devoted companionship, in the comforts of a pleasant and happy home to which she had long and earnestly looked forward, and so richly deserved, she is snatched from me and I am left alone.[20]

His professional achievements now seemed to be of little worth. "I have been ambitious," he admitted, "and in my efforts to accomplish my ends [I] have been favored with a marked degree of success." But it seemed so pointless now. "Age," he wrote, "is creeping upon me, and I must ere long follow her, whose death I solitarily mourn, to that bourn whence no traveller returns."[21]

68

For some time he considered the possibility of placing Josephine in a boarding school and taking an extended trip to Europe.[22] Finally he decided to rent the house to friends and board with them. He and Josephine became tenants in the room which he had originally designed as a study.[23]

The decision to remain in Chicago seems to have been prompted in part by an unexpectedly favorable court decision in a suit involving a sixty-acre tract of land on the South Branch of the Chicago River about two miles from the city. His share of the tract amounted to about twenty-five acres. The entire river front was becoming a center for the growing lumber and packing industries. Evans told his father: "I have no fears of realizing $500 per acre if sold at an early day for my 25 acres and by hanging on to it I hope to make it pay me $1,000 per acre." He had only about $50 per acre invested in the land, so he stood to make an enormous profit.[24]

This unforeseen development helped to revive his lagging spirits, and he again began to take a lively interest in his investments, his teaching, and his medical practice. With the money from this one tract, he said, "I will be able to do as I please for I will be rich enough."[25]

Aside from a few personal letters, records of his financial affairs in Chicago are almost nonexistent. Whether he actually made the expected profit on this plot of ground is not known. It is clear, however, that he made a considerable fortune in Chicago real estate. It was this or a similar tract that brought him what he later called "the first money I made."[26] By the mid-fifties his wealth ran to six figures, and in 1862 his income from Chicago real estate alone was $20,608.24.[27]

By 1852 Anne and Dr. John Nutt, his sister and brother-in-law, had moved to Chicago. John Nutt became a partner in practice with Evans, and they continued in this joint practice until 1857.[28] Evans was not satisfied with the treatment Josephine received from the tenants, so he rented the house to his sister and brother-in-law and boarded with them.[29]

Grandfather David and grandmother Rachel were apparently willing to care for Josephine, but John could not bear to part with her for any extended period. He referred to her repeatedly in his letters as "a very *good child*,"[30] "very affectionate,"[31] and "a great comfort to me."[32]

In 1853 John's youngest brother Jason came to Chicago to attend Rush Medical College. He also boarded at 92 Washington Street,[33] and Dr. Evans and Dr. Nutt acted as his preceptors. Jason did poorly at Rush, and he ultimately returned to Waynesville. Complaining that it was impossible to study in the office of Evans and Nutt with the constant clamor about investments and publishing, as well as medicine, Jason determined to transfer to Cincinnati.[34] John was forced to admit that his brother's complaints were well founded, although he and Dr. Nutt felt that Jason had not applied himself to his studies.[35] Jason had been sent to Chicago to stay with John partly because of the fact that his father did not approve of the friends he associated with at home.[36] Jason's behavior in Chicago was evidently only one of a long series of disappointments to his father. When David Evans died in 1861, he directed in his will that Jason's inheritance be $1,500 less than the shares of his brothers and sisters, "he having," as the will put it, "done less for me and cost me more than . . . the others."[37]

John's sister Hannah also lived with the family in Chicago during this period. She had met and fallen in love with a young lawyer, James F. Conover. Her father opposed the marriage and sent her to Chicago in the hope that she would forget the young man. After the exchange of some angry letters, David finally relented and gave his approval to the marriage. In a letter to John he stated that "if she cannot be happy and reconciled to her lot without a communion with Conover we had better submit to it than to cause her to pine away and die."[38] Not only did David give his blessing, but he also offered to help the young couple financially in establishing a home in Detroit,[39] where they raised a large family and lived happily thereafter.[40]

John Evans and his daughter Josephine,
"a very good child," *in the early 1850's.*

In the meantime John Evans' business affairs continued to prosper. While his basic investments seemed to be concerned mainly with real estate,[41] he also spent a good deal of time promoting other business ventures. He realized that Chicago's growth depended on its continued importance as a trading center.[42] When he first came to Chicago with some friends from Attica to sell farm produce,[43] steamboats were offering regular service between Chicago and Buffalo.[44] Wheat would bring from thirty-seven to sixty-six cents more per bushel in Chicago than if it were sold to traders on the Illinois or Ohio Rivers.[45]

From the first Evans was convinced that Chicago had the potential for becoming one of the largest cities in the country.[46] After analyzing population growth in the city for the period 1843-1850,[47] he concluded that Chicago would continue to attract people in increasing numbers. In 1855 he told his father that the "streets near the center of the city are full of men & waggons so that it is a jamb all the time." The development of Chicago, he continued, "has always far exceeded my expectations and I can now see reasons for more rapid advances than ever."[48]

In this expanding economy, investment capital was at a premium, and Evans recognized the need for new banking facilities.[49] A number of private banks had opened, and Evans for a time joined with N. P. Inglehart and R. K. Swift in one such bank.[50] The partners invested in land southwest of the city, which they ditched and drained and subdivided as the new suburb of Brighton.[51] Investments of this sort sometimes required more cash than Evans had available. On one occasion he asked for a loan of several thousand dollars from his father. "As my reputation for ability would be worsted by asking it here," he said, "I would much prefer not to try it if I could get it of thee."[52]

In about 1850 Evans and an Indianapolis friend, Jesse L. Williams, conceived the idea of a railroad connecting Chicago with Ft. Wayne, which was located on the Wabash and Erie

Canal.[53] They organized a company in 1852, the Ft. Wayne and Chicago Railroad. On April 1, 1853, Evans was elected to the board of directors and, together with another director, William B. Ogden, was appointed to superintend construction of the Chicago end of the road.[54] Ogden, one of the organizers of the Galena and Chicago Union Railroad, was then mayor of Chicago, and Evans had been a member of the city council since 1852, as will be described more fully later.

In June, 1853, acting as agent for the Ft. Wayne and Chicago, Evans purchased a forty-acre tract of land in the city of Chicago from Ogden, who was acting as attorney for the owners of the land.[55] The price of $35,000 was probably much more than the land was worth at the time. But the lot was in the industrial area, and Evans' judgment was vindicated the following year when half the tract was sold to the Burlington as a depot site at a price of $140,000.[56] Evans and his father owned property near this site, and the value of these lots also rose, as he had expected.[57]

Because of his position on the city council, Evans was able to push through an ordinance allowing the Ft. Wayne and Chicago to enter the city. He also put his promotional talents to work in securing the right-of-way from Chicago to the Indiana state line. Much of the land in which Evans had invested south of the city was swamp land and had to be drained before it could be sold. At that time the Ft. Wayne and Chicago "hadn't any money to pay for anything," and Evans reported that he "got the right of way by ditching and draining land."[58]

To raise money for the railroad Evans and his agents sold stock to the farmers who lived along the projected right-of-way. These people usually had no cash, but gave mortgages on their farms in payment for the Ft. Wayne stock. The railroad, in turn, issued bonds secured by the mortgages[59] and sold the bonds on the New York market.[60]

Lack of capital led to a consolidation of the Ft. Wayne and Chicago with the Ohio and Pennsylvania Railroad Company and the Ohio and Indiana Railroad Company.[61] The name of the newly-consolidated organization became the Pittsburgh, Fort Wayne, and Chicago Rail Road Company.[62] This reorganization did not produce the needed financial stability, and following the Panic of 1857 the consolidated company was forced into bankruptcy.[63]

J. F. D. Lanier, president of Winslow, Lanier and Company, the railroad's New York broker, formed a committee to reorganize the company. Ultimately the committee, which included Samuel J. Tilden and J. Edgar Thompson in its membership, secured the appointment of William B. Ogden as receiver, while Evans remained as one of the thirteen directors of the road. Ogden's efforts proved fruitless, and Lanier and his associates purchased the road at auction on October 24, 1861, for $2,000,000. No cash seems to have been involved in this transaction; the owners of the old stock and bonds simply exchanged their holdings for a new issue.[64]

The financial position of the Pittsburgh, Fort Wayne and Chicago continued to deteriorate, and in 1869 the road was again reorganized and leased on a long-term basis to the Pennsylvania Railroad.[65] By this time Evans was no longer a member of the board, having resigned in 1862 when he moved to Colorado.[66] At the former date, the road was still not out of the woods financially, but according to Evans, "every man got his money back if he held onto his stock long enough, and most of them with liberal interest."[67] Evans, presumably, was one of those who held on.

Evans also purchased several tracts of land at the sales held by the trustees of the Illinois and Michigan Canal, and he invested heavily in plank roads in the Chicago area.[68] By June, 1855, he was able to report that "at a moderate estimate my assets are worth 200 thousand dollars over my liabilities."[69]

In the 1852 municipal election Evans won a seat on the city council. The Chicago public schools then had a poor reputation, and, as Evans pointed out, "the better class of people did not patronize" them.[70] He therefore ran for office with a promise to reform the schools, and was elected. Because of his special interest, he secured an appointment as chairman of the Committee on Schools.[71]

"The first thing I did," he recalled later, "was to recommend and introduce an ordinance for the appointment of a superintendent of public instruction." The ordinance was approved, and John C. Dore of Boston was given the new post in 1854. One of Superintendent Dore's first proposals was that a public high school be opened.[72] The council asked Evans' committee to prepare an ordinance for this purpose,[73] and it was presented to the council in January, 1855.[74] By the time Evans left office in March of that year the committee had approved his plans for a three-story building of "Milwaukee brick."[75]

One important reason for the sad plight of the Chicago schools was the fact that much of the land in the federal government's donation of section sixteen of each township had been sold over the years at extremely low prices. The remaining land, called the "School Section Addition," was located in the heart of Chicago, the northern boundary being only two blocks south of the Evans Block and the Sherman House.[76] Under Evans' prodding the council decided to keep the remaining land and to offer it for lease only.[77] Evans also urged the purchase of lots in the suburbs for use in future school construction,[78] and he gave a number of lots in his own subdivisions to the city for this purpose.[79]

In his final report to the city council Evans said:

> The education both of the heads and the hearts of the people is an essential element of the public weal; the only sure ground of hope for the improvement of our social and political condition; the only guarantee of the perpetuity of our free institutions.[80]

He pointed to the improvements made by the new superintendent, and said that many parents were transferring their children from private schools in order "that they might enjoy the better advantages offered by the public schools." He estimated

*John Evans feared that the railroad
would "spoil the beauty and pleasantness"
of Chicago's lakefront, shown here in 1853.*

the value of school land in 1855 at $500,000 and stated that while the cash school fund contained only $40,000, the land which had been sold to create the fund was now worth $6,000,000. He begged his successors to keep for the schools what land they yet had, promising that if they did so, "the next generation may be in possession of a revenue adequate to support the grandest system of public schools in the world."[81]

While Evans was still a member of the council, "a Lake street property owner" petitioned the council to order his neighbor to lower his sidewalk three steps. Evans thought that "instead of putting the man's side walk down the other man should be made to put his side walk up, because the city was so in the mud." A majority of the council members evidently agreed with him, and accordingly the city was surveyed and grades were established for each street.[82]

While the expense of this policy to the taxpayers and property owners caused bitter complaints, there was little doubt of the ultimate wisdom of the move.[83] In the rainy season the streets often became so muddy that vehicles were abandoned until they could be dug out. The story has recently been repeated of the wag who erected a sign in the street in front of the city's leading hotel with the inscription, "No Bottom Here."[84] Evans himself in 1853 wrote that he was reluctant to build a home on Michigan Avenue because it was so poorly drained. "I am very fearful," he said, "that the Rail Road is going to spoil the beauty and pleasantness of the Avenue by forming a stagnant pool in front of it."[85]

When the street grades were changed, the fill in front of the Evans Block was so deep that the building had to be raised six feet. Since it was a brick building, fifteen hundred screw jacks were needed to do the job. Evans took advantage of the opportunity and put a basement under the building, thus adding materially to the value of the property.[86]

At Evans' insistence the city council in January, 1855, petitioned the state legislature to create a reform school for juveniles. He condemned the current system which placed youthful offenders "in common and congregate confinement with old, experienced and hardened offenders."[87]

Evans also led in the move to create the Board of Sewerage Commissioners in 1855.[88] This was partly the result of a study of sanitary conditions in the city made by a committee of the Chicago Medical Society under the direction of Dr. N. S. Davis,[89] Evans' colleague at Rush. Davis had written about the need for a sewage system in 1850, and along with the Chicago Medical Society had continued to urge the adoption of other public health measures.[90]

When the annual supper for the members of the Common Council was held at the Sherman House in early March, 1855, with both old and new council members present, John Evans was the featured speaker. He reviewed the development of Illinois and Chicago, after beginning his talk with a customary anecdote. Unlike most of his early public addresses, this one was preserved, since an interested reporter recorded the story substantially as Evans told it.

> When immigration came West entirely in wagons, one of the hundreds daily entering the State at various points contained a family where the mother was a pious old lady of Methodist persuasion. Being slightly unwell she had taken an anodyne and fallen asleep, while the wagon kept on without awaking her, and in the meantime had emerged from a gloomy forest into the center of one of our grand prairies. It was one of the most lovely days in June; the air and sky were glorious, the vast prairie was a rolling sea of velvet verdure, upon whose heaving waves a spray was roses and lilies and countless curious flowers, while the gay birds floated and fluttered above them, filling the air with the sweetest music. The old lady partially awoke and opened her eyes. "Glory," shouted she, faintly at first, but louder as the beautiful vision grew clearer,—"Glory! Here I am in Heaven at last."[91]

His years in Chicago had not only brought Evans a substantial fortune, but they had given him valuable experience in a number of business fields. A personal tragedy failed to defeat him. His initial training in politics in Indiana was broadened in city council and committee work. He had the background for more demanding administrative tasks and awaited the opportunity to put his experience to work.

7

"A Friend to Education"

Tentative plans for a Methodist university in Chicago had been formulated by John Evans and Bishop Matthew Simpson before Evans moved away from Indiana.[1] Nothing came of these plans, however, until 1850. On May 31 of that year nine of the leading citizens of Chicago, who were also members of the various Methodist churches in the city, held an organizational meeting in Grant Goodrich's law office on Lake Street. Goodrich was named chairman of the group, and Andrew J. Brown, an attorney, was named secretary. The meeting was opened with a prayer by the pastor of the Indiana Street Church and a formal address by the pastor of the Clark Street Church. John Evans then spoke on the pressing need for a Methodist university in the city. Members of the group had already made up their minds to take action; before the meeting adjourned, Evans was appointed chairman of a committee to draft a charter for the school, which did not yet have a name.[2]

The committee lost no time in preparing a charter and at a second meeting, held on June 4, 1850, the document was approved. A board of trustees was selected "under the name and style of the 'Trustees of the North Western University.' " Evans was made president of the board, and Andrew J. Brown was named secretary. Grant Goodrich and Dr. N. S. Davis were elected to the executive committee. Among the other prominent Methodists serving on the board was a man named Orrington Lunt. In one of their first official moves, the trustees invited the Rock River, Wisconsin, Michigan, North Indiana, Iowa, and Illinois Conferences of the Methodist Episcopal Church each to name four members to the board of trustees.[3]

The charter was largely the work of Grant Goodrich, since Evans did not have the legal training necessary for drafting such a document. It was also largely through the efforts of Goodrich that the charter was approved by the legislature, January 28, 1851.[4]

Financing the new university proved to be a real problem. The various Methodist conferences had their own plans for educational institutions, and their lack of response to the plea for aid was not unexpected.[5] A memorial was sent to Congress, asking for a grant of land to support the school, but nothing came of this request.[6] Evans then made a determined effort to secure some financial support from the state. Meanwhile, other men were formulating proposals for state and federal school support. One of these was Jonathan Baldwin Turner, former professor at Illinois College. In November, 1851, Turner addressed a convention of farmers at Granville, Illinois. He outlined to the farmers a "Plan for an Industrial University for the state of Illinois."[7] In Turner's view the crying educational need of the day was "a *University for the Industrial Classes* in each of the States, with their consequent subordinate institutions, lyceums, and high schools, in each of the counties and towns."[8] This plan had tremendous appeal to the farmers and mechanics of the state, who felt that existing public and private education was conducted mainly for the benefit of the wealthier professional groups.[9] The convention not only supported Turner's plan, but it printed a thousand copies of his address and sent them to newspapers, congressmen, public officials, and educators throughout the state.[10]

Jonathan Baldwin Turner later led the campaign to establish a state university in Illinois.

A few months later Turner suggested that the "Industrial University" be financed by a federal land grant. Acting for the committee appointed at Granville, he called a new convention to meet at Springfield in June to reconsider the plan and recommend legislative action. Partly as a result of the agitation of the Turner forces, the governor of Illinois called a special session of the legislature, also to meet in June, to consider appropriations from the state's College and Seminary Fund.[11]

Turner's ideas stimulated the supporters of private colleges to action, and they turned out at Springfield in force. The unofficial leader of this group was John Evans,[12] representing not only the infant Northwestern University, but also Rush Medical College, on whose faculty he still served.[13] Evans had developed a counter-plan, and he went to Springfield prepared to work for its adoption.

The convention opened at 9:00 A.M., June 18, 1852, in the courthouse, with Dr. J. A. Kennicott presiding. Evans immediately asked the chairman to name those who were eligible to participate in the convention. Kennicott replied that membership was open to "all persons . . . who, by their own showing, are the friends of practical industrial education."[14] With this decision, Evans and his supporters were admitted to membership. At the first business meeting held that same evening, Evans announced that as "a friend to Education," he would present his own plan to the convention.[15]

Turner immediately raised a point of order, contending that the convention had been called to discuss "*the* plan" which had been presented at Granville. Since Evans and his friends opposed "*the* plan," they were not entitled to participate. Evans responded by simply asking for "the reading of the resolution admitting gentlemen to a seat in the Convention." The secretary read Kennicott's resolution, and the president sustained Evans, who yielded the floor to another opponent of Turner's plan. The outcome of the evening's wrangling was a vaguely worded resolution to recommend "some specific plan . . . to the legislature, with a view to obtaining appropriations to carry it out."[16]

Overnight, a chance for harmony developed. Turner counted noses and found that the Evans forces were hopelessly outnumbered. He magnanimously moved, then, to change the agenda and allow Dr. Evans to present his scheme.[17]

In describing his proposal Evans first asked that the legislature appoint seven citizens to serve as the "Regents of the Industrial University of Illinois" and that "the proceeds of the College and Seminary Fund be placed at their disposal." The regents were to appoint six professors, whose duties, in addition to teaching, would include giving lectures at "mechanical, agricultural and horticultural fairs" and publishing "from time to time such matter of interest pertaining to their departments as they may deem valuable to the public."[18]

The six instructors were to include "a Professor of the Chemistry of Agriculture and the Arts," "a Professor of Practical Agriculture, Horticulture and Botany," "a Professor of Mechanical Philosophy, and the nature and use of tools and machinery," "a Professor of Natural History, Comparative Anatomy, and Veterinary Surgery," "a Professor of Geology, Meterology, and Hygiene," and "a Professor of Normal Instruction in English Literature." These men were to be paid out of the College and Seminary Fund, and the necessary equipment for their teaching was to be purchased from this fund.[19]

The regents were to accredit "as many of the colleges of the state as they may deem expedient." Each professor was to travel about the state giving courses at the accredited colleges "by turns." The colleges, for their part, were to supply laboratory space and lecture halls at a fixed rent, and to establish a suitable course of instruction leading to a bachelor of science degree.[20]

George Lumsden, a Turner disciple, ridiculed the professorships as "travelling menageries" and pointed out the waste in travel expense and in duplicated equipment. He moved that the Evans proposal be tabled, and his motion carried.[21]

The initiative then passed to Turner. At the afternoon session he requested the chairman to appoint a committee of five, including Kennicott himself, to present a memorial to the legislature calling for the establishment of a "State Industrial University." Kennicott, who favored Turner's plan, termed this motion a compromise, inasmuch as no specific plan would be mentioned in the memorial. Evans then asked Kennicott to appoint to the committee an equal number from each side of the question, but the chairman refused. A member of the Evans group then moved to amend the motion by naming Evans, Turner, and a member of each faction to serve on the committee. The amendment failed, but the motion carried.[22]

Realizing at last that their cause was defeated, Evans and his group made strong protest statements and walked out of the convention.[23] The local newspaper gave this summary of their position:

> They desired the old system, which has been mostly used for the benefit of the professional classes, to be improved by adding professorships for the benefit of the laboring classes. This is the *Old School* system,[24] and is opposed to the project of education for the masses, first started here in the winter of 1850-51, and ably seconded by the Granville Convention.[25]

The memorial prepared by Chairman Kennicott's committee was just what Evans had expected. The committee condemned the whole idea of aid to private colleges, saying:

> The equal distribution of . . . [the school funds] among the ten or twelve colleges in charge of the various religious denominations of the State, either now in existence or soon to arise and claim their share of these funds, and the equally just claim of Medicine and other Institutions for their share, it is thought by your memorialists, would produce too great a division to render these funds of much practical value to the people of the state.[26]

Undaunted by the defeat at Springfield, Evans and the other

trustees continued to work for the establishment of their new university. A site was still to be chosen, and when it became known that John Evans and Orrington Lunt had been appointed to find a suitable location, the two men were besieged by real estate promoters. One of them, however, had a proposition that seemed acceptable. He was P. F. W. Peck, whom Evans called "one of the largest real estate dealers in Chicago." Peck offered to sell the university sixteen lots on the corner of La Salle and Jackson Streets at a price of $500 per lot.[27] When Evans told him that they had no money, Peck replied: "I will sell you cheap and give you time."[28] Peck was willing to accept a down payment of $2,000, followed by three annual installments of $2,000 each. Thinking the site would be suitable for a preparatory school, Evans and the other trustees subscribed enough for the first payment.[29] Yet before the final payment came due, the trustees had picked another site for the university and had decided not to open a preparatory school.[30] Nevertheless, the land was retained, and it became an important source of income for the university, serving as a site for the Grand Pacific Hotel and later for the Illinois Trust and Savings Bank.[31]

It was through board member Orrington Lunt that Evans met the young lady who was to become his second wife. Lunt's wife Cornelia had three unmarried sisters, "famous for their beauty and accomplishments." These girls visited Cornelia in Chicago, and all met, later marrying prominent Chicagoans.[32]

The sister who was to become the wife of John Evans was Margaret Patten Gray. She was born in Bowdoinham, Maine, August 21, 1830, one of the nine children of Samuel and Susan Gray.[33] Margaret's father had moved to Bowdoinham from Rhode Island and was soon established as a prosperous lawyer, shipowner, and shipbuilder.[34] The Gray family was ardently Methodist, and Margaret had been baptized a Methodist in the stream that ran by her home.[35] Her sister Cornelia Augusta Gray had married Orrington Lunt, a native of Bowdoinham, in January, 1842. A few months later the young couple moved to Chicago, and Lunt soon made a fortune for himself in grain speculation and other investments.[36]

It seems likely that John Evans and Margaret Gray first met at a social gathering in the Lunt home. By July, 1853, John and Margaret had decided to be married, and on the twenty-second of that month he wrote to Margaret's parents asking for her hand.[37]

Remembering the ill feeling caused by his father's reaction to the proposed marriage of Hannah and James Conover, thirty-nine-year-old John Evans wrote to ask his father's permission to marry. "I would respectfully ask thy consent, and that of Mother to our Marriage," he said.[38] By chance David Evans' reply was delayed in the mail, and John feared for a time his father opposed the marriage.[39] David's approving letter was finally delivered on August 15, just as John was leaving for Bowdoinham.[40]

A lively and attractive girl, Margaret brought back John's former optimism and enthusiasm. It was almost as though he were in his twenties again. His letters to Margaret are full of youthful protestations of love. "I long for the elapse of the two weeks that must pass before we are united by the *Legal* bonds of Matrimony," he wrote to Margaret, "which with the silken chords that have already been entwined, will put us into the blissful relation of husband & wife. But I fancy I see you blush so I desist."[41] In another letter, he chided Margaret for her reluctance to let him kiss her. "I shall contend that a bad pledge is more honored in the breach than the observance," he declared, "remembering that you do sometimes vary from the strict observance of pledges."[42] Never an early riser,[43] John even promised to get up early in the morning for an occasional horseback ride with Margaret.[44] He carried a daguerreotype of "Maggie" in a pocket "next my heart" and placed it under his pillow at night.[45]

He and Margaret planned to move into the house which

Margaret Gray Evans, the second wife of John Evans.

John and Hannah had built, then being rented to John and Ann Nutt. Since his brother-in-law and sister were having difficulty finding another house, John tried to rent a suite of rooms in the Tremont House.[46] Rates were high, but Evans did not want to forfeit his "seat on the council by moving out of the ward." The matter was still not settled when he left Chicago for Bowdoinham, but it seems apparent that they lived either in the Tremont House or the Mattison House for a time after their marriage.[47]

Regardless of these difficulties, Margaret was determined to live in a home furnished just as lavishly as that of her parents in Bowdoinham. Her purchases of household furnishings caused John to complain, half seriously: "I must try & get my plain Quaker notions of style revised and *improved*."[48] It was planned that his daughter Josephine, who was staying with her grandparents in Waynesville, would live with them in Chicago, and apparently Margaret's sister Elizabeth was also invited to stay.[49] The Irish maid, Bridget, who had helped care for Josephine before, agreed to work for the family. John wrote that "we are certainly very fortunate in securing her as she is so neat, trustworthy, faithful, active and good to Josey." Still, as he pointed out, "she is not a very good cook [but] every thing will have the credit of perfect cleanliness."[50]

The wedding took place at the Gray home in Bowdoinham, Maine, August 18, 1853, and John later commented on the "delightful time we had on the occasion."[51] There is apparently no description of Margaret's wedding gown, but there is a record of what John planned to wear: "a black dress coat . . . black pants—a white silk vest with very small tinsel spots— patent leather boots, . . . white kids & hat."[52] It was probably the first time he had ever worn such splendid attire. His "plain Quaker notions" had temporarily undergone considerable revision.

Just before Evans left for Bowdoinham the trustees of the university purchased a site for the campus. It was located on the lake shore north of Chicago in an area that had not been seriously considered before because it was thought to be too swampy.[53] Orrington Lunt discovered the place accidentally while out driving with a friend, and he was at once certain that this was what they wanted.[54]

On July 4, 1853, the entire board of trustees traveled to the site to inspect it. They drove down a cow path through the marsh and suddenly found themselves in a "splendid oak forest" overlooking the lake.[55] Lunt later recalled that the view was so impressive that some of the men tossed their hats into the air and cheered.[56]

The ground which the trustees thus visited comprised a 379-acre farm[57] owned by Dr. J. H. Foster, whom Evans later described as "a rich, close man."[58] The asking price was $25,000, and Foster refused to consider anything less. If the price seemed high, the terms were attractive—$1,000 down and the balance in ten years at 6 per cent interest,[59]

Evans thought that the land beside the lake was worth no more than $25.00 per acre, so before agreeing to purchase the property, he talked to Walter S. Gurney, president of the Chicago and Milwaukee Railroad. Gurney stated that the railroad would probably run right through the site. Evans then felt justified in paying the Foster asking price, since the railroad connection would improve accessibility and enhance the value of the land.[60]

An agreement to buy the land was drawn up on August 11, 1853. Evans apparently furnished a good part of the down payment, as his gifts to the university in 1854 totaled more than $900.[61] After buying the land, the trustees were faced with the serious problem of finding a name for that "delightful spot," as Evans called it.[62] At first some members of the board wanted to call the proposed university town "Luntsville" or "Orrington" in honor of the man who discovered the site for them.[63] However, the executive committee proposed to the trustees "that the university town be called 'Evans.' "[64] At the meeting held on February 3, 1854, the trustees considered "Evans" and "University Place," but could not agree on either name.[65] Evans himself seems to have wanted to name the town in honor of his old friend Matthew Simpson,[66] whom he had been trying to retain as president of the school.[67] The board would not accept such a proposal, and, as Evans recalled later, "the board of trustees voted to call the town 'Evanston' as was understood for a compliment to me."[68]

The trustees then proceeded to raise money for the construction of suitable buildings. Streets were laid off, and lots were offered for sale at $500 each. Evans and Lunt started the ball rolling by buying two lots apiece. The trustees offered liberal credit terms, and with the example of Evans and Lunt, plus a good bit of promotional work by Evans, the home sites began to sell rather quickly.[69]

Andrew J. Brown and Harvey B. Hurd purchased an adjoining 248-acre tract and began to sell lots in that area. The partners donated a right-of-way to the Chicago and Milwaukee Railroad, with the condition that all passenger trains must stop in Evanston.[70] The railroad reached Evanston in September, 1854, and had pushed north to Waukegan by January 1, 1855, when the first building was dedicated on the campus.[71]

The board also began to sell tuition certificates "at the *extremely low price of one hundred dollars.*" These certificates guaranteed free tuition "to the purchaser, to all his sons, to all his legally adopted sons, and all his grandsons, one at a time during the purchaser's life, and descends by will forever."[72] Evans bought the first such tuition certificate and later used it to send his sons, William Gray Evans and Evan Elbert Evans, to Northwestern.[73]

The attorney regularly employed by Elizabeth Clark Garrett, a wealthy Chicago widow, was Grant Goodrich, one of the Northwestern trustees. Through his efforts and those of her pastor and other prominent Methodists, Mrs. Garrett was persuaded, early in December, 1853, to leave the bulk of her

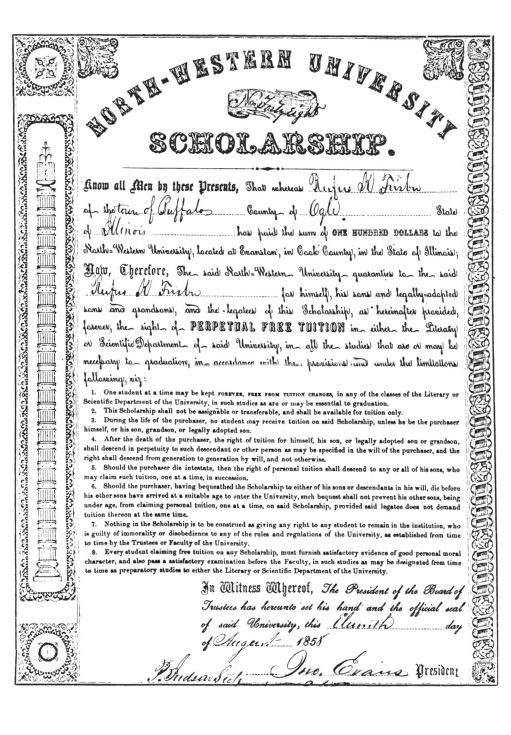

NORTH-WESTERN UNIVERSITY

SCHOLARSHIP.

Know all Men by these Presents, That whereas Rufus K Fisher of the town of Buffalo County of Ogle State of Illinois has paid the sum of **ONE HUNDRED DOLLARS** to the North-Western University, located at Evanston, in Cook County, in the State of Illinois;

Now, Therefore, The said North-Western University guaranties to the said Rufus K Fisher for himself, his sons and legally-adopted sons and grandsons, and the legatees of this Scholarship, as hereinafter provided, forever, the right of **PERPETUAL FREE TUITION** in either the Literary or Scientific Department of said University, in all the studies that are or may be necessary to graduation, in accordance with the provisions and under the limitations following, viz:

1. One student at a time may be kept FOREVER, FREE FROM TUITION CHARGES, in any of the classes of the Literary or Scientific Department of the University, in such studies as are or may be essential to graduation.

2. This Scholarship shall not be assignable or transferable, and shall be available for tuition only.

3. During the life of the purchaser, no student may receive tuition on said Scholarship, unless he be the purchaser himself, or his son, grandson, or legally adopted son.

4. After the death of the purchaser, the right of tuition for himself, his son, or legally adopted son or grandson, shall descend in perpetuity to such descendant or other person as may be specified in the will of the purchaser, and the right shall descend from generation to generation by will, and not otherwise.

5. Should the purchaser die intestate, then the right of personal tuition shall descend to any or all of his sons, who may claim such tuition, one at a time, in succession.

6. Should the purchaser, having bequeathed the Scholarship to either of his sons or descendants in his will, die before his other sons have arrived at a suitable age to enter the University, such bequest shall not prevent his other sons, being under age, from claiming personal tuition, one at a time, on said Scholarship, provided said legatee does not demand tuition thereon at the same time.

7. Nothing in the Scholarship is to be construed as giving any right to any student to remain in the institution, who is guilty of immorality or disobedience to any of the rules and regulations of the University, as established from time to time by the Trustees or Faculty of the University.

8. Every student claiming free tuition on any Scholarship, must furnish satisfactory evidence of good personal moral character, and also pass a satisfactory examination before the Faculty, in such studies as may be designated from time to time as preparatory studies to either the Literary or Scientific Department of the University.

In Witness Whereof, The President of the Board of Trustees has hereunto set his hand and the official seal of said University, this Eleventh day of August 1858

P. Sudson Sec'y   Jno. Evans President

estate to found a school for the training of Methodist ministers. A few weeks later, it was arranged that the school be built on the university campus.[74] Although it had a separate corporate status, the theological school became very closely identified with the university. Most of the members of the board of trustees of the seminary also served as members of the university board. Evans, Goodrich, and Lunt were named executors of the Garrett will, and it was contemplated that construction of the seminary buildings would begin after Mrs. Garrett's death.[75]

Plans for the seminary were changed abruptly in 1854 after John P. Dempster arrived in Chicago. He had helped to start a Methodist theological school at Concord, New Hampshire, and was on his way to Bloomington, Illinois, to start another one there. Goodrich met him in Chicago and asked him to work on the seminary at Evanston.[76]

Dempster replied that he would accept the proposal if the university would agree to erect a building and provide $2,500 per year to pay the faculty. Evans and four others agreed to contribute $500 apiece each year for five years, and the university agreed to provide the building. Mrs. Garrett, who was still involved in the settlement of her husband's estate, agreed to begin paying the expenses after five years.[77]

Dempster was named president of the school,[78] which was called Garrett Biblical Institute.[79] The building, called Dempster Hall, was completed in late 1854, and opening ceremonies were held January 1, 1855. No charge was made for tuition or room rent, and the cost of meals and laundry was to be shared by the students.[80]

At about this same time Evans decided to give up his medical practice and move to Evanston. In 1852 he had traded the medical journal for five acres of land on Chicago's West Side,[81] and now he found that his numerous investments left little time for medicine. He practically retired from medical practice in the fall of 1855, when the family moved to

Evanston,[82] but he did not resign his chair at Rush Medical College until 1857.[83]

In the last part of June, 1855, with Margaret expecting their first child, John let the contract for the construction of their new home in Evanston.[84] It was a rambling, two-story structure facing east on Judson Avenue. The half-block lot was bordered on the west by Hinman Avenue and on the south by Clark Street. A broad expanse of oak-shaded lawn stretched east to the park on the lake shore. A formal garden was placed on the west side of the house, filled with "flowers and shrubs, among which gravel walks wound in geometric design." A barn and a handyman's cottage stood on the north end of the property, surrounded by orchard, "hot beds and vegetable garden."[85]

After moving to Evanston late in the fall of 1855,[86] Evans commuted by train between his Evanston home and his Chicago office.[87] His niece, Cornelia Gray Lunt, has written a charming story of her Uncle John's morning trip to the station:

> Its funny to see Uncle John Evans take his breakfast as if he had a whole month to do it in—every minute the train time getting nearer and nobody can ever hurry him. I've laughed inside seeing them all try with that buggy always waiting at the door and Aunt Margaret saying "Now Pa, you know its getting late," and he slowly swallowing the last of his coffee. Perhaps he'll say "Plenty of time," or perhaps he'll only smile and ask for another cup of coffee, which he'll relish to the last drop and it seems as if the whole of Evanston couldn't make him hasten over it. "That's good," he often says with keen approval; then up without one evidence of hurry getting leisurely, sometimes with the whole family standing nervously by, into his coat and hat, and giving some last direction or farewell words with undisturbed composure. Then—a swift turn from that door and with one jump he's inside, grabs the reins and dashes off like mad. Its all in a second and you can't see the trap as it tears around the corner and makes one shiver for fear it'll turn over—but it never does. I suppose the train waits if he's not there—They say he comes up steaming every morning, and every morning just the same he alights coolly from his Buggy. The boy is always waiting

to take it back—and he throws down the reins and calmly gets. into the waiting Cars. He never will hurry beforehand and he was never known to miss that train.[88]

Those who built new homes in Evanston seem to have been a congenial group. In the homes of the leading families there were frequent social evenings, involving "students, teachers, trustees and citizens." Mrs. Harriet S. Kidder remembered that

at those gatherings, after a substantial supper was served, there was singing, sometimes short talks, and always prayer before separating. In all the social gatherings of that day we met early, and generally left before eleven o'clock.[89]

Mrs. Andrew J. Brown recalled that "Governor and Mrs. Evans had a beautiful home on the Lake Shore, always open to the young people."[90] Mrs. Oliver Marcy, who moved to Evanston in 1862, said that John and Margaret "were quite distinctive features of Evanston society in the early days. Mrs. Evans was a woman of superb presence, and the daughter, Josephine, a favorite among young people."[91] Cornelia Gray Lunt always liked to visit the Evans home, particularly in the summer, when she and Josephine could swim in the lake, using their nightgowns as bathing suits. According to her *Sketches*, the people in Evanston "all have nice houses," and there were "trees, trees, trees everywhere," making the whole village "a green loveliness."[92]

As was usual throughout most of his adult life, Evans frequently journeyed away from home. When he was gone, Margaret found pleasant companionship among the ladies of Evanston, many of whom had a similar New England background.[93]

A temperance advocate since his youth in Waynesville,[94] Evans helped to organize the Indianapolis chapter of the Sons of Temperance in 1846.[95] In the summer of 1855 Evans and some friends formed the Maine Law Alliance of the State of Illinois to sponsor an amendment which would have provided for state-wide prohibition.[96] The measure was defeated, largely in "the South part of the state," which "rolled up great majorities" against it.[97] Nonetheless, all was not lost. An amendment to the Northwestern University charter had been approved on February 14, 1855, providing that

> no spirituous, vinous, or other fermented liquors shall be sold under license, or otherwise, within four miles of the location of said university, except for medicinal, mechanical, or sacramental purposes.[98]

Another charter amendment, approved at the same time, declared that "all property of whatever kind and description belonging to or owned by said corporation shall be forever free from taxation for any or all purposes."[99] In speaking of both these amendments Evans said: "I do not claim that I did this but my associates and I did."[100]

Northwestern University began operation in November, 1855, with the registration of ten students;[101] Garrett Biblical Institute had started in January of the same year; and J. W. Johns, "originator of the panorama of the route to California," had founded the nearby Northwestern Female College. All three institutions were housed in wooden buildings, but all expected soon to improve their condition.[102]

Anticipating the growth of the town and a corresponding increase in land values, Evans urged the Northwestern Board of Trustees in 1855 to stop selling land in Evanston. He proposed that the university lease its property at 6 per cent of the market value, with reappraisal every ten years. The trustees tabled his resolution.[103] Still intent on achieving this purpose, on November 22, 1866, John and Margaret Evans deeded to the university property in Chicago worth $25,000. Their only stipulation was that this property be held "in trust . . . by said institution in perpetuity, for Lease, Rent, or permanent improvement . . . and that the rents arising therefrom shall be applied to the support of the Chair of Mental and Moral Philosophy."[104] In accepting this endowment the trustees agreed to

The original "Old College" building of Northwestern.
The rear wing was added in later years.

withhold from sale "in perpetuity at least one quarter of each and every block in the village of Evanston, and in such addition as it shall make thereto, for lease, rent, or permanent improvements."[105]

In later years, when expenses mounted, the trustees regretted their bargain and pressed Evans to allow a revision of the terms. Replying in a letter dated June 22, 1875, Evans refused to accede to their request and in doing so enunciated some of the principles on which his own fortune was based. "To buy only when property is low, and sell only when it is high," he said, "is the rule that makes individual fortunes, and it is equally wise for an institution." The population of Evanston, then five thousand, would increase for years to come. "It is a fair estimate," he told the board, "that the value of the real estate of a city is doubled by every one hundred per cent increase in its population. The parties who hold the real estate," he said, "enjoy the benefits of the advance." Thus, "the fact that people now prefer to purchase rather than to lease, is the strongest possible argument in favor of the reservation."[106]

In 1882 the indebtedness of the university rose to alarming proportions,[107] and John Evans agreed to contribute $25,000, if the university would raise another $75,000.[108] The trustees accepted his offer and obtained the requisite donations, assisted greatly by a matching $25,000 gift from William Deering. In September, 1883, the trustees accepted the notes of Evans and Deering for $25,000 each,[109] and on February 7, 1884, Evans paid his note with $25,000 cash.[110]

In September, 1888, Evans offered the university an additional $50,000 worth of property in Chicago. This was a dock on the lake front, which Evans valued at more than $75,000 and which was subject to a $25,000 lien. Since the dock would be free from taxation under university ownership, Evans judged that it "would be more valuable to the university than to any private party." His two previous gifts of $25,000 were to constitute a $50,000 endowment for a "chair of Moral and

Intellectual Philosophy." The dock property was to be used to endow a "chair of Latin." In return, Evans promised "to modify the condition restricting indebtedness (which has not been regarded) made in my last donation, as it is liable to embarrass the Institution in carrying out its grand designs."[111]

The board accepted Evans' offer, and on September 24, 1889, it set aside $100,000 worth of property as a perpetual trust to maintain the *"John Evans Chair of 'Moral and Intellectual Philosophy,'* and the *John Evans Chair of the 'Latin Language and Literature.'* " Evans, in turn, released his previous gifts of Chicago real estate from the restrictions that he had imposed.[112] This endowment brought the total value of John Evans' contributions to Northwestern University to $106,370 in cash and property.[113]

Although he retained his post as president of the board of trustees, Evans naturally took less of an interest in Northwestern after he moved to Denver and became involved in the affairs of another university. In 1875 Orrington Lunt became vice president of the board of trustees and acting president. Finally, in 1894, Evans resigned the presidency and was succeeded by Lunt.[114]

Through his connections with Rush Medical College and the *North-Western Medical and Surgical Journal,* Evans played a leading role in raising the standards of medical education. He worked on the city council's committee on schools and was one of the founders and one of the most ardent promoters of Northwestern University and Garrett Biblical Institute, both of which had the dual purpose of improving education and fostering religion. Seeming to prefer private control of colleges and universities, Evans made a vigorous effort to obtain state financial support for the private institutions with which he was associated. When his efforts here were unsuccessful, he worked just as hard to support these schools through private contributions, and he gave generously of his own time and money in their behalf.

100

8

"The Blighting Influence of Slavery"

Although he had been a Whig all his life, as his father was before him, John Evans announced his candidacy for Congress on August 11, 1854, as what a newspaper called an "Independent Democrat." In a statement which he issued to the press at that time, Evans said he had been invited to become a candidate by that "portion of the good and true of the Democratic party with which I have heretofore acted." Similar requests had come from "citizens generally," he said, "in whose discrimination and judgement I place confidence." He had decided not to seek the regular party nomination, because of "the corruption, the buying and selling, and the intrigues that have characterized the action of conventions."[1] His platform was simple:

> I shall oppose the Kansas-Nebraska bill so far as [it] relates to the repeal of the Missouri Compromise, believing that it was an uncalled for and unwarranted offering to the spirit of slavery propagandism, accepted in bad faith by the South, by which a vast extent of territory long and sacredly consecrated to freedom has been thrown open to the blighting influence of slavery.[2]

The Chicago *Daily Democratic Press* endorsed his candidacy,[3] as did the Aurora *Guardian*.[4] His opponent was James H. Woodworth, former mayor of Chicago, member of the Illinois General Assembly, and since 1848, a Free Soiler. Woodworth received the support of the Know-Nothing Party, and his election seemed like a shoo-in, considering the Know-Nothing strength in the city.[5]

In a letter to Evans on August 23, 1854, W. B. Plato of Geneva, Illinois, complained that Evans' stand on the slavery question was not specific enough. He posed four questions which he wanted Evans to answer for publication. Evans gave his reply on September 4,[6] and his statement was published in the Chicago *Tribune* a week later.[7]

Evans opened with a general condemnation of slavery, saying that the government "*in all cases where it has authority over the subject*" must "exercise its positive influence in favor of freedom and against slavery." A neutral policy "would be a spectacle of degeneracy too humiliating to be contemplated."[8]

Plato's first question asked whether Evans thought Congress had the authority to prohibit slavery in the territories. Saying that Congress had the power to prohibit the introduction of "any great moral, social and political evil" into a territory under Article IV, Section III of the Constitution, Evans stated categorically that Congress could prohibit slavery in the territories. He did not, however, answer the second part of this question, which asked: "If elected, will you endeavor to procure such prohibition?"[9]

The second question involved slavery in the District of Columbia. In Evans' opinion, the Constitution gave Congress authority to legislate on all matters in the District of Columbia, including slavery. "I should, if elected, certainly use my best endeavor," he said, "to remove from our nation that blackest spot upon her fair fame, Slavery in the National Capitol."[10]

In reply to the third question, Evans stated that he would vote against the admission of any more slave states to the Union. The fourth question involved a possible repeal of the Fugitive Slave Law. Evans stated that he favored amending this law to restore the writ of habeas corpus and trial by jury, and he said that if such an amendment could not be passed, he would vote to repeal the law.[11]

Evans appears, then, to have opposed slavery in the territories and in new states seeking admission to the Union. He thought that it might be excluded under the Constitution from areas under the jurisdiction of Congress, but he seemed to doubt that such action would be proper elsewhere. Moreover, he failed to specify how he would exclude slavery from the territories; and his preference for a revision of the Fugitive Slave Law rather than outright repeal indicated a cautious approach that was unacceptable to "both the slavery extension party and the abolition party," as one critic was quick to indicate.[12] His opinions were surprisingly close to the ideas later expressed by Lincoln in his speech at Peoria on October 6.[13] Evans occupied what Lincoln called "the middle ground . . . the good old Whig ground."[14]

A state convention which met at Aurora on September 20, 1854, took the name "Republican," as similar conventions in surrounding states had done that year.[15] This convention nominated Woodworth for Congress, although Evans worked hard to secure the nomination. As Evans pointed out in a letter to a Chicago newspaper, the platform adopted at Aurora "occupied the independent ground I had assumed as a candidate for congress." He withdrew gracefully, however, and asked his supporters to vote for Woodworth,[16] privately ascribing his own defeat to a refusal to accept the "Know Nothing Creed."[17]

An interesting sequel, according to Evans, occurred when Woodworth made a fumbling, incoherent speech to the Aurora convention. Evans countered him with "a speech which made a warm impression on the people, who were sorry they had nominated Woodworth."[18] Nonetheless, Woodworth triumphed at the polls, and the Know-Nothings captured most of the important municipal offices in Chicago.[19]

Evans remained interested in politics, primarily because of

the slavery issue. In February, 1856, a convention of news-paper editors with the assistance of Abraham Lincoln drew up a list of resolutions calling for the restoration of the Missouri Compromise and objecting to the further extension of slavery into the territories. Before adjournment a ten-man state central committee was appointed to plan a state convention to be held at Bloomington on May 29, 1856. John Evans was chosen to represent Chicago on the committee.[20]

The state central committee announced that the convention would choose candidates for state offices and appoint "dele-gates to the National Convention."[21] They carefully skirted the name "Republican," which had too many abolitionist im-plications,[22] preferring to call themselves the "Anti-Nebraska Party of Illinois."[23] Even though they elected delegates to the Republican National Convention, the delegates to the Anti-Nebraska Party convention refused to adopt that name for themselves and continued to identify themselves by the Anti-Nebraska label.[24]

Through these gradual steps Evans moved into the Repub-lican party and become identified as one of the influential political leaders in the Chicago area. His bid for Congress was not successful, but a curious promotional venture fostered by Evans in 1857 was destined to have political implications which were not at all apparent at the time. Several events helped to set the stage.

John Dempster, president of Garrett Biblical Institute, had planned to establish a series of ministerial training schools in the West and particularly in Nebraska.[25] In addition, in 1856 Congress had provided a grant of land to bring the Burlington and Missouri Railroad across Iowa to the mouth of the Platte River.[26] Moreover, it was popularly supposed that the railroad was required by law to cross the Missouri River on the exact point at which the Platte flowed into it.[27]

Led by these considerations, Evans "joined with some friends"[28] in organizing the Oreapolis Company,[29] and on

104

October 30, 1857, the town of Oreapolis was founded. The town site occupied approximately two sections of land on the south bank of the Platte River at its junction with the Missouri.[30] Oreapolis was less than a mile north of Plattsmouth, which was vying for the honor of becoming the site of the railroad bridge.[31]

So many towns had been organized by speculators that the territorial legislature on November 4, 1858, felt constrained to pass restrictive legislation.[32] In spite of this legislation, Evans, whose project was evidently considered sounder than the others, was able to secure a charter for a proposed Methodist seminary and a university at Oreapolis during that session.[33] In April, 1859, Evans appeared before the Kansas-Nebraska Conference of the Methodist Episcopal Church at Omaha City to obtain their support for three proposed educational foundations in Oreapolis, a seminary, a biblical institute, and a university.[34] The seminary and the university, which had already been chartered by the state, were approved by the conference.[35] Dr. John Dempster's Oreapolis Biblical Institute was approved after he promised to open it in the fall of 1860 with at least ten students; Dr. Dempster was also invited to join the conference.[36]

The Oreapolis Company had given each of these institutions a grant of land, but the largest grant—a "thirty acre site plus one-tenth of the company's lots and other land"—was donated to form an endowment for Oreapolis University.[37] The Nebraska City delegation fought hard to have their Olin University adopted by the conference, but the delegates decided to accept the Oreapolis institution.[38]

Evans stayed in Nebraska to supervise the development of the town. Before the end of April he was able to report the arrival of a steam ferry to provide service across the Missouri River.[39] In early June, Evans and the other seminary trustees awarded a contract to Loudin Mullin for the erection of the seminary building. It was to consist of a three-story brick structure, eighty feet long and thirty-eight feet wide, capable of accommodating 250 students.[40] Evans predicted that a hundred houses would be erected by the end of the year and that by the fall of 1860 the town would contain a thousand inhabitants.[41]

Before returning to Evanston, Evans personally undertook to survey a road west from Oreapolis to the county line.[42] He wrote to his wife that "no one here seems to appreciate the fact that a high hill is any objection in the way of a good route," and he vowed to "make a road that will be a great thorough-fare to the gold regions [of Colorado] Salt Lake Oregon & California." He hoped to make Oreapolis the starting point of the overland route to these places and said that "these roads are of so much importance to our Enterprise that to have neglected them would have been suicidal."[43]

John Evans' friend Bishop Matthew Simpson, who had been in poor health, wanted to change his episcopal residence to some city other than Pittsburgh.[44] In April, 1851, Evans offered Simpson the presidency of Northwestern University at an annual salary of $2,000,[45] but Simpson declined the offer.[46] In March, 1858, when he heard of the Bishop's ill health, Evans again asked Simpson to move to Evanston, promising this time to try to purchase a parsonage for him.[47] Simpson accepted, but at the time he decided to move to Evanston, Bishop Ames announced that he had chosen Evanston for his residence. It took some very delicate negotiating to change Bishop Ames' plan, but Evans and his friends managed it.[48] When Evans heard in June, 1859, that Bishop Simpson planned to attend the Northwestern commencement at the end of the month, he quickly returned home.[49] Bishop Simpson had decided that his episcopal duties could be performed just as well in Evanston, and in addition he would become "nom-inally president" of Garrett Biblical Institute.[50]

Back in Illinois, Evans wrote a glowing report on Oreapolis, urging families to settle there with the slogan: "The early settlers make the money."[51] He reported that steamboat connections with St. Louis and St. Joseph were "good most of the year" and that Oreapolis was the eastern terminus of "the best wagon road from the Missouri River to the New Gold Mines, to Oregon and California."[52]

The first building had not been started until early in 1859, yet by June some fifty buildings were under construction, including a lumber mill, a bank, several stores, a hotel, and the seminary.[53] The latter building was due to be completed before winter and was free from debt.[54] The grant of land to Oreapolis University provided that the land was to lie idle for ten years after it was chartered so that it would increase in value to an extent sufficient to provide an adequate income.[55] The Oreapolis Biblical Institute had obtained a pledged endowment of $30,000 and was to open in the fall of 1860.[56] Four public school sites had been donated to the city by the company, and "about 200 acres of a fractional School Section" were located near the business district and promised to be very valuable.[57]

The company offered its town lots at cost—"about $32 per acre"—to anyone who agreed to move to Oreapolis and build on one of the lots. A rudimentary building code was also in operation; each house had to be "at least 15 x 20 feet, one story high, or its equivalent in size, with a neat cornice and exterior finish, and if frame, painted with two coats." Evans reported that a number of lots secured in this manner were currently worth two or three hundred dollars and certain to increase in value.[58]

The company also offered parcels from a two-hundred-acre reserve at cost to commercial firms that located in the town and, as an added inducement, promised "a LARGE BONUS, according to the amount of capital invested," to twenty-one specific types of business. These included a grocery store, a hardware store (stocking "MINER'S AND OTHER TOOLS"), a drugstore, a flour mill, an agricultural implement factory, a tannery, a cooper shop, a gunsmith shop, "and in fact any and all other legitimate business or manufacturing establishments." Many of the enumerated occupations were boosted by such phrases as "will do a busy trade," "a fine opening," "cannot fail," and "sure to do well."[59]

In spite of these rosy predictions, when Evans returned to Oreapolis in October, he found that the boom was over. "The times in the county are so hard," he confided in a letter to Margaret, "that all looks gloomy[.] It makes me sick to think of a failure in our enterprise and yet it may come to us." Apparently he had promised Margaret that he would not invest any great amount of money in the town, and he now said that he would try to keep the promise "let the consequences be what they may."[60] Within a week he had decided to dispose of his investments in Oreapolis. He recognized an obligation to continue "to work for the founding of the town for the purpose of building up the institutions," but he seems to have realized that there was not much hope for the enterprise.[61]

Although Dr. Dempster announced to the Kansas-Nebraska Conference in the spring of 1860 that he was still willing to operate the Biblical Institute, the school was apparently never opened.[62] The seminary was under roof by December 1, 1859, but the interior was not completed until September, 1861. It was operated for two or three years, but few students attended, and it was ultimately dismantled.[63] By 1865 all the buildings at Oreapolis were being torn down or moved to Plattsmouth,[64] and nothing was left to mark the site.[65]

Upon his return to Chicago Evans immediately launched a campaign for a "Chicago to Pikes Peak Express" that would connect with "the Mines" by way of Oreapolis and the Platte River. The routes through Omaha, Council Bluffs, Oreapolis, and Nebraska City to Chicago, he said, were better and perhaps a hundred miles shorter than those through Leavenworth City and St. Joseph to St. Louis. Evans also suggested the establishment of a federal mint and assay office at Chicago so that the city might be more attractive to miners and bankers.[66]

He realized that an express line was only a temporary expedient, but he felt that such a route would hasten the completion of a railroad across Iowa to the mouth of the Platte.[67] When the express line proposal failed to generate much enthusiasm among Chicago investors,[68] Evans switched to a plan for completing the railroad from Cedar Rapids to the Missouri River. In July, 1860, he was appointed to a "committee of ten" to solicit stock subscriptions for the Cedar Rapids and Missouri River Railroad.[69]

Nothing came of these efforts, however, and Oreapolis soon dwindled into oblivion. Perhaps the last communication Evans received from there was a plaintive letter from a citizen of Plattsmouth who refused to believe a report that Evans was using his influence to back a railroad through Omaha.[70] Commenting thirty years later on the failure of Oreapolis, Evans said: "They were so long building and it was so close to Plattsmouth, that most of the people moved away afterwards."[71]

By 1860 the Anti-Nebraska people in Illinois had decided to accept the name Republican. John Evans was chosen as one of the forty-seven delegates to the 1860 Republican State Convention at Decatur, Illinois, where Abraham Lincoln was designated as the convention's choice for president.[72] The candidate had been given a boost when John Hanks and Isaac Jennings carried into the Wigwam two fence rails emblazoned with the legend "Abraham Lincoln, the Rail Candidate for President in 1860." These rails, so the inscription said, were "from a lot of 3,000 made in 1830 by Thomas [John] Hanks and Abe Lincoln."[73] The deafening applause which followed this event lasted for ten or fifteen minutes before Lincoln was finally allowed to speak.[74] Almost thirty years later Evans was able to recall the gist of Lincoln's speech.

> Now says he, I don't know whether I split that rail or not, but one thing I do know, that down where that was made, John Hanks and I did in such a winter split a great many oak rails.[75]

Evans seems to have known Lincoln casually before he was nominated, but during the campaign, he said, they "became quite well acquainted."[76] This phrase seems to mean only that Lincoln knew Evans as a prominent political and social leader in the Chicago area. Evans stated that Lincoln once stayed at his home in Chicago "when he was there attending a lawsuit."[77] There is also a story—perhaps true, although Evans did not mention it himself—that John Evans sat on the speaker's platform during one of the Lincoln-Douglas debates.[78] It is clear from their correspondence, however, that Lincoln and Evans were not close friends,[79] for there is no evidence of any personal correspondence between them.

The Illinois delegation to the National Republican Convention in Chicago did not include Evans, and if he attended, there is no record of it.[80] However, Evans did campaign actively for Lincoln, traveling throughout a good portion of the state in the process.[81]

Even though Evans was not a delegate at Chicago, a good friend of his was. The friend, Samuel H. Elbert of Plattsmouth, Nebraska, served as a member of the Nebraska delegation and was placed on the "committee to prepare the order of business."[82]

Elbert and Evans had met in 1858, when Evans appeared before the legislature in Omaha City to secure a charter for the Oreapolis schools.[83] Evans had made a number of other friends in the Nebraska Legislature, and they "fixed up a plan," as Evans said, "that when Lincoln was inaugurated I should be appointed Governor of Nebraska."[84] Accordingly, on December 27, 1860, a letter was addressed to Lincoln by the President of the Council of the Legislative Assembly and the Speaker of the House of Representatives of Nebraska Territory, asking that Evans be appointed governor. The letter said:

> We cordially unite in recommending Doctor John Evans of Chicago & your own State for Governor of this Territory. He has

been identified with us in interest for more than two years and
he is generally throughout the Territory regarded as one of us.
He is a western man . . . and has an extensive acquaintance and
thorough knowledge of Nebraska. . . . The appointment of Doctor Evans would be hailed with Satisfaction by the people &
would doubtless give general Satisfaction to the great majority
of the Republican party of this Territory, whose destiny is a
part & parcel of Nebraska.[85]

When this letter failed to produce the desired result, Bishop
Simpson wrote on February 20, 1861, to Senator Henry S.
Lane of Indiana and asked him to use his influence to have
Evans appointed to the Nebraska governorship. The sketch of
Evans' qualifications presented in Simpson's letter included the
founding of "our University & Theological School" at Evanston
and similar work in Nebraska. The bishop concluded with the
remark that he would regard Lane's help as a personal favor.[86]
He also wrote in Evans' behalf to James Harlan, a former student of Simpson's at Indiana Asbury University and currently
serving as a senator from Iowa.[87] In reply Harlan suggested
that Evans might be approved as governor of Colorado.[88]

Bishop Simpson then wrote to Lincoln urging the appointment of Evans. "It will be a matter of peculiar gratification,"
he said, "if you, in your wisdom see fit to appoint Dr. Evans
as Governor of one of the Western Territories, either Nebraska
or Colorado."[89] On March 8, 1861, the New York *Herald*
announced: "Dr. Evans of Chicago will be governor of Nebraska." Still nothing happened. By the middle of the month,
Evans could only report to Bishop Simpson: "Nothing unfavorable to my appointment has yet come to my knowledge."[90]

Their disappointment at the end of March when they heard
of the appointment of Dr. William Jayne as Governor of Nebraska can only be imagined. When Evans was later presented
to Lincoln by Senator Harlan, Lincoln explained that he had
not received the request of the Nebraska territorial legislature.
"Somebody captured it on the way," Evans learned afterwards.[91]

The bishop was angry. He believed that qualified Methodists were being passed over while members of other religious groups received political appointments solely because of their religious affiliation.[92] He complained immediately to Lincoln and secured a promise that Evans would be the next man from Illinois to be considered for appointment as territorial governor.[93]

Evans still managed to remain in the picture politically. In the summer of 1861 a Cook County convention adopted a resolution presented by Evans which called for the "emancipation and arming of the slaves." As might be expected, the resolution caused quite a bit of controversy,[94] and Judge Walter Bennett Scates of the Illinois Supreme Court took particular exception to it. The dispute between Evans and Scates reached the pages of the Chicago *Evening Journal* where it waxed hot and heavy for a time.[95]

Finally, in October, 1861, Lincoln had the opportunity to make good on his promise to Bishop Simpson. William H. Wallace had resigned as governor of Washington Territory,[96] and Lincoln offered the post to Evans. He asked Congressman Isaac N. Arnold to tell Evans that he could have the post if he wanted it. Evans declined the job in a letter to Lincoln, saying: "But for the remoteness of that Territory rendering a residence there incompatible with occasional attention to my interests in Illinois I would have accepted your kind offer gladly."[97]

The bishop and other Methodists kept up the pressure for more Methodist appointments.[98] Evans, too, was making efforts in his own behalf. In early December, 1861, he was sent to Washington as part of the "Joint Armory Committee" which sought support for building a federal armory in Chicago.[99] It may be that Evans heard then of the move to replace William Gilpin as governor of Colorado. On January 30, 1862, Evans wrote to Senator Harlan, saying that he would accept the governorship of Colorado Territory and asking Harlan to speak to Lincoln about it. "I suppose he will not appriciate my claim unless his attention is called to it," his letter concluded.[100]

Senator Harlan urged the appointment in a letter to Lincoln on February 6,[101] and a similar request from Senator Lyman Trumbull and others followed on February 19.[102] A month later, President Lincoln responded by nominating Evans as governor of Colorado for a four-year term. The nomination was approved by the Senate, and Lincoln signed the commission on March 26, 1862.[103] This development marked the beginning of a new area of responsibility and activity for the Chicago businessman and founder of Northwestern University.

It had all seemingly started at the mouth of the Platte River, where Evans envisioned a fine new city for Nebraska Territory. Influential friends in the Nebraska legislature first nominated him for the Nebraska executive post. Leading Methodist spokesmen then urged his appointment to any available territorial governorship. Their insistent letters obviously had some influence on Lincoln, but in the end John Evans received the appointment because he was a prominent Republican whose wide experience in business, education, and politics qualified him for the office.

9

Governor of Colorado Territory

Uppermost in John Evans' mind after he received news of his appointment as Governor of Colorado was the selection of a territorial secretary with whom he could work harmoniously. Such a secretary had certain administrative duties to perform and was authorized to serve as acting governor during the governor's absence from the territory.[1] Evans was determined to have a secretary of his own choosing, and, even though a great deal of pressure was brought to bear on him to support various candidates, he ultimately secured the appointment of the man of his choice. This was Samuel Hitt Elbert, his friend from Nebraska.[2]

Apparently Evans was in Illinois when he learned of his own appointment. He immediately left for Washington, which he reached early in April, 1862. His efforts to secure the appointment of Elbert bore fruit on April 7, when Lincoln ordered that he be given the secretary's post.[3] Evans also asked Seward to allow William Gilpin to continue as governor until Evans should arrive in Denver,[4] and this was apparently done. On April 11, 1862, Evans took his oath of office before Associate Justice James M. Wayne of the United States Supreme Court.[5]

Samuel H. Elbert.

There is a story, probably apocryphal, though related by the man concerned, of Evans' using his influence to have a Methodist missionary appointed as the secretary of the territory. The missionary, John Lewis Smith, later declared that he received letters from both Bishop Simpson and John Evans asking for a private meeting with him during the sessions of the North Indiana Conference of the Methodist Episcopal Church at Ft. Wayne, April 10 to 15, 1862. Smith maintained that both the bishop and Evans had agreed that Smith should assume superintendence of the Methodist missions in Colorado and that Evans would appoint him secretary of the territory. In Smith's words: "The doctor insisted that there would be no difficulty in having the work of the secretary's office done by a deputy, so as not to hinder the evangelistic services of the superintendent." Yet, according to Smith, he declined the appointment mainly because his wife did not want to take the children out of their school in Indiana and expose them to the crudities of western society.[6]

Several points in Smith's story fail to stand up under close scrutiny. For example, Lewis L. Weld resigned as secretary of Colorado on April 7, and Lincoln appointed Elbert to succeed him on the same date, three days before the North Indiana Conference opened. The appointment was confirmed by the Senate on April 14,[7] while the Conference was still in session, and Elbert took the oath of office on April 19.[8] Then, too, Evans did not have the power of appointment to this post, although he could use his influence as he did in the case of Elbert. Finally, there is no other evidence to support Smith's story, which in any case was not published until thirty years after the meeting was supposed to have taken place. Nonetheless, there were charges that Evans was using his office to favor Methodists.[9] It seems clear that both Evans and Elbert were appointed at least partly because of their church affiliation, although Evans' professional accomplishments and political prominence were also major considerations.[10]

In addition to his administrative duties, the governor was required by the 1861 "Organic Act" for Colorado to live in the territory, be "commander-in-chief of the militia," and "perform the duties and receive the emoluments of superintendent of Indian affairs." The governor's salary was set at $1,500 per year, and he was to receive another $1,000 per year for acting as Superintendent of Indian Affairs. The secretary of the territory received an annual salary of $1,800. The salaries were to be paid quarterly by the Treasury of the United States.[11] A special appropriation of $2,000 was provided to cover "incidental and office expenses" which Evans might incur as superintendent of Indian affairs.[12]

Evans journeyed to Denver without his family, arriving on May 16, 1862. He was greeted by an official delegation, and that evening at about eight o'clock "The Rocky Mountain Band," accompanied by a large crowd, serenaded the new governor at the Tremont House, where he was staying. After the band played several selections, the crowd gave three cheers for their new territorial executive, and Evans appeared on the hotel balcony to make a speech.[13]

The crowd met a big man—he was nearly six feet tall and weighed 180 pounds[14]—with a broad grasp of their problems. One of the points that Evans emphasized was the need for a railroad connection with the East. He blamed the "famine prices for food" on the lack of a railroad and said that he was encouraged by the fact that Congress had finally passed the Pacific Railroad Bill. He also noted the farms of the South Platte Valley and predicted that the area would soon become "fertile and populous."[15]

On May 18, 1862, his first Sunday in Denver, the new governor received a chilling introduction to the Indian problem, when he witnessed a war dance staged by a victorious Sioux, Arapahoe, and Cheyenne war party. The Indians had raided a Ute band and had taken a scalp. This was carried on an eight-foot pole by a "young squaw . . . in gorgeous attire

Governor John Evans.

with a big cape . . . made out of Eagle's feathers, and other feathers that were gaudy and red."[16]

The celebrating Indians had camped for the night near Denver, and the next morning Evans went with some troops from Camp Weld to visit the camp. After having the soldiers fire a cannon to impress the Indians, Evans gave them a speech on the senselessness of their war. He said later that the only result of his talk had been to make these people think that he had taken the side of the Utes in their controversy. This conclusion was reaffirmed the following day when a delegation of Utes paid him a visit. The superintendent needed all his diplomatic skill to keep the fight from being renewed then and there. The Utes later confided to him that "the best thing that could be done with an Arapahoe or a Cheyenne was to kill him."[17] Obviously, Indian affairs were going to require a lot of attention.

William Gray, the Governor's brother-in-law, had accompanied him to Colorado, and on Monday the twenty-sixth they rode to Central City with Ben Holladay, proprietor of the stage line, to visit the Gregory diggings. Here Evans saw "mill after mill in a narrow ravine close together to the number of a hundred or more pounding the stone and taking out the precious metal . . . some of them producing over a thousand dollars a day."[18]

The second session of the territorial legislature was scheduled to begin on the first Monday in June. Evans had not yet had an opportunity to make a personal investigation of the needs of the territory, so he was somewhat relieved when he received a message from Colorado's delegate to Congress, H. P. Bennet, informing him that the session was to be delayed a month.[19] Evans had told Bennet that he wanted to delay the session until February, 1863, but he was not to be allowed to do this.[20]

Besides desiring time to become better acquainted with the needs of the territory, Evans also wished to devote his attention to Indian matters, which would require some weeks of travel away from Denver. He hoped to be able to return to Chicago for his family before the end of the summer.[21] In any case, there was a serious question about the legality of the proposed legislative session, since the legislature had already met once within the previous twelve months.[22] The members of the legislature, however, successfully contended that their meeting was not really a second session but a continuation of the first session, and Secretary of State Seward advised Evans to recognize the body when it met.[23]

In spite of his disappointment Evans was prepared to appear before the delegates. At the last session they had agreed to move the capital to Colorado City. Evans visited that city early in June and returned convinced that the legislature would be so disappointed with the place that they would immediately return to Denver—"really the only tolerable place" in the territory. He told his wife that Colorado City reminded him of nothing so much as "a deserted Nebraska village at or near the Mouth of the Platte river."[24]

So sure was he in his prediction that Evans did not go to Colorado City but waited for the legislature to adjourn to Denver, which it did on July 11.[25] On July 15 Evans officially approved the legislature's decision to return to Denver,[26] and on July 18 he delivered his first message to a joint session of that body.[27]

Since some counties were too sparsely populated to pay the expenses of county government, Evans first proposed that these counties be consolidated on a population basis and that a single individual be charged with the responsibility for several county offices. He suggested that the territorial legislative districts be redrawn and that the scheduled election be postponed until fall.[28]

The Governor also requested revision of the law on mining claims. The existing law, which gave permanent possession to the claimant, should be revised, the Governor believed, to require "a certain amount of actual development on claims within a given time." This requirement would discourage speculative buying by people who had no intention of working the claim.[29]

He asked for an amendment to the militia law which would render it "less complex and expensive and more closely adapt it to the convenience of the people."[30] Although his wording seems a bit vague, the Governor's intentions are clear. The militia law of 1861 contained no provision for mounting members of the militia or for paying individual members for the use of their horses.[31] Obviously, infantry would be of little use in the field against mounted Indians. An equally serious shortcoming was that all male inhabitants of the territory between the ages of eighteen and forty-five—with the exception of public officials, Quakers, clergymen, lunatics, idiots, and prisoners—were required to serve in the militia and to provide their own uniforms and equipment.[32] Moreover, there was no provision for supplying these men while they were on active duty.[33] In addition, members of the militia were required under threat of fine and imprisonment to serve at the pleasure of territorial officials, and only a few officers could expect to receive pay for their efforts.[34]

The basic problem with the militia was money—money for horses, money for forage, money for food, money for arms and equipment. The territory simply did not have the funds to pay for its own defense. The obvious answer was to use regular army units for this purpose. As Evans pointed out, however: "The General Government has called away to posts of danger our volunteers as fast as they could be enlisted."[35] Governor Evans could offer no solution to the militia dilemma then, nor was he ever able to find a satisfactory answer.

Evans thought the school lands provided for in the act creating the territory would be of little value to the territory, since they could not be sold or leased until surveyed. By that time, he said, the desirable land would already have been pre-empted by settlers or claimed by miners. To provide a school fund, then, he suggested the passage of a law "that shall secure to the Territory, for the use of schools, a claim on every newly discovered lode," and he also asked that Congress be petitioned to approve the law.[36]

In addition, he asked for a corporation law that would not grant "exclusive right and privileges," the appointment of a committee to draft "a full code of Statute Law," new measures to insure adequate collection of taxes, amendment of the probate laws, and legislative request for a federal subsidy to build a territorial prison.[37] Moreover, he recommended that the legislature memorialize the Commissioner of Indian Affairs, the Secretary of the Interior, and Congress,

> asking that treaties be authorized with the Ute, Apache, Kiowa, and Camanche Indians of the South and West, and with the Ogillalla Sioux for the extinction of their title to such parts of the Territory as may not be permanently reserved to them.[38]

The Pacific Railroad Bill had been approved by Congress, and Evans had been named as one of the 158 "Commissioners."[39] He had initiated a survey of the Berthoud Pass route,[40] and he told the assembled legislators that he expected Surveyor General F. M. Case to submit the results of his survey within a very short time. He promised to report on the route in a forthcoming special message to the legislature.[41]

The Governor's message was a masterly summary of the legislative problems of the territory, and it met the enthusiastic approval of the legislators. They wrote, passed, and sent to him for signature acts reorganizing the militia,[42] granting an absentee ballot to soldiers in service outside the territory,[43] creating a school fund by reserving one claim in each quartz lode,[44] and providing new legislative districts.[45] The legislature also sent a petition to the Secretary of the Interior regarding Indian land titles,[46] as recommended by the Governor. Evans signed all of these.

An unacceptable bill allowing district judges to decide for themselves the time and place for holding court was returned unsigned, with the observation that it contravened the provisions of the Organic Act of 1861.[47] The legislature then passed a suitably revised bill, and it was approved by the Governor.[48]

Governor Evans also vetoed an act granting a divorce. He told the legislators that a law already existed whereby a divorce could be obtained in the courts "in all proper and meritorious cases." Only a court decree, he said, could "properly adjust the equities in such cases," and it was "unwise" for the legislature "to assume the discharge of the functions thus already assigned to the courts."[49]

Meanwhile, after the Legislative Assembly had been in session for only a week, Evans received crushing news from home. His five-year-old daughter Margaret Gray Evans, whom everybody called Maggie, had died on July 8 of scarlet fever. There had been an epidemic of this dread disease in Chicago for more than a month, and just as it seemed that his three children had escaped unscathed, the news reached him of Maggie's death.[50]

Just how she caught the disease is uncertain.[51] Her mother had visited the home of John and Ann Nutt, where it was suspected that at least one of the children had scarlet fever. John wrote his wife that he hoped she had been "careful enough to be thoroughly aired and ventilated and washed &c before going to our own dear little children." He reminded her that he "was always so much afraid of that malignant scarlet fever—by all odds the worst scourge of children and the most fatal of any other malady."[52] When Margaret's next letter told him that the Nutt children did not have scarlet fever,[53] and when a letter of June 22 said that the Evans children were still quite well, John assumed that the danger had passed.[54] The news of the child's death, then, must have been a stunning blow.

Inasmuch as Evans did not learn of the death until a week

after it occurred,[55] and since it would require nearly a week simply to travel as far as the Missouri River,[56] there was no question of his going home for the funeral. But he determined to remain in Denver only until the close of the Legislative Assembly in mid-August.

The surveyor's report of a possible railroad route over Berthoud Pass had been a great disappointment to the citizens of Denver. They had contributed almost $200 to finance the study[57] and Evans had said, after a personal investigation,[58] that Berthoud Pass looked to him as though it had "been designed by the Great Master Mechanic" as a railroad route.[59] Yet Surveyor Case reported that while a wagon road was possible, a railroad—well, Case gave the figures on the grade and said that the people could draw their own conclusions.[60]

Although the Governor sent Case back for another look,[61] the report was still unfavorable. The grade was too steep, and a tunnel at least three and a half miles long would be required. When Evans suggested that gold might be discovered in digging the tunnel,[62] Case replied:

> I might say in this connection, that there would be a *possibility* of striking [a] rich gold lode in the construction of the tunnel . . . yet, I would not like to undertake the construction of the tunnel with the understanding that I should take this "possibility" in "part payment."[63]

Former Governor William Gilpin immediately seized upon the unfavorable survey as a political weapon. He had blamed Evans for his own removal from office,[64] and now he was campaigning for Congress on an anti-administration platform.[65] Even before the results of the survey were made public, he accused Evans of being opposed to a Colorado route because it would mean that Chicago would not be the eastern terminus.[66]

Governor Evans attempted to answer Gilpin's charges in a letter to the *Rocky Mountain News*. Gilpin responded with the implication that Evans was "a hypocrite" and said that the coming election would allow the people to judge who was right and who was wrong.[67] Evans was content with this arrangement. The territorial legislature responded by instructing Governor Evans to attend the meeting of the Board of Corporators of the Union Pacific in Chicago and by recommending that Evans be given a place on the permanent board of directors.[68] The people of the territory gave their verdict on October 7, when they rejected Gilpin and re-elected Bennet to Congress by "a very large plurality."[69]

Evans left Denver on August 18, 1862.[70] At the Chicago meeting of the railroad board, he attempted to gain approval of the Colorado route, pointing to the mineral resources of the territory as a guarantee of the future growth of the state.[71] The best that Evans could get was a resolution stating:

> The development of prosperous settlements in Colorado, Utah and Nevada Territories . . . has furnished one of the greatest desiderata to the construction and maintenance of the Pacific Railroad, and encouraged us in our efforts.[72]

Having done what he could to bring the Union Pacific through Colorado, Governor Evans went to Washington in early October to arrange for more troops to guard the territory from possible Indian raids.[73] The recent massacre at New Ulm, Minnesota, had raised fears in Colorado that the Indians might try to take advantage of the isolated condition of the settlements.[74] Evans had written to Secretary of War Edwin M. Stanton asking for troops to guard the Platte River route, and with the support of the influential Ben Holladay he received the promise of military aid.[75] The First Colorado Regiment was to be converted to cavalry,[76] and the Platte route would be guarded.[77]

While he was in Washington, Evans told William P. Dole, Commissioner of Indian Affairs, that the Cheyenne and Arapahoe Indians looked upon his efforts to end their long-standing hostility against the Utes as "unwarranted intervention." Another cause of disaffection among these Indians lay in the fact that some of their bands had not been included in the arrangements made in the 1861 Treaty of Fort Wise. "Further negotiation with them will be required," Evans reported, "to induce them" to accept the treaty.[78]

Following his visit in Washington, Governor Evans entrained for Chicago to revisit his family. Then early in November he departed with them for Colorado. He chartered a coach in Atchison, Kansas, on November 6,[79] and ordered that it be driven straight through to Denver. Although the party stopped to eat at the stations along the way, they did not stop at night but simply covered over the space between the seats to make a bed. Mrs. Evans recalled later (in 1889): "Some of us slept a little." They arrived in Denver on November 11, after nearly a week of travel.[80] Evans had purchased land for a home in Denver before leaving for the East in August.[81] The new home was yet to be built, however, so the Governor's family stayed in a suite of rooms at the Tremont House.[82]

Early in the morning of April 19, 1863, a fire broke out in the business section of Denver and destroyed most of the district. Many of the buildings were of flimsy construction, and the greater part of the $250,000 loss consisted of merchandise.[83] Although there is no record of the Governor's reaction to this disaster, the destruction of such a great quantity of goods must have increased his realization of the isolated position of Denver.

During the early months of 1863 Evans had a home built for his family at the corner of Fourteenth and Arapahoe Streets in Denver. It was a small house, one and a half stories high, of red brick with white trim. It was not as elaborate as the home in Evanston, and on Monday morning, April 27, 1863, when the family moved in, Margaret recalled the child she had lost last summer—"our precious little Maggie."[84]

Perhaps this was the reason that three days later John took her for a week-long trip to Central City.[85] Two months after, on June 26, 1863, her second son was born.[86] He was named

*The Evans home, built in 1863, in Denver
on the corner of Fourteenth and Arapahoe Streets.*

Evan Elbert, after the Governor's good friend, Territorial Secretary Samuel H. Elbert. With a new baby to care for, Margaret soon forgot her sorrow over the death of "precious little Maggie."

Shortly thereafter, in early July, 1863, Governor Evans received a telegram from Indian Commissioner William P. Dole, advising him to arrange a Ute treaty conference for September 1.[87] Evans had been planning to hold a conference on that date with the Cheyenne and Arapahoe tribes—about which more will be said later—and Dole's order upset his plans. He informed Dole that since messengers had already been sent to these tribes, it was really too late to change the conference dates.[88] As though to force Evans into compliance, Dole mentioned in his reply that John Nicolay, Lincoln's secretary, was leaving for Colorado to attend the conference with the Utes "whom I suppose you will get together by 1st Sept."[89] Not the least overawed, Evans answered: "As to Mr. Nicolay coming, I am glad of it—I know him well."[90] Only then did Dole tell Evans that when the Utes were in Washington in the spring he had promised them that a conference would be held with them in August or early September.[91] The Governor informed Dole that the Cheyenne-Arapahoe conference could not be postponed and that Nicolay, in any case, would be of more help at this conference.[92] No damage was done in this instance by the Commissioner's long-distance meddling; but it serves as an example of the needless pressure put on Evans by the Indian Bureau, and it illustrates Dole's complete failure to understand problems in the field.

The 1861 Treaty of Fort Wise required the government to establish a reservation for the Arapahoe and Cheyenne Indians on the Arkansas River. The treaty was proclaimed December 5, 1861, but no effort had been made to put it into effect before Evans arrived in Denver in May, 1862.[93] Realizing that the Indians expected some action in compliance with the treaty, Evans urged Commissioner Dole in the summer of 1862 to allow him to settle as many Arapahoes and Cheyennes as possible on the Upper Arkansas reservation, so that they could be more easily guarded. Commissioner Dole replied that there was no appropriation and none could be expected until the following year. Supplies could not be purchased, and the treaty would simply have to stand in abeyance for a year.[94]

A serious misunderstanding with the Cheyennes and Arapahoes over the boundaries of their new reservation was also in the making. The Treaty of Fort Wise had been concluded with the advice of Agent William Bent that a confederated band of Cheyenne and Arapahoe claimed as their tribal ground the area between the North and South Platte Rivers. A similar confederated band occupied the area between the South Platte and the Arkansas Rivers. In 1863 it appeared that the Indians involved were not aware of any such distinctions and were balking at being moved onto the Upper Arkansas reservation. Governor Evans was given the unpleasant task of convincing these Indians and all the non-signatory Cheyennes and Arapahoes that they should accept the land provided in the Fort Wise Treaty.[95] According to one author this was nothing less than an attempt by "a novice Commissioner in distant Washington" to shift responsibility for the "explosive state of affairs" to Governor Evans.[96]

In spite of dismal reports from his messengers,[97] Evans left Denver on August 27 to meet the Cheyennes and Arapahoes on the Republican River.[98] He was dismayed to find that disaffection had spread throughout the Cheyenne and Arapahoe bands. When he reached the treaty area on the Red Fork of the Republican River a few days later, not an Indian was in attendance.[99] He immediately dispatched squaw-man Elbridge Gerry to try to bring them in. One of the chiefs asked Gerry just what the superintendent had in mind. Gerry replied that the Indians were "to settle down and live like white men."[100] The chief answered: "You can just go back to the governor and tell him we are not reduced quite that low yet."[101] Another chief, who had consented to attend after being promised a horse as a gift, later changed his mind when the others threatened him with severe punishment.[102]

The Indians gave several reasons for not attending the conference and for refusing to live on the reservation established in the Treaty of Fort Wise. One good reason, which they did not give, was that their buffalo hunt had been extraordinarily successful—so much so that there seemed to be no need to go onto the reservation where food would be doled out to them.[103] However, the main contention of those who had not signed the treaty seemed to be that they still retained the right to roam about the country as they pleased, and they would not be coerced into giving up this right.[104]

A quarter of a century later, Evans called it "ridiculous" to suppose that "a country a thousand miles long and five hundred miles wide, one of the most fertile in the world, should belong to a few bands of roving Indians." The correct view in his opinion was "that they had a right to hunt on the land, but that right must be subject to the higher occupation of the land, for a larger population and for civilization."[105]

Evans realized that the Bureau's policy of trying to place the Indians on farms would not be practical. A more likely policy, he felt, would be to train them in the herding of cattle and sheep. In a report to the Commissioner he said:

> Cattle and sheep here thrive and fatten the year round without any other care than that of herding; and from the care these Indians take of their horses, which are kept in large droves, I am confident they would soon learn to herd cattle and sheep so as to fully sustain themselves, if not to become wealthy from the increase of their flocks and herds.[106]

Evans had discussed this plan with the Commissioner in Washington the previous fall and had been invited to submit a full report "as to the best means of concentrating these Indians upon their reservation, and introducing them into their new mode of life."[107] Evans did so, but his plan was not included in

131

the Commissioner's report for that year,[108] nor were his suggestions adopted for the Arapahoe and Cheyenne Indians. The Commissioner simply went ahead with his plan to establish small farms at the Upper Arkansas Agency.[109] This may be one of the reasons for the fear on the part of Evans that "my course as Superintendent of Indian affairs does not meet the cordial approbation of the Dept.,"[110] and for his believing the rumor that he would probably be removed from office.[111]

From the fruitless journey to the Republican River, Evans went to the San Luis Valley to meet the Utes for negotiations which were more successful. On October 7, 1863, Evans and Nicolay met with Tabeguache Utes at Conejos. They were accompanied by Agents Lafayette Head and Simeon Whiteley, as well as Michael Steck, the Superintendent of Indian Affairs in Santa Fe, all of whom had members of the Tabeguache band under their supervision.[112] It was absolutely essential to conclude a treaty with these Indians, since, as Evans noted in his 1862 report, "several of the organized counties of this Territory, and many of the richest and most extensive mining districts, are in the country belonging to or claimed by this tribe."[113] The Indians were growing restive under this intrusion,[114] and Dole had promised them a satisfactory settlement.[115]

Having seen the armed might of the Army of the Potomac in a recent trip to Washington,[116] the Utes decided to stage a military show of their own for the edification of the treaty commissioners. On the day of the council, with Evans and the others of his party atop a house to watch the show, the Indians marched into the agency in military formation. "The commanders were mounted and they rode as hard as they could ride around each platoon . . . with their feathers and gew-gaws and trappings making a grand show."[117] Evans called it "one of the finest Indian performances you ever saw."[118] The Utes themselves were impressed with the show of strength, according to Evans, and it was only through the efforts of Ouray, who had taken the trip to Washington, that a few hotheads were dissuaded from "going to war with the United States."[119]

In the treaty that was subsequently drawn up, a reservation was set aside for the Tabeguaches, with the understanding that the Muache band could also join them. The Indians were to receive each year for a period of ten years $10,000 worth of trade goods and another $10,000 worth of provisions. If the Utes should manifest any interest in agriculture or pastoral pursuits, the government would furnish them with as many as 150 head of cattle annually for five years. The government also agreed to give up to 1,000 head of sheep for the first two years and 500 head of sheep for the next three years. Furthermore, a blacksmith was promised to repair guns and agricultural implements. After the negotiations were concluded, Evans decorated seven of the chiefs with silver medals,[120] and on October 7 the treaty was signed.[121]

In the treaty the Utes ceded "one of the largest and most valuable tracts of land in the United States," in the words of Commissioner Dole. Included in the cession were "nearly all the important settlements thus far made in Colorado, and all the valuable mining districts discovered up to this time."[122]

While at Conejos, Evans and his party narrowly escaped being murdered by the Espinosa brothers, who had been terrorizing the non-Spanish settlers in the area. One of the brothers had written to Evans, saying that the murders were intended as retaliation for the seizure of his land by the U.S. government. He offered to end the killings if Evans would pardon him and pay for the land.[123] One of the Espinosas was said to have spied on the Conejos camp, but either because he feared to attack such a large group, or because he was not aware of their identity, he left without firing on the group or making his presence known to the party.[124]

The Ute treaty seemed acceptable to all concerned, and the *Rocky Mountain News* called it a guarantee of "permanent peace and friendship."[125] The Arapahoes and Cheyennes, however, continued their warlike gestures, and some Ute bands, not included in the treaty negotiations, also caused trouble.[126] The Ute Indians at the Middle Park Agency were so unruly that summer that it was not thought safe for Agent Whiteley and his family to remain there without military protection.[127] When the troops were finally withdrawn, the agent left also.[128]

The First Colorado Cavalry had been returned to the territory in January, 1863, to provide additional defense against the Indians. But that military unit had no sooner arrived than the Second Colorado Regiment was ordered to Fort Leavenworth. In addition, some units of the First were assigned to duty in western Kansas and eastern Colorado, outside the jurisdiction of the Commander of the Military District of Colorado.[129] Citizens of Denver complained to Governor Evans about such moves,[130] but there was little he could do about it.

Evans had asked Secretary of State Seward to approve a three-month leave of absence from the territory to begin in November, 1863.[131] The Secretary was not inclined to grant the request,[132] and as a result John Nicolay wrote the Secretary, stating that Evans' assistance at Washington was necessary to secure passage of the Conejos Treaty.[133] Evans also wrote to the Secretary again, explaining that he had official business to transact which could not be handled properly through correspondence.[134] It is not clear whether Seward officially granted him leave. Evans had simply assumed permission in the fall of 1862 to go East and notified Seward after the fact.[135] Perhaps he did the same in 1863.

Before Evans could leave Colorado this time, however, news reached him of several serious Indian raids. A group of Ute Indians had stolen livestock from a stage station near Conejos.[136] A band of Arapahoe Indians stole provisions and sixteen horses from a rancher east of Denver and killed an ox belonging to the same man.[137] After the last incident Evans requested Colonel Chivington to try to recover the missing livestock but cautioned the Colonel "to avoid any collision with the Indians or any cause of ill feeling." Evans also asked that the chiefs of any bands encountered be invited to Denver to confer with him.[138]

A squaw-man named John North then came to Denver and informed Evans that he was present in an Arapahoe camp during the discussion of a plan for the Comanche, Apache, Kiowa, Northern Arapahoe, Cheyenne, and Sioux Indians to confederate for a general war against the whites in the spring. North said that the plan was to "shake hands and be friendly with the whites" until enough guns and ammunition were secured. Although he had lived with the Arapahoes most of his life and had an Arapahoe wife, North declared: "I am yet a white man and wish to avoid bloodshed." He told Evans that he was making the statement at the risk of his own life.[139] This testimony agreed with information which Evans had from Agent Colley and from Agent Lorey of the Upper Platte Agency.[140]

At about the same time, on November 9 and 10, Evans conferred in Denver with the Arapahoe chief Roman Nose and attempted to get him to sign the Treaty of Fort Wise. Roman Nose refused to sign but professed his friendship for the whites. Colley and his interpreter were present, and both told Evans they thought Roman Nose was a party to the conspiracy that North had revealed.[141]

A conference on the eleventh with a group of Northern Arapahoe chiefs proved fruitless, although these Indians did agree to pay for the stock their people had killed.[142] In spite of this gesture the depredations continued.[143]

Evans had previously instructed the military commanders not to allow Indians to loiter near the forts or to purchase supplies there.[144] He now ordered Agent Colley to stop supplying the Indians with guns and ammunition.[145] There was little else that he could do for the time, and with the approach of winter it was not likely that any serious difficulty with the Indians would arise. He determined that the wisest course was to request aid again in Washington, since a personal appeal had proven partially successful in 1862. Consequently on November 17, 1863, he departed for Washington.[146]

By that time Evans had shown himself to be an able and tireless territorial governor. His grasp of legal matters was surprisingly good, and his relations with the Legislative Assembly had been excellent. In the field of Indian relations he was less successful. This was an area in which he had no experience and for which he could hardly be expected to be prepared. It probably had come as a surprise to him when Commissioner of Indian Affairs William P. Dole wrote on April 9, 1862:

> Having been appointed by the President, by and with the advice and consent of the Senate to be Governor of the Territory of Colorado, in virtue of . . . [this] you will Ex-Officio assume the duties of Superintendent of Indian Affairs for said Territory. . . .[147]

There was no chance to refuse this position. He could only try to make the best of what must then have seemed a less-than-happy bargain.

In his favor it must be said that he approached the Indian problem with imagination and determination. With more help from the Indian Bureau, he might have been successful in preserving peace. But, as events were to prove in the coming months, Washington underrated the Indian threat and overestimated the Governor's ability to deal with the problem on his own.

10

"Murdering Horse-Stealing Indians"

The problem to which John Evans was introduced quite casually in the spring of 1862, when Indian Commissioner William P. Dole informed him that he was ex officio superintendent of Indian affairs,[1] was to become the major concern of the Evans administration. This was the problem of maintaining peaceful relations with the Cheyenne and Arapahoe Indians. Although Evans tried patiently to settle the grievances of these Plains tribes, his efforts were frustrated by his political opponents in the territory and by indecisive and inept officials in Washington.

The positions of governor and Indian superintendent were not really compatible. The governor had the duty of protecting the rights of citizens in the territory, while the Indian superintendent had a corresponding duty with regard to Indians, who were not citizens. In case of a dispute it was often impossible to satisfy both parties. If an uprising occurred—as happened with the Sioux in Minnesota in the fall of 1862 when seven hundred white men, women, and children were killed in seven days—it would be highly improbable that the officeholder could remain impartial.

The same Sioux Indians who had participated in the Minnesota outbreak, after being driven out onto the Plains, began to agitate among the Plains Indians in Colorado Territory to bring about a similar war in their area.² Two tribes in particular were more than a little inclined to listen to the proposition.

As stated in the previous chapter, the Cheyenne and Arapahoe Indians were unhappy about the treaty of Fort Wise, which gave them a reservation on the upper Arkansas River. Several bands which had not signed the treaty were to be crowded onto the reservation with no readjustments for the original signers. These two tribes also felt aggrieved because of the fact that Fort Wise was built on the reservation without compensation to the Indians for the land or for the ensuing destruction of game.³ According to the resident Indian agent there was "not a buffalo within two hundred miles of the reservation" and very little other game in the area;⁴ nevertheless, the government was not prepared to provide food and clothing during the difficult period of transition to reservation life.

In addition, the government seemed to be in no hurry to carry out the treaty commitments made at Fort Wise in 1861. In this treaty the United States had agreed to convert the arid reservation land to agricultural use and to help the Indians adapt to a sedentary way of life.⁵ By mid-1864 the agreement still had not been fully honored.

The Cheyennes and Arapahoes, for their part, were not eager to become farmers. Evans had seen that this would be a difficult change for them to make, had seen a growing shortage of irrigation water in the Arkansas River, and had suggested in writing that both the Indians and their reservation were better suited to ranching than farming. Commissioner Dole, who had asked Evans for his ideas on the subject, apparently paid no attention to this proposal.⁶ The Commissioner proceeded instead with his plan to divide the reservation into small forty-acre plots that the unskilled Indians were expected to work as irrigated farms.⁷ In the fall of 1863 when Evans made one of several attempts to get the tribes to enter the reservation, one of the chiefs said that farming was beneath

138

the dignity of the warriors, and the tribesmen refused to enter the reservation.[8]

Trouble with these tribes had started as soon as Evans arrived in Denver. On a Sunday in May, 1862, Evans was visited by a band of Sioux, Arapahoe, and Cheyenne Indians who had recently raided a Ute camp and scalped one of the braves there. Conscious of his duty as superintendent of Indian affairs, Evans told these braves to end their senseless feud with the Utes. For his trouble, Evans was accused of having sided with the Utes in the ancient rivalry, something that the Cheyennes and Arapahoes never forgot.[9]

Even as early as the summer of 1862 the Cheyennes and Arapahoes were threatening the white settlers. In one serious incident, a raiding party struck at ranches along the Platte, and Evans went out with the army unit to track down the miscreants and send them back to the Arkansas River.[10] Conscious that Indians were usually not punished for such theft and pillage, Evans proposed to deal with the offenders through the ordinary judical process, but the commissioner of Indian affairs seems to have disapproved his attempt to send the thieves to jail.[11]

A major shortcoming of the Bureau of Indian Affairs was the tightfisted policy of Commissioner William P. Dole. By a tragic coincidence the very tribes that Evans had identified as potential sources of trouble were the ones to suffer most from Dole's austere budget policy, which made them even more disgruntled. An outstanding example of his penurious attitude is found in his directive that a delegation of Utes, Comanches, Kiowas, and Apaches be sent to Washington for a conference and a look at the mighty Army of the Potomac. Since the Cheyennes and Arapahoes had already signed a treaty favorable to the government, he said their chiefs could come only if they agreed to pay their own way![12]

In the summer of 1863 Evans began to receive reports from soldiers, Indian agents, and Indians themselves that the Sioux were agitating among the Plains tribes. Both Indian Agent Samuel Colley at the Cheyenne-Arapahoe reservation on the Arkansas and Agent John Lorey on the South Platte felt that the danger of a war was serious.[13]

Evans conducted an investigation to determine the truth of the reports and then notified the authorities of the results of his investigation. He found not only that the Plains Indians did plan an uprising, but that Agent Colley was about to distribute guns and ammunition to these tribes, and that arms and whiskey were available from the sutlers at military posts. Evans ordered Colley to halt the distribution of arms;[14] he had already asked the military authorities to keep the Indians away from the forts.[15]

To add to the Governor's worries, the territory had no adequate defense against a possible Indian war. Although two volunteer regiments had been recruited in the area, they were immediately federalized and sent to posts outside the territory.[16] Militia, as the Governor repeatedly explained, could not do an effective job against the Indians. There were several good reasons for this. For one thing the territory had no money to purchase equipment, and it had no funds to pay salaries to men who might be called into temporary service. In addition, the militia would be of little use as infantry, but there were no funds for mounting the militia or even for food, should the militia be sent into the field.[17] Most important of all, Evans did not feel qualified to organize a military campaign, and moreover, he did not feel that a territorial governor should have to undertake such a task when the army could provide trained regulars.[18]

In April, 1864, just as Evans had predicted, the confederated tribes began a series of raids on ranches, settlements, and routes of communication.[19] The Indians seemed to be completely fearless, attacking military and civilian targets without discrimination. Immigrant trains, freight wagons, and stagecoach and telegraph lines were hit by Indian raids that grew

140

increasingly fierce; and for varying periods in the summer of 1864 communication with the East was cut off altogether.[20] By the end of the summer, according to one estimate, some two hundred people had been killed[21] and untold amounts of property stolen and destroyed. Many people were rendered destitute when members of the family were killed, their homes burned, and their livestock slaughtered or driven off.[22]

Early in June General Samuel R. Curtis, commander of the Department of Kansas, ordered Colonel Chivington to move the First Colorado Volunteers to the Arkansas River east of Fort Lyon (the new name for Fort Wise) with the intention of attacking the hostile Indians and perhaps of invading Texas.[23] Although this meant leaving Denver and the other settlements in an exposed position, Evans approved of the move. He even provided Chivington with two friendly Cheyennes to act as guides, saying that he hoped they might "be instrumental in bringing about a peace."[24]

No sooner had the troops left the area, however, than a warring band attacked the Hungate ranch thirty miles east of Denver. They murdered the Hungates and their children, raping Mrs. Hungate before she died.[25] The army unit camped near Denver en route to Fort Lyon could not be recalled because the telegraph line to headquarters was down. By the time General Curtis could issue new orders to the company, the murderers had managed to get away.[26]

Fearing that this was a prelude to an attack on Denver, Evans ordered two volunteer militia companies to stand in readiness for emergency action. He urged the citizens to organize new volunteer militia companies,[27] and he sent telegrams both to General Curtis, commander of the military district, and to the War Department asking for authority to federalize the militia so that they would be under regular military control.[28] Curtis answered that he could not accept the responsibility for such a move.[29] The War Department ignored the message.[30]

Realizing what might happen if the civilian population began to panic, Evans carefully kept his frantic official correspondence out of the newspapers.[31] This led to charges by his political opponents that Evans did not appreciate the gravity of the Indian menace and that he was deliberately sending soldiers away from the territory.[32] When this happened, Evans finally allowed some of his correspondence with the authorities in Washington and in army headquarters to be published.[33]

In spite of the Governor's efforts to prevent panic, on one occasion a false rumor of an impending raid caused the citizens of Denver to barricade themselves behind hasty fortifications. Evans himself refused to credit the reports,[34] and he later ordered that in the future all such rumors should be cleared through his office in order to prevent unnecessary alarm.[35] Thereafter, there was no repetition of such a false scare.

As the situation continued to deteriorate with no likelihood of aid from higher authority, Evans devised a plan to invite friendly Indians to settle on special reservations where food and protection would be given them. This move would accomplish the dual task of protecting the Indians from attack by troops in the field and at the same time providing "a nucleus for peace" which might induce the hostile Indians to lay down their arms. He hoped that eventually all of those at war would grow tired of fighting and come in to the camps.[36]

One of the main reasons for taking this action was that hostile Indians occupied the buffalo country and tried to coerce the friendly Indians into joining them.[37] If they were ever to be brought back to a friendly relationship, some plan such as that proposed by the Governor was going to have to be adopted to feed and clothe them.

Although Commissioner Dole at first telegraphed a guarded approval of the plan, a later message from Acting Commissioner Mix thoroughly emasculated it. It was all right, he said, to call in the friendly Indians, but no additional money was to be spent for their subsistence. Instead, Mix suggested that the friendly Indians be "collected about the buffalo range," which is exactly where they were already.[38] In spite of the Commissioner's order to expend no extra funds, Evans attempted to carry out his own plan, which promised to end hostilities.[39]

Realizing that this procedure might very well conflict with the commanding general's operations in the field, Evans asked General Curtis and the War Department to approve his plan or to suggest an alternative.[40] He did not even receive an acknowledgement of his letters carrying these requests.

Ten days later, on June 27, 1864, with only partial support from Commissioner Dole, and still no word from General Curtis on how the scheme might fit in with his military plans, Evans sent a notice "To the Friendly Indians of the Plains."

Colorado Superintendency Indian Affairs.

Denver, June 27th, 1864.

To the Friendly Indians of the Plains:

AGENTS, INTERPRETERS, and TRADERS, will inform the friendly Indians of the Plains that some members of their tribes have gone to war with the white people. They steal stock and run it off hoping to escape detection and punishment. In some instances they have attacked and killed soldiers and murdered peaceable citizens. For this the Great Father is angry, and will certainly hunt them out and punish them. But he does not want to injure those who remain friendly to the whites. He desires to protect and take care of them. For this purpose I direct that all friendly Indians keep away from those who are at war, and go to places of safety.

Friendly Arapahoes and Cheyennes, belonging on the Arkansas River, will go to Major COLLEY U. S. Indian Agent at Fort Lyon, who will give them provisions and show them a place of safety.

Friendly Kiowas and Camanches will go to Fort Larned, where they will be cared for in the same way.

Friendly Sioux will go to their Agent at Fort Laramie for directions.

Friendly Arapahoes and Cheyennes of the Upper Platte, will go to Camp Collins on the Cache la-Poudre where they will be assigned a place of safety, and provisions will be given them.

The object of this is to prevent friendly Indians from being killed through mistake. None but those who intend to be friendly with the whites must come to these places. The families of those who have gone to war with the whites must be kept away from among the friendly Indians.

The war on hostile Indians will be continued until they are all effectually subdued.

JOHN EVANS,

Governor of Colorado, and Superintendent of Indian Affairs.

In his proclamation Evans directed the Indians to assemble at designated camp sites and promised to supply them with food.[41] Although the agents were to see that hostile Indians did not send their families in and themselves continue to fight, all Indians who agreed to remain peaceful were to be welcomed at the camps. As Evans said to Agent Colley: "Many who are now hostile may come to the friendly camps and when they all do the war will be ended."[42]

The reaction of the Indians was disappointing. Only two groups responded to the proclamation; one left its assigned camp shortly after coming in, and the other was confined with meager rations to a small area near Camp Collins.[43] It is impossible now to determine what effect was produced by the Interior Department directive to "use the utmost economy" in providing supplies,[44] but the hostile tribesmen were by this time aware of the government's attitude in money matters. More generous treatment might well have convinced them that it was time to end the war.

Six weeks after the June proclamation was issued it became apparent that the Plains tribes were not interested in peace, and even their good friend Agent Colley said: "I now think a little powder and lead is the best food for them."[45] The last of the messengers who had been sent out with the proclamation returned and stated that the offers had been almost universally spurned.[46]

On August 8, 1864, a series of Indian attacks was made on Overland Stage stations between Denver and Leavenworth, and some thirty persons were murdered or taken into captivity. At the Ewbank Station on the Little Blue River one of the murdered women was found with a wooden stake driven through her loins.[47]

With this atrocity in mind Evans issued his famous proclamation of August 11, 1864, authorizing all citizens to arm themselves and to hunt down the hostile Indians. He cautioned the people against rash measures and admonished them to take

144

action only after organizing into proper militia companies.[48] When Charles Autobees told the Governor of his plan to raise a company and attack the Indians in their villages, Evans urged him to do so only after organizing a regular militia company. Then, said Evans, he would authorize Autobees "to punish and exterminate these murdering horse-stealing Indians of the plains."[49]

In reply to those who had criticized his policy of inviting Indians to places of safety, Evans pointed out that to kill friendly Indians would "only involve us in greater difficulty. It is important," he said, "to fight only the hostile [Indians], and no one has been or will be restrained from this."[50]

Baseless as the accusations against Evans were, they at least tend to show that the Governor did not exaggerate the danger from the Indians. Fortunately for the territory, it was just at this time that the War Department finally answered his plea for military aid and authorized him to enlist a volunteer regiment for one hundred days to search out and destroy the hostile tribesmen.[51] The regiment soon proved its worth. An Indian plot to attack a number of settlements simultaneously on the night of August 20 was discovered, and armed troops were dispatched immediately to the danger points. The Indian plan was completely frustrated, and what promised to be a major raid was thwarted by the militia and the hundred-day troops.[52]

One incident in this affair helps to show Evans' concern for the friendly Indians. Militia Captain Samuel E. Browne, who was also U.S. attorney and one of the Governor's bitterest political foes, told Evans on the morning of the twentieth that he intended to attack the band of peaceful Indians near Camp Collins. Evans ordered him not to do so, but he later learned that Browne intended to raid the village anyway. He then sent Browne a written message in which the officer was "peremptorily ordered not to go to Friday's Camp." Near midnight Evans found that Browne still intended to ignore the order, and he was forced to send a second written dispatch ordering Browne to keep away from these friendly Indians. Only then did the Captain obey the Governor's command.[53]

In spite of the fact that the Indian raids of August 20, 1864, had been thwarted, the danger was still not ended. Successive attacks by Indians along the Platte route kept that road closed from August 25 to the end of September.[54] In the face of these hostile raids, General Curtis mounted a major offensive against the confederated tribes. With more than six hundred troops and five mountain howitzers Curtis began to move against the tribes on the Plains south of the Platte River.[55]

Territorial Governor John Evans was greatly surprised, then, to receive a letter from Major Edward Wynkoop, commander of Fort Lyon, that he was bringing several Cheyenne and Arapahoe chiefs to Denver with a "proposition for peace."[56] Knowing of Curtis' foray along the Republican and Smoky Hill Rivers, Evans was reluctant to interfere in the military operations.[57]

According to Wynkoop's later testimony before a congressional committee, however, Governor Evans had another reason for his unwillingness to talk of ending the war. According to the major, Evans said that since he had raised a storm of protest to get the hundred-day volunteers, he could hardly allow them to be mustered out without seeing action.[58] A good deal has been made of this bit of testimony by Wynkoop, yet it should be noted that his account of the affair changed materially each of the several times that he testified.[59]

Although seriously ill at the time of Wynkoop's arrival, Governor Evans presided at a conference with the seven chiefs at Camp Weld, near Denver, on September 28, 1864.[60] While little importance was attached to it at the time, within three

One Eye's mark appears at the bottom of this letter from Black Kettle and "other Chieves" to Colley.

146

Cheyenne Village Aug. 29th/64

Maj. Colley.

Sir

We received a letter
from Bent, wishing us to make peace
We held a consel in regard to it & all
came to the conclusion to make
peace with you providing you make peace
with the Kiowas, Commenches, Ar-
opahoes, Apaches and Siouxs.
We are going to send a messenger to the
Kiowas & and to the other nations
about our going to make with you.
We heard that you some prisoners
in Denver. We have seven prisoners
of you which we are willing to give
up providing you give up yours.
There are three war parties out yet and
two of Arrapohoes. they been out some
time and expect now soon.
When we held this counsel there
were few Arrapohoes and Siouxs
present. we want true news from
you in return, that is a letter

Black Kittle &
other Chiefs

Brought to Mr Lym Sunday Sept
4th 1864 by One Eye—

*Denver residents waited near
Sixteenth and Lawrence Streets
for the Indians to arrive
for the Camp Weld conference
in September, 1864.*

months the conference was to become the center of the Sand Creek controversy. Agent Whiteley kept a record of the proceedings, the only one that has ever come to light.[61]

Whiteley's report shows that Black Kettle and the other chiefs were evasive, but that they finally admitted having been involved in hostile raids. It was Neva, however, an Arapahoe sub-chief, who revealed the Indians' real purpose—to have Agent Colley resume the distribution of treaty goods.[62] Evans refused to commit himself on this point, feeling, apparently, that hostilities had nullified the old treaty and that a new one should be negotiated.[63]

The fact that the chiefs had not been able to prevent the war in the spring or bring it to an early close made him doubt that they would "be able to make a peace which will last longer than until winter is past." His offer to "the friendly Indians" was still good, however, and he would "be glad to have them all come in under it."[64] A peace treaty was different. The Indians who had been at war would have to make peace with the military authorities, who were even then in the field hunting the hostile bands. Evans advised them to surrender unconditionally, and Colonel Chivington assured the Indians these were the only terms that would be acceptable.[65]

The Governor also doubted the sincerity of the Indian peace offer. Some of the Indians represented at the council had come to Camp Collins in answer to Evans' proclamation of June 27, accepted supplies, and then had gone back on the warpath.[66] Evans, therefore, wanted some guarantee that they intended to remain at peace. "Show, by your acts," he said, "that friendly disposition you profess to me."[67] He later told Dole that to make peace without better evidence of their sincerity "would be the most *cruel* kindness and the most *barbarous* humanity."[68]

Moreover, a reasonable delay in making peace would not endanger the lives of the citizens. With new militia units and the hundred-day volunteers, the territory was in a good defensive position. The approach of winter would also help. "You, so far, have had the advantage," Evans told them, "my time is just coming." When one of the chiefs protested that his people back in camp were in danger of attack by soldiers, Evans replied: "There is great danger of it."[69] The chief saw the point. Wynkoop had risked his life and that of his troops in visiting the Indian camp; the Indians might now consider themselves in a similar position.

One of the important questions in the Sand Creek affair is: "Why did Wynkoop bring the Indians to Denver?" Fort Lyon was not in the Military District of Colorado, and he should logically have reported to Fort Riley. Perhaps the best explanation is that he feared General Curtis, commander of the Department of Kansas, would not approve of any easy end to the war.

Evans determined to gain what advantage he could from the Indian peace offer. It was clear that the Indians wanted to enter the reservation, and the Governor approved of their going and staying there. He warned Agent Colley the day after the conference at Camp Weld, however, to have no official dealings with them. The Governor's real problem here was to keep Colley from distributing annuities to the tribes before they had surrendered unconditionally. This is what he had in mind when he wrote to Colley that the Indians "must deal with the military authorities until peace; in which case alone they will be in proper position to treat with the government in relation to the future."[70] Evans did not want to furnish the Indians with the means to continue the war the following spring, and he feared Colley might do just that.

His fears were well founded. Dexter Colley, the agent's son, was the trader at the agency, and Colley himself, together with the interpreter, John Smith,[71] was probably a partner in the trade. Both William Bent and Robert Bent testified that Smith and the Colleys sold annuity goods to the Indians.[72] Gossip at Fort Lyon said that Mrs. Colley's fruit pies, so popular at the fort, were made with treaty goods intended for the Indians.[73] Colley ignored the Governor's instructions about trading, and on October 18 another copy of Governor Evans' letter was sent to him.[74] Finally, on November 10, 1864, Evans sent Colley a sharp letter repeating his instructions and saying: "Until Genl Curtis has treated or made peace with the Indians, we cannot interfere."[75]

Colley's position in the affair is obscure. Although nominally under the direction of the Governor, for the most part he acted independently of Evans, and he even submitted his reports directly to Commissioner Dole, whom he addressed as "Dear Cousin."[76] He ignored Evans' letter of November 10, just as he had ignored the previous letters. When Chivington's "Hundred Dayzers" struck the sleeping camp at Sand Creek, Colley had a wagonload of trade goods there, which he had just sent under the supervision of Smith.[77] Exactly why Chivington decided to attack the camp is uncertain, but it is clear that Evans knew nothing about the plan.[78]

In any case Governor Evans had trouble enough over the statehood question.[79] Territorial Judges Charles Lee Armour, Stephen S. Harding, and Allen A. Bradford, together with U.S. Marshal Alexander Cameron Hunt and U.S. District Attorney Samuel E. Browne had all opposed the statehood movement, and they now were trying to oust Evans and the other federal appointees who had supported it. Evans had written to Secretary of Interior Usher in protest,[80] but he finally decided he must go to Washington to plead his case personally. The need to confer on "the disturbed state of the affairs of the Colorado Indian Superintendency" was an additional reason for his trip.[81]

Governor Evans wrote to the Secretary of State in mid-October, asking for a two-month leave of absence, to begin the first of November.[82] When a month passed with no answer from Seward, Evans simply assumed permission to leave the territory,[83] as he had done in previous years,[84] and he left for Washington with his family on November 16, 1864.[85] The maneuvers for his removal from office in the fall of 1864 doubtless made that year's leave seem even more urgent.

In Washington Evans received the unqualified support of James M. Ashley, chairman of the House Committee on Territories. With Ashley's backing Evans asked Lincoln to remove those appointees in Colorado who had opposed "the Union ticket and statehood."[86] Ashley said: "I am in favor of removing every man appointed by the administration to any office in the territories who opposes the *regularly nominated Union ticket.*"[87] Lincoln apparently shared these sentiments, and he told Evans to continue his dealings with Ashley.[88]

News of the surprise attack by Chivington on the Indians encamped at Sand Creek broke in Washington while Evans was there. Information that filtered through from the West indicated that the hundred-day volunteers had attacked a peaceful camp without warning, slaughtered women and children, and committed other unspeakable atrocities in the process.[89] The Governor's political opponents turned the resulting investigations into an open attack against him.[90] John W. Wright, who harbored a grudge against Evans for questioning the propriety of his conduct in surveying the reservation on the Arkansas, immediately began circulating a pamphlet accusing Evans of responsibility for Sand Creek.[91] Some of Evans' political enemies from Colorado had the ear of "a member of the committee charged with the investigation of the Chivington Affair," or so a Washington friend of the Governor said.[92]

When the report of the committee was published in the summer of 1865, Evans found it riddled with half-truths, innuendoes, and outright lies about himself and others in the territory. On August 6, 1865, he published an item-by-item refutation of the report,[93] but the damage had been done. President Johnson was unwilling to listen to Evans' plea for a fair hearing. On July 18, 1865, Secretary of State Seward asked for his resignation, and Evans submitted it on August 1, as soon as he received the Secretary's letter.[94]

Evans' removal was not only unfair to the Governor, but it was to have an adverse effect on the later efforts of the citizens to achieve statehood. Evans' refusal to make peace at Camp Weld was a prudent decision based on good evidence that the Indians were not sincere in their request for peace. His August 11 proclamation, which authorized all citizens to pursue and destroy hostile Indians and to appropriate their property, was severely criticized by the Joint Committee on the Conduct of the War. The phrase seems less objectionable, however, in light of Evans' statement that it was not his own. He said: "I quoted the language of the Secretary of War in his complimentary order to General Rosecrans. The same language which he used in regard to the rebels I used in regard to the Indians."[95]

His reply to the report of the Committee on the Conduct of the War was weak, but the weakness of his defense lay precisely in the area where Evans thought he had given it the greatest strength. He was determined to use only "official correspondence and accredited testimony," available in "public documents."[96] Evans refused to engage in any personal feud with his detractors because he hoped to get a rehearing before the committee or a chance to present his case to some other official body.[97] The chance was never given to him, and his privately-printed *Reply* had to bear the burden of refuting the slanderous report of the Committee on the Conduct of the War and the report of the military investigation, which was not released until 1867.[98] If Evans had known in the fall of 1865 that he would not be given a rehearing, he undoubtedly would have chosen to make a much more complete defense of his performance as superintendent of Indian affairs.

Regardless of his efforts, the Governor's enemies were successful in connecting him with the massacre. As one consequence Colorado statehood was delayed for another dozen years.

11

"All Hail the State of Colorado"

In spite of Territorial Governor John Evans' support of
statehood in 1864, the proposition encountered serious ob-
stacles. The vote on the question was taken in September,
1864, at the peak of the Indian crisis, and statehood went
down to defeat in a deluge of opposition votes. No one could
have foreseen the outcome when the proposal was first
introduced six months earlier.

The enabling act was approved by President Lincoln on
March 21, 1864,[1] and Territorial Governor John Evans immediately issued a call for a constitutional convention. With support from almost all the newspapers in the territory, approval
seemed assured from the very start. Simeon Whiteley, agent
to the Ute Indians at the abandoned Middle Park Agency, put
the announcement in his *Commonwealth* under the headline,
"All Hail the State of Colorado!"[2] In spite of this auspicious
beginning, opposition to the plan soon came to the surface.

The Spanish-speaking people in the southern part of the
territory were almost universally opposed to statehood. As a
minority group, they felt their interests would be better protected by the federal government than by an unknown body
of new state officials. A considerable group of other people
throughout the territory opposed statehood because the federal

155

draft law would then apply to Colorado.[3] Probably the most important reason for opposition arose from a widely held opinion that the population was too small to pay the expenses of state government,[4] but other factors also contributed to the defeat of the measure.

One of these was the Indian War of 1864, which revealed the unsettled condition of the territory and the need for a great deal of continued federal assistance. On the night of May 19, 1864, disaster in another form struck the capital city. Only a scant year before, fire had destroyed a large portion of the business district.[5] Now torrential rains on the headwaters of Cherry Creek brought a flood that threatened to wipe out the city. The governor's offices were flooded, and such buildings as the *Rocky Mountain News* plant and the Methodist Episcopal Church were swept away altogether. Public buildings in West Denver were inundated, and important records were destroyed. Homes, too, were flooded, and a large number of people were left destitute.[6] The terrible destruction, in the opinion of editor Frank Hall, graphically exposed the isolated condition of Colorado and furnished additional evidence of the need for continued federal assistance.

Since statehood had been proposed for Colorado, Nebraska, and Nevada in order to provide additional electoral votes for Lincoln in the fall and to help pass reconstruction legislation through the Senate,[7] it was natural that opposition to statehood should be closely tied to opposition to the Lincoln administration. As Lincoln's appointee, Evans found all his own acts, official and otherwise, open to criticism by his political opponents.

The voice of the anti-statehood forces was the Black Hawk *Mining Journal.* The Central City *Miners' Register* at first joined the *Journal* in charging that Evans had deliberately brought on the Indian war by sending the Colorado troops out of the territory.[8] When Evans wrote to the editors showing the absurdity of this charge, the *Register* shifted its ground and became an ardent supporter of Evans.[9] The attacks by the *Journal*, though, became more personal, and there was little attempt at consistency. When the price of mining stocks tumbled on the New York market, Evans was blamed. He was accused of selling worthless mining property and of conspiring to inflate the price of good mining stock.[10] At the same time, he was accused of making derogatory statements about the value of Colorado mines and of supporting discriminatory legislation.[11]

Although everyone in Colorado agreed that the Indian menace was real,[12] the opposition charged that Evans had caused the war or that he had failed to take steps to end it. At first Evans refused to answer these charges, feeling that "general charges without fact to sustain them are well understood by an intelligent public to be groundless for no one making them would omit the facts when they exist."[13] He was continually pressed to publish his correspondence with the military authorities but declined to do so on the ground that it might frighten the citizenry.[14] When he finally received permission to enlist a regiment for a hundred-day campaign against the hostile Indians, the Black Hawk *Mining Journal* observed sulkily—and unrealistically—that he should have ordered the First Colorado Volunteers back to the territory on his own authority. He had, instead, ordered local militia companies to take charge of local defense needs, and the *Journal* said that "calling out militia" was "a humbug second only to state organization."[15]

Aside from the fact that he hoped to avoid giving the citizens any reason for panic, Evans had another good reason for not publishing his correspondence with the military authorities. The opposition forces were using the Indian menace as an argument against statehood. After the raid on the Plum Creek station in early August, the Overland Stage Line withdrew its equipment and effectively cut communications between Colorado and "the states." The telegraph lines were cut as often as they could be repaired, and Colorado was virtually isolated by the Indian warriors.[16] In spite of the governor's repeated requests for military assistance, no effective aid was given until after the first of September, when President Abraham Lincoln wrote directly to General Curtis and asked him "to do the very best you can" to guard the Overland Mail.[17] Even then, regular mail service was not established until the end of the month, when the statehood question had already been defeated.[18]

The proposed state constitution itself offered additional grist for the opposition mill. In an effort to forestall arguments that statehood would mean higher taxes, the convention wrote into the document what would probably have been the lowest salary schedule in effect for state officers anywhere in the nation at that time. With pay rates of a thousand dollars for secretary of state, four hundred dollars for attorney general, and three dollars a day for members of the state legislature, the offices were singularly unattractive to ambitious territorial politicians.[19]

Because the Indian menace occupied so much time and attention during the summer, the statehood vote was not taken until September. With time growing short, the decision was made to elect state officers at the same time the constitution was voted on, September 13, 1864.[20] In early August the Republican convention named Evans as one of its candidates for the Senate, but the attacks of the anti-statehood forces had convinced many voters that he was unfit for the office. In the convention itself there was some indication that this was the general belief. When Evans' name was proposed as the candidate for the seat in the House of Representatives, the motion was defeated, and Colonel John M. Chivington was named to fill that position on the ballot.[21]

Republicans who had not been designated for state office quickly grew cool toward the statehood proposal. Even some of those who had won in the convention were less than enthusiastic about the plan. D. T. Towne, who had been named as the gubernatorial candidate, asked that his name be with-drawn.[22] A number of territorial officers also joined the opposition. These included the three members of the supreme court, the marshal, and the U.S. attorney.[23]

The Denver Council of the Union League, whose primary reason for existence was to "use all proper and legal efforts" to secure the election of Union Party candidates,[24] had debated the statehood question in late March.[25] At the meeting of July 25, 1864, a bitter argument ensued when the following motion was offered:

> Resolved, That [in] the present Condition of Our Country in this Great Struggle for nation[al] existence Her pressing need for all the aid Loyal hearts and heads can give demands of all the Union men in Colorado that they come to her rescue by adopting a State Government.

The question was carried over to the July 27 meeting and was then postponed for an additional two weeks. The opponents of statehood then deserted the organization. Finally, on September 5, a quorum was assembled with considerable difficulty, and the motion carried. On September 12, the eve of the election, the secretary made his last official entry in the minute book, noting that "the attendance indicated there was little more need" for the Denver Council to meet.[26]

By the end of August, Evans saw that his senatorial candidacy would have an adverse effect on the statehood vote, and he withdrew from the race.[27] It was too late. The statehood proposal was defeated by a sizable majority, 4,672 to 1,520.[28] As Frank Hall, one of the editors of the *Journal*, wrote later: "The people were not strong enough to support an independent commonwealth, and they knew it."[29]

If this were true, then why did Evans support the plan so strongly, almost blindly? There were a number of reasons. First, he was intensely loyal to President Lincoln, who had asked him to bring Colorado into the Union.[30] He also felt that Colorado's interests could best be protected by a voting representation in Congress.[31] A "seigniorage" bill had been proposed in Congress, levying a tax on the production of minerals, and Evans hoped to defeat the proposal.[32] Then, too, if Colorado were fully represented in Congress, it might be possible to have the railroad legislation changed to bring the transcontinental route through Colorado.[33] Added to these was Evans' obvious desire—one which he never lost—to be sent to Congress or to hold some other high national office.

Although the active opponents of the statehood measure had their own reasons for their position, Evans thought that the average voter had a less complex reason for his negative vote. In a letter to his brother Joel on October 31, 1864, Evans said:

> We have had a terrible time here during the past summer. The floods first washed us out and then the Indian war interrupted our commerce on the plains so that the Territory has had a severe back set. Our State movement was lost in consequence.[34]

On November 11, he repeated this reasoning in a letter to the President. "The great discouragements of floods and Indian wars," he said, "conspired to defeat the measure."[35] The favorable vote on the statehood question in the following year, when the flood damage and the Indian war were both only bitter memories, seems to support his analysis.

Although he did not believe their protestations of peace, Evans felt that the Indians at the Camp Weld conference had indicated their intention of halting the campaign at least for the winter. It would be safe, then, for him to go to Washington and try to make some definite arrangement to provide adequate protection for the territory's communication lines and, hopefully, bring out enough soldiers to end the war altogether. He wrote to Secretary of State Seward on October 18, asking for a leave of absence for this purpose, to begin November 1. Seward ignored the request, and, since there had been no objection raised in the fall of 1862 and 1863, Evans simply assumed that there would be no objection now.[36]

Evans had called a meeting in Central City on November 8 to consider the proposed "seigniorage" bill, and the meeting adopted his proposal to convey outright title to the miner, with no lease or royalty payments. This is the resolution that Evans presented to the Secretary of the Interior; the resolution was incorporated into the secretary's annual report for 1864, and this is the proposal which eventually became law.[37]

The anti-statehood group, supremely confident after its overwhelming success at the polls, now determined to remove Evans and his supporters from territorial office. Evans had previously written to Secretary Usher about the matter, and he now proceeded to bring other allies into the fight. He recommended the removal of all territorial officers who had opposed the statehood movement. This included the three members of the territorial supreme court, A. A. Bradford, Charles L. Armour, and Stephen S. Harding. It also included U.S. Attorney Samuel E. Browne, who had tried to attack the peaceful Indian band at Camp Collins, and Marshal A. C. Hunt.[38]

Evans received support in his fight from James H. Lane and Samuel C. Pomeroy, the senators from Kansas;[39] from James M. Ashley of Ohio, chairman of the Committee on Territories and the man who had originally proposed the Colorado statehood bill;[40] and from Congressmen William M. Stewart of Nevada, Samuel J. Tilden of New York, Joseph A. Wright of Indiana, and Richard Yates of Illinois.[41] President Lincoln determined not to desert the men who had worked so hard to advance his program. Even after the Sand Creek scandal, he supported Evans[42] and told him, in effect, to arrange with Ashley for suitable appointees to replace the opponents of statehood.[43]

Matters had taken a similar turn in Colorado during the governor's absence. Under the leadership of Representative Worrall of Central City, an attempt was made to petition for the removal of the Governor because he supported statehood. Evans' friends threatened to ask for the removal of those who had opposed statehood, and the plan was dropped.[44]

While he was in Washington, Evans was called to testify before the Committee on the Conduct of the War, which had been authorized to inquire into the battle at Sand Creek. Having been assured by the chairman that the committee had no authority or wish to investigate his handling of Indian matters, Evans confined his testimony to what he knew about the massacre—which was very little.[45] The chairman, Senator Benjamin F. Wade, was absent during the proceedings, and later said that he did not understand the full import of the committee report, which he signed.[46] Only three members of the committee were present: Senator C. R. Buckalew and Representatives D. W. Gooch and B. F. Loan. Evans' enemies, including John W. Wright, who had clashed with him in 1863 during the survey of the Upper Arkansas reservation, seem to have had the ear of at least one of these men.[47] In any case, the report was completely at variance with the facts and was obviously intended to blacken Evans' character and force the administration to remove him from office.

A special joint committee of Congress under Senator James F. Doolittle investigated the Sand Creek battle in the summer of 1865 and placed the blame for it elsewhere. The committee report was not published until 1867, however, too late to repair the damage to Evans' reputation and too late to help the statehood movement in Colorado.[48]

After Lincoln's death, Evans returned to Denver to resume his efforts for statehood. The former opposition group in Colorado, with few exceptions, now supported the statehood proposal.[49] Opposition, however, soon arose in another quarter. The Comittee on the Conduct of the War had recommended the removal of Evans as governor,[50] and the committee's criticism of Evans became one of the major arguments in Congress against statehood for Colorado.[51]

Evans, however, had influential friends in Washington who worked hard to promote his interests. There was, for example, Senator James Harlan of Iowa, who had cooperated with

Methodist Bishop Matthew Simpson in securing for Evans the appointment as governor of Colorado.[52] Evans had returned the favor on his recent trip to Washington by urging Lincoln to appoint Harlan to the post of Secretary of the Interior.[53] When Harlan won the appointment, he made strenuous efforts to have Evans retained as governor of Colorado. Although the appointments of Evans and Harlan were parts of Bishop Simpson's program of placing Methodists in high office, Evans and Harlan seem to have cooperated with each other more on the basis of friendship and mutual admiration than on religious grounds.[54]

Despite such support as that of Secretary Harlan, the new territorial delegate, Allen A. Bradford, worked feverishly to have Evans removed. He was motivated partly by the fact that Evans had criticized him for his opposition to statehood, and partly by Evans' efforts to have new territorial officers appointed without consulting him.[55]

The efforts of men like Bishop Simpson,[56] Congressman Ashley,[57] Senator Doolittle,[58] Senator Colfax,[59] and Secretary Harlan[60] seemed for a time to be bearing fruit. Simpson, for example, not only worked closely with Harlan, but also had other men exert pressure on the President and the Secretary of State. He made no secret of the fact that the removal of Evans would be considered a direct rebuff to the Methodist Church.[61] When the President refused to see him, Bishop Simpson went to Seward, who was vacationing at Cape May, New Jersey. Seward told him frankly that, because of the report of the Committee on the Conduct of War, he could not keep Evans in office "without having trouble in Congress."[62]

The bishop wanted to propose Samuel H. Elbert, then territorial secretary, as the next governor, but Seward would not agree to this. He then suggested Alexander Cummings, and Seward accepted the proposal. He also expressed his willingness to retain Elbert as secretary. "He says he wishes to do nothing unpleasant which he can avoid," the bishop wrote, "and that as Mr. Elbert is not named [in the committee report] he will retain him."[63]

John Evans forwarded his resignation to the President on August 1, 1865.[64] He wrote to Seward at the same time, asking that its acceptance be delayed until the return of Senator Doolittle, who had been in Denver the previous week.[65] Seward felt, however, "in view of the published action of the Committee on the War, . . . that a change was necessary to prevent attacks on the administration."[66]

In the meantime the statehood movement had been gathering fresh steam. Jerome B. Chaffee directed the move, and W. A. H. Loveland took a prominent part in the proceedings.[67] Henry M. Teller, named as candidate for senator in the previous statehood campaign, seemed less enthusiastic on this occasion.[68] The Spanish-speaking people in the San Luis Valley remained unalterably opposed, although there was considerable evidence that they would approve statehood if their area were joined to New Mexico.[69]

In spite of the many objections, the new proposal was approved at the polls on September 5, 1865, by a vote of 3,025 to 2,870.[70] As in the vote on the same question in 1864, there were charges of fraud. The question was not voted on in one county, and another county was not informed of the election until noon of the day on which it was held; nonetheless, full returns were reported for both counties.[71] As Frank Hall later observed: "Notwithstanding the apparent majority of one hundred and fifty-five, . . . there were many who believed that it was more apparent than real."[72]

One blunder of the previous campaign was not repeated in 1865. Candidates for state offices were not chosen until the constitution was approved by the voters. The Republicans again named John Evans as senatorial candidate, but Henry M. Teller, perhaps because of his lukewarm support for the campaign, was beaten in the party race for the other seat by Jerome B. Chaffee. Teller then refused to run for the House seat, and he became one of the more vocal opponents of statehood.[73]

On December 18, 1865, the newly-elected Colorado state legislature made Evans its unanimous choice for the Senate and appointed Chaffee to the other seat.[74] Although it should have come as no surprise, the statehood forces were shocked when Governor Cummings almost immediately loosed his first blast against the new constitution.

On December 22, Cummings notified Seward that the entire campaign had been "conducted wholly irrespective of the National or Territorial authority." He sent the Secretary a copy of the proposed state constitution and took pains to point out that Negroes were excluded from the ballot.[75] Thus Cummings drew the line on which the statehood question would be fought in Congress. Frank Hall later said that "his turbulent excellency"[76] was "the chief factor in the ultimate defeat of our admission as a state."[77]

Cummings followed this first attack with a message to the territorial legislature on January 23, 1866. Referring to an action of the 1864 legislature, excluding Negroes from the franchise, he said: "It seems incredible, and were it not for the record, it would be incredible, that such a measure could have been adopted at such a time." He also pointed to the fact that, while their parents were taxed for the support of public schools, Negro "children are not permitted to attend them." Cummings urged the legislators to "erase this odious record from the statehood book."[78] He then added a supporting petition signed by "a committee of colored citizens, acting for the colored citizens of the territory," and sent both documents along to Seward.[79]

Evans reacted with his usual vigor. Under date of January 29, 1866, he and Chaffee, together with Congressman-elect Chilcott, presented a memorial to Congress, giving their side of the case. While they made no attempt to defend the fact that the proposed constitution denied Negroes the right to vote, they did claim that there were probably not more than a hundred and fifty Negroes in the territory and that "nineteen of the twenty-five loyal states of the union" had the same provision in their constitutions.[80]

The battle was soon joined in the halls of Congress. When the statehood bill was introduced in the Senate, Benjamin F. Wade attacked it because the population of Colorado was too small.

> To say that a population of twenty-five or thirty thousand, which is the utmost extent of the population in this Territory now, shall have two Senators on this floor and a Representative in the other House is an inequality amounting to almost the old rotten-borough system of England.[81]

Senator Charles Sumner, who helped lead the opposition, attacked Evans personally on the basis of the report of Wade's Committee on the Conduct of the War,[82] but he based his opposition mainly on the exclusion of Negroes from the franchise.[83] Others pointed out that the question of Negro suffrage had never before been raised in the admission of any state.[84] It was also stated that Negroes in Nevada were specifically excluded from voting on the statehood question in 1864 and still could not vote, and that this had not been raised as an objection to statehood for Nevada.[85] Senator Doolittle came to Evans' defense in answer to Sumner's attack,[86] as did Senator Lane of Indiana.[87] Lane made the additional point that even if the charges were true, "it does not in the slightest degree affect the right of Colorado to admission as a state."[88]

In spite of the opposition, the statehood measure passed both houses of Congress and was sent to the President for his signature. Johnson had recently vetoed the Civil Rights Bill,[89] and by April 9, 1866, both houses had passed it over his veto.[90] The vote in the Senate on this measure had been 33 to 15, only slightly more than the necessary two thirds.[91] If there had been two additional senators supporting Johnson, the vote would have been 33 to 17, just short of the required two thirds.

With the statehood question hanging in the balance, President Johnson offered a deal to the senators from Colorado; he would approve the statehood measure only if they would sign an agreement to support "my policies." Evans and Chaffee turned the offer down flat.[92] As a result, the President vetoed the bill on May 15, 1866.[93]

He gave several reasons for his veto. First, the population was much too small, the most generous estimate being only forty thousand, while the current ratio for representation in Congress was one for a hundred and twenty-seven thousand. Secondly, the president doubted that the small majority of a hundred and fifty-five in favor of statehood reflected the sentiments of the citizens of the territory, particularly when the overwhelming vote against statehood in 1864 was considered. On this latter point he challenged the proponents of statehood to hold "another election under the authority of Congress,"[94] but they refused to take up the challenge.

Radicals in the Senate soon realized that the question of additional votes was a two-edged sword. Their margin in passing the Civil Rights Bill over Johnson's veto was distressingly thin. Two additional votes might be very useful in the future. After the Senate heard the veto message, Senator Wade changed his position on Colorado statehood, saying that on the previous vote he "had not got hold of all the facts."[95] Sumner, however, refused to reconsider; Negro suffrage was, for him, still the paramount issue. "I, for one," he said, "mean always to stand by the principle that no State shall be received into this Union from this time forward with a constitution which disavows the first principle of the Declaration of Independence."[96] There he stood, and he could not be moved. In any case, the Colorado bill was not passed over the President's veto.

The question was brought up again in the next session, and Congress once more passed a statehood bill. Again Johnson vetoed the bill, and again the Senate failed to muster the votes to override the veto.[97] In a letter to his brother, Evans offered little hope for a new attempt in that session. "Congress is likely to adjourn too soon to pass it over a veto."[98] Meanwhile, some pressure had been brought on Evans and Chaffee to agree to vote for the Radical program. Their refusal to do so[99] probably accounts for the Senate's failure to override the veto in 1867. Nebraska, which was admitted in 1867, gave two votes for Johnson's impeachment.[100]

Early in 1868 a last attempt for approval of the Colorado statehood bill was made by Evans and Chaffee. This time Henry M. Teller's anti-state group had the support of Roscoe Conkling, and the bill failed to carry. Teller had taken the pulse of the territory and knew that the citizens were no longer interested in statehood. He challenged Evans and Chaffee to submit the question to the voters in Colorado, but the would-be Senators knew Teller was right and refused to ask for the vote.[101]

Senator-elect Evans did not spend all his time in Washington pressing the statehood measure. On July 5, 1868, he wrote to his wife:

> I am very busy with my R. R. bill as well as in helping get our appropriations through. We shall get the penitentiary money, . . . an appropriation for geological surveys and in fact all the measures we are asking before Congress adjourns. Even they say the state bill shall be passed.[102]

He was wrong on the last point, but the "R. R. bill" did pass the Senate.[103]

12

"For Denver and my Railroad"

Almost simultaneously with the rejection of the statehood bill in 1868, John Evans' efforts to secure favorable railroad legislation for the territory began to show some promise of success. Railroading was not a new field for Evans. All of his previous experience had shown that business success was tied directly to transportation. His father's own considerable fortune had been based on investments in toll roads, railroads, and canals, and on land that appreciated in value after transportation facilities were improved.[1] John Evans' wealth in Chicago had demonstrated the validity of this principle. The town promotion at Oreapolis failed largely because the railroad was not built to the site. Denver might suffer the same fate, but Evans was determined that it should not.[2]

On May 16, 1862, his first evening in Denver, the new governor spoke to the assembled citizens in front of the Tremont House and told them that the proposed Pacific railroad would become "the great commercial auxiliary" of Denver.[3] By the end of June, Governor Evans had dispatched Surveyor General F. M. Case to the mountains west of Denver to determine whether the Berthoud Pass route, discovered the previous year by Captain E. L. Berthoud, would be practical for a railroad or a wagon road.[4] Evans and Case had made a personal inspection earlier in the month, and they felt the results warranted a more thorough survey of the pass.[5]

Late in July, Case made his report, which declared that a wagon road would be practical, but a railroad was something else again.[6] Nothing daunted, Evans had Case go back for another look, but the report was still unfavorable. According to Case, the only way the railroad could be built would be by putting a three-and-a-half-mile tunnel under the pass.[7] When Evans suggested that gold might be discovered in constructing the tunnel, Case replied that it was possible, but not very likely.[8]

In spite of the discouraging report, Evans continued to promote the Colorado route. He had been named by Congress as one of the 158 "commissioners" charged with the duty of organizing "the Union Pacific Railroad Co." to build a transcontinental railroad.[9] Armed with a joint resolution from the territorial legislature, asking that the route be located in Colorado,[10] Evans attended the meeting of the "commissioners" in Chicago in September, 1862, and urged them to approve the Colorado route.[11] The strongest commitment he could get from the assembled commissioners was a resolution stating that "the development of prosperous settlements in Colorado, Utah and Nevada Territories . . . has furnished one of the greatest desiderata to the construction and maintenance of the Pacific Railroad, and encourages us in our efforts."[12]

Although the railroad project was suspended during the war, Evans did not forget it. In his message to the territorial legislature on February 3, 1864, the Governor declared that there was still a strong possibility that the transcontinental railroad would come through Colorado. The Union Pacific Eastern Division (later called the Kansas Pacific) had received a land grant extending to the hundredth meridian. This grant would bring the road to a point only 250 miles east of Denver. Evans felt confident that Congress could be persuaded to extend the grant to Denver and urged that "the entire energies of the Territory be brought to bear in co-operation with the branches from Kansas City and Atchison for their extension to the heart of our Territory." The promotional work must be done in a dignified manner, however. "Our Territory is not to be regarded in the light of the suppliant for the favor for she has quite as many benefits to confer as to receive in consideration of such location."[13]

The Governor had attended a meeting of the "Managers of the Pacific Railroad" in New York in December, 1863, and had apparently received considerable support for the plan to run the railroad through Denver, over Berthoud Pass, through Middle Park, and to Provo, Utah.[14] It is not possible to say what effect his efforts had on Congress, but on July 2, 1864, legislation authorized the Union Pacific Eastern Division, to build on west to meet the Central Pacific, provided it reached the hundredth meridian before the line from Omaha did so.[15]

After his abortive election to the U.S. Senate in the fall of 1865, Evans continued to use his influence to bring the transcontinental railroad through Denver. During the following February, he asked Surveyor General John Pierce, Case's successor and a member of Case's 1862 survey party, to give his "opinion of the feasability of crossing the main range of the mountains in Colorado as I desire to secure more thorough surveys of the various proposed routes for the same." He also asked Pierce to give his "opinion as an Engineer . . . of the practicability of a temporary crossing while a tunnel might be in course of construction at or near the Berthoud Pass."[16]

Pierce replied that a temporary track could be run over Berthoud "with no trouble," and that the summit could be easily reached "either by stationary power or by a series of zig zag tracks." On the other hand, an even better route would follow the South Platte River through South Park. Here the average grade would be only forty feet per mile, and the tunnel through the divide would be only a mile in length—both less than half the requirement on the Berthoud route. "The richness of the country," he concluded, "and the abundance of fuel on the line through Colorado as well as the fact that it is 150 miles shorter certainly demand that these passes should at least be surveyed in a thorough manner."[17]

Senator-elect Evans also engaged in extensive correspondence with John A. Dix, president of the Union Pacific, but he received little encouragement. Dix had apparently agreed with W. A. H. Loveland and Henry M. Teller of the newly organized Colorado Central and Pacific Railroad to cross Colorado, if indeed the territory were crossed at all, on the line of Cache la Poudre River, considerably to the north of Denver.[18] Although Dix promised that the proposed line would "connect with Denver,"[19] this was not quite what Evans had in mind.

He apparently continued to press for favorable congressional action, and on June 27, 1866, the Union Pacific Eastern Division was authorized to join the main line no more than fifty miles west of Denver.[20] Evans' part in securing this legislation is not known, but as soon as it passed Congress, he wired the editor of the *Rocky Mountain News* from Washington that the railroad would "build direct to Denver now." *News* editor William Byers greeted the announcement with the headline, "Hurrah! Hurrah!"[21]

Within a few short months joy changed to gloom. The Eastern Division was openly considering a swing south into New Mexico,[22] and General Grenville M. Dodge, chief engineer for the Union Pacific, advised his board of directors that neither the Berthoud route nor any other Colorado route would be practical. The Union Pacific soon decided to build through Cheyenne.[23] A frantic telegram from fellow Senator-elect Jerome B. Chaffee brought Evans to New York to make a final plea in the case, but to no avail.[24]

When this occurred, Loveland announced that his Colorado Central and Pacific Railroad would build to Cheyenne. His proposal received the support of the Denver people until it became clear that the main line would terminate in Golden and that only a branch would be built to Denver.[25] During the summer and fall of 1867 the Colorado Central proposal was argued by the opposing groups, and it was finally doomed when the voters refused to approve the requested county bonds.[26] Civic gloom deepened when a representative of the Union Pacific Eastern Division told the Denver voters that unless $2,000,000 in Arapahoe County bonds were made available, the road from the east would also probably decide to bypass Denver.[27]

A representative of the Union Pacific, George Francis Train, then visited the city, and suggested that Denver organize its own railroad and build to Cheyenne with Union Pacific help.[28] This was the spark the city needed. A Board of Trade was organized in the fall of 1867, with John Evans as one of its principal supporters.[29] Through the efforts of the board, the Denver Pacific Railroad Company was incorporated, with John Evans as a member of the road's board of directors.[30]

In an obvious effort to restore peace with the Colorado Central, whose Union Pacific alliance apparently had been preempted by the Denver Pacific, Evans pushed a resolution through the Denver Board of Trade, supporting the efforts of Loveland's road to build west to Black Hawk and Central City.[31] The honeymoon was short. The Union Pacific Eastern Division soon stepped in to offer assistance to the Denver Pacific, and the Union Pacific made financial assistance again available to the Colorado Central.[32]

The Denver Pacific Railroad was capitalized at $2,000,-000,[33] and the citizens of Arapahoe County voted $500,000 in bonds to purchase one-fourth of the stock.[34] Nonetheless, Denver's railroad future was still uncertain. The first president of the Denver Pacific resigned, and the second died before he had been in office four months. In March, 1868, John Evans was elected president of the road.[35] He assumed the responsibility for marketing the county bonds and found that no one would buy them.

Late in the same month, Evans spoke to the Chicago Board of Trade, asking its support. That group agreed to use its influence to place $200,000 worth of the Arapahoe County bonds.[36] Sales were discouragingly slow, however. Only eleven of the $1,000 bonds were sold, and these went at a discount of ten per cent.[37]

With no hope of building the road through local effort alone, Evans met with Sidney Dillon and Thomas C. Durant of the Credit Mobilier Company and concluded an agreement for the construction of the road. According to this contract, which the Denver Pacific board approved on May 4, 1868, the Denver Pacific was to increase its capital stock from $2,000,000 to $4,000,000. Acting as sub-contractor to the Union Pacific, the Denver Pacific was to grade the right-of-way, construct the bridges, and lay the ties. The Denver Pacific was also to apply for a land grant and to incorporate a branch to go to the mountain mining camps. "Durant and Dillon and their associates" agreed to lay the rails and furnish the rolling stock in return for $3,500,000 of the stock of the Denver Pacific, and, upon completion, the road was to be leased to the Union Pacific.[38] The agreement meant loss of local control, but it seemed the only way to build the road.[39]

On June 26, 1868, Senator Harlan of Iowa introduced the Denver Pacific land grant bill in the Senate.[40] Congressman Chilcott had tried the same thing in the House, and the bill was referred to the Committee on the Pacific Railroad, where it died.[41] When the Senate bill failed to excite any enthusiasm, the lesson became clear. Additional support was necessary.

Senator-elect Evans then concluded an agreement with the Union Pacific Eastern Division, whereby that road agreed to back the move for a Denver Pacific land grant in return for Denver Pacific support of an addition to their own grant.[42] Consequently, Harlan introduced an amendment on July 25, which in effect would give the Eastern Division an additional subsidy of $800,000.[43]

Apparently doubting that the amended bill had any chance to pass, Evans first had the Eastern Division's officers execute a written agreement with the Denver Pacific, giving the Denver Pacific any claim they might have to a grant of land north of Denver. When the amended bill failed to pass the House before adjournment, the Denver Pacific at least had a relinquishment by the Eastern Division on the land grant between Denver and Cheyenne.[44]

Evans then had a bill introduced giving the Denver Pacific a land grant between Denver and Cheyenne and bonding authority similar to that given the Union Pacific. Under the terms of this act, which passed both houses of Congress and was approved on March 3, 1869, the Denver Pacific was granted a right-of-way to Cheyenne, alternate sections of land for twenty miles on each side of the line, and the right to mortgage the line with first-mortgage bonds at the rate of $32,000 per mile.[45]

Durant and Dillon, in the meantime, were having their own problems. Evans met with the two in their private railroad car at a tie siding in Utah called Quaking Asp. The tie cutters had not been paid for their work, and they were holding the two directors under guard until payment was made. "I was hospitably entertained," said Evans, but he found the two men unable to keep their agreement to finish and operate the Denver Pacific.[46]

One of the reasons for their refusal was that they simply did not have the money, but another may be found in the legislation granting the Eastern Division a perpetual right-of-way over the Denver Pacific tracks.[47] This was something less than the complete control Durant and Dillon had envisioned in their original contract.

With sixty miles of the line graded and ties and bridge timbers floating down the Cache la Poudre, the situation again looked hopeless.[48] But John Evans had saved the line from disaster before; perhaps he could do it again.

The Denver Pacific board offered Evans "all of the assets of the company," if he would agree to build the road. He agreed to try and resigned his position as president. John Pierce was elected in his place.[49]

Under the terms of the contract Evans signed with the road, June 4, 1869, he was to receive the $3,500,000 capital stock left in the Denver Pacific treasury,[50] the remaining $300,000 in Arapahoe County bonds, $2,500,000 in Denver Pacific first-mortgage bonds and about 100,000 acres of the 900,000-acre land grant. In return, Evans agreed to build and equip the road and to pay off the $200,000 debt incurred in the preliminary construction work.[51]

Although they had a nominal value of some $6,000,000, the stock and bonds had been singularly unsuccessful in attracting investment capital. The land grant would not be valid unless the road were built. Then the stock and bonds might grow to be worth their face value, and yet they might not. Under the prodding of W. A. H. Loveland and William J. Palmer, the Arapahoe County Commissioners later complained bitterly about the increase in capital stock, which reduced the county's interest from one-fourth to one-eighth. In 1869, however, they were eager to have John Evans accept the terms of the construction contract, which seemed to offer the only hope for saving their investment.[52] In early 1870, when the success of the road seemed assured, Evans promised to donate another half-million dollars worth of stock to the county, and this he subsequently did.[53]

With the construction contract in hand, Evans proceeded to look for capital to build the road. He first offered the contract to Durant and Dillon, but the two men refused to accept it.[54] Then he went to the Kansas Pacific, which, tired of the confusion of names, had dropped the label Union Pacific Eastern Division and assumed the new title.[55]

R. E. Carr, one of the Kansas Pacific directors, agreed to purchase a half interest in the construction contract. So a new construction company was formed, named Evans and Carr. John Evans, Walter S. Cheesman, and David H. Moffat held a half interest in the firm, and General Carr held the other half.[56] As part of the agreement, the Denver Pacific was to pool its gross receipts with those of "an equal length of the Kansas Pacific next to Denver." The Kansas Pacific also received 15,000 shares of Carr's portion of the Denver Pacific stock, and thus the Denver Pacific became a virtual subsidiary of the Kansas Pacific.[57]

The Denver Pacific board gave its enthusiastic approval to this agreement on August 3, 1869. As Evans said later, after the pooling agreement began to work to the disadvantage of Denver, pooling was "an absolutely necessary condition of receiving aid to iron the road."[58] Then too, the agreement could be advantageous to Denver. As President John Pierce noted: "This ensures to your company the full benefit of one half the business of Colorado at all times, and at the same time relieves you [the stockholders] from the burden of competition." Moreover, said Pierce, there was no other way to build the road.[59]

With Kansas Pacific cooperation, the new firm of Evans and Carr proceeded to build the road. By mid-December, 1869, the road was completed from Cheyenne to Evans, forty-eight miles from the outskirts of Denver, and three locomotives began pulling passenger and freight cars over the line.[60] Taking advantage of the fertile land at the railhead, Evans and Carr had platted the town of Evans and had begun selling lots. The Loveland forces complained sourly that construction had been deliberately stopped in order to enhance the value of Evans and Carr land.[61] They overlooked the fact that the Denver Pacific lands would also increase in value, but the railroad's board did not miss this point, and the company's annual report happily looked forward to the sale of several thousand acres.[62]

In January, 1870, John Evans was elected president of the Denver Pacific. The board positions were divided between

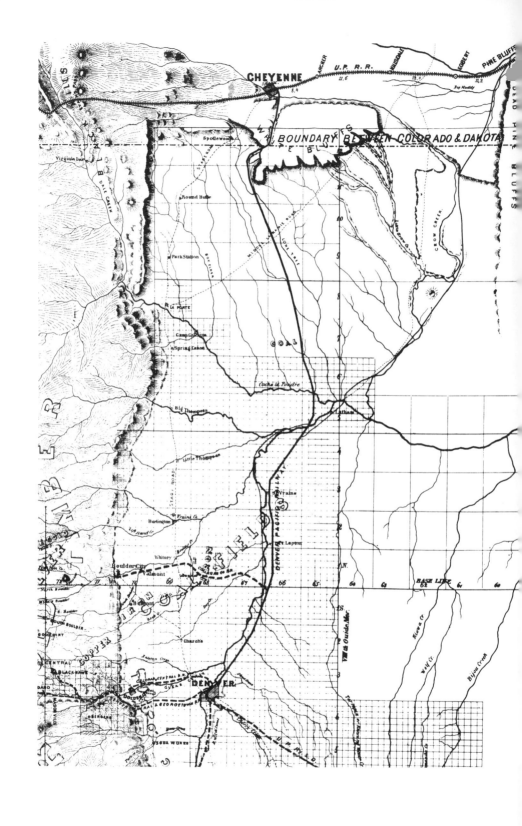

Denver Pacific and Kansas Pacific men. The Kansas Pacific was building on to Denver under the direction of William J. Palmer, who also became a member of the Denver Pacific board.[63]

President Evans pushed construction of the Denver Pacific, and the tracks reached the Denver depot on June 23, 1870. A branch line, the Denver and Boulder Valley Railroad, had been surveyed, and Evans immediately began the construction of that line to the company's rich coal fields.[64] This gave the Denver Pacific a very cheap supply of coal, lowering operating costs and enabling the road to control the coal business in northern Colorado.[65]

With the completion of the Denver Pacific, Colorado railroad construction developed at an astounding pace. The Kansas Pacific reached Denver on August 15, 1870. The Union Pacific, fearful of Kansas Pacific control of the Colorado business, made funds available to W. A. H. Loveland, and his Colorado Central joined the Denver Pacific on September 2 of the same year.[66] John Evans' dream of making Denver a railroad center had been realized.

It is impossible to tell how much profit Evans and his associates realized from the Denver Pacific venture. The available records offer only a few clues. The Evans and Carr Company received securities with a face value of some $6,000,000, plus 100,000 acres of land. The cost of constructing the railroad line was about $2,000,000. The land brought perhaps four dollars per acre, or somewhat less than another $500,000.[67] Evans and his Denver associates seem to have invested very little cash in the road.[68] Indeed, Denver's lack of investment capital was what inspired the original promoters to insist that Evans accept the construction contract. Obviously he would

An 1868 map of the Denver Pacific showing the "final location with prospective connections" of the line.

179

not have done so unless there were some chance to make a considerable profit. He was too good a businessman to do otherwise. Profits were undoubtedly uppermost in Evans' mind when he sold his interest to the Kansas Pacific in February, 1872.[69]

More than three years earlier, that is in November, 1868, Evans had become interested in building a railroad from Denver to Georgetown. His Denver, Central and Georgetown Railway Company was intended to tap the mining region west of Denver, a development that Dillon and Durant had specified in their original agreement with the Denver Pacific.[70] With construction promised as soon as the Denver Pacific was built,[71] the people of Georgetown began to consider the Denver Pacific as their own road, even going so far as to contribute the silver spike to mark completion of the line.[72] Evans tried unsuccessfully to combine that road with Loveland's Colorado Central,[73] and when the attempt failed, he determined to build his own line to Georgetown.[74]

Evans visited Brigham Young in Salt Lake City early in 1872 and secured a promise of enthusiastic cooperation for the newly-organized Denver, Georgetown and Utah Railway Company.[75] The new railroad had banked heavily on assistance from the Kansas Pacific.[76] When this aid was not forthcoming, and when the Colorado Central blocked plans to build along Clear Creek, Evans organized a new railroad, the Denver, South Park and Pacific.[77]

When the South Park line was incorporated on October 1, 1872,[78] the owners planned to utilize the tracks of the Denver, Georgetown and Utah into Bear Creek canyon and to enter South Park near Fairplay.[79] In June, 1873, the road was reorganized, and new plans were made to go through the South Platte canyon to South Park. Branches were also to be built to Morrison, to Middle Park, and to the San Luis Valley. Capitalization was increased from $2,500,000 to $3,500,000.[80]

When the South Park asked for an Arapahoe County bond

election to enable the county to buy $300,000 worth of stock, William J. Palmer, whose new Denver and Rio Grande also wanted to build into South Park, began to attack the proposal.[81] Evans soon saw that Palmer's attacks on him and his railroad could be turned to the advantage of the South Park, and he entered into a public debate with Palmer through the Denver newspapers. Evans cleverly allowed Palmer to ruin his own case, letting the General make it appear that Colorado Springs was "dictating" to Denver.[82]

But there was apparently more than one way to influence voters. The Denver *Republican*, for example, later charged that the South Park "Campaign Committee" spent $763 at a local brewery "for beer furnished to carry that election."[83]

Whatever was involved, the project succeeded. On July 28, 1873, the citizens of Arapahoe County approved the bonds by a vote of 1,867 to 588.[84] The county commissioners accordingly cancelled the bonds—some $200,000 worth—that had been previously voted for the Georgetown road, and issued new bonds worth $300,000 to the South Park.[85]

Before work could be started, the Panic of 1873 struck the financial centers of the country and made it extremely difficult to market the securities.[86] Two companion firms, with which Evans was closely associated, had already been organized, however, and this made it easier to set temporary objectives for the road. One of these companies, the Morrison Stone, Lime and Townsite Company, organized in 1872, was even then platting a town at the mouth of Bear Creek canyon and was preparing to exploit the stone quarries there.[87] The second firm, the Bear Creek Wagon Road Company, had also begun work on a road into South Park, and the railroad could utilize its surveys to build out of Denver.[88]

In spite of the financial stringency, a few of the county bonds were sold; in addition, the South Park had raised $150,000 on its own securities during the past year. John Evans' brother Seth was a partner in some Cincinnati rolling mills, and it was apparently from these firms that enough track was obtained to run the line to Morrison.[89] The line was open to Morrison in June, 1874,[90] and at the end of the year a total of forty-six miles of track had been laid.[91]

The Morrison stone quarries furnished enough revenue to pay expenses, although not enough to make the stock or bonds attractive. The $300,000 in Arapahoe County bonds also proved disappointing, bringing in only $211,400 in cash.[92]

Evans went to New York for several months in the winter of 1874, but had little success in selling the South Park securities. In the spring of 1875 he sailed for London, remaining there until the end of October; yet again he could not find any investment capital.[93]

The Morrison Stone, Lime and Townsite Company suffered badly from mismanagement while Evans was away, endangering not only the town investments, but also the railroad. The trouble was that the manager, Bailey, had been "selling stone for about half what it cost to get it out [,] and a very large business at that rate" had put the concern "hopelessly in debt." In addition, the Bear Creek Wagon Road had been allowed to deteriorate to such an extent that the South Park trade was going through Colorado Springs.[94]

In Denver there was some criticism of the South Park management, and Evans found it necessary to defend his efforts before the Board of Trade. "I don't care if they do abuse me," he wrote to his wife, "if they will only let me work for Denver & my R.R.—I can't afford to quit either nor wont."[95]

Evans had expected assistance from the Kansas Pacific, then in the midst of a quite active rivalry with the Atchison, Topeka and Santa Fe. The Kansas Pacific was expected to build south to Trinidad, but the Santa Fe, he thought, would control the portion of the South Park trade which came through Colorado Springs and Pueblo. This control was expected to force the Kansas Pacific into an alliance with the South Park.[96] Evans' hopes on this score were dashed when the

Kansas Pacific, the Santa Fe, and the Rio Grande signed a pooling agreement to be effective in September, 1876.[97]

This agreement meant the South Park investors were strictly on their own, and Evans put the matter squarely to "the merchants and capitalists of Denver." In a letter to his wife, he reported that he told them he was "under no more obligation to build the South Park road than they and if they want it they must help."[98] He informed the members of the Denver Board of Trade that the "whole world" was in bad condition financially and that the road could be extended only if they contributed their own funds. As a beginning, he suggested $150,000 for use in building on to Buffalo Creek.[99]

Although Evans continued to talk to other investors, including a representative of London's Credit Fonciere and Baring Brothers, the best arrangement seemed to lie with local investors. J. W. Smith, of Denver, began to talk of forming a new construction company. After much discussion, the Denver and San Juan Construction Company was organized, with an initial subscription of $150,000.[100]

In the South Park firm, as in the Denver Pacific, John Evans was the driving force. Criticism of his management once led him to resign his position as board chairman of the former, but the resignation was not accepted.[101] After the new construction company was organized, Evans again considered getting out of the management of the South Park. "J. W. Smith takes hold energetically and I guess will run the enterprise successfully," he told his wife Margaret. "I have half a mind to slip out altogether." Second thoughts kept him from taking this step. "I fear," he wrote, "they could not get on without me."[102]

Then, too, he felt a moral obligation to continue the work. In writing to Margaret about Bailey's mismanagement of the Morrison business, he confessed that it seemed impossible to avoid bankruptcy, "but my honor is at stake in many of the debts and I must raise the money and put them right."[103] During August, 1876, when the money subscribed for the new construction was slow in arriving, Evans wrote to Margaret: "I propose to come through now honorably and squarely if I have to sacrifice half [of what] I am worth to do so."[104]

Smith finally started construction in mid-August,[105] but by the next year work had ground to a halt.[106] The company was again reorganized, again placed under the direction of J. W. Smith, and again local funds—$120,000—financed the operation.[107] This time construction was carried through to completion. The silver discoveries in Leadville removed all doubt that the line would pay. Evans' brother Seth, in Cincinnati, helped to obtain rails, as he had done for the line to Morrison.[108]

Once the road entered the South Platte canyon, Jay Gould began to show an interest in the project. Early in 1878, Gould, who had just begun to invest in the Rio Grande,[109] wrote to Evans: "We should arrange our extensions so as not to get in each others way. There is plenty of room for us all and I shall be glad to confer with you with that end in view."[110] Evans preferred, however, to retain local control for the South Park.[111] Sale of the Denver Pacific had resulted in receivership for that road in 1874,[112] and Evans had no wish to see that step duplicated.

According to J. Sidney Brown, Gould actually made an offer for a half interest in the South Park railroad, but the board turned him down flat. Brown quoted Evans' summation of the offer in these words: "If we would give him all of the property, he would give half of it back."[113]

When an offer of money failed to move the South Park board, Gould decided to try other methods. His attorneys opened suit for receivership, charging Evans with mismanagement.[114] No one seems to have taken the suit seriously, and within a few days it was dropped.[115]

Gould maintained his determination to acquire an interest in the South Park, while Evans continued to negotiate to strengthen the road's competitive position. In May, 1879, he corresponded with M. D. Thatcher, the Pueblo banker who

The Denver, South Park and Pacific at Buffalo Park.

represented the Santa Fe's interests. Only a few months before, the Santa Fe had leased the Rio Grande, and during May both Evans and Thatcher tried to arrange a pool for the Leadville traffic. A rate war, as Evans pointed out, would depress rates to the injury of both roads. "It seems too bad," he declared, "that we should build two roads from Trout Creek to Leadville when one track ought to answer."[116]

In the meantime the Santa Fe lost control of the Rio Grande,[117] only to see the latter road come under the control of Jay Gould.[118] Gould seems to have had the idea of building a transcontinental railroad to compete with the Union Pacific.[119] He had acquired control of the Kansas Pacific and Denver Pacific in 1878,[120] and the railroads through South Park were logical extensions of his proposed transcontinental system. William J. Palmer had allowed the Rio Grande to fall under Gould's sway, only because Gould offered financial aid that Palmer had not been able to get elsewhere.[121] With the Rio Grande at least partially under his control, Gould could use Palmer's road as a wedge to gain entry to the South Park line's board of directors. He accordingly visited Evans and made a personal inspection of the line in May, 1879, and by September was said to be negotiating a stock purchase.[122]

What Gould offered to the South Park board was a pooling agreement with the Rio Grande, joint operation of the line from Buena Vista to Leadville, a more cooperative attitude on the part of the Union Pacific and the Kansas Pacific, and financial aid to complete the South Park road to Buena Vista.[123] He also promised aid in building the line on to Gunnison and into Utah.[124] What he sought in return was the right to purchase a quarter interest in the capital stock of the Denver, South Park and Pacific.[125]

Gould made the South Park road a valuable offer, but to accept it would be expensive for the South Park stockholders. He wanted a fourth of the stock held by the Denver men, yet he would pay only "$2.00 for every $1.00 paid in."[126] It is not possible to say how much money was involved here, since the records are not available, but Evans said that the stockholders considered the price very low. Only the other terms, which were attractive, caused them to sell at that price. What apparently led Palmer to accept the pooling agreement and the joint line to Leadville was the distinct possibility that Gould would withhold financial aid from the Rio Grande's planned extensions beyond Buena Vista and Alamosa.[127]

Gould also offered to buy the $300,000 worth of South Park stock held by Arapahoe County. In December, 1879, the voters of Arapahoe County accepted his offer of $150,000 for the stock.[128] It is interesting to note in this regard that W. A. H. Loveland, allied with Gould through the Colorado Central, had purchased the *Rocky Mountain News* in July, 1878.[129] During the latter part of 1878 and the early part of 1879, Loveland's paper continually attacked Evans for alleged mismanagement of the South Park.[130] But when Jay Gould began to show an interest in the railroad, the *News* reversed its stand, declaring:

> The South Park road is an institution which Denver and Colorado, not less then Gove. Evans and his associates in the management, may feel proud of.[131]

Undoubtedly the favorable attitude of the *News* had a good deal to do with approval of the stock sale.[132]

Most Denver newspapers of the latter nineteenth century were openly, and sometimes violently, partisan. Under William N. Byers the *News* had always supported Evans, and even when Byers began to take a less direct interest in the paper, he went to some pains to continue this policy.[133] During the political campaign of 1876 a short-lived paper called the *Mirror* apparently practiced journalistic blackmail, taking on each candidate in succession until he paid for relief. According to a letter from John Evans to his wife, the editor of the *Mirror*, Stanley G. Fowler, would "give them all a dose unless they 'step in to the Captains office' and settle. I know of no remedy for such freedom of the press," Evans wrote, "except to go with a club and break the fellows head." Speaking of Henry C. Brown's *Independent*, Evans said: "It is democratic & dirty."[134]

When the *News* in 1879 renewed its support of Evans, the *Tribune* stepped into the fray, and by early 1881 the latter paper was openly supporting Palmer's Rio Grande in opposition to the Evans road. On one occasion Evans went to see O. H. Rothacker, one of the editors, to ask him to correct one of his statements about the South Park line. According to Evans, Rothacker "seemed to think . . . that *facts* were unimportant if public opinion was against them."[135]

The *Tribune's* assaults on Evans reached a new low in September, 1881. The managing editor, Eugene Field, reported in a tongue-in-cheek article that John Evans was an enthusiastic member of the theater audience when Miss Emma Abbott took part in the bedroom scene from *Fra Diavolo*. It was obviously a piece of satire that Field expected no one to take seriously, but Evans felt that the *Tribune* had gone too far, especially when, as a grand jury noted, Miss Abbott "did indecently disrobe herself" during the performance. He sued the *Tribune* and editors Rothacker and Field for libel.[136] The case was still pending when Rothacker and Field left town, so that it was never settled.[137] Regardless of the outcome, the *Tribune* and other Denver papers continued to play an important role in Colorado railroad affairs.

After Gould's purchase of the South Park stock, he was able to exert considerable influence in the operation of the road. It was apparently understood by everyone that Gould intended to gain complete control of the road, so Evans and the other Denver stockholders placed all their stock in the hands of a trustee, J. S. Brown, and agreed that it must be voted or sold only as a block.[138]

Jay Gould's purchase of the stock held by Arapahoe County was a major step toward obtaining complete control of the

South Park line. The citizens who voted to approve this sale seem to have believed that Gould's purchase of the road would be of great benefit to Denver, perhaps because this arrangement would make the South Park an integral part of his system. Indeed, Jay Gould seems to have felt that by purchasing the stock he was conferring a valuable benefaction on the city, for he told Evans: "My object in paying Denver $100,000 was two fold—1st to help carry through the Denver and So Park purchase & 2nd to keep the friendship of the good people of Denver."[139] In Gould's opinion this was "a big price,"[140] and the voters seem to have shared that opinion.

Gould's money and influence provided just the stimulus the South Park line needed.[141] By February 6, 1880, Evans reported that the tracks had reached across South Park to the Arkansas River.[142] The agreement with the Rio Grande would assure the South Park access to Leadville, and a similar arrangement was to give the Rio Grande entree into Gunnison over the South Park tracks.[143]

Work on the Gunnison extension had hardly started before the agreement was cast aside by the Rio Grande. Palmer started to build his own line to Gunnison.[144] Gould and Evans looked at the agreement and found to their surprise that, while the Rio Grande could demand equal rights on any line that the South Park might build to Gunnison, there was nothing to keep the Rio Grande from building an independent line— exactly what the agreement was intended to avoid.[145]

Gould wrote furiously to Evans: "As I understood the contract the D&RG were not to build an *independent* line into the Gunnison Co." The only possible way to avoid renewing the old rivalry was to consolidate both roads, and he urged Evans to do what he could to achieve this end.[146]

Evans, for his part, was quite willing to comply—if he could sell the South Park, and if the price were right. The Gunnison Town Company, which he had helped to organize, had split into rival factions, and it seemed as though nothing but trouble

The Denver, South Park and Pacific's
Engine No. 15, the Breckenridge, is shown
at the Massachusetts plant where it was built in 1879.
The photograph below, also taken in 1879,
shows Engine No. 2 hard at work on the road.

could be expected from this direction.[147] Since General Palmer seemed determined to complete his road to Gunnison,[148] Gould's suggestion offered really the wisest solution. Evans immediately began active negotiations with Palmer.[149]

Palmer seems to have been taking a calculated risk by building an independent line to Gunnison. If he really feared that Gould and the Union Pacific would discriminate against his road, as Robert Athearn has suggested,[150] building an independent line to Gunnison could hardly make them less inclined to fight. As a matter of fact, only a ruinous rate war could result, as Gould himself observed.[151] Palmer's real intention seems to have been to force Evans to sell him the South Park, thus preventing Gould from acquiring control of the Gunnison route to Utah and forcing him to deal with the Rio Grande on Palmer's own terms.

The pooling agreement had been made with the objective of eventually consolidating the Rio Grande and the South Park.[152] Gould, however, had apparently wanted both of these roads for himself, and he had previously obtained the right to buy the pooled South Park stock at the price offered to any other prospective purchaser. In the face of Palmer's new threat, Gould relinquished this right and told Evans and Palmer to continue negotiations for a sale to the Rio Grande.[153]

Palmer offered to trade Rio Grande stock share for share. The stock was selling then at about $60 or $70 per share.[154] While there was no market price for South Park stock, since none was for sale on the open market, the road was proving enormously profitable,[155] and the Denver stockholders considered it to be worth at least its par value, that is, $100 per share. Palmer, aware of this difference in stock value, offered to make an additional payment of $700,000.[156]

This latter payment proved to be a real stumbling block. It was to be given in the form of a note payable in nine months. Palmer at first offered no security for the note, although he seems ultimately to have agreed to pledge enough Rio Grande bonds to cover the amount. Evans wanted the $700,000 to be paid in cash or in negotiable paper. Since Gould was a large shareholder and also represented the Kansas Pacific, Evans decided to accept the offer only if Gould approved.[157]

Gould, when he learned of the terms, shared Evans' reaction; the Palmer proposal seemed a little "too complicated." He offered to purchase the South Park himself at $90 per share, and, as an added inducement, offered to let Evans remain as president.[158]

Evans countered suspiciously: "Why should I be president afterwards?"[159] Somewhat taken aback, Gould replied: "I thought you might like to remain as president and be identified with the Union Pacific."[160] Not to be led astray with a promise of this sort, Evans told Gould that the stockholders had refused to accept an offer of less than par from Palmer, and he supposed they would react the same way to Gould's offer. He could, however, "get a cash par offer accepted at once."[161]

To this Gould replied: "Make me a cash offer. Answer quick as Mr. Ames [president of the Union Pacific] and other directors are in this city now."[162] Evans immediately wired: "We will take cash par for our railroad stock."[163] Gould answered as quickly: "Your offer is accepted."[164]

With these brief messages, Evans concluded the biggest financial transaction of his career, and the most profitable. Evans at one time estimated that the Denver stockholders had made about 2,500 per cent profit on their original investment.[165]

Of the 22,992 shares held by J. S. Brown in 1880 under the trust agreement, Evans owned 5,600.25 shares, and his wife Margaret owned 375 shares.[166] In addition to this, Evans seems to have owned some stock that was not included in the trust. He had sold Gould one-fourth of his stock in October, 1879, and Gould had later offered to resell the stock to him at the same price—$14,000—plus interest.[167] There seems to be no reason to doubt that Evans accepted the offer, which would mean that he probably owned nearly 2,000 additional shares not included in the original trust.[168]

It is possible to estimate Evans' dollar investment in the stock he owned. In 1879 Gould purchased one-fourth of the stock held by each stockholder, paying twice as much as this quarter-interest had cost the original owner.[169] This seems to indicate that Evans had invested only about $28,000 in the road before October, 1879.[170]

Evans is probably not the only Denver stockholder to have stock outside the original trust. Of the 35,000 shares, 22,992 were held in trust by J. S. Brown, the Kansas Pacific owned 3,000 shares, and Jay Gould owned 5,716 shares, a sum which apparently included the 3,000 shares purchased from Arapahoe County.[171] Since Gould paid the Denver stockholders $2,590,800, several thousand shares are still not accounted for, but Gould's method of payment—four checks—indicates the existence of three other trust agreements. One check was for $2,299,200 (the amount of the original trust), and the three others were for $249,800, $22,500, and $19,300.[172]

Evans received $560,025 from J. S. Brown for his trust stock, and his wife received $37,500 for hers. In addition, the 2,000 shares which he seems to have held outside the original trust would have brought him another $200,000. Thus he apparently realized nearly $800,000, a sum which tallies closely with his own estimate of a 2,500 per cent profit on his original investment.

Palmer, however, seems to have had the last laugh, for the Rio Grande stock soon rose to $100 per share, thus making his offer, in retrospect, more profitable than Gould's.[173]

Evans and six other Denver men retained ownership of one share of stock apiece, and Evans was retained as president of the road.[174] But the heavy hand of Union Pacific general manager S. H. H. Clark soon made itself felt in the operation of the South Park, and what was once a profitable road was headed toward bankruptcy.

By early January, 1881, Evans complained to Gould of the arbitrarily high freight rates which were driving South Park customers to the Rio Grande.[175] Clark also suspended work on the branch to the Gunnison coal fields, even though most of the construction expense had already been incurred. His worst blunder, however, was the surrender of the joint trackage agreement to Leadville, and the subsequent construction of the grossly inefficient "high line" in an attempt to compensate for this loss.[176]

Because of his many heated complaints about Clark, Evans was not re-elected to the presidency of the South Park.[177] Gould had sold his interest in the road to the Union Pacific almost as soon as he received Evans' first letter about Clark's disastrous policies in January, 1881.[178] Within a few years the South Park was sold at foreclosure.[179]

Supporting Evans' contention that Clark was responsible for the ruin of the Denver, South Park and Pacific, is an estimate of Clark's abilities by Charles Francis Adams, who became president of the Union Pacific in 1884. In a letter to G. M. Dodge, Adams called Clark "utterly incompetent." "He turned over the road . . . in a wholly demoralized condition," Adams said, "and materially in condition which could not stand six months hard work. Why the thing did not tumble to pieces of itself is now incredible to me."[180]

The sale of the South Park to Gould had hardly been consummated before Evans was embarked on a third major railroad project. This was the plan to build a direct rail line between Denver and the Gulf of Mexico, probably Evans' most visionary railroad venture and one on which he had been working for some time.

As early as 1870 Evans had discussed the plan in public. By 1873 the Denver Board of Trade voted to support his scheme for making Denver a customs port of entry. Government approval of the proposal would mean that merchandise from abroad shipped to Denver would not be appraised or

194

examined in the actual seaport where it was unloaded. Instead, it would be brought to Denver in bonded railroad cars with duties payable there as though Denver were a seaport.[181]

The advantages of such an arrangement were obvious. European goods could be landed at New Orleans or Galveston at nearly the same rates as in New York. The subsequent rail haul to Denver was a thousand miles shorter than the Denver-New York route. For that matter, the rail haul on a direct line from Galveston to Portland, Oregon, would be seven hundred miles shorter than from New York to Portland. Even the domestic trade between Denver and the Atlantic ports would benefit by taking advantage of the lower water rates available at Galveston.[182]

Evans' arguments must have been convincing Early in January, 1881, he and a group of Denver investors, including many of those who had been prominent in South Park affairs, organized the Denver and New Orleans Railroad Company.[183] Evans originally seems to have intended to have his line connect with the Texas and Pacific at Fort Worth, with the idea of using that line's tracks to continue to New Orleans. A similar meeting with the Texas Central would give the Denver and New Orleans a through route to Galveston.[184] No sooner were his construction plans announced than an official of the Fort Worth and Denver City Railway Company wrote to tell Evans that his line, building from Fort Worth, had had similar plans since 1872. Perhaps there could be a joint operation between the two cities.[185]

In April the new plans were formalized in a contract between the new Evans line and the Fort Worth and Denver. Both roads would build to a junction at the Canadian River. Furthermore, there were plans that the Texas and Pacific, the Missouri Pacific, and the Missouri, Kansas and Texas, would operate their roads as through lines in conjunction with the new system.[186]

Opposition, however, soon appeared at a familiar stand. The Rio Grande had acquired control of two Denver papers

—or so Evans charged—and these journals delivered almost daily tirades against the Denver and New Orleans railroad. In a public speech delivered in the fall of 1881, Evans said: "They [the Rio Grande] own fifty-five per cent of the capital stock of the Denver *Tribune* and one hundred per cent of the *Republican* and can direct the course of these papers." Evans also said that the Colorado Springs *Gazette* was an "echo . . . which chimes in on proper occasions."[187]

In support of Evans' charges, Champion Vaughan, former editor of the *Tribune*, wrote to him on July 24, 1881, saying:

> When I first became connected with Colorado Journalism I was surrounded by persons & influences particularly hostile to yourself. . . . For many years past I have been conscious of the mistake & have sincerely regretted it.

Vaughan went on to say that the various accusations against Evans made by the *Tribune* were completely without foundation.[188] A few weeks later Evans wrote to a friend regarding the *Tribune's* present editor: "Of course except as a party willing to hire himself out, as a blackguard, to the services of the Corporation that owns the paper, the D. & R. G., the Editor is not responsible."[189] Perhaps the best evidence indicating the partisanship of editors Rothacker and Field of the *Tribune* is that they left town rather than face the libel suit that Evans brought against them in the fall of 1881.[190]

The newspaper war against the Denver and New Orleans started in July, 1881. The *Tribune* charged that it was financed by Jay Gould and would be a virtual tool of the Union Pacific.[191] Within a few days the paper added an accusation that Evans had victimized Arapahoe County when the county purchased stock in the South Park and the Denver Pacific.[192]

The *Tribune* did not stop there. Other charges appeared in succeeding issues. One asserted that Evans "bribed or offered to bribe the County Commissioners, and paid or promised to pay their Chairman, Frank Cran[e], twenty per cent of the proceeds of a certain subscription by the county for South Park bonds." Another charge claimed that he manipulated the price of the Denver Pacific bonds in order to buy them at an extremely low rate and use them to purchase land from the railroad. Finally, the *Tribune* alleged that Gould had paid Evans to change the original plans of the Denver and New Orleans, to the detriment of the stockholders.[193]

The *Republican* soon joined the fray with a statement that Evans used the Arapahoe County bonds to build the South Park to Morrison solely in order to exploit the stone quarries there. According to that paper, the quarries were "commonly assumed to be owned in large part by Governor Evans." The *Republican* also had discovered that Jay Gould was the "worst enemy of Denver,"[194] apparently in reference to the Union Pacific's mismanagement of the South Park.

Both Evans and the Denver and New Orleans countered with libel suits against the *Tribune*.[195] Evans observed, in an obvious jibe at the *Republican*, that he found it "extraordinary" that the recent purchase of "nearly all the stock of the *Tribune* by the attorney of the Denver & Rio Grande railway company for his client should call forth no comment on the dangers of railroad influence on the press."[196] Although the law suits had no immediate effect on the *Tribune*, Evans explained to a friend that he thought it essential that "the real authors of the foul means used against the D. & N. O." be exposed.[197] In any case, the *Tribune's* charges seem to be without any factual basis.[198]

The railroad issue had also become a factor in the political arena. The Rio Grande had used its influence with the county commissioners to embarrass Evans and his new railroad. The railroad secured the aid of sheriff's officers and a court injunction in an attempt to prevent the Denver and New Orleans construction crews from laying track across the Rio Grande right of way in Denver. [199] In addition, the Rio Grande had managed to capture the Republican Party in the state, and both the *Tribune* and the *Republican* were supporting the move—

at least it seemed that way to Evans and his supporters.[200]

The *Rocky Mountain News* rallied to the support of Evans. In early October it quoted a Republican politician as declaring:

> We must show the *Tribune-Republican* gang that the Republican Party of Colorado cannot be delivered over to a few bad . . . men whose purpose is to defeat [Senator] Teller and place Ed. Wolcott in [Representative] Belford's place.

This same politician was quoted as asserting that Evans was "too good a Republican" to support such a ticket.[201]

As though worried about losing Evans' support for the Republican ticket, the *Tribune* temporarily dropped its hostile attitude.[202] But if this was a conciliatory move, it came too late. On October 21, Evans and a number of other Republicans—J. S. Brown, Theodore F. Brown, D. J. Cook, W. A. Smith, and others—joined with a number of prominent Democrats—Thomas M. Patterson, W. A. H. Loveland, J. M. Strickler, and others—to name a coalition ticket for the coming city and county elections.[203] Although the organizers liked to think of themselves as the "Citizens' Party"[204] or the "People's Party,"[205] the opposition referred to them as "The Mongrels."[206] Evans, in turn, called the *Tribune*, the *Republican*, and the Colorado Springs *Gazette* "the newspaper department of the Denver and Rio Grande Railway company." He based his opposition to the Republican ticket on the Rio Grande's threat of discrimination against Denver[207] and the possibility of "ring rule" in the city.[208]

The *News*, to no one's surprise, came out in favor of "John Evans and fair play for the Denver & New Orleans."[209] The *Times* said that regular Republicans could hardly blame Evans and his friends for deserting the party. "Their business, characters and enterprises have been assailed in so bitter and vindictive a manner by a portion of the press of their own party," said the *Times*, "that they think self-respect will not permit them to support nominations . . . by this element."[210]

Evans felt that his support of the People's Party was a service to the Republican Party in Colorado. As he saw it, the entire Republican slate was in the pay of the Rio Grande.[211] If this were allowed to continue, that is, if the "People's ticket" failed to carry, it would mean certain defeat for the Republicans in the 1882 senatorial contest.[212]

The voters, however, and not the newspapers, had the last word at the polls, and the Republican instincts of the electorate were too strong for Evans to overcome. Republican nominees won every post except coroner and justice of the peace.[213] Still, Evans seems to have gained a partial victory. According to the *News*, both the *Tribune* and the *Republican* were anxious to find some safe way to "let go" of Evans. "If somebody will hold Governor Evans while we retreat," the *News* quoted them as saying, "we will never be caught in such a fight again."[214]

In the meantime, a few of the Denver and New Orleans construction problems had been solved. A favorable court decision in late October allowed the Denver and New Orleans to cross the Rio Grande tracks near Denver, and track was being laid at the rate of a mile and a half per day.[215] The Pueblo merchants were said to have been quite anxious to welcome the Denver and New Orleans to their city, in the hope of breaking the monopoly of the Tripartite Agreement.[216] The truth of this rumor was graphically proven on May 3, 1882, when a rejoicing Pueblo delegation met the first train from Denver and treated Evans and the other passengers to a sumptuous banquet.[217]

The Tripartite group—the Rio Grande, the Santa Fe, and the Union Pacific—had signed a "peace treaty" on March 27, 1880, whereby they agreed to pool all Colorado traffic among themselves.[218] When the rails of the Burlington reached Denver in May, 1882, that road, for various reasons, was also admitted to the alliance.[219] The Denver and New Orleans, however, was pretty effectively excluded. The Tripartite group refused to exchange freight, even when the goods had been specifically consigned to the Denver road by the shippers.

Denver and New Orleans finances had always been precarious, and without the cooperation of the Santa Fe and the Rio Grande at Pueblo, disaster seemed imminent. Evans had the attorneys for his line bring suit against the Santa Fe to compel them to do business with his railroad. The Evans road lost the suit on appeal, and the members of the Tripartite alliance continued to discriminate against their new rival.[220]

It was then that two real estate purchases, which Evans had made earlier for the Denver and New Orleans, proved their worth. He had very quietly retained a young lawyer to buy up land in downtown Denver. Before the other roads realized what was happening, the attorney had assembled a parcel of about a hundred acres in the heart of town to be used as a railroad yard. The ground lay between Fifteenth Street and the Platte River, and, as Evans boasted to an interviewer, there was "no street crossing it for nearly half a mile, making it the best yard that any company has."[221]

Evans had also purchased for the Denver and New Orleans 1,140 acres in a valuable coal deposit at Franceville, east of Colorado Springs. All that remained was to build a spur from the main line to Franceville, and the railroad would not only have a cheap source of fuel but a readily saleable commodity.[222]

Although the road had been completed to Pueblo, the work was not paid for, and there was no money available for the vital four-mile spur to Franceville or the nine-mile line to Colorado Springs. Consequently, all of the assets, including the valuable Franceville coal land and the downtown Denver yards, both of which were owned by the construction company, were placed in trust by the construction company as security for a mortgage of $1,400,000. The loan was to be prorated among the stockholders, but a few refused to pay their assessments. Because of this refusal, the company defaulted on the loan, and in September, 1883, the assets of the construction company were transferred by the trustee, the Mercantile Trust Company of New York, to the Denver and New Orleans Railroad.[223]

It is not clear what motives lay behind these arrangements, but the result was the transfer of control of the line from the stockholders of the construction company to the stockholders of the railroad company. Evans himself made little distinction between the two firms, and Poor's *Manuals* treat them as almost the same entities.[224] These rather complicated arrangements were probably nothing more than a convenient way to transfer the Denver real estate and the Franceville coal lands to the railroad company, thus improving the financial position of that firm. Both pieces of land had been purchased by Evans with construction company funds; in all probability the purchases had to be made in this way because the assets of the railroad were pledged in payment of construction. Now, when consolidation was in the offing, it was essential to restore the assets to the railroad.[225]

Evans himself must have been one of the largest stockholders of the Denver and New Orleans Railway Construction Company, for he held about a quarter of a million dollars of trust notes at the time of the sale in September, 1883. Russell Sage, Jay Gould's associate, held a similar amount.[226]

That this foreclosure sale was little more than a paper transfer of assets seems clear from Evans' statement that "when the construction company could not pay, we sold the property all out, or had the Mercantile Trust Company do it." There was no cash involved. Evans and his associates simply "gathered all the trust notes in" and "bought it in with these notes."[227]

All of these actions were a prelude to the consolidation of the Denver and New Orleans with the Fort Worth and Denver. At the board meeting in March, 1884, Evans "declined re-election," and his place was taken by G. M. Dodge, who then controlled the Fort Worth line[228] and was "practically the head of the Gould system of railroads in Texas."[229] On March 21, the new president of the Denver and New Orleans, Cyrus W. Fisher, announced that Gould had, "with the consent of the company, acquired a large interest in the trust bonds."[230]

On March 15, 1884, the New York firm of Winslow, Lanier and Company, then acting as "transfer office" for the Denver and New Orleans[231] had wired Evans an offer for purchase of the road.[232] Evans replied: "Negotiations for completing through line pending."[233] Evans had apparently concluded an agreement with Dodge, based on Dodge's assurance that his stockholders would approve. Under the terms of this agreement, Evans was to complete the line from Denver to Wichita Falls, the terminus of the Fort Worth road, and Dodge would pay Evans the stock and bonds still in the Fort Worth and Denver treasury.[234] Dodge's directors proved to be less tractable than he had supposed, and they would agree only to a renewal of the old contract to meet at the Canadian River.[235]

Evans' role in these negotiations was an attempt to repeat a previously successful venture. He had resigned from the presidency of the Denver Pacific in order to head the construction company which successfully completed the road. Perhaps he could do the same with the Denver and New Orleans.

Finding the Fort Worth and Denver terms unsatisfactory,[236] Evans approached Collis P. Huntington of the Southern Pacific and signed a traffic contract with the Houston and Texas Central, a Southern Pacific subsidiary.[237] He also negotiated with William B. Strong for a sale to the Santa Fe,[238] and, in the most imaginative deal of all, he incorporated with Jay Gould the Denver, New Orleans, and Missouri Pacific Railroad Company to build from Pueblo to the Missouri Pacific tracks in Kansas.[239] None of these plans came to fruition, although a sale to the Missouri Pacific looked quite promising for a time.[240]

With Evans off the board, the Denver and New Orleans made no progress, and Evans' own plans to finish the line came to nought. Jay Gould suggested reorganizing the road, because its financial affairs had become "too complicated."[241] Consequently, on May 29, 1885, John Evans was re-elected to the presidency of the Denver and New Orleans Railroad, and a successor line, the Denver, Texas and Gulf Railroad Company was immediately incorporated.[242]

Transfer of the assets was held up by the refusal of Winslow, Lanier and Company to acquiesce in the arrangement. The banking firm claimed $80,000 due from the Denver and New Orleans as commission on bond sales, and filed suit to prevent the transfer. Evans and the other directors charged that the Winslow, Lanier claim was fraudulent, since they had not actually sold the bonds in question. Moreover, the firm had prevented a potential sale by referring to the Denver and New Orleans as a "wreck."[243]

The court refused to issue an injunction to prevent the transfer,[244] but Russell Sage now feared that other suits might be brought if the transfer were made simply through an "exchange of bonds."[245] Sage recommended "a regular foreclosure by law."[246] Accordingly, a court order for the sale was obtained, and the transfer was made in March, 1886. The Mercantile Trust Company again acted as trustee, and J. S. Brown, acting for the holders of the trust notes, made the purchase for the Denver, Texas and Gulf.[247]

As with the previous foreclosure of the construction company, no cash was involved in the sale. The holders of the Denver and New Orleans trust notes received an average of $1,610.36 in stock and $1,206.30 in bonds of the new line for each $1,000 worth of trust notes. This meant that Evans, for example, received $422,032.27 in Denver, Texas and Gulf stock and $316,139.17 in bonds for his $262,027.97 in Denver and New Orleans notes. Russell Sage received $419,009.66 in stock and $313,874.96 in bonds for his trust notes.[248] Clearly, this was a grand bargain, if the new securities ever reached a value near par. The stockholders seemed determined to see that the securities reached par, for they appointed J. S. Brown as trustee and agreed to leave the stock and bonds in his hands until a junction was made with the Fort Worth and Denver, when both lines would be consolidated.[249]

The opposition of the Tripartite Agreement still had to be overcome. Evans had tried court action and legislative action, but to no avail.[250] The only course left was to join forces with the other railroads, and that is what he proceeded to do.

The Santa Fe, he learned, was now interested in purchasing the Denver, Texas and Gulf, in order to end its dependence on the Rio Grande's line from Pueblo to Denver. Gould and Sage, as well as David Moffat and some of the Denver stockholders, were anxious to accept the Santa Fe offer. Evans held them off, and with the help of Augustus Kountze, he convinced Strong that the Santa Fe should raise its offer to $2,000,000. When the other investors saw that Strong valued the Denver, Texas and Gulf so highly, they apparently changed their own opinions of the road, and the Santa Fe offer was refused.[251]

Events then proceeded swiftly to a conclusion. A new road, called the Denver, Texas and Fort Worth, was to be incorporated, with Sidney Dillon of the Union Pacific as president, John Evans as first vice president, and Morgan Jones of the Fort Worth and Denver as second vice president.[252] The Denver, Texas and Fort Worth was to complete the line from the end of the Fort Worth and Denver tracks to Trinidad; construction was to be under the direction of G. M. Dodge. From Pueblo to Trinidad the line was to operate on the tracks of the Rio Grande, to which a third rail would be added.[253] Construction was finished on March 14, 1888.[254]

Following the completion, the officers set about integrating the management of the roads. As Overton observed, "by 1889 virtually every traffic and operating officer of each company held a similar position with one or both of the others."[255] In the summer of 1888, the Denver, Texas and Fort Worth began to exchange its stock for that of the other companies.[256]

204

The road had hardly been completed before it began to experience serious financial trouble. In February, 1889, Evans wrote gloomily to Morgan Jones that he feared Dodge was try-ing to sell the property. Evans was unalterably opposed to such a move. "If we sell out we are gone so far as making our stock valuable," he told Jones. "If we go into the hands of a receiver we may recover the property again."[257]

Nonetheless, Dodge proceeded to do just what Evans had feared. Under heavy pressure from Dodge and others, Evans consented to allow the Denver, Texas and Gulf to be consoli-dated with a new Union Pacific subsidiary, called the Union Pacific, Denver and Gulf Railway Company.[258] The companies were to exchange securities on a "share-for-share and bond-for-bond basis."[259] This consolidation went into effect on April 1, 1890, so that "the Gulf-to-Rockies line was a part of the Union Pacific system."[260]

In November, 1890, when Sidney Dillon became president of the Union Pacific, Evans was finally convinced that consoli-dation had been the correct move. He wrote to Dillon that he had "never sold a share" of his Union Pacific, Denver and Gulf stock and did not intend to "until it gets up to par or near that point." He also told Dillon that he was confident now that the stock would soon reach par, particularly since his "old time friends" Gould and Sage were now on the board.[261]

Evans had good reason for his optimism. It was to Gould and Sage that he had made the profitable sale of the South Park. These two had also been early investors in the Denver and New Orleans.[262] Moreover he had bought a block of Union Pacific stock at or below par and sold it at 116 shortly after selling the South Park.[263] Perhaps the same thing would hap-pen under the Dillon regime.

Realizing that the future of the road depended to a great extent on good connections with ocean traffic, Evans began to use his influence to back the proposal for a federal appropria-tion to deepen the harbor at Galveston. With improved facilities at that port, the Gulf Road would be in an excellent competitive position. In August of 1888 Evans became a member of the Deep Harbor Committee of the Denver Chamber of Commerce.[264] He was very active in promoting this venture,[265] and, although Evans was out of the picture by 1897, the deep harbor at Galveston was a major factor in the financial recovery of the road by that time.[266]

In spite of his early optimism, the new management proved to be quite as disappointing to Evans as the old one. Before many months had passed, Evans was conferring with his attorney, E. T. Wells, regarding possible legal moves against the Union Pacific. The parent company, it seems, was forcing the Gulf Road to carry coal "in great amounts and at less than a fair price." Moreover, the Union Pacific was discriminating against the Gulf Road on the interchange of freight.[267]

By January, 1892, Evans had begun serious discussions aimed at the creation of an independent line between Denver and Galveston.[268] Within two months he also had a far-reaching plan to build new lines from Denver to El Paso, Duluth, and the Black Hills, as well as to Galveston.[269] Evans does not appear to have been completely serious about these roads, a fact which seems to have been apparent to everyone. He was nearly eighty years old and his health was failing rapidly.[270] Although three of the roads eventually were organized and Evans was made president of all three, his election was little more than a gesture on the part of the directors, and his efforts in behalf of the new roads were quite limited.[271]

His main interest was still the Gulf Road. At a stockholders' meeting on April 12, 1892, he introduced resolutions calling for a reorganization of the road, but his proposals were voted down. Similar efforts in 1893 met the same fate.[272] Finally, in August of 1893, after a dozen Denver banks had closed their doors, Evans took legal action. He asked the U.S. Circuit Court in Denver to appoint a receiver for the Union Pacific, Denver and Gulf Railway Company. His proposal meant, in effect, the re-establishment of the independence of the Gulf Road.[273] On December 12, 1893, after much maneuvering on both sides, Judge Moses Hallett named Frank Trumbull as receiver, with the full approval of John Evans.[274] The thirty-five-year-old Trumbull moved the main office of the Union Pacific, Denver and Gulf back to Denver,[275] and by the end of 1898, when the company was about to be reorganized as the Colorado and Southern, the road's future seemed assured.

Evans now began to retire from railroad matters. In April, 1894, he was dropped from the board of directors of the Union Pacific, Denver and Gulf.[276] There had been some question in 1892 as to whether Evans actually owned any stock in the firm in his own name.[277] Perhaps after Trumbull's appointment Evans disposed of his remaining stock; by January 1, 1895, he apparently held considerable amounts of Union Pacific, Denver and Gulf bonds, but there is no evidence to show that he held any stock in the road.[278]

In reviewing his years of promoting railroad construction, it is clear that Evans contributed greatly to the development of western transportation. While still living in Chicago, he realized that civic development was closely tied to railroad building. In the sixties he tried to bring the Union Pacific through Denver, and when that effort failed, he built a line from Denver to join the Union Pacific at Cheyenne. In order to bolster Denver's position as a western rail center, he built the South Park line to bring the Leadville trade through the capital city. He later sold the road to Jay Gould, partly because Gould seemed determined to make it a part of a transcontinental system. When this plan seemed to falter, he joined enthusiastically in the move to build a direct line to the Gulf of Mexico and give Denver the advantage of lower freight rates on imports. All of his railroad enterprises were intended to help himself, Denver, and Colorado, in about that order. He was a hardheaded businessman, but also civic-minded. He built, he once wrote his wife, "for Denver and my railroad."[279]

13

"The Personal Interests of John Evans"

The Denver home built by John and Margaret Evans in 1863 was simply styled but ornately furnished. Here their second son Evan Elbert Evans was born, just after the family moved in. A few months later, in January, 1864, when Josephine Evans graduated from Wesleyan Academy in Wilbraham, Massachusetts, she also joined the family in the new home.[1]

In the previous year Josephine had met Territorial Secretary Samuel H. Elbert, who visited her at Wilbraham at her parents' request. The plump and solemn little child had become a pretty, slender, dark-eyed girl of eighteen. The territorial secretary, who was then a bachelor of thirty, asked whether he might write to her, and a romance was soon in full bloom.[2] After a two-year courtship, Josephine and Samuel were married in June, 1865.

The wedding took place at the Evans home in Evanston, on the shores of Lake Michigan. The marriage was solemnized by Evans' old friend Bishop Matthew Simpson. Josephine's wedding took place "upon a little mound in her father's yard adjoining the lake, and surrounded by a large company of her friends." The garden, said Bishop Simpson, "had been handsomely arranged, the mound and walks carpeted, the branches of the trees were hung with lamps."[3] It was, in the Bishop's words, "a remarkably pleasant occasion."[4]

The newlyweds made their home in a small cottage near the Evans house in Denver. Their son, John Evans Elbert, was born there in March, 1868, but he was a sickly baby and died before the summer was over.[5] Josephine's own recurrent illness became worse that summer, and her father recommended "the traveling treatment."[6] But nothing seemed to help, and on October 22, 1868, Josephine died of consumption in the little wedding cottage, surrounded by the members of her family.[7]

John and Margaret were affectionate and understanding parents to their two little boys, William and Evan. John begrudged every day that his business and political affairs forced him to spend away from his wife and children. His letters to Margaret are filled with references to the boys and with advice on how they should be trained. In July, 1868, when he was in Washington making a last attempt to secure a favorable vote on the statehood bill, he told Margaret: "I wish I could have been home on Evans birthday to see our 5 year old. I keep his photograph on my table all the time and look long & earnestly in its face."[8] Regarding Willie, who was having trouble with his studies, Evans wrote:

> The main point for him is to get accurate knowledge of everything rather than to hurry on. Honesty (& thorough acuracy is the sole of truth) is the best foundation for a good character. Teach him this and his ability and fondness for learning will make him a great & good man. He will command the love of his parents & friends in a ten fold greater measure.[9]

Although business took him often to the mountains of Colorado, John Evans did not like outdoor life. He tried trout fishing once, didn't like it, and never tried again. The rest of the family, however, enjoyed excursions in the mountains.[10] On one family outing in the summer of 1868, Evans and Elbert discovered a bit of land on Bear Creek, which they liked. Together they purchased 320 acres and built a summer home.

"Kuhlborne," as the place was called, was in a valley lush with grass, and surrounded by tree-covered slopes. The delightful summer breezes, however, were the chief attraction.[11] As Evans later punned: "Up in the mountains . . . it is always *Kuhl*."[12]

Several years later, when twenty-year-old Will had determined to try his hand at ranching, part of the Kuhlborne ranch was almost sold. Will had agreed to sell the land to a local rancher, and although John Evans did not approve, he would not back out of the deal that Will had made. The buyer eventually decided not to take up his option, so the family was able to "keep the land and Willie's promises too."[13]

Early in May, 1870, when the Denver Pacific Railroad was nearing completion and John Evans' financial affairs were in good order, he took his family to New York so that he could put Margaret and the children aboard ship for a few months of travel abroad.[14] Evans himself returned to Denver to preside at the completion of the Denver Pacific Railroad.[15] He later joined his family in England in late November, 1870.[16]

Margaret Evans and Mary Lincoln, the widow of the President, apparently met in London that fall. When John arrived in London, Mrs. Lincoln decided to ask his "candid advice" about sending her son Tad back to the United States to attend school.[17] Evans must have advised her to keep the boy in England, for in February, 1871, Tad and Will Evans were attending school together there.[18]

On January 23, 1871, while they were in London, a daughter Anne was born to John and Margaret.[19] Possibly because the baby was too young for an ocean voyage and because Margaret herself became violently ill at sea, she decided to remain in Europe through the rest of 1871. With his investments at home demanding attention, Evans decided to return to the United States and come back to get Margaret and the children at the end of the summer. He left England in March and was back in Denver before the month was out.[20]

Margaret's health caused Evans a great deal of concern. In order to make her return trip more comfortable, he devised for her use a bed that would remain level in spite of the motion of the ship. The bed was pivoted at the sides and at the ends and counterbalanced in such a way that the force of gravity caused it to remain level.[21] The fact that this was not Margaret's last trip abroad indicates that the device was successful.[22] In any case, John Evans thought enough of the invention to take out patents on it in several foreign countries.[23]

He returned to England in August, 1871, to tour Europe with his wife and children and accompany them on the ocean voyage back.[24] Margaret and the younger children seem not to have joined in the tour of the Continent, where a blood bath had recently ended the Commune's control of the French capital. But young Will and his father were not so easily discouraged. Taking a hurried trip across Europe, they were in Switzerland when news arrived about the disastrous Chicago fire of October 8 and 9, 1871. Even this news did not dampen their enthusiasm for the strange sights of the Old World. The sale of the Evans Block in Chicago had been negotiated before Evans' departure in August, and the vacationer's main concern was for the safety of his relatives and friends in the stricken city. Father and son went on to Genoa, Rome, and Naples,[25] and rode donkeys up Mount Vesuvius.[26] Then, with the special berth for Margaret installed in the parents' stateroom,[27] the Evans family made the return trip to the United States, leaving England in November,[28] and arriving in New York on December 7.[29]

Some time after the return from Europe—one source says 1873—the Evans home in Denver was remodeled into a three-story dwelling with a mansard roof. A four-story addition was also added at the rear of the house; a formal staircase was placed in the entry hall; and a conservatory was built off one side. Within a few years the gardens became the envy of Denver.[30] Son-in-law Samuel Elbert, who lived with the Evans

In this drawing the remodeled Evans house is shown as it looked about 1880.

family, became territorial governor in April, 1873, and the Evans home was again the executive mansion.[31]

Shortly after Elbert's appointment, President Grant and his family arrived for a visit. The Grants were entertained at the Evans home, and the two families became close friends. Less than a year later, after a political dispute, the friendship was put to a severe test. The President removed Elbert from office and re-appointed Edward McCook as territorial governor.[32] Evans tried in vain to secure some other federal appointment for Elbert. In June, 1876, while in the East on business, Evans called on the Grants at the White House to ask that Elbert be named as federal judge after the admission of Colorado as a state. Grant still harbored suspicions about Elbert and would not agree to the appointment, but Mrs. Grant asked Evans to stay for lunch with the family.[33] Mrs. Grant had disagreed sharply with her husband on the question of Elbert's removal, but she apparently could not influence him in the matter.[34] She had told the President: "Ulys I do hope you will appoint Governor Elbert." And he replied: "Well suppose I vacate and let you run the office."[35]

In the spring of 1875, Margaret decided to take her children again to Europe for an extended visit. Even her newly remodeled home did not make life in Denver pleasant for her, and she particularly missed the congenial people she had known in Chicago and Evanston.[36] She was also troubled by violent headaches, which might well be alleviated by a change of climate, although a New York physician diagnosed the trouble as "a tumor or abscess in or under the dura mater."[37] A lesser annoyance was her son-in-law, who was at loose ends since his loss of the governorship and spent most of his time at the Evans home, reading and brooding.[38]

On May 22, 1875, the family sailed on a Cunard liner for Europe.[39] Little Evan had gone the previous October with Governor Elbert,[40] with the rest of the Evans family planning to meet them in the spring. After spending the summer with his family in England and on the Continent, Evans rented a house at 39 Arundel Gardens, Notting Hill, London, for Margaret, Evan, and Anne. He and Elbert then returned home to look after their investments.[41] Evan was enrolled in a boarding school in London,[42] perhaps the same one that Will Evans and Tad Lincoln had attended. For a Christmas holiday, mother and son went to Belgium and had their Christmas dinner in Antwerp.[43] Evan sent regular expense reports home to his father, who felt that this practice would help his son "to acquire habits of accuracy and candor . . . that will last him all of his life."[44] Apparently impressed with his own bookkeeping, the twelve-year-old boy announced that he intended to become a banker. Margaret later wrote to John: "I told him if that were the case he should be very careful and exact about his accounts, or we would never consent to it."[45]

Throughout the winter, John's letters to Margaret stressed the critical state of his investments and the lack of ready cash. After several months of gloomy reports from her husband, Margaret began to think she should come home. "Maybe you will find difficulty to make the ends meet," she wrote to John, "and I would be in the lurch here among strangers."[46] She even suggested taking her children to Germany, because it would cost less to live there.[47]

John was greatly surprised to find his wife so worried about their finances. But his surprise changed to exasperation when he learned that she had written similar letters to Elbert and to her brother Horace Gray. "I am mortified," said Evans, "for I judge the Capt. & Gov. Elbert think I have been scolding you about your expenses." Not being noted for his "liberality in personal expenses," Evans said: "I fear they think I am mean to you, and that this is the cause of your extraordinary proposition about breaking up and coming home."[48]

Now it was Margaret's turn to be angry. "Everybody wrote so dismally," she said, "and it seemed as though you were keeping back worse troubles." Moreover, John had apparently implied that her professed concern was not genuine. "You ought not to have said that I was acting under resentment," she said, "and I do not like it, but I forgive you and feel sorry for the trouble that I have caused you."[49]

Will Evans, who was attending Northwestern University, was a source of genuine worry to his father. He had wanted for some time to quit school and become a rancher.[50] His father managed to convince him that he should stay at Northwestern until graduation, but in early June, 1876, Evans learned that Will had been neglecting his studies. "Willie dont attend his recitations regularly," he said, and the father was determined to find the cause.[51] It turned out that Will had been spending all his time playing baseball, and as a result he would have to stay at Northwestern part of the summer to make up his class work.[52]

Margaret decided in the latter part of the summer to give up the London house when the lease expired in August. She wanted to visit Paris and Brussels again, and the expense of running the London house was too great for her to keep the place while she traveled. She and the children moved to Brussels in August and were soon established in a charming pension.[53] She wrote such delightful letters home from Belgium that her husband asked her whether she would want to live there permanently. "How would you like [for me] to be Minister to Brussels or some nice place over there?" he asked. "If Hayes is elected I guess I could get an appointment by a systematic effort." His wife was "so averse to Denver" that Evans was quite willing to try for a diplomatic post if it would make her happy.[54]

> If I thought you wanted to stay in Europe *very* bad I might try for a mission. It would give us *position* and be a nice place for a few years. I guess I would not have to do much work myself to get it. What do you say?[55]

Apparently Margaret said she wanted to come home, and in early November Evans sailed for Europe to bring them back.

Margaret Gray Evans posed for this portrait in Dresden in the 1870's.

Evans intended to stop in London for a month to try to sell some South Park railroad bonds, so he asked the family to meet him there.[56] They later journeyed through Belgium and France and stopped in Italy for the winter, coming back to Denver in April, 1877.[57]

After their return from Europe, the Evans family began to entertain more extensively than they had ever done before. More than two hundred guests were present at a reception in the Evans home on December 30, 1879. "The refreshment rooms and parlours," according to the *News* report, "were odorous with the perfume of rare exotics, and ornamented profusely but tastily with gems from every clime."[58]

A year later, when Evans had just made a fortune in the sale of the South Park railroad, the *Tribune* reporter hardly seemed to know how to describe another Evans social occasion. The two hundred guests represented "the wealth, beauty and culture of Denver." The house was "brilliantly illuminated, the windows festooned with evergreens and flowers and the company of guests were welcomed by the sweet, soft strains of orchestral music." The floral decorations had exhausted the stock of seven Denver florists, and other "rare flowers" were imported from St. Louis and Chicago. The main staircase was decorated with calla lilies, poinsettias, and thousands of small flowers. On the upper part of the staircase was a canopy of "brilliant feather grass, sea moss from the West Indies, sea oats, and various novel grasses." It was "a new feature in floral decorations in the West." Each of the two dining rooms was decorated in a different style. In one, the centerpiece was "a lake of real water, containing real fish, bordered on one side by a rocky cliff." In the middle were "an island, a bridge, boat and swans, and around this was a silver railing supporting waxen tapers." The other dining room was "an arctic scene," with masses of snow-covered evergreens and holly at the end of the room, and a centerpiece representing "a ship among real icebergs—its rigging a mass of sleet and

218

ice—and sporting about it were seal and polar bears." The ladies, of course, were singularly beautiful, their costumes "conspicuous more for their ornate tastefulness than extravagance of display." Their escorts "represented the models of style."[59]

Another highlight of the Denver social scene was the marriage of William Gray Evans to his cousin Cornelia Gray on December 12, 1883. The wedding chapel was brilliantly ornamented with flowers, and the guest list was a roster of Denver's social elite. "The bride's dress," according to the *Republican*, "was of crepe of lily whiteness, the train of ottoman silk, the trimmings being of point Duchess lace. The veil was of almost transcendant transparency and fineness."[60]

The ceremony took place in the Evans Chapel, which John Evans had built as a memorial to his daughter Josephine. Begun in 1873, the little church was not finished until October, 1878. Evans' old friend, Bishop Matthew Simpson, came to Denver to preside at the dedication.[61]

John Evans had for years been actively engaged in religious affairs, particularly in the work of the Methodist Episcopal Church. He was one of the main contributors to the fund for the construction of the Lawrence Street Church,[62] and for many years he gave a standard contribution of $100 to any new church, regardless of denomination.[63] He seldom failed to attend the annual conferences of the Methodist Episcopal Church, although on at least one occasion, when his finances were in a precarious state, Margaret advised him not to attend. "It seems to me," she wrote, "that you will avoid a great deal of *disagreeable pressure* to help disabled church institutions when you have empty pockets if you should not go to the conference."[64]

Probably his most significant contribution to the Methodist Church in Colorado was the founding of Denver University. The first planning meetings for the new institution were held in the fall of 1862, and within a week more than $2,500 had

The Evans Chapel, shown here in 1880,
was moved to the University of Denver campus in 1960.

been subscribed.[65] Although the name Denver University was used in newspaper reports in 1863, by the time a charter was secured from the territorial legislature, in March, 1864, the institution was called Colorado Seminary.[66] The original charter for the new school included a provision that "such property as may be necessary for carrying out the design of the seminary in the best manner, while used exclusively for such purpose, shall be free from all taxation."[67] Twenty-eight trustees were named in the charter, their successors to be named by the Colorado Conference of the Methodist Episcopal Church. At the first meeting of the board Amos Steck was elected president; Samuel H. Elbert, vice president; D. H. Moffat, treasurer; and William N. Byers, secretary. John Evans was named to the executive committee.[68]

Evans donated four lots on the corner of Fourteenth Street (then called E Street) and Arapahoe Street, across from his own home, as the site for the seminary. A building contract was awarded in July, 1863, and by December it was so nearly completed that a bell could be hung in the cupola. The school was opened in November, 1864, and by early December more than fifty students were in attendance.[69]

In spite of this auspicious start, Colorado Seminary did not prosper. It was closed in 1867 with an unpaid debt of $3,000.[70] By October, 1868, a mortgage on the building in excess of $4,000 was held by John Evans and Edwin Scudder, both trustees of the seminary. The building mortgage was foreclosed in 1870, apparently to keep the property from falling into other hands. John Evans, Samuel H. Elbert, and other trustees immediately began to buy title to the ten lots that made up the seminary grounds.[71] They purchased the property with the clear intention of holding the seminary facilities for eventual reopening.[72] "We are glad to note that the building known as the Colorado Seminary is still in the possession of the excellent brethren who have saved it from falling into unmethodistic hands," said an 1872 Colorado Conference report, "and these brethren are rapidly reducing the debt, with a view to the restoration of the property to the use and the possession of the Conference."[73] By 1874 John Evans had acquired sole title to the building and lots, but there was a $5,000 mortgage on the property.[74]

During the years after the closing, Evans made every effort to rent the seminary building so that the income might be used for maintenance and debt reduction. In the winter of 1867 the territorial executive offices and the lower house of the territorial legislature occupied the building.[75] Probably the most bizarre tenant was Dr. Case's Hygienic Institute. John Evans described it to his wife as "a great bathing establishment—a hydropathic cure." As Evans said: "If it dont do anything else for us it will get our money out of the old Seminary."[76]

In 1874 Evans announced a plan to organize a Union Evangelical University, using, it is assumed, the facilities of the old Colorado Seminary. Although the proposal was supported with varying degrees of enthusiasm by the Methodists, Episcopalians, Presbyterians, and Baptists,[77] nothing came of the venture. Evans himself ascribed the failure of the scheme to the fact that a tax-free charter could not be obtained,[78] but it has also been suggested that the various denominations were not prepared to accept this type of ecumenism.[79]

By 1879 the Methodists were ready to try again on their own. Early in that year John Evans told the Preachers' Aid Society that he would return the seminary property to the Colorado Conference, if the conference would agree to reopen the school. His offer was immediately accepted, and at a special meeting in Denver in early June, the necessary steps were taken to reopen the seminary.[80] Probably because he doubted that a tax-exempt charter for a new school could be secured, Evans opposed the move to change the name of the school to Denver University, but a committee was appointed at his suggestion to investigate the tax question.[81] When the Colorado Conference met later that summer, a new board of trustees

*This contemporary sketch shows
Colorado Seminary in the 1860's.*

was appointed.[82] Evans was later elected president of the board, and it was announced that Colorado Seminary would reopen the following year.[83]

In 1880, when it was ascertained that a tax-exempt charter for a new school could not be obtained, the University of Denver incorporated as the degree-granting body, while all property was to be held in the name of Colorado Seminary. A seven-member board of trustees was created for the new university, and John Evans was elected president of that body. Evans transferred the old seminary property back to the institution and gave $3,000 for laboratory equipment.[84]

A four-story dormitory wing was added to the old building at a cost of $16,000, of which Evans appears to have paid half.[85] Work on the new wing was still in progress when the school opened on October 4, 1880. Some forty or fifty students enrolled on the first morning,[86] and before the year was out, enrollment had reached a hundred and fifty.[87]

Two of the Evans children attended the school. Young Will Evans was a student at Colorado Seminary in 1864, when it was a preparatory school.[88] Evan Evans went to Northwestern University for two years but apparently did not graduate.[89] Anne Evans, who first attended a "private school in Berlin,"[90] also attended the University of Denver.[91]

Within a few years of reopening the university was faced with another serious crisis. Unoccupied university land had been sold for taxes by Jefferson County on the threefold ground that it was not being used for educational purposes, that the charter granted by the territorial legislature became invalid when Colorado became a state, and that the tax-exemption violated the state constitution. The Supreme Court ultimately upheld the charter and tax-exempt status of the university, but tax exemption was limited to that property used directly for educational purposes.[92]

Realizing that the university's real estate income was threatened by the court decision, Evans stepped immediately into

the breach with a proposal for an amendment to the state constitution exempting all of the property owned by educational
institutions.[93] The *Rocky Mountain News* attacked Evans'
plan with a headline calling it "State Aid for Religion."[94]
According to Evans, Dr. David H. Moore, former chancellor
of the university, was behind the attack of the *News*. Dr.
Moore, he explained, was bitter because he had not been re-
elected to the chancellor's post.[95] But Evans saw that his fight
for a constitutional amendment was doomed, when Catholics
in the state began to support his position. It was a familiar
scene. The state constitution had been approved in 1876, he
thought, largely because the Catholics of the territory opposed
it.[96] Now that he had their support on a similar question, he
knew the result would be the same. In a letter to the *News* he
tried to disavow the fatal friendship of this group. "If Catholics
approve of our proposition so much the better," he wrote. "It
shows they are very right on one question at least."[97] It was
no use. The proposal died before the year was out.

After the new University Park campus for the University of
Denver was begun in 1890, the board of trustees decided to
make a concerted effort to put the institution on a sound financial footing. In January, 1891, a drive to collect $100,000 in
contributions was announced. Evans pledged $25,000 "as a
starter."[98] By April he had determined to raise his donation.
He offered, and the board accepted, downtown Denver property valued at $100,000. The gift consisted of lots 23, 24, and
part of lot 25 in block 42 of East Denver (1500 block of
Blake Street).[99] Other gifts by Margaret Evans, Samuel Elbert,
and Mary Lowe Dickinson brought the year's contributions to
$125,000.[100] With this gift, John Evans had donated more
than $130,000 to the University of Denver,[101] and this was his
last major gift to the school.

John Evans' benefactions were not confined to Methodist
institutions. His financial records show frequent small donations to individuals and institutions, religious and secular.[102]

He was also interested in projects aimed at civic betterment. Evans was one of the incorporators of the State Historical Society of Colorado,[103] one of the organizers and leaders of the Denver Chamber of Commerce,[104] and one of the organizers of the United Charities of Denver.[105]

In 1887 he supported the proposal to enlarge City Park with an additional 320 acres of school land, even though the addition would cost more than $1,000 an acre.[106] A few years later, in 1894, John Evans found himself in the middle of another dispute about parks. He proposed that the city begin to acquire land for parks in all parts of Denver, and that plans be made for wide boulevards leading to the parks. The *Rocky Mountain News* opposed the park plan on the ground that it would cost too much to irrigate the parks. Moreover, said the *News*, the Denver Tramway Company, of which John Evans and his son Will were major stockholders, would be the main beneficiary, since the firm would build lines to all the parks for picnic excursions. Because of this opposition, the park proposal failed.[107]

Old age and the crippling depression of the 1890's finally brought an end to John Evans' long and productive career. Nearly eighty years old in 1893, he was no longer able to bounce back from such severe financial blows. His Railroad Building, erected in 1888 at a cost of $100,000,[108] was soon foreclosed by the mortgage holder.[109] The Evans Block, built in 1872 at the corner of Fifteenth and Lawrence,[110] was the only piece of downtown real estate saved, but it was mortgaged to the hilt.[111] By 1895 it was clear to the family that old John could no longer manage his own financial affairs.[112] Evan was called home to help bring some order out of the chaos.[113] When Will and Evan went through the books to see what could be done with his investments, they found that many transactions had never been entered, and that for years the books had been kept in a slapdash manner.[114] As his sons continued to try to straighten out his tangled accounts, the old gentleman began

John Evans about 1880.

to retreat further from reality. Finally, on November 18, 1896, the Arapahoe County Court appointed Margaret Evans conservatrix of the estate.[115]

Realizing that the end was near, John Evans determined to see that his place in history was adequately marked. Although he had refused all previous solicitations for inclusion in subscription biographies, including Hubert Howe Bancroft's *Chronicles of the Builders*,[116] in 1895 Evans signed a contract with the James T. White Company for a two-page biographical sketch with five illustrations. The $1,500 biography appeared in Volume VI of the *National Cyclopedia of American Biography*, published early in 1896,[117] and it is still one of the most accurate brief summaries of his life ever printed.

In the spring of 1896 old John Evans' health began to fail more rapidly. He was no longer conscious of those about him, but spent his days in an easy chair by the parlor window, watching the streetcars go by.[118] In November his wife was appointed guardian of the estate. The cold and formal phrases of the legal documents for Margaret's conservatorship spoke of him as "a distracted person."[119]

Within a few months, Evans was confined to his bed. In the words of a *News* report: "Extreme old age has succeeded in overcoming nearly every faculty." A series of "comatose states" had come upon him, any one of which might be the last. In the first days of July, 1897, it became obvious that death was imminent. Ropes were strung across the intersection of Fourteenth and Arapahoe to keep traffic away from the house. Streetcars were rerouted along other lines, and policemen were stationed near the house to ward off casual visitors.[120]

Death came to John Evans at 4:30 P.M. on July 3, 1897, with his wife and children at the bedside.[121] At that very hour, some of the ladies from the Denver Fortnightly Club noted a strange phenomenon, which they described in a note to Margaret Evans.

We are wondering if you have been told of the wondrous way in which Nature herself seemed to feel the passing away of Governor Evans from Earth: from half-past three until about five o'clock on Saturday afternoon, while the rest of the mountain range from Pikes Peak to Long's presented a clear and unclouded outline, a long thin white veil hung from the sky to the base of Mt. Evans, hiding the whole Mountain from view, in so peculiar and defined a manner, as to impress us all with awe, as we said one to another, "Can it be that perhaps his Spirit is just now passing away?" And we afterward found that while his Mountain veiled its face, that spirit had ascended.[122]

His body lay in state in the Capitol from 10:00 A.M. until 1:30 P.M. on July 6. The cedar casket was then escorted to Union Lodge for the Masonic memorial observances, after which a brief funeral service was held at the Evans home. Most Denver businesses closed at noon on the day of the funeral, and this helped to swell the crowds that accompanied the body to Riverside Cemetery for the reading of "the majestic burial service of the Masons."[123]

The *Rocky Mountain News*—less than friendly to Evans in his later years—called him "a valuable citizen for any community" and "a man of brains, of culture and of irreproachable personal character." His enduring monument, said the *News*, would not be a granite shaft, but the "Magnificent Metropolis" of Denver, for which he had worked so tirelessly.[124] But the *News* had managed to catch the essential nature of the man's motivations in an article published exactly seven years earlier.

While he has been very careful to look after the personal interests of John Evans there are few . . . that have done so much towards building up and making Colorado great. Governor Evans has been a really useful man.[125]

NOTES

Chapter 1 *"Arise and Flee"*

1. John Belton O'Neall, *The Annals of Newberry, Historical, Biographical and Anecdotal* (Charleston, S.C.: S. G. Courtenay & Co., 1859), p. 40; H. E. Smith, "The Quakers, Their Migration to the Upper Ohio, Their Customs and Discipline," *Ohio Archaeological and Historical Publications,* XXXVII (1928), 49.

2. Quoted in Luke Smith Mote, *Early Settlements of Friends in the Miami Valley,* ed. Willard Heiss (Indianapolis: Indiana Quaker Records, 1961), p. 2.

3. Bancroft MS, P-L329 (Bancroft Library, Berkeley, Calif., interviews made about 1889), Fol. IV, 10.

4. Smith, *Ohio Archaeological and Historical Publications,* XXXVII (1928), 52.

5. Stephen B. Weeks, *Southern Quakers and Slavery: A Study in Institutional History* ("Johns Hopkins University Studies in Historical and Political Science," Extra Volume XV; Baltimore: Johns Hopkins University Press, 1896), pp. 266-68, 279-81.

6. O'Neall, *Annals of Newberry,* p. 40.

7. Weeks, *Southern Quakers and Slavery,* p. 267.

8. Smith, *Ohio Archaeological and Historical Publications,* XXXVII (1928), 55; Weeks, *Southern Quakers and Slavery,* pp. 280-81.

9. Charles Meredith Dupuy and Herbert Dupuy, *A Genealogical History of the Dupuy Family* (Philadelphia: J. B. Lippincott Co., 1910), p. 86. See also *The History of Warren County, Ohio* (Chicago: W. H. Beers & Co., 1882), p. 839.

10. John Belton O'Neall, who seems to have known the Evans family in Newberry, stated that the inventor was Benjamin Evans. See his *Annals of Newberry,* p. 41. John Evans worked at auger-making in

his father's shop in Waynesville. He said that the device was invented by Benjamin's brother Owen. See his account in Bancroft MS, P-L329, Fol. IV, 11. George Leland Summer stated that the tool was invented by Benjamin Evans, who "sold his rights to another Quaker, John Edmondson." See his *Newberry County South Carolina, Historical and Genealogical* (n.p.: George Leland Summer, 1950), p. 104. The records of the United States Patent Office fail to show that either Owen Evans or Benjamin Evans applied for a patent on the tool. Patent records for the period before 1837 are incomplete, but the failure of John Evans to mention a patent probably indicates that there was none. Moreover, Isaac Fleischmann, director of the Office of Information Services, the Commissioner of Patents, Washington, D.C., stated that "the screw auger patents listed do not include any issued to an Evans and none in this category were issued prior to 1827." Letter from Isaac Fleischmann to author, April 12, 1962. Nonetheless, there is no doubt that the family manufactured screwaugers. See the letter from David Evans to Alfred Vail, January 16, 1852, David Evans Papers, Ohio Historical Society, Columbus, cited hereafter as David Evans Papers. Xerox copies of pertinent portions of these papers are now in the John Evans Collection, State Historical Society of Colorado, Denver, cited hereafter as the John Evans Collection.

11. Edgar Carlisle McMechen, *Life of Governor Evans, Second Territorial Governor of Colorado* (Denver: Wahlgreen Publishing Co., 1924), p. 6. In conducting research for his biographical study, McMechen was given a great deal of assistance by John Evans' son, William G. Evans, who had gathered and preserved a considerable body of material regarding his father's life and accomplishments. See also Bancroft MS, P-L329, Fol. IV, 11.

12. Letter from David Evans to Alfred Vail, January 16, 1852, David Evans Papers. See also Quantrille D. McClung, "Colorado Governors: John Evans—2nd Territorial Governor, 1862-65," *The Colorado Genealogist*, XV (July, 1954), 67; Bancroft MS, P-L329, Fol. IV, 11; William Wade Hinshaw, *Encyclopedia of American Quaker Genealogy* (Ann Arbor: Edward Roos Bros., Inc., 1936), V, 52; and *History of Warren County*, p. 840.

13. Dupuy, *History of the Dupuy Family*, p. 91.

14. Bancroft MS, P-L329, Fol. IV, 10; *History of Warren County*, pp. 839-40; Smith, *Ohio Archaeological and Historical Publications*, XXXVII (1928), 55.

15. Bancroft MS, P-L329, Fol. IV, 10; Fol. V, 4. Her father died when Rachel was very young, and her mother remarried. After her

mother's death, an uncle brought Rachel to live with her grandparents in Middletown, Ohio. Letter from David Evans to Alfred Vail, January 16, 1852, David Evans Papers.

16. McMechen, *Life of Governor Evans*, p. 7. Rachel Burnet was born October 18, 1794. See the letter from David Evans to Alfred Vail, January 16, 1852, David Evans Papers.

17. Letter from David Evans to Alfred Vail, January 16, 1852, David Evans Papers; McMechen, *Life of Governor Evans*, p. 7. This date and place are also confirmed by an obituary article concerning Rachel Evans which appeared in the *Miami Gazette* [Waynesville, Ohio], May 9, 1885, clipping in the John Evans Collection.

18. *Miami Gazette* [Waynesville, Ohio], May 9, 1885, clipping in the John Evans Collection.

19. Bancroft MS, P-L329, Fol. IV, 11.

20. *Ibid.*

21. *Ibid.*; letter from David Evans to Alfred Vail, January 16, 1852, David Evans Papers; letter from John Evans to his brother Joel, January 17, 1836, John Evans Collection.

22. *Miami Gazette* [Waynesville, Ohio], May 9, 1885, clipping in the John Evans Collection. Dates of birth for the Evans children are found in the *History of Warren County*, p. 840, and in the letter from David Evans to Alfred Vail, January 16, 1852, David Evans Papers.

23. *Ibid.*

24. Letter from David Evans to Alfred Vail, January 16, 1852, David Evans Papers; *Miami Gazette* [Waynesville, Ohio], May 9, 1885, clipping in the John Evans Collection; letter from Joel Evans to John Evans, February 24, 1836, John Evans Collection.

25. Letter from John Evans to Margaret Evans, July 9, 1876, John Evans Collection.

26. *History of Warren County*, p. 840.

27. *Ibid.*, 582. An indication of the value of these properties is found in the fact that the mill sold for $14,000 in 1840.

28. Letter from Seth Evans to John Evans, March 5, 1836; letter from Jason Evans to John Evans, January 30, 1836, John Evans Collection.

29. Letter from Benjamin Evans to John Evans, March 10, 1836, *ibid.*

30. Letter from D. S. Burson to John Evans, July 6, 1837, *ibid.* See also a letter from J. P. Compton to John Evans, March 4, 1836, *ibid.*, in which Compton expressed his surprise at not having seen a drunken man on the street for three days. "It is court week," he wrote, "and

Long has shut up his establishment."

31. McMechen, *Life of Governor Evans*, p. 7.

32. Bancroft MS, P-L329, Fol. IV, 12.

33. Neall's contract is quoted in full in Mote, *Early Settlements of Friends*, p. 35.

34. *Ibid.*, 38.

35. Letter from John Evans to his cousin Margaret Evans, January 23, 1836, John Evans Collection.

36. Letter from J. P. Compton to John Evans, March 4, 1836, *ibid.* Copies of this chart are apparently no longer extant, but some idea of the illustrations may be gained from the pictures in C. P. Bronson's *Abstract of Elocution and Music, in Accordance with the Principles of Physiology and the Laws of Life, for the Development of Body and Mind* (Auburn, Ind.: Oliphant, 1842), pp. 61-73.

37. Letter from Benjamin Evans to John Evans, March 10, 1836, John Evans Collection.

38. Letter from J. P. Compton to John Evans, March 4, 1836, *ibid.*

39. Letter from Noah S. Haines to John Evans, July 28, 1840, *ibid.*

40. Bancroft MS, P-L329, Fol. IV, 12.

41. Typed copy of a letter from John Evans to Benjamin Evans, August, 1834, John Evans Collection. The original letter is not now available. Edgar McMechen commented on its disappearance from the John Evans Collection in his letter to Richard C. Overton, January 2, 1951, a copy of which is in the John Evans Collection.

42. David Furnas, "History of Miami Monthly Meeting, Hicksite— From 1828 to 1903," *Proceedings, Centennial Anniversary Miami Monthly Meeting, Waynesville, Ohio, 10th Month, 16-17, 1903* (Waynesville, Ohio: Press of Miami Gazette, n.d.), p. 43. The Hicksite controversy stemmed from the preaching of Elias Hicks of New York. In the view of Hicks every man received a manifestation of God at some time during his life, and this alone was sufficient for salvation. Christ was not divine, but simply a man with a unique mission. He received extraordinary power to aid in fulfilling this mission. His death had no meaning for men except as an example of sacrifice. The Bible had only a limited value, because much of what it related was probably untrue. Those who called themselves Hicksites accepted at least a portion of the Hicks theology. The Orthodox, on the other hand, believed in the inspiration of the Scriptures, the unity of Christ with the Father and the Holy Spirit, and the death of Christ on the cross as a necessary prerequisite for salvation. Both factions accepted the Inner Light as the guide for the individual on the road to salvation. The controversy came into the open at the New York Yearly Meeting

in 1828. Following this, a division occurred in Ohio "which was the most disorderly of any," and about half the Ohio members became Hicksites. A few Indiana Quakers also joined with Hicks. See Allen C. Thomas and Richard Henry Thomas, *A History of the Friends in America* (Pennbury Series of Modern Quaker Books; 6th ed.; Philadelphia: John C. Winston Co., 1930), pp. 123-28, 140. There are important theological manuscripts by Hicks in the David Evans Papers.

43. John T. Plummer, "Reminiscences of the History of Richmond," *A Directory to the City of Richmond, Containing Names, Business and Residence of the Inhabitants, Together with a Historical Sketch* (Richmond, Ind.: R. O. Dormer & W. R. Holloway, 1857), p. 60; Andrew W. Young, *History of Wayne County, Indiana, from Its First Settlement to the Present Time, with Numerous Biographical and Family Sketches, Embellished with Upwards of Fifty Portraits of Citizens and Views of Buildings* (Cincinnati: R. Clarke & Co., 1872), pp. 397-98.

44. Letter from John Evans to Benjamin Evans, August, 1834, John Evans Collection. It might be noted that John Evans' grammar and spelling were somewhat erratic, as was the case with many of his contemporaries; it is not at all unusual to find a word spelled three different ways on the same page. In order to avoid repeated interruptions of the narrative, spelling, capitalization, and punctuation in quotations will be reproduced exactly as given in the original, with no attempt to indicate deviations from currently accepted standards.

45. Letter from John Evans to Benjamin Evans, August, 1834, John Evans Collection.

46. *Ibid.*

47. *Ibid.*

48. Letter from Benjamin Evans to John Evans, November 20, 1835, *ibid.*; letter from Benjamin Evans to John Evans, January 22, 1836, *ibid.*

49. Letter from John Evans to Samuel Hill, November 15, [1834,] *ibid.* For references to David Evans' opposition to his son's educational plans see the letters from John Evans to Claiborne Cooke, November 18, 1835; from Joel Evans to John Evans, November 29, 1835; from John Evans to Benjamin Evans, December 9, 1835; from John Evans to Benjamin Evans, January 6, 1836; from Joel Evans to John Evans, January 17, 1836; and from John Evans to David Evans, January 21, 1836, all of which are in the John Evans Collection.

235

"Tu et Ego Erimus Medici"

1. "*Tu et ego . . .*": "You and I will be doctors." Letter from John Evans to Benjamin Evans, January 1, 1836, John Evans Collection.

2. Letters from Benjamin Evans to John Evans, November 20, 1835; December 19, 1835; January 17, 1836; February 17, 1836; from Joel Evans to John Evans, February 24, 1836; from Benjamin Evans to John Evans, March 10, 1836; from Seth Evans to John Evans, November 7, 1836; and from Elias Fisher to John Evans, November 7, 1836, all in the John Evans Collection.

3. Letters from John Evans to Claiborne Cooke, November 18, 1835; from Benjamin Evans to John Evans, November 20, 1835; from Joel Evans to John Evans, November 29, 1835; and from John Evans to Benjamin Evans, December 9, 1835, *ibid*.

4. Letters from John Evans to Claiborne Cooke, November 18, 1835; from John Evans to Benjamin Evans, December 9, 1835; January 6, 1836; and from John Evans to David Evans, January 21, 1836, *ibid*.

5. A receipt signed by John Evans on November 2, 1835, shows that David Evans gave John $330 before he left. Of this amount $250 was for goods, which John was to purchase for the store in Waynesville, and the remainder was for "traveling and school expenses." David apparently gave the money to John in Cincinnati, a day or two after leaving Waynesville. See the letter from Joel Evans to John Evans, November 29, 1835. Both the letter and the receipt are in the John Evans Collection.

6. Letter from John Evans to Benjamin Evans, December 9, 1835, *ibid*.

7. *Ibid*.

8. Letter from John Evans to Claiborne Cooke, November 18, 1835, *ibid*.

9. Letter from John Evans to Benjamin Evans, December 9, 1835, *ibid*.

10. Letter from John Evans to Margaret Evans, January 23, 1836, *ibid.*

11. *Ibid.*

12. *Ibid.*

13. Letter from John Evans to Benjamin Evans, December 9, 1835, *ibid.*

14. Letter from John Evans to Benjamin Evans, January 6, 1836, *ibid.* The performance in question took place on New Year's Eve, but it was, presumably, like the first two.

15. Letter from Benjamin Evans to John Evans, December 19, 1835, *ibid.*

16. Letter from John Evans to Benjamin Evans, January 6, 1836, *ibid.*

17. Letter from John Evans to Claiborne Cooke, December 18, 1835, *ibid.*

18. Letter from Joel Evans to John Evans, November 29, 1835, *ibid.*

19. Letter from John Evans to Benjamin Evans, January 6, 1836, *ibid.*

20. Letter from Rachel Evans and Seth Evans to John Evans, February 1, 1836, *ibid.*

21. Letter from John Evans to David Evans, January 21, 1836, *ibid.*

22. Letter from Joel Evans to John Evans, January 17, 1836, *ibid.* Although his father provided some funds (see the letter from John Evans to David Evans, December 23, 1836, David Evans Papers), much of the money came from other sources. This seems clear from the fact that John signed a note on October 22, 1836, promising to pay Robert Head $100 in ninety days at ten per cent interest. See also the letters from Elias Fisher to John Evans, February 22, 1838, and Isaac Fisher to John Evans, February 23, 1838, John Evans Collection, in which both men speak of lending money to John. McMechen, *Life of Governor Evans*, p. 22, states that "John received no financial assistance from David Evans while attending his last course of lectures in Cincinnati." This statement evidently refers to the academic year 1837-38, and seems to be based on the letters from the Fishers cited above. In Bancroft MS, P-L329, Fol. V, 4, it is said that "his father supplied the money to defray the expenses of his education except those of the last course of lectures." John himself said: "My father assisted me until I got halfway through." See Bancroft MS, P-L329, Fol. I, 4. Whether David's assistance was in the form of a loan or a gift is not clear.

23. Letter from John Evans to Benjamin Evans, December 9, 1835, John Evans Collection.

24. Letter from John Evans to Benjamin Evans, January 6, 1836, *ibid.*

25. *Ibid.*

26. Letter from John Evans to Margaret Evans, January 23, 1836, *ibid.*

27. Letters from John Evans to David Evans, January 21, 1836, and from John Evans to Benjamin Evans, January 6, 1836, *ibid.*

28. Letter from Noah S. Haines to John Evans, September 21, 1837, *ibid.*

29. Letter from John Evans to Benjamin Evans, January 6, 1836, *ibid.*

30. Letters from John Evans to Benjamin Evans, January 1, 1836, and February 3, 1836, *ibid.*

31. *Ibid.* See also Richard C. Wade, *The Urban Frontier: The Rise of Western Cities, 1790-1830* (Cambridge, Mass.: Harvard University Press, 1959), pp. 69-70.

32. Letter from John Evans to Benjamin Evans, January 1, 1836, John Evans Collection.

33. Letter from John Evans to Samuel Hill, November 15, 1834, *ibid.*

34. Letter from John Evans to Benjamin Evans, January 1, 1836, *ibid.*

35. Letter from John Evans to Benjamin Evans, January 6, 1836, *ibid.*

36. Letter from John Evans to Benjamin Evans, January 1, 1836, *ibid.*

37. Letter from John Evans to Benjamin Evans, February 3, 1836, *ibid.*

38. Letter from Benjamin Evans to John Evans, March 10, 1836, *ibid.*

39. Roscoe Carlyle Buley, *The Old Northwest: Pioneer Period, 1815-1850* (2 vols.; Bloomington: Indiana University Press, 1951), II, 472-73.

40. Letter from John Evans to Benjamin Evans, January 1, 1836, John Evans Collection.

41. *Ibid.*

42. *Ibid.*; letter from John Evans to David Evans, January 21, 1836, *ibid.*

43. Letter from John Evans to Margaret Evans, January 23, 1836, *ibid.*

44. Letter from John Evans to Benjamin Evans, January 6, 1836, *ibid*. In 1826 Horner first published his *Treatise on Special and General Anatomy*. For years the standard text, it ultimately went through seven editions. See William Fredcrick Norwood, *Medical Education in the United States before the Civil War* (Philadelphia: University of Pennsylvania Press, 1944), pp. 82-87.

45. Letter from John Evans to Benjamin Evans, January 6, 1836, John Evans Collection.

46. Letters from John Evans to Benjamin Evans, January 6, 1836, January 17, 1836, and March 10, 1836, *ibid*.

47. Letter from Benjamin Evans to John Evans, February 17, 1836, *ibid*.

48. Letters from Benjamin Evans to John Evans, February 17, 1836, and March 10, 1836, *ibid*.

49. Norwood, *Medical Education*, pp. 32-33.

50. Buley, *The Old Northwest*, I, 278-79.

51. Letter from Benjamin Evans to John Evans, March 10, 1836, John Evans Collection.

52. Letter from Joel Evans to John Evans, February 24, 1836, *ibid*.

53. Letters from Elias Fisher to John Evans, February 22, 1838, and from Isaac Fisher to John Evans, February 23, 1838, *ibid*. See also Evans' statement in Bancroft MS, P-L329, Fol. I, 4.

54. Letter from Noah Haines to John Evans, April 7, 1837, John Evans Collection.

55. Letter from John Evans to Samuel Hill, October 13, 1836, *ibid*.

56. Letter from Noah Haines to John Evans, July 20, 1837, *ibid*.

57. Dr. Isaac Fisher of Waynesville is listed as a student at Cincinnati College during the time that John and Benjamin attended. See *A Catalogue of the Officers and Students of the Cincinnati College in Its Medical, Law and Academical Departments for 1836-7* (Cincinnati: N. S. Johnson, 1837), p. 5.

58. The promissory note is deposited in the John Evans Collection.

59. Letter from Seth Evans to John Evans, November 7, 1836, and letter from Noah Haines to John Evans, December 4, 1836, John Evans Collection.

60. Letter from Elias Fisher to John Evans, November 7, 1836, and letter from Seth Evans to John Evans, November 7, 1836, *ibid*.

61. Raymond Walters, *Historical Sketch of the University of Cincinnati* (Cincinnati: Mountel Press, 1940), p. 15; Buley, *The Old Northwest*, I, 278; Nathan Smith Davis, "History of the Medical Profession from the First Settlements of the British Colonies in America to the Year 1850," *The North-Western Medical and Surgical*

Journal, III (November, 1850), 282; this last article was a chapter from Dr. Davis' book, published later under the title, *History of Medical Education and Institutions in the United States from the First Settlement of the British Colonies in America to the year 1850; with a Chapter on the Present Condition and Wants of the Profession, and the Means Necessary for Supplying Those Wants, and Elevating the Character and Extending the Usefulness of the Whole Profession* (Chicago: S. C. Griggs & Co., 1851).

62. Norwood, *Medical Education,* p. 312. See also Daniel Drake, *Pioneer Life in Kentucky, 1785-1800,* ed. Emmett Field Horine (New York: Henry Schuman, 1948), p. xxiii.

63. Walters, *Historical Sketch of the University of Cincinnati,* p. 8.

64. Otto Juettner, *Daniel Drake and His Followers: Historical and Biographical Sketches* (Cincinnati: Harvey Publishing Co., 1909), p. 65.

65. *Ibid.,* 59.

66. Walters, *Historical Sketch of the University of Cincinnati,* p. 8; and Buley, *The Old Northwest,* I, 278.

67. Norwood, *Medical Education,* pp. 318-19. See also "Medical Department of Cincinnati College" *The Western Journal of the Medical and Physical Sciences,* XI (April, May, and June, 1837), 168.

68. "Catalogue of the Medical Department of the Cincinnati College for 1837-8," *The Western Journal of the Medical and Physical Sciences,* XI (January, February, and March, 1838), 670. According to advertisements in 1835, all candidates were required to be at least twenty-one years old and to have completed a minimum of three years of work "under some reputable practitioner." When Benjamin Evans and John Evans graduated, these requirements were not in the catalogue, and neither John Evans nor Benjamin Evans had practiced for three years prior to graduation. See Buley's *The Old Northwest,* I, 278. An early medical historian stated that the three years usually included the time spent at a medical college. See Davis, *History of Medical Education,* p. 119.

69. Norwood, *Medical Education,* p. 319; *Catalogue of the Officers and Students of Cincinnati College for 1836-7,* p. 10.

70. *Ibid.*

71. John Allen Wyeth, *With Sabre and Scalpel: the Autobiography of a Soldier and Surgeon* (New York: Harper and Bros., 1914), p. 328.

72. *Catalogue of the Officers and Students of Cincinnati College for 1836-7,* p. 11.

73. *Ibid.*

74. "Medical Department of Cincinnati College," *The Western Journal of the Medical and Physical Sciences*, XI (1837), 168.

75. Letter from Benjamin Evans to John Evans, February 28, 1837, John Evans Collection.

76. *Ibid.*

77. The library at the beginning of the 1837-38 term contained thirteen hundred volumes, including a number added in the summer of 1837. See the "Catalogue of the Medical Department of the Cincinnati College for 1837-8," *The Western Journal of the Medical and Physical Sciences*, XI (1838), 670.

78. Letter from Benjamin Evans to John Evans, February 28, 1837, John Evans Collection. See also *Catalogue of the Officers and Students of Cincinnati College for 1836-7*, p. 12.

79. J. Wesley Whicker, *Historical Sketches of the Wabash Valley* (Attica, Ind.: n.p., 1916), typed extract in the John Evans Collection. See also J. Wesley Whicker, "Attica's Most Illustrious Citizens," *Ledger* [Attica, Indiana], July 6, 1917, newspaper clipping in the Evan E. Evans Scrapbook, John Evans Collection. The date and place of birth are also shown in a photograph of the inscription on Hannah's tombstone, Evan E. Evans Scrapbook, *ibid.*

80. Hannah's parents were Joseph Canby and Lydia (Pedrick) Canby. Lydia's younger sister Hannah Pedrick married Thomas Evans, the older brother of John's father David Evans. Hinshaw, *Encyclopedia of American Quaker Genealogy*, V, 52; McClung, *The Colorado Genealogist*, XV (1954), 66-67. See also the letter from Benjamin Evans to John Evans, December 19, 1835, in which Benjamin calls Dr. Canby "Uncle J. Canby"; in the letter from Margaret Evans (Benjamin's sister) to John Evans, July 2, 1837, Hannah Canby is spoken of as "cousin Hannah." Both of these letters are in the John Evans Collection.

81. Typed copy of a letter from John Evans to Hannah Canby; the date of the letter has not been established. The letter is headed "Fisher's Office, Monday Morning." See also the letters from David S. Burson to John Evans, September 22, 1837, and from Noah S. Haines to John Evans, September 21, 1837, John Evans Collection. The informality of the heading leads to the supposition that the letter was to be delivered immediately, perhaps personally. Most of the originals of the correspondence between Hannah Canby and John Evans are missing, although Edgar C. McMechen had them when he wrote his *Life of Governor Evans*. McMechen made the existing typed copies from the originals and returned the originals to W. G. Evans, after which time

they were lost. See the letter from Edgar C. McMechen to Richard C. Overton, January 2, 1951, John Evans Collection.

82. Letter from Noah S. Haines to John Evans, June 26, 1837, John Evans Collection.

83. Letter from Elias Fisher to John Evans, June 1, 1837, *ibid.*

84. Letter from Margaret Evans to John Evans, July 2, 1837; letter from David S. Burson to John Evans, July 6, 1837, *ibid.*

85. Letter from Elias Fisher to John Evans, June 1, 1837, *ibid.*

86. Letter from Elias Fisher to John Evans, July 27, 1837, *ibid.* This letter also mentions that Joseph C. Cooper, who the year before had married Benjamin's sister Lydia, was quite ill and that Isaac Fisher had just recovered. See also the letter from Thomas Evans to John Evans, July 27, 1837, *ibid.*

87. Letter from Elias Fisher to John Evans, July 27, 1837; letter from Thomas Evans to John Evans, July 27, 1837, *ibid.* Both of these letters state that Benjamin died "last evening." Hinshaw, *Encyclopedia of American Quaker Genealogy*, V, 52, gives the date of Benjamin's death as July 23, 1837.

88. Letter from Elias Fisher to John Evans, July 27, 1837, John Evans Collection.

89. Letter from John Evans to Margaret Evans, October 4, 1837, *ibid.*

90. Letter from David S. Burson to John Evans, September 22, 1837, *ibid.*

91. Letter from John Evans to Margaret Evans, October 4, 1837, *ibid.*

92. Letter from John Evans to Margaret Evans, October 4, 1837; letter from John Evans to Hannah Canby, November 13, 1837, *ibid.*

93. *Ibid.*

94. Daniel Drake, "Our Institution," *The Western Journal of the Medical and Physical Sciences*, XI (July, August, and September, 1837), 335.

95. See the bulletin issued by Transylvania University, July 25, 1837; a note from Cross to John Evans is inscribed on the fly sheet; below it is the remark in Evans' hand, "Who Cares." The bulletin is deposited in the John Evans Collection.

96. Registration information is contained in Drake, *The Western Journal of the Medical and Physical Sciences*, XI (1837), 335-36.

97. Letter from John Evans to Hannah Canby, November 13, 1837, John Evans Collection.

98. Walters, *Historical Sketch of the University of Cincinnati*, 7.

99. *Catalogue of the Officers and Students of Cincinnati College for 1836-7*, p. 10.

100. Letter from John Evans to Hannah Canby, December 4, 1837, John Evans Collection; letter from John Evans to David Evans, December 23, 1836, David Evans Papers.

101. Letter from John Evans to Hannah Canby, April 17, 1838, John Evans Collection.

102. Letter from Isaac Fisher to John Evans, February 23, 1838; letter from Elias Fisher to John Evans, February 22, 1838, *ibid.*

103. *Ibid.*

104. "Catalogue of the Medical Department of the Cincinnati College for 1837-8," *The Western Journal of the Medical and Physical Sciences*, XI (1838), 665.

105. *Ibid.*, 666, 669.

"Some Chance for Distinction"

1. Letter from John Evans to Hannah Canby, April 17, 1838, John Evans Collection; Bancroft MS, P-L329, Fol. IV, 13.

2. The actual facts here are not clear. Evans said, some years later, that after graduation, "I had to scratch for myself" (Bancroft MS, P-L329, Fol. IV, 13). McMechen, however, states that "David Evans unbent to the extent of furnishing his son a pony, a saddle and a ten-dollar bill" (see his *Life of Governor Evans*, p. 22). F. D. DuSouchet recounts the same incident and adds a bridle to the pony's equipment (see his article "John Evans," *Dictionary of American Medical Biography*, eds. Howard A. Kelly and Walter Burrage [New York: D. Appleton & Co., 1928], p. 390). Neither author indicates the source of his information, and, although DuSouchet's article appeared four years after McMechen's book, it is quite possible that his information was obtained independently. DuSouchet had begun his rather careful research on the life of John Evans as early as 1917 (see his letters to William G. Evans, May 12, 1917, and July 6, 1917, John Evans Collection). Evans' own reminiscences credit David Evans with aid only in paying the first year's college expenses. Of his own expenses after graduation he said, in part: "I traded first for a black mare" (Bancroft MS, P-L329, Fol. IV, 13). The inference here is that the "black mare" was not a gift horse.

3. Letter from John Evans to Hannah Canby, June 8, 1838, John Evans Collection.

4. Letter from Elias Fisher to John Evans, June 1, 1837, *ibid*.

5. Letters from John Evans to Hannah Canby, April 17, 1838; May 7, 1838, *ibid*.

6. *Ibid*.

7. *Ibid*.

8. Letter from John Evans to Hannah Canby, May 7, 1838, *ibid*.

9. Letter from John Evans to Hannah Canby, May 25, 1838, *ibid*.

10. Letter from Noah S. Haines to John Evans, June 26, 1837, *ibid*.

244

11. Letter from John Evans to Hannah Canby, May 7, 1838, *ibid.* The miniature painting has apparently been lost.

12. Letter from John Evans to Samuel Hill, November 15, [1834], *ibid,*

13. Letter from John Evans to Samuel Hill, October 13, 1836, *ibid.*

14. Letter from John Evans to Hannah Canby, May 25, 1838, *ibid.*

15. *Ibid.*

16. Letter from John Evans to Hannah Canby, June 8, 1838, *ibid.*

17. *Ibid.*

18. *Ibid.*

19. *Ibid.* The letter was finished June 9, and a copy of that issue of the paper, which included Evans' railroading article, was enclosed.

20. Letter from John Evans to Hannah Canby, postmarked July 25, 1838, *ibid.*

21. *Ibid.*

22. *Ibid.*; Bancroft MS, P-L329, Fol. I, 3. See also Webster B. Lamphier, "Gov. John Evans" (unpublished manuscript in the John Evans Collection [1873]). Both the original handwritten manuscript and a typed copy are in the collection. A penciled notation on the typed copy says "written about January 1873," and the year is substantiated by internal evidence. The pages in the manuscript are not numbered. Although it is not so stated in the manuscript, it seems pretty clear that the material was obtained from a personal interview with Evans.

23. Letter from John Evans to Hannah Canby, July 25, 1838, John Evans Collection. Evans also seems to have considered moving to Memphis, Tennessee. See his letter to Hannah Canby Evans, postmarked May 28, [1842]. Supporting this statement McMechen in his *Life of Governor Evans*, pp. 25-26, cites a letter from John Evans to Hannah Canby, September, 1838. This letter has apparently been lost, as it is not now catalogued in the John Evans Collection.

24. Letter from John Evans to Hannah Canby, July 25, 1838, John Evans Collection.

25. Lamphier, "Gov. John Evans," MS in the John Evans Collection; Bancroft MS, P-L329, Fol. I, 3; Fol. IV, 4.

26. While it is clear that the wedding took place soon after his return from Illinois, there is some discrepancy regarding the actual date. F. D. DuSouchet lists the date as December 11, 1838 (DuSouchet, "John Evans," *Dictionary of American Medical Biography*, p. 391). Quantrille D. McClung gives December 24, 1838 (*Colorado Genealogist*, XV [1954], 68). Both these authors seem to have had access to family records which are not now available. See the letters

from DuSouchet to William G. Evans, March 26, 1917; April 2, 1917; May 12, 1917; and June 16, 1917, in the John Evans Collection. In a personal letter dated June 19, 1962, Miss McClung stated that her source was a "hand written page of dates . . . labelled 'Family Record,' " but she could not remember the location of the original document. Even sources evidently based on information supplied by Evans himself are not in agreement. *The National Cyclopedia of American Biography* says that the wedding took place "early in 1839" ("John Evans," *The National Cyclopedia of American Biography* [New York: James T. White & Co., 1896], VI, 446). Jerome Smiley, on the other hand, has the marriage ceremony in 1838 (*History of Denver: with Outlines of the Earlier History of the Rocky Mountain Country* [Denver: Times-Sun Publ. Co., 1901], p. 587). Webster Lamphier is a little more explicit, placing the ceremony in the month of December, 1838 ("Gov. John Evans," MS in the John Evans Collection).

27. Neither the records of the Logan County Clerk nor of the Probate Court of Logan County show that a marriage license was issued to John and Hannah; however, John stated unequivocally that the marriage took place in Bellefontaine (Bancroft MS, P-L329, Fol. IV, 13).

28. R. P. Kennedy, *Historical Review of Logan County, Ohio* (Cincinnati: S. J. Clarke Publ., 1903), p. 670; Hinshaw, *Encyclopedia of American Quaker Genealogy*, V, 35.

29. It was clearly not a Quaker ceremony, since both were disowned by the Miami Monthly Meeting for marrying "out of unity" (Hinshaw, *Encyclopedia of American Quaker Genealogy*, V, 53). Disowning of the two was delayed for several years, probably in the hope that they would eventually become reconciled with the Society. The fact that the marriage was "contrary to discipline" was reported to the Society on May 27, 1840. Hannah was disowned April 21, 1841. Perhaps out of respect for his parents, who still lived in Waynesville and remained faithful to the Quaker religion, John was not disowned until October 27, 1852. It was then officially noted that he had not only violated the Quaker marriage ordinances, but had also joined another church (*ibid.*).

30. Letter from John Evans to Hannah Canby, May 25, 1838, John Evans Collection.

31. *History of Warren County, Ohio*, p. 840; letter from John Evans to Hannah Canby, December 4, 1837, John Evans Collection.

32. Letter from John Evans to Hannah Canby, December 4, 1837, John Evans Collection.

33. Letter from Lydia Evans Cooper to John Evans, March 13, 1839, John Evans Collection. Lydia was a sister of Benjamin and cousin of both John and Hannah. She told John that her money was out on loan. She offered to let him have it as soon as it was repaid to her, but she feared that the borrower "intends taking his own time to repay it." When the money was repaid (some two hundred dollars), in June of that year, she immediately offered it to John. See the letter from David S. Burson to John Evans, June 12, 1839, John Evans Collection.

34. Bancroft MS, P-L329, Fol. I, 3.

35. Lamphier, "Gov. John Evans," MS in the John Evans Collection. It is not certain just when Fisher moved to Attica, but John's letter to Hannah, dated September 29, 1839, seems to indicate that Evans did not have a partner at that time. Fisher was living in Attica in December, 1840. See John Evans, "Indiana Hospital for the Insane," *The North-Western Medical and Surgical Journal*, IV (January, 1852), 371.

36. Letter from John Evans to Hannah Canby Evans, September 29, 1839, John Evans Collection.

37. *Ibid.*

38. *Ibid.*

39. *Ibid.*

40. McClung, *Colorado Genealogist*, XV (1954), 68.

41. J. Wesley Whicker, "Dr. John Evans," *Indiana Magazine of History*, XIX (September, 1923), 226-27. Letter from Louise Rhode, April 2, 1968.

42. Lamphier, "Gov. John Evans," MS in the John Evans Collection. For a good description of the grain traffic down the Wabash to New Orleans in the thirties and forties, see John G. Clark, *The Grain Trade in the Old Northwest* (Urbana: University of Illinois Press, 1966), pp. 23-25 and 37-41.

43. Letter from John Evans to Hannah Canby, postmarked May 28 [1842], John Evans Collection. Evans started the letter on April 29 and finished it on May 20.

44. Lamphier, "Gov. John Evans," MS in the John Evans Collection.

45. Clark, *Grain Trade in the Old Northwest*, p. 25.

46. Letter from John Evans to Hannah Canby, postmarked May 28, [1842], John Evans Collection.

47. Lamphier, "Gov. John Evans," MS in the John Evans Collection. Lamphier's paper, which was written more than thirty years after the event, is in surprisingly close agreement with Evans' letter

to his wife relating the same story. Lamphier's main error was in placing the incident in 1841 rather than 1842. See the letter to Hannah Canby Evans, May 28 [1842], John Evans Collection.

48. *Ibid.*

49. *Ibid.*

50. Letter from Noah S. Haines to John Evans, September 21, 1837, John Evans Collection.

51. Robert D. Clark, *The Life of Matthew Simpson* (New York: Macmillan Co., 1956), pp. 72-73.

52. Bancroft MS, P-L329, Fol. I, 7. Frances E. Willard quotes a story by Mrs. Simpson that this lecture was on the subject of education. See her book, *A Classic Town: The Story of Evanston* (Chicago: Women's Temperance Publ. Assoc., 1892), p. 1. McMechen also confirms this statement in his *Life of Governor Evans*, p. 36, naming as his source "Anon. Mss.—Governor Evans private papers."

53. McMechen, *Life of Governor Evans*, p. 35.

54. Bancroft MS, P-L329, Fol. I, 7.

55. McMechen, *Life of Governor Evans*, p. 35.

56. Bancroft MS, P-L329, Fol. I, 7; in an earlier interview Evans said: "I have been a Methodist since 1852." Since the date was contradicted in the later statement, it was probably an error on the part of the interviewer. See Bancroft MS, P-L23, 4. The date 1842 would agree closely with a statement by Bishop Matthew Simpson that Evans joined the Methodist church in 1843. See Matthew Simpson (ed.), *Cyclopedia of Methodism; Embracing Sketches of Its Rise, Progress, and Present Condition, with Biographical Notices and Numerous Illustrations* (Philadelphia: Evarts & Stewart, 1878), p. 350. This article is very brief and reads as though Simpson composed it from memory, although he wrote to Evans on July 10, 1877, asking for a "sketch of the facts and dates in your life" for use in this work.

57. Weeks, *Southern Quakers and Slavery*, pp. 293-94.

58. Herbert L. Heller, *Indiana Conference of the Methodist Church, 1832-1956* (Greencastle, Ind.: Historical Society of the Indiana Conference, 1956), p. 80.

59. Carl F. White, "Lengthened Shadow of a Man," *The Indiana Freemason*, XXIV (May, 1947), 14, 30. See also "The Mountain and the Man; A Tribute to Our First Worshipful Master," *The Booster of Marion Lodge No. 35, F. & A. M.*, XXIII (May-June, 1947), 4.

60. See the correspondence with his father in the David Evans Papers.

Politics in the Amen Corner

1. Evans himself said: "When I settled in Attica, Indiana, practicing medicine, I commenced publishing articles in relation to founding institutions for taking care of the insane, who were then kept in poor houses and jails throughout the state." Quoted in McMechen, *Life of Governor Evans*, p. 38.

2. In 1847 there was one insane person for every 2,786 of the population in Indiana. Indiana, Commissioners and Superintendent of the Hospital for the Insane, *Third Annual Report of the Commissioners and Superintendent of the Hospital for the Insane to the General Assembly of the State of Indiana* (Indianapolis: John D. Defrees, 1847), p. 70.

3. John Evans, "Indiana Hospital for the Insane," *The North-Western Medical and Surgical Journal*, IV (January, 1852), 371.

4. *Ibid.*, 371-72. In this article Evans erroneously referred to Ritchey as head of the Senate Committee on Education, although Ritchey did not enter the Senate until the session of 1842-43. Letter to the author from Miss Louise Wood, Reference Librarian, Indiana State Library, August 24, 1962. See also Bancroft MS, P-L329, Fol. IV, 13, where Evans mentions using similar strategy in 1843.

5. Evans, *North-Western Medical and Surgical Journal*, IV (1852), 372.

6. Whicker, *Indiana Magazine of History*, XIX (1923), 227, 229.

7. Jacob P. Dunn, *Indiana and Indianans* (Chicago: American Historical Society, 1919), II, 993.

8. Evans, *North-Western Medical and Surgical Journal*, IV (1852), 372.

9. *Ibid.*, 14.

10. Barbara Brandon, "The Care of the Insane in Indiana, 1840-1890" (unpublished Master's thesis, University of Chicago, 1938), p. 13.

11. Whicker, *Indiana Magazine of History*, XIX (1923), 227.

12. Brandon, "The Care of the Insane in Indiana, 1840-1890," pp. 14-15.

13. Dunn, *Indiana and Indianans*, p. 996; Evans, *North-Western Medical and Surgical Journal*, IV (1852), 372; Whicker, *Indiana Magazine of History*, XIX (1923), 228.

14. Dunn, *Indiana and Indianans*, p. 997.

15. *Ibid.*, 996.

16. *Ibid.*

17. Whicker, *Indiana Magazine of History*, XIX (1923), 230; Evans, *North-Western Medical and Surgical Journal*, IV (1852), 372. Evans did not mention the fact that Bigger failed for a year to act on the legislature's recommendation, so his account is a little confusing on this point. He probably omitted mentioning this on purpose, not wanting to pour salt into old wounds.

18. William Warren Sweet, *Indiana Asbury-DePauw University, 1837-1937: A Hundred Years of Higher Education in the Middle West* (New York: Abingdon Press, 1937), pp. 28-29; and Robert D. Clark, *Life of Matthew Simpson*, p. 72.

19. Clark, *Life of Matthew Simpson*, p. 105.

20. *Ibid.*, 105-06.

21. Sweet, *Indiana Asbury-DePauw University*, p. 29; and Clark, *Life of Matthew Simpson*, pp. 106-09.

22. Whicker, *Indiana Magazine of History*, XIX (1923), 228.

23. Clark, *Life of Matthew Simpson*, p. 107.

24. Quoted in *ibid.*, 109.

25. *Ibid.*, 107-09, quoting the *Indiana State Journal* [Indianapolis], July 4, 1843, and the *Indiana State Sentinel* [Indianapolis], June 27, 1843, and August 1, 1843.

26. Whicker, *Indiana Magazine of History*, XIX (1923), 229.

27. *Ibid.*, 231-32.

28. Clark, *Life of Matthew Simpson*, pp. 109-10, quoting the *Indiana State Journal* [Indianapolis], August 23, 1843.

29. Quoted in Sweet, *Indiana Asbury-DePauw University*, pp. 29-30.

30. Whicker, *Indiana Magazine of History*, XIX (1923), 232.

31. *Ibid.*, 230.

32. Evans, *North-Western Medical and Surgical Journal*, IV (1852), 372.

33. Whicker, *Indiana Magazine of History*, XIX (1923), 230.

34. James V. Z. Blaney, review of *Address on Insanity and the Establishment of a Lunatic Asylum* by John Evans, *Illinois Medical and Surgical Journal*, I (April, 1844), 30-31. The changed political

climate was apparent in the fact that the meeting took place in a Methodist church.

35. Berry R. Sulgrove, *History of Indianapolis and Marion County, Indiana* (Philadelphia: L. H. Everts & Co., 1884), p. 95; Bancroft MS, P-L329, Fol. IV, 13.

36. Bancroft MS, P-L329, Fol. IV, 13.

37. Whicker, *Indiana Magazine of History*, XIX (1923), 230.

38. Brandon, "The Care of the Insane in Indiana, 1840-1890," p. 16.

39. *Ibid.*, 17.

40. George F. Edenharter, "History and Notes of the Central Indiana Hospital for the Insane, 1832-1915," *Sixty-Seventh Annual Report of the Board of Trustees and Superintendent of the Central Indiana Hospital for Insane at Indianapolis, Indiana, for the Fiscal Year Ending September 30, 1915* (Indianapolis: Wm. B. Burford, 1915), p. 105.

41. Evans, *North-Western Medical and Surgical Journal*, IV (1852), 372.

42. Edenharter, *Sixty-Seventh Annual Report of the Board of Trustees and Superintendent of the Central Indiana Hospital for Insane*, p. 107.

43. Indiana, Commissioners of the Lunatic Asylum, *Report of the Commissioners of the Lunatic Asylum to the General Assembly*, Document No. 16 in *Documents of the General Assembly of Indiana* (Indianapolis: J. P. Chapman, 1845), Part II, 175.

44. *Ibid.*, 176.

45. In his 1852 article Evans mentions the trip, and, since he was describing his own part in the building of the hospital, it seems safe to assume that he would also have mentioned that he was not reimbursed, if this were the case. Evans, *North-Western Medical and Surgical Journal*, IV (1852), 372.

46. John Evans, *Report on the Subject of Hospitals for the Insane, Made to the Commissioners of the Lunatic Asylum of Indiana, June 22, 1845*, Document No. 17 in *Documents of the General Assembly of Indiana* (Indianapolis: J. P. Chapman, 1845), Part II, 185.

47. For a discussion of the miasmatic theories see Iago Galdston, *Progress in Medicine: A Critical Review of the Last Hundred Years* (New York: Alfred A. Knopf, 1940), pp. 14-30.

48. Evans, *Report on the Subject of Hospitals for the Insane*, p. 186.

49. *Ibid.*, 187.

50. *Ibid.*

51. *Ibid.*, 188.

52. *Ibid.*, 189.

53. *Ibid.*, 192.

54. *Ibid.*, 188-89.

55. Indiana, Commissioners of the Lunatic Asylum, *Report, 1845,* p. 176; Sulgrove, *History of Indianapolis,* p. 123; and Whicker, *Indiana Magazine of History,* XIX (1923), 235. Bolton was the first newspaper editor in Indianapolis, having operated for a time the *Indiana Democrat.* By this date he had given up the paper and, together with his wife, the noted Indiana poetess Sarah T. Bolton, operated the farm and converted the farmhouse into the popular Mount Jackson Tavern. See Harris Elwood Starr, "Sarah Tittle Barrett Bolton," *Dictionary of American Biography* (New York: Charles Scribner's Sons, 1929), II, 424.

56. Indiana, Commissioners of the Lunatic Asylum, *Report, 1845,* pp. 176, 180.

57. *Ibid.*, 177.

58. *Ibid.*, 179-80.

59. *Ibid.*, 56; Evans, *North-Western Medical and Surgical Journal,* IV (1852), 372.

60. Indiana, Commissioners of the Hospital for the Insane, *Second Annual Report of the Commission and Superintendent of the Hospital for the Insane, to the General Assembly, of the State of Indiana, October 31, 1846,* Document No. 5 in *Documents of the General Assembly of Indiana* (Indianapolis: J. P. Chapman, 1846), Part II, 55-56.

61. Letter from John Evans to John McLean, February 14, 1846, John Evans Collection.

62. Letter from F. D. DuSouchet to William G. Evans, March 26, 1917, *ibid.*

63. Letter from John Evans to John McLean, February 14, 1846, *ibid.*

64. Bancroft MS, P-L329, Fol. I, 5.

65. Indiana, Commissioners of the Hospital for the Insane, *Second Annual Report,* p. 55.

66. Bancroft MS, P-L329, Fol. I, 5.

67. Indiana, Commissioners of the Hospital for the Insane, *Second Annual Report,* pp. 57-62.

68. Indiana, Commissioners of the Hospital for the Insane, *Third Annual Report,* pp. 60-71; Whicker, *Indiana Magazine of History,* XIX (1923), 235.

69. Indiana, Commissioners of the Hospital for the Insane, *Third Annual Report*, p. 61. The board, in any case, had already proposed to reduce Evans' salary, if an architect were employed. See Indiana, Commissioners of the Hospital for the Insane, *Second Annual Report*, p. 57.

70. *Ibid.* The adjustment was evidently not made, at least in the case of Evans. He received only $450 for his services from October 31, 1847, to July 31, 1848, which would indicate that he was still being paid at the rate of $600 per year. See Indiana, Commissioners of the Hospital for the Insane, *Fourth Annual Report of the Commissioners and Superintendent of the Hospital for the Insane to the General Assembly of the State of Indiana*, Document No. 1 in *Documents of the Indiana General Assembly* (Indianapolis: John D. Defrees, 1848), Part II, 16.

71. Evans, *North-Western Medical and Surgical Journal*, IV (1852), 372-73.

72. Indiana, Commissioners of the Hospital for the Insane, *Third Annual Report*, pp. 7-9. Dr. Nutt had been a student of Evans at Rush, had worked for him at the Insane Hospital in the summer of 1847, and had just graduated from Rush Medical College in the spring of 1848. Indiana, Commissioners of the Hospital for the Insane, *Third Annual Report*, p. 77; John Evans, review of *Fourth Annual Report of the Commissioners and Superintendent of the Hospital for the Insane to the General Assembly of the State of Indiana*, appearing in *The North-Western Medical and Surgical Journal*, I (February and March, 1849), 502.

73. Blaney, *Illinois Medical and Surgical Journal*, I (1844), 30-31.

74. Evans, *North-Western Medical and Surgical Journal*, IV (1852), 372; James V. Z. Blaney, *Illinois Medical and Surgical Journal*, II (April, 1845), 10.

75. John Evans, "Observations on Insanity and Its Treatment in Private Practice," *Illinois and Indiana Medical and Surgical Journal*, I (October, 1846), 315-19.

76. Bancroft MS, P-L329, Fol. IV, 13.

77. Dunn, *Indiana and Indianans*, II, 1001.

"The Great Institution of the Northwest"

1. *Dedicatory Exercises of the New Building of Rush Medical College, Introductory Lecture to the Thirty-Fourth Annual Session, October 4, 1876. With an Appendix, Containing a Historical Sketch of the College; Proceedings at the Laying of the Cornerstone, Nov. 20th, 1875, Etc., Etc., Etc.* (Chicago: C. H. Blakely & Co., 1876), p. 31. See also James Nevins Hyde, *Early Medical Chicago: An Historical Sketch of the First Practitioners of Medicine, with the Present Faculties, and Graduates since Their Organization, of the Medical Colleges of Chicago* (Chicago: Fergus Printing Co., 1879), p. 32; and Bessie Louise Pierce, *The Beginning of a City, 1673-1848*, Vol. I of *A History of Chicago* (2 vols.; New York: Alfred A. Knopf, 1937), 192, 284.

2. Norwood, *Medical Education in the United States before the Civil War*, pp. 58, 340.

3. Letter from John Evans to John McLean, June 21, 1847, John Evans Collection; Thomas Neville Bonner, *Medicine in Chicago, 1850-1950: A Chapter in the Social and Scientific Development of a City* (Madison, Wis.: American History Research Center, Inc., 1957), p. 50.

4. *Dedicatory Exercises of the New Building of Rush Medical College*, p. 31.

5. Letter from John Evans to John McLean, February 14, 1846, John Evans Collection. The arrangement for lecturing only once a day was intended to go into effect in the 1846-47 session.

6. Letter from John Evans to John McLean, June 21, 1847, *ibid.*

7. *Dedicatory Exercises of the New Building of Rush Medical College*, p. 3; Norwood, *Medical Education in the United States before the Civil War*, p. 341.

8. *Dedicatory Exercises of the New Building of Rush Medical College*, pp. 31-33.

9. Letter from John Evans to John McLean, February 14, 1846,

John Evans Collection; J. Wesley Whicker, *Historical Sketches of the Wabash Valley* (Attica, Ind.: n.n., 1916), p. 151.

10. Letter from John Evans to John McLean, February 14, 1846, John Evans Collection.

11. Blaney, *Illinois Medical and Surgical Journal*, I (1844), 30-31.

12. John Evans, "Treatment of the Fracture of the Clavicle," *Illinois Medical and Surgical Journal*, I (December, 1844), 133-34.

13. John Evans, "Two Cases [of] Uterine Hydatids," *Illinois Medical and Surgical Journal*, II (May, 1845), 17-20.

14. Letter from John Evans to Margaret Evans, November 21, 1837, John Evans Collection.

15. Pierce, *History of Chicago*, I, 44.

16. Letter from John Evans to John McLean, February 14, 1846, John Evans Collection.

17. *Ibid.*

18. *Ibid.*

19. Bonner, *Medicine in Chicago*, p. 49.

20. Letter from John Evans to John McLean, February 14, 1846, John Evans Collection. Evans spoke of this as "a proposal to publish . . . a journal." It is not certain that this meant Knapp wanted Evans to participate; still, Evans' statement in his letter to McLean was phrased so that it could be interpreted to mean that he had received a firm offer from Knapp, and Brainard evidently got the message.

21. Bonner, *Medicine in Chicago*, pp. 50-51. See also the letters from John Evans to John McLean, February 14, 1846; February 7, 1847; March 9, 1847; June 21, 1847, and July 11, 1849, John Evans Collection. See also John Evans, "Rush Medical College," *The North-Western Medical and Surgical Journal*, I (February and March, 1849), 548.

22. The lot for the original building was donated by an interested citizen. The building was financed partly by loan, partly by public subscription, and the remainder by faculty contributions. *Dedicatory Exercises of the New Building of Rush Medical College*, pp. 31-33. See also Bonner, *Medicine in Chicago*, p. 50.

23. See the letters from John Evans to John McLean, dated February 14, 1846; February 7, 1847; March 9, 1847; June 21, 1847, John Evans Collection.

24. Pierce, *History of Chicago*, I, 284.

25. Bonner, *Medicine in Chicago*, p. 51.

26. John Evans, "American Medical Association," *The North-Western Medical and Surgical Journal*, II (July, 1849), 173.

27. John Evans, "The Concours," *The North-Western Medical and Surgical Journal*, II (January, 1850), 458.

28. Evans, *The North-Western Medical and Surgical Journal*, II (1849), 173.

29. W. B. Herrick, "Appointment of Demonstrator of Anatomy in Rush Medical College," *The North-Western Medical and Surgical Journal*, II (January, 1850), 457-58.

30. *Dedicatory Exercises of the New Building of Rush Medical College*, pp. 33-34.

31. Evans, *The North-Western Medical and Surgical Journal*, II (1849), 165-66.

32. Letter from John Evans to John McLean, June 16, 1849, John Evans Collection; Isaac Newton Danforth, *Life of Nathan Smith Davis, A.M., M.D., LL.D., 1817-1904* (Chicago: Cleveland Press, 1907), p. 25; "Rush Medical College," *The North-Western Medical and Surgical Journal*, II (July, 1849), 176; William Allen Pusey, "High Lights in the History of Chicago Medicine," *Bulletin of the Society of Medical History of Chicago*, V (May, 1940), 172.

33. Bonner, *Medicine in Chicago*, p. 52.

34. "Free Medical Schools," *The North-Western Medical and Surgical Journal*, II (November, 1849), 365. Evans was co-editor of the journal at this time, and it is possible that he was the author of this article.

35. *Ibid.*, 367-68.

36. John Evans, "Free Medical Schools," *The North-Western Medical and Surgical Journal*, III (September, 1850), 259.

37. Norwood, *Medical Education in the United States*, p. 342; see also the Rush College advertisement on the back cover of *The North-Western Medical and Surgical Journal*, IV (July, 1851). The reduced rate was still in effect in 1851. See the letter from John Evans to David Evans, March 19, 1851, David Evans Papers.

38. James V. Z. Blaney, "Dr. Drake and the Rush Medical College," *Illinois Medical and Surgical Journal*, I (December, 1844), 135; letter from John Evans to John McLean, July 11, 1849, John Evans Collection; *The North-Western Medical and Surgical Journal*, IV (July, 1851), back cover.

39. Letter from John Evans to David Evans, March 19, 1851, David Evans Papers.

40. Bonner, *Medicine in Chicago*, p. 241.

41. Hyde, *Early Medical Chicago*, p. 47; Bonner, *Medicine in Chicago*, p. 51.

42. Letter from John Evans to John McLean, February 7, 1847, John Evans Collection; Bonner, *Medicine in Chicago*, p. 55.

43. A dispensary was already in existence and furnished clinical facilities for the college. See the letters from John Evans to John McLean, dated February 7, 1847, and March 9, 1847, John Evans Collection. See also Hyde, *Early Medical Chicago*, p. 42, and Constance Bell Webb, *A History of Contagious Disease Care in Chicago Before the Great Fire* (Chicago: University of Chicago Press, 1940), p. 40. A rough board structure was constructed on the edge of town in 1843, mainly for cholera patients, but it burned in 1845 (*ibid.*, 40, 59).

44. Bonner, *Medicine in Chicago*, p. 148. It it not known just when this first general hospital closed, but there was no hospital in operation in Chicago when Davis arrived in 1849. See Nathan Smith Davis III, "Nathan Smith Davis, M.D., A.M., LL.D.," *A History of the American Medical Association, 1847 to 1947*, ed. Morris Fishbein (Philadelphia: W. B. Saunders Co., 1947), pp. 8-9. Tippecanoe Hall was empty in the fall of 1850 and was being considered as the site for a new hospital. See John Evans, "Illinois General Hospital of the Lake," *The North-Western Medical and Surgical Journal*, III (September, 1850), 263; Webb, *Contagious Disease Care*, pp. 51-53.

45. Hyde, *Early Medical Chicago*, p. 44.

46. A. T. Andreas, *History of Chicago from the Earliest Period to the Present Time*, Vol. I: *Ending with the Year 1857* (3 vols.; Chicago: A. T. Andreas Co., 1884), p. 597; Hyde, *Early Medical Chicago*, p. 45.

47. *Ibid.*

48. Evans, *North-Western Medical and Surgical Journal*, III (September, 1850), 263.

49. Andreas, *History of Chicago*, I, 598.

50. "Illinois General Hospital," *The North-Western Medical and Surgical Journal*, III (March, 1851), 493; Andreas, *History of Chicago*, I, 597-98.

51. Robert M. Sweitzer, *The Sisters of Mercy and Chicago* (Chicago: Sisters of Mercy, 1921), pp. 12-13; and "Illinois General Hospital," *The North-Western Medical and Surgical Journal*, III (1851), 492-93.

52. "Illinois General Hospital," *The North-Western Medical and Surgical Journal*, III (1851), 493. At this time students at Rush were paying $2.00 to $2.25 per week for board. *The North-Western Medical and Surgical Journal*, IV (July, 1851), back cover.

53. Evans, *The North-Western Medical and Surgical Journal*, III (1850), 263; Sweitzer, *Sisters of Mercy*, p. 12.

54. Sweitzer, *Sisters of Mercy*, p. 12; Davis, "Nathan Smith Davis," *History of the American Medical Association*, pp. 8-9; Bonner, *Medicine in Chicago*, p. 148.

55. McMechen, *Life of Governor Evans*, p. 47.

56. Webb, *Contagious Disease Care in Chicago*, p. 51.

57. "Chicago Medical Society," *The North-Western Medical and Surgical Journal*, III (May, 1850), 88. A stillborn attempt by Dr. Levi D. Boone to organize such a group in 1836 is sometimes listed as the first medical society in the city. See Hyde, *Early Medical Chicago*, p. 54, and Bonner, *Medicine in Chicago*, p. 72. Evans was already a member of the Indianapolis Medical Society, which he helped to organize in February, 1848. Dunn, *Indiana and Indianans*, II, 805.

58. Bonner, *Medicine in Chicago*, p. 73.

59. Andreas, *History of Chicago*, I, 466.

60. *Ibid.* The name was again changed in 1858, and the organization has been known as the Chicago Medical Society ever since that date. See Bonner, *Medicine in Chicago*, p. 73.

61. John Evans, "American Medical Association," *The North-Western Medical and Surgical Journal*, III (July, 1850), 172.

62. John Evans, "The Obstetrical Extractor—A Paper Read before the Chicago Medical Society," *The North-Western Medical and Surgical Journal*, III (May, 1850), 55. Evans apparently did not specialize in obstetrics until he came to Rush and began to lecture on the subject.

63. *Ibid.*, 56-58.

64. *Ibid.*, 54, 58.

65. John Evans, "Observations on the Use of the Obstetrical Extractor," *The North-Western Medical and Surgical Journal*, IV (May, 1851), 45-46.

66. Letter from John Evans to Margaret Evans, July 13, 1855, John Evans Collection.

67. John Evans, *Observations on the Spread of Asiatic Cholera, and Its Communicable Nature*, (Chicago: n.n., 1849), reprinted from *The North-Western Medical and Surgical Journal*, II (September, 1849), 246-85.

68. Bonner, *Medicine in Chicago*, p. 207; and Nathan Smith Davis, "The Cholera, and the Influences Which Favor or Retard Its Spread or Diffusion," *The North-Western Medical and Surgical Journal*, II (September, 1849), 482.

69. Evans, *Observations on the Spread of Asiatic Cholera*, p. 38.

70. *Ibid.*, 42.

71. U.S. Congress, Senate, *Memorial of Doctor John Evans, Praying the Establishment of a System of Quarantine for the Prevention of the Spread of Cholera*, 39th Cong., 1st Sess., 1866, Misc. Doc. No. 66.

72. U.S., *Congressional Globe*, 39th Cong., 1st Sess., 1866, Part III, 2120, 2581-89, 2795, 2807, and Appendix, 428. For an example of opposition arguments see U.S. Congress, Senate, *Memorial of Edwin Snow, M.D.*, 39th Cong., 1st Sess., 1866, Misc. Doc. No. 85.

73. Morris C. Leikind, "Quarantine in the United States," *Ciba Symposium*, II (September, 1940), 582.

74. Andreas, *History of Chicago*, I, 384.

75. *Illinois and Indiana Medical and Surgical Journal*, I (April, 1846), front cover; letter from John Evans to John McLean, February 14, 1846, John Evans Collection.

76. Letter from John Evans to John McLean, February 7, 1847, *ibid.*

77. By February, 1849, there were 1,050 subscribers and the editors decided to publish 200 additional copies for another subscription drive. See "To Our Patrons," *The North-Western Medical and Surgical Journal*, I (February and March, 1849), 535.

78. *The North-Western Medical and Surgical Journal*, III (May, 1850), front cover.

79. Letter from John Evans to David Evans, March 3, 1851, David Evans Papers.

80. John Evans, "Notice to Subscribers—Extension of Time," *The North-Western Medical and Surgical Journal*, IV (March, 1852), 471.

81. John Evans, "Notice to Subscribers: New Arrangement," *The North-Western Medical and Surgical Journal*, IV (January, 1852), 381. Evans had made this same offer to delinquent subscribers two years earlier. See "To Subscribers," *The North-Western Medical and Surgical Journal*, II (March, 1850), 548.

82. *The North-Western Medical and Surgical Journal*, II (April and May, 1849), 90.

83. Letter from John Evans to David Evans, March 17, 1851, David Evans Papers.

84. Andreas, *History of Chicago*, I, 384.

85. Bancroft MS, P-L329, Fol. IV, 14.

86. *Ibid.*

87. Personal letter from Ruth Cibulka Gilbert, reference librarian,

Chicago Historical Society, July 27, 1961. Mrs. Gilbert's letter contains a listing of the business and home addresses of John Evans for the period 1849-1868, collated from the Chicago directories of that period.

88. Indiana, Commissioners of the Hospital for the Insane, *Third Annual Report*, p. 77; Evans, *North-Western Medical and Surgical Journal*, I (1849), 502; Hyde, *Early Medical Chicago*, p. 57.

89. Bancroft MS, P-L329, Fol. IV, 11; personal letters from Ruth Cibulka Gilbert, reference librarian, Chicago Historical Society, July 27, 1961, and October 13, 1961; Rush Medical College, Sophomore Class, *The Pulse: Rush Medical College* (Chicago: Rogers & Wells, 1895), II, 257.

90. See, for example, the unsigned editorials in *The North-Western Medical and Surgical Journal*, I (April and May, 1848), 86-88; II (September, 1849), 230.

91. *The North-Western Medical and Surgical Journal*, IV (March, 1852), 465.

"A Stranger in a Strange Land"

1. Bancroft MS, P-L329, Fol. I, 5.

2. McClung, *The Colorado Genealogist*, XV (1954), 68. The three children are buried in a family plot in the Attica cemetery. The exact dates of birth are not known. McClung lists 1839 as the year of Joseph's birth, 1841 for David, and 1846 for John. The accuracy of at least the first two dates is supported by Evans' reference to his "dear little children" in a letter written in the spring of 1842. See his letter to Hannah Canby Evans, April 29, 1842, John Evans Collection. The date of Josephine's birth is given as September 30, 1844, in Helen Cannon's "First Ladies of Colorado: Josephine Evans Elbert," *The Colorado Magazine*, XXXIX (October, 1962), 264.

3. Letters from John Evans to David Evans, October 14, 1850; January 15, 1851, David Evans Papers.

4. According to Evans, "the city was . . . in the mud." See his statement in Bancroft MS, P-L329, Fol. IV, 3. See also D. W. Yungmeyer, "John Evans: Chicago's Forgotten Railroad Pioneer" (paper read at the Centennial Observance of Northwestern University, Evanston, Illinois, February 21, 1951), pp. 2-3.

5. "Chicago in 1856," *Putnam's Monthly Magazine*, VII (June, 1856), 606-13, quoted in Bessie Louise Pierce and Joe L. Norris (eds.), *As Others See Chicago; Impressions of Visitors, 1673-1933* (Chicago: University of Illinois Press, 1933), p. 157.

6. Letter from John Evans to David Evans, October 14, 1850, David Evans Papers.

7. Letters from John Evans to John McLean, June 16, 1849; July 11, 1849, John Evans Collection.

8. Letter from John Evans to David Evans, October 14, 1850, David Evans Papers.

9. Bancroft MS, P-L329, Fol. IV, 14.

10. McMechen, *Life of Governor Evans*, pp. 75-76; Bancroft MS, P-L329, Fol. II, 2-3; Yungmeyer, "John Evans: Chicago's Forgotten

Railroad Pioneer," p. 4; *The Chicago Tribune*, July 4, 1897; Walter Dill Scott, *John Evans, 1814-1897: An Appreciation* (Evanston, Illinois: Lester J. Norris, 1939), p. 25.

11. McMechen, *Life of Governor Evans*, p. 76; Scott, *John Evans*, p. 25.

12. Letter from John Evans to David Evans, October 14, 1850, David Evans Papers; personal letter from Ruth Cibulka Gilbert, reference librarian, Chicago Historical Society, July 27, 1961.

13. Letter from John Evans to David Evans, January 15, 1851, David Evans Papers.

14. In March, 1851, Evans estimated his income from teaching at $500 and from the journal at $1,000; he said that his income for the year should total $2,000 after all living expenses were deducted. See his letter to David Evans, March 17, 1851, David Evans Papers.

15. Letter from John Evans to David Evans, October 14, 1850, *ibid.*

16. *Ibid.*

17. *Ibid.*

18. Whicker, *Indiana Magazine of History*, XIX (1923), 237; there is a photograph of the gravestone in the Evan E. Evans Scrapbook, John Evans Collection.

19. Letter from John Evans to David Evans, January 15, 1851, David Evans Papers.

20. *Ibid.*

21. *Ibid.*

22. Letters from John Evans to David Evans, January 15, 1851, and March 17, 1851, *ibid.*

23. Letter from John Evans to David Evans, January 15, 1851, *ibid.*

24. *Ibid.*

25. *Ibid.*

26. Bancroft MS, P-L329, Fol. IV, 4, 14; in this interview he stated that the land was purchased in 1847, which is the date referred to in his letter to David Evans, January 15, 1850, David Evans Papers.

27. Letter from John Evans to Margaret Evans, June 8, 1855, John Evans Collection; letter from Hy Brookes to John Evans, June 6, 1863, *ibid.*

28. Bancroft MS, P-L329, Fol. IV, 11; letters from Ruth Cibulka Gilbert, July 27, 1961, and October 13, 1961. Mrs. Gilbert's letters include business and residential addresses for Evans and Nutt during the period of their residence in Chicago. See also the letter

from David Evans to Alfred Vail, January 16, 1852, David Evans Papers.

29. Letters from John Evans to David Evans, March 3, 1851; August 11, 1853; and August 19, 1853, David Evans Papers; personal letters from Ruth Cibulka Gilbert, July 27, 1961, and October 13, 1961; and letters from John Evans to Margaret Gray, August 6, 1853, and August 12, 1853, John Evans Collection.

30. Letter from John Evans to David Evans, March 3, 1851, David Evans Papers.

31. Letter from John Evans to David Evans, January 15, 1851, *ibid.*

32. *Ibid.*

33. Letter from John Evans to David Evans, August 11, 1853, *ibid.*

34. Letter from David Evans to John Evans, August 11, 1853, *ibid.* Cincinnati College had been absorbed by the Medical College of Ohio in 1846; the Medical College of Ohio became the Medical Department of the University of Cincinnati in 1896. Mohr, *American Medical Directory*, pp. 67-68.

35. Letter from John Evans to David Evans, August 19, 1853, David Evans Papers.

36. Letter from David Evans to John Evans, August 11, 1853, *ibid.*

37. The will is filed in the records of the Probate Court of Warren County, Ohio.

38. Letter from David Evans to John Evans, April 19, 1853, David Evans Papers. W. P. Sugars, *Tales of a Forgotten Village* (Ypsilanti: University Lithoprinters, Inc., 1953), pp. 91-94.

39. Letter from Hannah Evans Conover to David Evans, November 15, 1853; see also the letter from James F. Conover to Mr. and Mrs. David Evans, October 3, 1853, David Evans Papers.

40. Bancroft MS, P-L329, Fol. IV, 11; *Detroit Evening News*, April 21, 1902, p. 5.

41. Bancroft MS, Fol. II, 3; Fol. IV, 4, 11.

42. Letter from John Evans to David Evans, October 19, 1855, David Evans Papers.

43. Whicker, *Historical Sketches of the Wabash Valley*, p. 151.

44. Pierce, *History of Chicago*, I, 76.

45. *Ibid.*, 127.

46. Bancroft MS, P-L329, Fol. I, 5; letter from John Evans to David Evans, October 19, 1855, David Evans Papers.

47. In *The North-Western Medical and Surgical Journal*, IV (May, 1851), 40, Evans lists the population of Chicago as follows: 7,580 in 1843; 10,170 in 1844; 12,088 in 1845; 14,169 in 1846; 16,859 in

1847; 19,724 in 1848; 23,047 in 1849; 28,620 in 1850. In her *History of Chicago*, I, 44, Bessie Louise Pierce gave substantially the same figures (with three exceptions) and said they were based on "the best available statistics."

48. Letter from John Evans to David Evans, October 19, 1855, David Evans Papers.

49. Letters from John Evans to David Evans, January 15, 1851; March 17, 1851; and October 19, 1855, *ibid.*

50. Bancroft MS, P-L329, Fol. II, 3. Frank Cyril James in his two-volume work on *The Growth of Chicago Banks* (New York: Harper & Bros., 1938) fails to indicate what part Evans played in the development of Chicago banking. He does state that in 1849 Swift "appears to have been closely associated with the domestic exchange market" (*ibid.*, I, 199-200). R. K. Swift and Company was one of "some twenty-five banking houses" in Chicago in the 1850's, and according to James, the firm was "as important as the incorporated banks had ever been." The firm closed its doors September 29, 1857 (*ibid.*, 255-68).

51. Bancroft MS, P-L329, Fol. II, 3; and letter from John Evans to David Evans, February, 1856, David Evans Papers. The exact date is not listed on the letter.

52. Letter from John Evans to David Evans, March 17, 1851, *ibid.*

53. Bancroft MS, P-L329, p. 4.

54. McMechen, *Life of Governor Evans*, p. 77; Bancroft MS, P-L329, Fol. II, 4. See also "John Evans," *The National Cyclopedia of American Biography*, VI, 446. This article, based on a question-naire completed by Evans, states that "for many years" Evans "acted as its [the railroad's] managing director in Chicago."

55. Yungmeyer, "John Evans: Chicago's Forgotten Railroad Pioneer," p. 8.

56. Bancroft MS, P-L23, p. 4.

57. Letter from John Evans to David Evans, August 11, 1853, David Evans Papers.

58. Bancroft MS, P-L329, Fol. II, 4.

59. *Ibid.*

60. James Franklin Doughty Lanier, *Sketch of the Life of J. F. D. Lanier* (second edition; n. p.: J. F. D. Lanier, 1877), pp. 21, 26-27.

61. *Ibid.*, 27; Bancroft MS, P-L329, Fol. I, 6.

62. Yungmeyer, "John Evans: Chicago's Forgotten Railroad Pioneer," p. 6.

63. Lanier, *Life of J. F. D. Lanier*, p. 26.

64. *Ibid.*, 27-30; Yungmeyer, "John Evans: Chicago's Forgotten Railroad Pioneer," p. 6.

65. Lanier, *Life of J. F. D. Lanier*, p. 32.

66. Bancroft MS, P-L329, Fol. II, 4; the sale was not effective until May 1, 1862 (Lanier, *Life of J. F. D. Lanier*, p. 30), by which time Evans was about to leave for Colorado. Evans was still a director in early 1862 (Pierce, *History of Chicago*, II, 480) but dropped out when the road was reorganized.

67. Bancroft MS, P-L329, Fol. I, 6.

68. *Ibid.*, Fol. IV, 4; letter from John Evans to Margaret Evans, June 8, 1855, John Evans Collection.

69. Letter from John Evans to Margaret Evans, June 8, 1855, John Evans Collection.

70. Bancroft MS, P-L329, Fol. II, 2.

71. McMechen, *Life of Governor Evans*, p. 71.

72. Bancroft MS, P-L329, Fol. II, 2; *Daily Democratic Press* [Chicago], March 9, 1855, p. 2. A committee had been appointed by the Board of School Inspectors of Chicago on November 27, 1852, "to enquire into the expediency of recommending to the city council a plan for the establishment of one high school for the city." See John Wesley Bell, *The Development of the Public High School in Chicago* (Chicago: University of Chicago Libraries, 1939), p. 2.

73. Bell, *The Development of the Public High School in Chicago*, p. 4.

74. *Daily Democratic Press* [Chicago], January 9, 1855, p. 3.

75. *Ibid.*, March 9, 1855, p. 2.

76. Bancroft MS, P-L329, Fol. II, 1; P-L23, p. 2.

77. *Ibid.; Daily Democratic Press* [Chicago], March 9, 1855, p. 2.

78. Bancroft MS, P-L329, Fol. II, 1; *Daily Democratic Press* [Chicago], January 2, 1854, p. 2, and March 9, 1855, p. 2.

79. In a personal interview, July 26, 1961, John Evans II said that the titles to these gifts of land usually contained a reversion clause providing for their return to Evans if the land were used for other than school purposes. Several years ago the Chicago Public Schools wanted to use such a plot for other purposes and asked for a quit-claim deed. The Evans heirs decided instead to assign their claim on the property to Northwestern University, which eventually realized about $30,000 on the transaction.

80. *Daily Democratic Press* [Chicago], March 9, 1855, p. 2.

81. *Ibid.*

82. Bancroft MS, P-L329, Fol. II, 2-3.

83. *Ibid.*, 3.

84. Yungmeyer, "John Evans: Chicago's Forgotten Railroad Pioneer," p. 3.

85. Letter from John Evans to Margaret Gray, August 6, 1853, John Evans Collection.

86. Bancroft MS, P-L329, Fol. II, 3.

87. *Daily Democratic Press* [Chicago], January 16, 1855, p. 3; February 10, 1855, p. 2; February 13, 1855, p. 3.

88. *Ibid.*, January 13, 1855, p. 3; March 6, 1855, p. 3.

89. Bonner, *Medicine in Chicago*, pp. 180-81.

90. *Ibid.*, 8.

91. *Daily Democratic Press* [Chicago], March 12, 1855, p. 3.

"A Friend to Education"

1. Bancroft MS, P-L329, Fol. I, 6.

2. Northwestern University, Minutes of the Board of Trustees, May 31, 1850, I, 1. A typed copy of volumes I through VII of these minutes is on microfilm in the John Evans Collection. See also Harvey B. Hurd and Robert D. Sheppard (eds.), *History of Northwestern University and Evanston* (Chicago: Munsell Publ. Co., 1906), pp. 53-54; James Alton James, "Northwestern University and the Christian Ideals of Its Founders," *The Methodist Movement in Northern Illinois*, ed. Almer M. Pennewell (Sycamore, Ill.: Sycamore Tribune, 1942), p. 132; Estelle Frances Ward, *The Story of Northwestern University* (New York: Dodd, Mead & Co., 1924), p. 7.

3. Northwestern University, Minutes of the Board of Trustees, June 14, 1850, I, 3-4.

4. Ward, *The Story of Northwestern University*, pp. 9-11; Hurd and Sheppard (eds.), *History of Northwestern*, p. 54.

5. See the copy of the letter to the Michigan Annual Conference, September 30, 1850, in Northwestern University, Minutes of the Board of Trustees, I. See also Bancroft MS, P-L329, Fol. I, 8.

6. Hurd and Sheppard (eds.), *History of Northwestern*, p. 57.

7. Burt E. Powell, *Semi-Centennial History of the University of Illinois*, Vol. I. *The Movement for Industrial Education and the Establishment of the University, 1840-70* (Urbana, Ill.: University of Illinois, 1918), pp. 12-16. Turner had already introduced this plan at a county teachers' convention at Griggsville in May, 1850. See Robert Francis Seybolt, "Jonathan Baldwin Turner," *Dictionary of American Biography* (Centenary edition; New York: Charles Scribner's Sons, 1946), XIX, 68.

8. Powell, *History of the University of Illinois*, I, 20.

9. *Illinois Daily Journal* [Springfield], June 14, 1852, p. 2.

10. Powell, *History of the University of Illinois*, I, 25.

11. *Ibid.*, 25-31.

12. *Ibid.*, 33.

13. Bonner, *Medicine in Chicago*, pp. 180-81. Evans joined the Rush faculty in 1845 and remained there eleven years. Bancroft MS, P-L329, Fol. IV, 14; in addition, he was a member of the board of trustees at Rush and may have served in this capacity in 1852. *The Press and Tribune* [Chicago], February 16, 1860, p. 1.

14. *Illinois Daily Journal* [Springfield], June 9, 1852, p. 2.

15. *Ibid.*, June 10, 1852, p. 2.

16. *Ibid.*

17. *Ibid.*, June 11, 1852, p. 2.

18. *Ibid.*, June 17, 1852, p. 2.

19. *Ibid.*

20. *Ibid.*

21. *Ibid.*, June 11, 1852, p. 2; Powell, *History of the University of Illinois*, I, 33.

22. *Illinois Daily Journal* [Springfield], June 11, 1852, p. 2.

23. *Ibid.*

24. As opposed to Turner's "*Progressive* system."

25. *Illinois Daily Journal* [Springfield], June 14, 1852, p. 2.

26. Quoted in Powell, *History of the University of Illinois*, I, 34. Turner's agitation, coupled with that of Justin Morrill of Vermont, ultimately resulted in Congressional approval of the Morrill Land Grant College Act of 1862.

27. Bancroft MS, P-L329, Fol. I, 8; Hurd and Sheppard (eds.), *History of Northwestern*, p. 57.

28. Bancroft MS, P-L329, Fol. I, 8.

29. The title was made out in Evans' name, and he signed a contract to deed it to the university after all the payments were made. *Ibid.*, 9; Hurd and Sheppard (eds.), *History of Northwestern*, p. 57. This transaction was made on September 22, 1852, and is also the date of Evans' first contribution to the university, the sum of $250. *Report of Business Manager and Treasurer of Northwestern University, Fiscal Year 1914-1915* (Evanston, Ill.: Northwestern University, 1915), pp. 90, 184; and letter from Florence Stewart, Northwestern University Archivist, December 20, 1962.

30. Clark Titus Hinman, who had been principal of Wesleyan Seminary in Albion, Michigan, suggested to the trustees that they should abandon the plan for a preparatory school in Chicago and should concentrate on building a university outside the city. His advice seemed so sound that on June 23, 1853, he was elected president of the university. He took charge of much of the planning and spent a good deal of his time in soliciting contributions. See Ward,

Story of Northwestern, pp. 19-22; Bancroft MS, P-L329, Fol. I, 9; "Clark Titus Hinman" *Appleton's Cyclopaedia of American Biography* (New York: D. Appleton & Co., 1888), III, 213.

31. *Ibid.; The Evanston Index* [Evanston, Illinois], May 31, 1873 (a typed copy of this article is on microfilm in the John Evans Collection); Hurd and Sheppard (eds.), *History of Northwestern*, p. 59.

32. J. Seymour Currey, "Evanston's Namesake—Governor John Evans," *Evanston News Index* [Evanston, Illinois], undated newspaper clipping in the John Evans Collection.

33. McClung, *The Colorado Genealogist*, XV (1954), 68. Samuel Gray was quite wealthy, and his family was one of the leading families in Bowdoinham; see Silas Adams, *The History of the Town of Bowdoinham, 1762-1912* (Fairfield, Maine: Fairfield Publ. Co., 1912), p. 89. Through his mother he traced his descent from two signers of the Mayflower Compact, Richard Warren and Francis Cooke; see Bancroft MS, P-L329, Fol. IV, 2. Through his father he traced his descent from Pardon Gray who served in the American army during the Revolutionary War; see Helen Cannon, "First Ladies of Colorado: Margaret Gray Evans," *The Colorado Magazine*, XXXIX (January, 1962), 19; McClung, *The Colorado Genealogist*, XV (1954), 66-68.

34. Bancroft MS, P-L329, Fol. IV, 2; Adams, *History of Bowdoinham*, pp. 81, 116-20.

35. Cannon, "Margaret Gray Evans," *The Colorado Magazine*, XXXIX (1962), 19.

36. *In Memoriam: Orrington Lunt* (n. p.: n.n., n. d.), p. 11.

37. Letter from Samuel and Susan Gray to John Evans, July 29, 1853, John Evans Collection.

38. Letter from John Evans to David Evans, August 1, 1853, David Evans Papers.

39. Letter from John Evans to David Evans, August 11, 1853, *ibid.*

40. Letters from John Evans to David Evans, August 11, 1853, and August 19, 1853, *ibid.*

41. Letter from John Evans to Margaret Patten Gray, July 31, 1853, John Evans Collection.

42. Letter from John Evans to Margaret Patten Gray, August 4, 1853, *ibid.*

43. Bancroft MS, P-L329, Fol. IV, 31.

44. Letter from John Evans to Margaret Patten Gray, August 10, 1853, John Evans Collection.

45. Letter from John Evans to Margaret Patten Gray, August 6, 1853, *ibid.*

46. *Ibid.*; letters from John Evans to Margaret Patten Gray, August 11 and 12, 1853, *ibid.*

47. Letters from John Evans to Margaret Patten Gray, August 11 and 12, 1853, *ibid.*

48. Letter from John Evans to Margaret Patten Gray, August 4, 1853, *ibid.*

49. Letter from John Evans to Margaret Patten Gray, August 6, 1853, *ibid.*

50. Letter from John Evans to Margaret Patten Gray, July 31, 1853, *ibid.*

51. Letter from John Evans to David Evans, August 19, 1853, *ibid.*

52. Letter from John Evans to Margaret Patten Gray, August 6, 1853, *ibid.*

53. Hurd and Sheppard (eds), *History of Northwestern*, p. 58.

54. Arthur Herbert Wilde (ed.), *Northwestern University, A History, 1855-1905* (New York: University Publ. Society, 1905), I, 128-31.

55. Hurd and Sheppard (eds.), *History of Northwestern*, p. 58, quoting the recollections of trustee Andrew J. Brown.

56. Ward, *Story of Northwestern*, p. 18.

57. Wilde (ed.), *Northwestern University*, I, 128.

58. Bancroft MS, P-L329, Fol. I, 10.

59. *Ibid.*; Hurd and Sheppard (eds.), *History of Northwestern*, p. 58.

60. Bancroft MS, P-L329, Fol. I, 10.

61. *Report of Business Manager of Northwestern, 1914-15*, pp. 90, 184.

62. Letter from John Evans to Margaret Patten Gray, August 11, 1853, John Evans Collection.

63. Ward, *Story of Northwestern*, p. 19.

64. Northwestern University, Minutes of the Board of Trustees, January 11, 1854, I, 36.

65. *Ibid.*, February 3, 1854, I, 37.

66. Willard, *Story of Evanston*, p. 2.

67. Letter from John Evans to Matthew Simpson, April, 1850, (day not specified), Matthew Simpson Papers, Library of Congress.

68. Letter from John Evans to W. H. Ballou, March 29, 1881, John Evans Collection; and Northwestern University, Minutes of the Board of Trustees, February 3, 1854, I, 37.

69. Bancroft MS, P-L329, Fol. I, 10.

70. Hurd and Sheppard (eds.), *History of Northwestern*, p. 62.

71. A. T. Andreas, *History of Cook County Illinois from the*

Earliest Period to the Present Time (Chicago: A. T. Andreas, 1884), p. 418.

72. *Daily Democratic Press* [Chicago], January 23, 1854, p. 2.

73. McMechen, *Life of Governor Evans*, p. 69. The university now considers that the certificates "may violate the rule against Perpetuities, and therefore all be void." Heirs who now attempt to use the certificates must surrender them for cancellation, and they are, in turn, credited with $250 in tuition payments. See the letter from the registrar of Northwestern University to Lillian Frisbec Johnson, June 12, 1964. A copy of the letter and a list of "Perpetual Scholarship Regulations" are in the John Evans Collection.

74. Horace G. Smith, "Garrett Biblical Institute," *The Methodist Movement in Northern Illinois*, ed. Almer M. Pennewell (Sycamore, Ill.: Sycamore Tribune, 1942), pp. 114-15.

75. *Ibid.*, 123-24; Bancroft MS, P-L329, Fol. I, 11-12.

76. This school at Concord, New Hampshire, later became the theological school of Boston University. See "John Dempster," *Appleton's Cyclopaedia of American Biography* (New York: D. Appleton & Co., 1887), II, 139; Bancroft MS, P-L329, Fol. I, 11-12.

77. Bancroft MS, P-L329, Fol. I, 12.

78. *Daily Democratic Press* [Chicago], November 14, 1854, p. 2.

79. The term "Biblical Institute" was decided upon in deference to current Methodist opposition to formal ministerial training, which, it was popularly supposed, would make the preaching formal and dull. See Smith, "Garrett Biblical Institute," *The Methodist Movement in Northern Illinois*, p. 116; Bancroft MS, P-L329, Fol. I, 12.

80. *Daily Democratic Press* [Chicago], November 14, 1854, p. 2; January 4, 1855, p. 2. It was originally planned that the university itself would dispense "Christian education . . . without money and without price," but this goal was soon abandoned as impractical. See the statement by John Evans in Bancroft MS, P-L329, Fol. I, 8.

81. Andreas, *History of Chicago*, I, 2.

82. Bancroft MS, P-L329, Fol. IV, 1, 14.

83. *Daily Democratic Press* [Chicago], July 20, 1857, p. 1; Evans was still a trustee of Rush in 1860. See *The Press and Tribune* [Chicago], February 16, 1860, p. 1.

84. Letters from John Evans to Margaret Gray Evans, June 30, 1855; July 6, 1855; July 13, 1855, John Evans Collection.

85. Henry Bixby Hemenway, "Medical History (Regular)," in Hurd and Sheppard (eds.), *History of Northwestern*, p. 246. See also the photograph of the Evans home in the Northwestern University Archives. There is some dispute about the location of the Evans

home, which is no longer on the original site; but James Taft Hatfield, vice president of the Evanston Historical Society, confirmed the fact that the house was located on Judson Avenue facing the lake. See his letter to an unidentified person, July 1, 1942, on microfilm in the John Evans Collection. See also the letter from John Evans to Margaret Gray Evans, June 30, 1855, John Evans Collection.

86. Letters from John Evans to Margaret Gray Evans, July 6, 1855, and July 13, 1855, John Evans Collection.

87. Bancroft MS, P-L329, Fol. I, 13.

88. Cornelia Gray Lunt, *Sketches of Childhood and Girlhood; Chicago, 1847-1864* (Evanston, Ill.: Cornelia Gray Lunt, 1925), p. 72. The punctuation and syntax used in the original are followed here.

89. Quoted in Emily Huntington Miller, "Social Life in the Early Days," in Wilde (ed.), *Northwestern University*, I, 410.

90. Quoted in *ibid.*, 416.

91. Quoted in *ibid.*, 414.

92. Lunt, *Sketches of Childhood*, p. 72.

93. Interview with Helen Cannon, July 18, 1961. Miss Cannon was given the opportunity of reading the diary of Margaret Gray Evans, and these impressions are based on her interpretation of that diary. John Evans II, who now has possession of the diary, has since closed it to inspection. See the excerpts from the diary quoted in Miss Cannon's "Margaret Gray Evans," *The Colorado Magazine*, XXXIX (1962), 21.

94. Letter from John Evans to Benjamin Evans, August, 1834, John Evans Collection.

95. Jacob P. Dunn, *Greater Indianapolis: The History, the Industries, the Institutions, and the People of a City of Homes* (2 vols.; Chicago: Lewis Publ. Co., 1910), I, 452. In 1850 Evans publicly commended the Committee on Arrangements of the American Medical Association Convention in Cincinnati because "they did not furnish intoxicating drinks" at their banquet; John Evans, "American Medical Association," *The North-Western Medical and Surgical Journal*, III (July, 1850), 172. In November, 1854, Evans had introduced an ordinance to discontinue the issuing of liquor licenses in Chicago, but the move was defeated; *Daily Democratic Press* [Chicago], November 17, 1854, p. 3. His opposition to liquor was not absolute, and he often prescribed some sort of alcoholic beverage for his patients. See, for example, his letter to Margaret Gray Evans, June 8, 1855. See also his offer to drink an apple-cider toast to his cousin Benjamin Evans (letter of January 6, 1836, John Evans Collection), and his offer of toasts at the Fourth of July celebration in

Hennepin, Illinois (letter to Hannah Canby, July 25, 1838, John Evans Collection).

96. *Daily Democratic Press* [Chicago], March 13, 1855, p. 3.

97. Letters from John Evans to Margaret Gray Evans, June 6, 1855, and June 8, 1855, John Evans Collection.

98. Quoted in James Alton James, "Northwestern University and the Christian Ideals of Its Founders," *The Methodist Movement in Northern Illinois*, ed. Almer M. Pennewell (Sycamore, Ill.: Sycamore Tribune, 1942), p. 139; see also Ward, *Story of Northwestern*, p. 14.

99. Quoted in Ward, *Story of Northwestern*, pp. 14-15.

100. Bancroft MS, P-L329, Fol. I, 11; an article on Evans in *The National Cyclopedia of American Biography*, VI, 446, states that Evans and Simpson lobbied the tax-exemption bill through the legislature.

101. *The Evanston Press* [Evanston, Illinois], July 10, 1897. A typed copy of the article in question is on microfilm in the John Evans Collection.

102. *Daily Democratic Press* [Chicago], July 30, 1856, p. 1.

103. Hurd and Sheppard (eds.), *History of Northwestern*, p. 66.

104. Cook County, Illinois, Records of the Clerk of the Circuit Court and Ex-Officio Recorder, filed December 8, 1866, Deed Book 370, p. 113, copy in the John Evans Collection.

105. Northwestern University, Minutes of the Board of Trustees, November 21, 1866, I, 368. Part of this land "was sold by condemnation to the Burlington Railroad" in 1888 for $55,000. Bancroft MS, P-L329, Fol. I, 14; *Daily Rocky Mountain News* [Denver], June 20, 1889, p. 1.

106. Letter from John Evans to the Board of Trustees of Northwestern University, May 22, 1875, in Northwestern University, Minutes of the Board of Trustees, June 22, 1875, II, 330-36.

107. The debt stood at $194,702.14 in June, 1883, according to the *Evanston Index* [Evanston, Illinois], June 23, 1883, p. 2.

108. *Ibid.*, June 10, 1882, p. 2.

109. Northwestern University, Minutes of the Board of Trustees, September 23, 1883, III, 389.

110. Bancroft MS, P-L329, Fol. IV, 15; and *Report of Business Manager of Northwestern University, 1914-1915*, p. 184.

111. Letter from John Evans to Orrington Lunt, September 6, 1888, in Northwestern University, Minutes of the Board of Trustees, September 22, 1888, IV, 327-28.

112. Northwestern University, Minutes of the Board of Trustees, September 24, 1889, V, 20-22.

113. Through an error in accounting, the university has credited Evans with $181,370. This total is apparently reached by counting the $25,000 cash donation of February 7, 1884, and the $50,000 dock property as separate contributions, rather than as part of the $100,000 endowment of the two chairs. See the *Report of Business Manager of Northwestern University, 1914-1915*, pp. 100, 123, and 184. In 1889 Evans told an interviewer the details of his gifts, as listed above, and concluded: "I have given altogether what was worth a hundred thousand dollars when I gave it. . . . That is about the bulk of what I have done for the University." This was in 1889, after all the donations included in the supposed $181,370 had been made. Bancroft MS, P-L329, Fol. IV, 15. In addition to the $100,000 endowment, he also gave cash sums in the amount of $250 in 1852, $950 in 1854, $300 in 1856, $3,500 in 1857, $50 in 1859, $120 in 1860, $200 in 1870, and $1,000 in 1880; all of which add up to $106,370. See the *Report of Business Manager of Northwestern University, 1914-1915*, pp. 90-93, 97, 184. It should be noted that the university does not recognize that such an error has been made. Letter from A. T. Schmehling, Controller and Assistant Business Manager of Northwestern University, December 27, 1962.

114. Letter from Florence Stewart, Northwestern University Archivist, December 28, 1962; Wilde, *Northwestern University*, I, 133; *In Memoriam: Orrington Lunt*, p. 14; and Northwestern University, Minutes of the Board of Trustees, July 2, 1894, VII, 17, and June 11, 1895, VII, 232. See also his letter to Northwestern University President Dr. H. W. Rogers, January 16, 1892, in which Evans explains his close connection with the University of Denver.

"The Blighting Influence of Slavery"

1. *Daily Democratic Press* [Chicago], August 15, 1854, p. 1.

2. *Ibid.*

3. *Ibid.*

4. *Ibid.*, August 21, 1854, p. 1.

5. Pierce, *History of Chicago*, II, 210; Bancroft MS, P-L329, Fol. II, 6.

6. Letter from John Evans to W. B. Plato, September 4, 1854, John Evans Collection. This draft copy conforms substantially with a quotation from the letter which appeared in the *Daily Democratic Press* [Chicago], September 26, 1854, p. 2.

7. Cited in the *Daily Democratic Press* [Chicago], September 26, 1854, p. 2.

8. Letter from John Evans to W. B. Plato, September 4, 1854, John Evans Collection.

9. *Ibid.*

10. *Ibid.*

11. *Ibid.*

12. Letter to the editor from S. S. Hayes, *Daily Democratic Press* [Chicago], September 26, 1854, p. 2.

13. Philip Van Doren Stern (ed.), *The Life and Writings of Abraham Lincoln* (New York: Random House, 1940), p. 349.

14. *Ibid.*, 372.

15. It was also called the "People's Convention" (Pierce, *History of Chicago*, II, 210), and Evans spoke of it as the "Mass District Convention." See his letter to the editors in the *Daily Democratic Press* [Chicago], September 22, 1854, p. 1. The "Independent Democrat" appellation seems to have been the idea of the editors of the *Press*, and Evans apparently never referred to himself in this manner. He stated later that he was a Whig until the party disintegrated, "when I became a Republican and have been one ever since." See

Bancroft MS, P-L329, Fol. II, 6; and *Daily Democratic Press* [Chicago], August 15, 1854, p. 1; September 22, 1854, p. 1; September 26, 1854, p. 2.

16. Letter from John Evans to the editors of the *Daily Democratic Press* [Chicago], September 22, 1854, p. 1; William N. Byers, "John Evans," *Encyclopedia of Biography of Colorado; History of Colorado* (Chicago: Century Publ. & Engr. Co., 1901), pp. 440-41.

17. Bancroft MS, P-L329, Fol. II, 6.

18. *Ibid.*

19. Pierce, *History of Chicago*, II, 211, 510.

20. William B. Ogden, who was the original choice as Chicago representative, was out of the state, and Evans was appointed in his place. Paul Selby, "The Editorial Convention of 1856," *Journal of the Illinois State Historical Society*, V (October, 1912), 346; Pierce, *History of Chicago*, II, 212; *Daily Illinois State Journal* [Springfield], May 5, 1856, p. 2. Perhaps it is significant that the name of John Evans was listed first in the signed newspaper announcement issued by the committee. The other members, in order of their signing, were S. M. Church, Ed. A. Dudley, Isaac C. Pugh, I. O. Wilkinson, Thomas J. Pickett, G. D. A. Parks, W. H. Herndon, Jos. Gillespie, and L. D. Phillips. *Daily Illinois State Journal* [Springfield], May 5, 1856, p. 2.

21. *Daily Illinois State Journal* [Springfield], May 5, 1856, p. 2.

22. Stern (ed.), *Life and Writings of Abraham Lincoln*, p. 55.

23. *Daily Illinois State Journal* [Springfield], May 5, 1856, p. 2.

24. *Ibid.*, May 30, 1856, p. 2; Stern (ed.), *Life and Writings of Abraham Lincoln*, p. 55.

25. "John Dempster," *Appleton's Cyclopaedia of American Biography*, II, 139.

26. George Minot and George P. Sanger (eds.), *The Statutes at Large and Treaties of the United States of America, from December 3, 1855 to March 3, 1859, and Proclamations since 1791, Arranged in Chronological Order with References to the Matter of Each Act and to the Subsequent Acts on the Same Subject* (Boston: Little, Brown & Co., 1863), XI, 9-10.

27. John Evans, *Oreapolis, Nebraska Territory: Its Institutions, Advantages in Site, etc., etc. Plan of the Co. for Building up the Town, Inducements Offered to Emigrants to Settle There. Bonus for Manufacturers, Tradesmen, etc.* (Chicago: Press & Tribune, 1859), p. 1; Nathan Howe Parker, *The Kansas and Nebraska Handbook for 1857-8 with a New and Accurate Map* (Boston: John P. Jewett & Co., 1857), p. 157.

28. Bancroft MS, P-L329, Fol. II, 7.

29. Evans, *Oreapolis*, p. 11.

30. *Ibid.*, 2; G. H. Gilmore, "Ghost Towns in Cass County, Nebraska," *Nebraska History Magazine*, XVIII (July-September, 1937), 181; see also the map prepared by Gilmore and bound inside the back cover of the magazine. The name of the town was said to be derived from Greek terms which signified "border city." Walter Dill Scott, *John Evans, 1814-1897: An Appreciation* (Evanston, Ill.: Lester J. Norris, 1939), p. 41.

31. Bancroft MS, P-L329, Fol. II, 7; and Parker, *Kansas and Nebraska Handbook*, p. 157.

32. Gilmore, *Nebraska History Magazine*, XVIII (1937), 181.

33. A. T. Andreas, *History of the State of Nebraska; Containing a Full Account of Its Growth from an Uninhabited Territory to a Wealthy and Important State; of Its Early Settlements; Its Rapid Increase in Population, and the Marvellous Development of Its Great Natural Resources. Also an Extended Description of Its Counties, Cities, Towns and Villages, Their Advantages, Industries, Manufacturers and Commerce; Biographical Sketches, Portraits of Prominent Men and Early Settlers; Views of Residences and Business Blocks, Cities and Towns* (Chicago: Western Historical Co., 1882), p. 475; and Evans, *Oreapolis*, p. 3.

34. *Minutes of the Fourth Annual Session of the Kansas and Nebraska Conference of the Methodist E. Church Held at Omaha, Nebraska April 14-18, 1859* (Omaha: Robertson & Clark, 1859), pp. 14-16; and letter from John Evans to Margaret Evans, April 2[0], 1859, John Evans Collection.

35. *Minutes of the Kansas-Nebraska Conference, 1859*, p. 10; and letter from John Evans to Margaret Evans, April 2[0], 1859, John Evans Collection.

36. *Minutes of the Kansas-Nebraska Conference, 1859*, pp. 14-16; and letter from John Evans to Margaret Evans, April 2[0], 1859, John Evans Collection.

37. Evans, *Oreapolis*, pp. 3-4.

38. *Minutes of the Kansas-Nebraska Conference, 1859*, p. 10; and letter from John Evans to Margaret Evans, April 2[0], 1859, John Evans Collection.

39. Letter from John Evans to Margaret Evans, April 2[0], 1859, John Evans Collection.

40. Letter from John Evans to Margaret Evans, June 12, 1859, *ibid.*; Andreas, *History of Nebraska*, p. 475.

41. Letter from John Evans to Margaret Evans, June 12, 1859, John Evans Collection.

42. *Ibid.*; and letter from John Evans to Margaret Evans, October 3, 1859, *ibid.*

43. Letter from John Evans to Margaret Evans, June 12, 1859, *ibid.*

44. Clark, *Life of Matthew Simpson*, p. 209.

45. Letter from John Evans to Matthew Simpson, April, [1851], Bishop Matthew Simpson Papers, Library of Congress.

46. George R. Crooks, *The Life of Bishop Matthew Simpson of the Methodist Episcopal Church* (New York: Harper & Bros., 1890), p. 255, quoting from an autobiographical sketch of Simpson.

47. Letter from John Evans to Matthew Simpson, March 15, 1858, Bishop Matthew Simpson Papers, Library of Congress.

48. Clark, *Life of Matthew Simpson*, p. 209.

49. Letter from John Evans to Margaret Evans, June 12, 1859, John Evans Collection.

50. "Matthew Simpson," *Appleton's Cyclopaedia of American Biography* (New York: D. Appleton and Company, 1888), V, 539.

51. Evans, *Oreapolis*, title page.

52. *Ibid.*, 1.

53. *Ibid.*, 2, 3, 6.

54. *Ibid.*, 2-3; *Minutes of the Kansas and Nebraska Annual Conference of the Methodist Episcopal Church, Fifth Session, Held in Leavenworth City, K. T., March, 1860* (Leavenworth, Kan.: Herald Book & Job Office, 1860), 12.

55. *Minutes of the Kansas-Nebraska Conference, 1860*, p. 12.

56. *Ibid.*; Evans, *Oreapolis*, p. 4.

57. Evans, *Oreapolis*, pp. 3-4.

58. *Ibid.*, 4.

59. *Ibid.*, 5-8.

60. Letter from John Evans to Margaret Evans, October 3, 1859, John Evans Collection.

61. Letter from John Evans to Margaret Evans, October 9, 1859, *ibid.*

62. *Minutes of the Kansas-Nebraska Conference, 1860*, p. 12.

63. Andreas, *History of Nebraska*, p. 475.

64. *Nebraska Herald* [Plattsmouth], May 3, 1865, p. 3.

65. Gilmore, *Nebraska History Magazine*, XVIII (1937), 181.

66. *The Press and Tribune* [Chicago], February 10, 1860, p. 1.

67. *Ibid.*

68. *Ibid.*, February 10, 1860, p. 1; February 13, 1860, p. 1; Feb-

ruary 16, 1860, p. 1; February 18, 1860, p. 1; February 29, 1860, p. 1.

69. *Ibid.*, April 14, 1860, p. 1; July 13, 1860, p. 2; July 14, 1860, p. 1.

70. Letter from C. H. King to John Evans, July 26, 1862, John Evans Collection.

71. Bancroft MS, P-L329, Fol. II, 7.

72. *Daily Illinois State Journal* [Springfield], May 12, 1860, p. 2; Bancroft MS, P-L329, Fol. II, 5.

73. *Daily Illinois State Journal* [Springfield], May 11, 1860, p. 2.

74. It was John Hanks who helped split the rails. See Wayne C. Temple, "Lincoln's Fence Rails," *Journal of the Illinois State Historical Society*, XLVII (Spring, 1954), 26.

75. Bancroft MS, P-L329, Fol. II, 5. Compare this with the report of the speech in the *Daily Illinois State Journal* [Springfield], May 11, 1860, p. 2.

76. Bancroft MS, P-L329, Fol. II, 5.

77. *Ibid.*

78. Whicker, *Indiana Magazine of History*, XIX (1923), 238.

79. In 1889 Mrs. Evans stated that "he was a personal friend of Abraham Lincoln and had known him for a number of years very well." Mrs. Evans was apparently not so precise in her recollection as John, as is evidenced by her statement that "he never took an active part in politics before we came" to Colorado. Bancroft MS, P-L329, Fol. II, 1.

80. See the list of delegates and alternates in the *Daily Illinois State Journal* [Springfield], May 12, 1860, p. 2; see also *Proceedings of the First Three Republican National Conventions of 1856, 1860, and 1864. Including Proceedings of the Antecedent National Convention Held at Pittsburg, in February, 1856, as Reported by Horace Greeley* (Minneapolis: Charles W. Johnson, 1893), pp. 173-74.

81. *The Rocky Mountain News* [Denver], March 31, 1862, p. 2; Evan E. Evans, "John Evans, Second Territorial Governor of Colorado," unpublished manuscript, dated December 3, 1913, in the John Evans Collection, pages not numbered. The daily *Rocky Mountain News* will be cited hereafter as *DRMN*; the weekly will be cited as *WRMN*.

82. *Proceedings of the First Three Republican National Conventions*, pp. 89, 174.

83. Bancroft MS, P-L329, Fol. II, 7-9; Andreas, *History of Nebraska*, p. 475.

84. Bancroft MS, P-L329, Fol. II, 7.

85. Letter from William H. Taylor and Henry W. DePay to Abraham Lincoln, December 27, 1860, Department of State, Applications and Recommendations for Office, 1861-69, National Archives.

86. Letter from Matthew Simpson to Henry S. Lane, February 20, 1861, filed in the Lane Papers, William Henry Smith Memorial Library, Indiana Historical Society, Indianapolis.

87. "James Harlan," *Appleton's Cyclopaedia of American Biography* (New York: D. Appleton and Company, 1888), III, 83; Earle Dudley Ross, "James Harlan," *Dictionary of American Biography* (Centenary Edition; New York: Charles Scribner's Sons, 1946), VIII, 268.

88. Letter from James Harlan to Matthew Simpson, March 15, 1861, Bishop Matthew Simpson Papers, Library of Congress.

89. Letter from Matthew Simpson to Abraham Lincoln, no date, Department of State, Applications and Recommendations for Office, 1861-69, National Archives.

90. *New York Herald*, March 8, 1861, p. 1. Letter from John Evans to Matthew Simpson, March 14, 1861, Bishop Matthew Simpson Papers, Library of Congress.

91. Bancroft MS, P-L329, Fol. II, 7.

92. Letter from Abraham Lincoln to Salmon P. Chase, July 26, 1861, cited in Carl Sandburg, *Abraham Lincoln: The War Years* (Sangamon Edition; New York: Charles Scribner's Sons, 1944), I, 310; letter from Abraham Lincoln to William Pickering, October 7, 1861, in Roy P. Basler (ed.), *The Collected Works of Abraham Lincoln* (New Brunswick, N.J.: Rutgers University Press, 1953), IV, 550; letter from Matthew Simpson to Simon Cameron, November 27, 1861, Robert Todd Lincoln Collection, Abraham Lincoln Papers, Library of Congress.

93. Letter from Abraham Lincoln to William Pickering, October 7, 1861, in Basler (ed.), *Collected Works of Abraham Lincoln*, IV, 550. See also footnote 1 on the same page.

94. Bancroft MS, P-L329, Fol. II, 8.

95. *Ibid.*; Henry Dudley Teetor, "Hon. John Evans, War Governor of Colorado," *The Magazine of Western History*, IX (April, 1889), 724; Byers, *Encyclopedia of Biography of Colorado*, p. 44; "Walter Bennett Scates," *Appleton's Cyclopaedia of American Biography* (New York: D. Appleton and Company, 1888), V, 414.

96. Basler (ed.), *Collected Works of Abraham Lincoln*, IV, 550.

97. Letter from John Evans to Abraham Lincoln, October 28, 1861, Robert Todd Lincoln Collection, Abraham Lincoln Papers, Library of Congress.

98. Letter from Matthew Simpson to Simon Cameron, November 27, 1861, *ibid.*

99. *Chicago Tribune*, December 11, 1861, p. 3.

100. Letter from John Evans to James Harlan, January 30, 1862, Department of State, Applications and Recommendations for Office, National Archives.

101. *Ibid.* The letter was endorsed to Lincoln by Harlan on February 6, 1862.

102. Letter from Lyman Trumbull and others to Abraham Lincoln, February 19, 1862, cited in Basler (ed.), *Collected Works of Abraham Lincoln*, V, 173.

103. A photostatic copy of the commission is in the John Evans Collection. McMechen (*Life of Governor Evans*, p. 88) infers that Lincoln offered Evans the Colorado post without any previous effort by Evans to obtain the appointment. He goes on to say that Evans then journeyed to Colorado to look over the state before he accepted the offer. This account errs not only in putting the initiative in Lincoln's hand, but it contradicts the clear implication in Evans' first speech that he had never before been to Colorado. See the transcript of Evans' address in *DRMN*, May 17, 1862, p. 2. McMechen's story may arise from an erroneous interpretation of the statement by Evans that he "took a week to inquire what was there" when Lincoln tendered him the appointment as governor of Washington Territory. See Bancroft MS, P-L329, Fol. II, 9.

Governor of Colorado Territory

1. See "An Act to Provide a Temporary Government for the Territory of Colorado," sec. 3, which is quoted in Colorado Territory, *General Laws* (1861), p. 24.

2. Bancroft MS, P-L329, Fol. II, 7-9.

3. Letter from Abraham Lincoln to William H. Seward, April 7, Basler (ed.), *Collected Works of Abraham Lincoln*, V, 182.

4. Letter from John Evans to William H. Seward, April 8, 1862, Department of State, Territorial Papers, Fol. LII, No. 28, National Archives.

5. John Evans, Record of Oath of Office, April 11, 1862, Territory of Colorado, Executive Record, Book "A", p. 93, Colorado State Archives, Denver.

6. John Lewis Smith, *Indiana Methodism, A Series of Sketches and Incidents Grave and Humorous Concerning Preachers and People of the West, with an Appendix Containing Personal Recollections, Public Addresses and Other Miscellany* (Valparaiso, Ind.: n.n., 1892), pp. 284-85. Smith wrote to Evans on June 10, 1892, enclosing an account of Evans' life and a history of Northwestern University. He asked Evans to make corrections and to remit $300 to help finance the publication of the book. Margaret Evans replied to the letter, stating that Evans was not interested in subscription biographies. Smith's letter and a copy of Margaret's undated reply are in the John Evans Collection. Smith's proposed biography was not published, and no copies of the draft are known to exist.

7. Letter from Abraham Lincoln to William H. Seward, April 7, 1862, in Basler (ed.), *Collected Works of Abraham Lincoln*, V, 182n.

8. Samuel H. Elbert, Record of Oath of Office, April 19, 1862, Territory of Colorado, Executive Record, Book "A", p. 93.

9. *The Daily Commonwealth* [Denver], November 9, 1863, p. 2.

10. Robert D. Clark calls Evans' appointment "the first political triumph of moment" for the Methodists. See his *Life of Matthew*

Simpson, p. 227. In a personal letter, dated January 16, 1962, Dean Clark pointed out that, religious considerations aside, these other factors qualified Evans for the appointment.

11. "An Act to Provide a Temporary Government for the Territory of Colorado," quoted in Colorado Territory, *General Laws* (1861), sec. 2, p. 24, and sec. 11, p. 29.

12. Letter from John Evans to Margaret Evans, July 6, 1862, John Evans Collection.

13. *DRMN*, May 17, 1862, p. 2.

14. Bancroft MS, P-L329, Fol. III, 1, which was an interview with Evans made in 1889, gave his height as 5' 11" and his weight as 170 pounds. Bancroft MS, P-L21, p. 7, which was an 1884 interview of Samuel H. Elbert, described Evans as "about 5 ft. 11 in. rather a large frame, but little flesh." In a letter to his wife in 1876, Evans gave his weight as "180# exactly." See his letter to Margaret Evans, August 12, 1876, John Evans Collection.

15. *DRMN*, May 17, 1862, p. 2.

16. Bancroft MS, P-L329, Fol. II, 11.

17. *Ibid.*

18. *DRMN*, May 26, 1862, p. 3; letter from John Evans to Margaret Evans, June 1, 1862, John Evans Collection.

19. See Evans' proclamation of May 24, 1862, Territory of Colorado, Executive Record, Book "A", p. 48.

20. Letter from John Evans to Margaret Evans, June 8, 1862, John Evans Collection.

21. See his letters to Margaret Evans, June 8, 1862, and July 6, 1862, *ibid.*

22. The first session of the territorial legislature convened at Denver on September 9, 1861. See Colorado Territory, *General Laws* (1861). See also the letter from H. P. Bennet to John Evans, June 17, 1862, John Evans Collection, and letter from Samuel H. Elbert to Elisha Whittlesey, June 27, 1862, Official Letters of the Secretary of Colorado Territory, I, 64.

23. *DRMN*, July 14, 1862, p. 2; Frank Hall, *History of the State of Colorado; Embracing Accounts of the Pre-Historic Races and Their Remains; the Earliest Spanish, French and American Explorations; the Lives of the Primitive Hunters, Trappers and Traders; the Commerce of the Prairies; the First American Settlements Founded; the Original Discoveries of Gold in the Rocky Mountains; the Development of Cities and Towns, with the Various Phases of Industrial and Political Transition, from 1858 to 1890* (Chicago: Blakely Printing Co., 1889), I, 293.

24. Letter from John Evans to Margaret Evans, June 15, 1862, John Evans Collection.

25. Hall, *History of Colorado*, I, 292.

26. Letter from John Evans to the Speaker of the House of Representatives of Colorado Territory, July 15, 1862, Territory of Colorado, Executive Record, Book "A", p. 53.

27. "Governor's Message, Delivered before Both Houses of the Legislature of Colorado on Friday, July 18th, 1862," Territory of Colorado, Executive Record, Book "A", pp. 54-63.

28. *Ibid.*, 54-55.

29. *Ibid.*, 55-56.

30. *Ibid.*, 56-57.

31. "An Act to Organize the Militia," Colorado Territory, *General Laws* (1861). Evans later cited this as one of the major defects of the Militia Law of 1862, which was essentially the same as the previous law. See *ibid.* (1862); telegram from John Evans to Major General Curtis, June 21, 1864, Indian Affairs Letter Book, John Evans Collection. This source will be cited hereafter as Indian Letter Book. See also the "Proclamation, Sep. 5th, 1862," signed by then Acting Governor Elbert, Executive Record, Book "A", p. 86.

32. "An Act to Organize the Militia," Secs. 1 and 11, Colorado Territory, *General Laws* (1861).

33. Three years later Evans listed this as a major hindrance to his recruiting efforts under the revised militia law. See his telegrams to Edwin M. Stanton, June 14, 1864, and to Major General Curtis, June 21, 1864, Indian Letter Book, John Evans Collection.

34. "An Act to Organize the Militia," Colorado Territory, *General Laws* (1861).

35. Message to the Legislature, July 18, 1862, Territory of Colorado, Executive Record, Book "A", pp. 54-55.

36. *Ibid.*, 57.

37. *Ibid.*, 57-59.

38. *Ibid.*, 58-59.

39. U.S. Congress, Senate, *An Act to Aid in the Construction of a Railroad and Telegraph Line from the Missouri River to the Pacific Ocean, and to Secure to the Government the Use of the Same for Postal, Military, and Other Purposes*, 37th Cong., 2nd Sess., 1862, Misc. Doc. No. 108, pp. 1, 2.

40. *DRMN*, July 8, 1862, p. 2.

41. Message to the Legislature, July 18, 1862, Executive Record, Book "A", p. 60.

42. Executive Record, Book "A", p. 72. A significant change incor-

porated into the new militia law was the provision for "active" and "reserve" units. Generally speaking, only those who volunteered for the active militia would be called to duty, and they would be paid $2.00 per day for each day of such service. The other shortcomings of the 1861 law remained.

43. *Ibid.*, 74.

44. *Ibid.*, 76; and "Governor's Message," February 3, 1864, p. 131.

45. Executive Record, Book "A", p. 77.

46. *Ibid.*, 75-76.

47. *Ibid.*, 65.

48. *Ibid.*, 77.

49. *Ibid.*, 66.

50. *DRMN*, July 16, 1862, p. 2; see also the letters from John Evans to Margaret Evans, June 8, 1862; June 15, 1862; July 6, 1862, John Evans Collection.

51. One story has it that Mrs. Evans "rode in a carriage with the casket containing a victim of scarlet fever, and on returning home took her little Margaret upon her knee." See Hemenway, "Medical History (Regular)," *History of Northwestern*, eds. Hurd and Sheppard, p. 246.

52. Letter from John Evans to Margaret Evans, June 8, 1862, John Evans Collection.

53. *Ibid.*, June 15, 1862.

54. *Ibid.*, July 6, 1862.

55. It was first announced in the *Daily Rocky Mountain News* [Denver], July 16, 1862, p. 2. Even the news of the Seven Days' battles did not reach Denver until July 7, nearly a week after they were ended. See the postscript of July 7, 1862, in the letter from John Evans to Margaret Evans, July 6, 1862, John Evans Collection.

56. When Evans brought his family to Denver the following November, they left Atchison, Kansas, on November 6 and arrived in Denver on November 12. See *WRMN*, November 13, 1862, p. 2, and November 20, 1862, p. 1.

57. *Ibid.*, July 8, 1862, p. 2.

58. *Ibid.*, June 21, 1862, p. 1.

59. *Ibid.*, June 27, 1862, p. 2.

60. *Ibid.*, July 25, 1862, p. 3.

61. *Ibid.*

62. Samuel D. Mock, "Colorado and the Surveys for a Pacific Railroad," *The Colorado Magazine*, XVII (March, 1940), 56.

63. Quoted in *ibid.*

64. Bancroft MS, P-L329, Fol. II, 9.

65. Hall, *History of Colorado*, I, 289.

66. *DRMN*, July 22, 1862, p. 2; *WRMN*, July 24, 1862, p. 2.

67. *DRMN*, July 26, 1862, p. 3.

68. *Ibid.*, August 16, 1862, p. 2.

69. Hall, *History of Colorado*, I, 291.

70. *DRMN*, August 18, 1862, p. 2.

71. *WRMN*, September 18, 1862, p. 2.

72. Quoted in Mock, *The Colorado Magazine*, XVII (1940), 56.

73. *Chicago Tribune*, October 11, 1862, p. 2.

74. "Proclamation, Sep. 5th, 1862," by then Acting Governor Elbert, Executive Record, Book "A", p. 86.

75. Letter from John Evans to Edwin M. Stanton, September 11, 1862, with endorsement by Ben Hughes, general agent for Holladay's Overland Mail Line, John Evans Collection; *WRMN*, October 16, 1862, p. 2.

76. Letter from John Evans to William P. Dole, October 30, 1862, in *Report of the Commissioner of Indian Affairs For the Year 1862* (Washington: Government Printing Office, 1863), p. 230; and Reginald S. Craig, *The Fighting Parson; The Biography of Colonel John M. Chivington* (Los Angeles: Westernlore Press, 1959), pp. 141-42.

77. *WRMN*, October 16, 1862, p. 2.

78. See Evans' report to Dole, October 30, 1862, in *Report of the Commissioner of Indian Affairs for the Year 1862*, p. 230. Dole gave his own summary in *ibid.*, 33-34.

79. *WRMN*, November 13, 1862, p. 2.

80. Bancroft MS, P-L329, Fol. IV, 2; *DRMN*, November 12, 1862, quoted in *WRMN*, November 20, 1862, p. 1.

81. *DRMN*, August 18, 1862, p. 2.

82. Cannon, "Margaret Gray Evans," *The Colorado Magazine*, XXXIX (1962), 22.

83. Hall, *History of Colorado*, I, 301-02.

84. Cannon, "Margaret Gray Evans," *The Colorado Magazine*, XXXIX (1962), 22, quoting from the diary of Margaret Evans, April 27, 1863. The house was apparently not finished yet, for the *Rocky Mountain News* of September 10, 1863, spoke of it as still "going up"; quoted in Ann W. Hafen and LeRoy R. Hafen, "The Beginnings of Denver University," *The Colorado Magazine*, XXIV (March, 1947), 59-60. See also Bancroft MS, P-L329, Fol. IV, 2.

85. *WRMN*, May 7, 1863, p. 4; May 14, 1863, p. 4.

86. *Denver Times*, June 17, 1921, p. 1; his place of birth is listed in error as Evanston in McClung, *The Colorado Genealogist*, XV (1954), 68; and Cannon, "Margaret Gray Evans," *The Colorado*

Magazine, XXXIX (1962), 23. The error apparently arises from an obituary of Evan E. Evans which appeared in *The Trail*, XIV (July, 1921), 30-31. The census of 1870, however, shows his place of birth as Colorado (see the enumeration of "Inhabitants in City of Denver," June 8, 1870, p. 32, microfilm in the Denver Public Library). His death certificate, with information supplied by his older brother William G. Evans, also shows his birthplace as Denver (Certificate No. 5335, June 17, 1921, State Bureau of Vital Statistics, Denver, Colorado).

87. Telegram from William P. Dole to John Evans, July 8, 1863, Records of the Office of Indian Affairs, Letters Sent, LXXI, 113, National Archives.

88. *Ibid.*, July 16, 1863, LXXI, 149.

89. Letter from William P. Dole to John Evans, July 16, 1863, John Evans Collection.

90. Letter from John Evans to William P. Dole, July 29, 1863, *ibid.*

91. Letter from William P. Dole to John Evans, July 28, 1863, Records of the Office of Indian Affairs, Letters Sent, LXXI, 200, National Archives.

92. Letter from John Evans to William P. Dole, July 29, 1863, John Evans Collection.

93. William E. Unrau, "A Prelude to War," *The Colorado Magazine*, XLI (Fall, 1964), 302-05.

94. Letter from William P. Dole to John Evans, June 17, 1862, citing Evans' letter of June 3, 1862, Records of the Office of Indian Affairs, Letters Sent, LXVIII, 356, National Archives; and *ibid.*, July 9, 1862, citing Evans' letter of June 24, 1862, 424-25.

95. Letter from William P. Dole to John Evans, May 18, 1863, Records of the Office of Indian Affairs, Letters Sent, LXX, 455-57, National Archives.

96. Unrau, *The Colorado Magazine*, XLI (1964), 311-12.

97. Letter from John Evans to William P. Dole, July 29, 1863, John Evans Collection; letters from John Evans to S. G. Colley, August 25, 1863; and to William P. Dole, August 26, 1863, Indian Letter Book, John Evans Collection.

98. Letter from John Evans to William P. Dole, August 26, 1863, Indian Letter Book, *ibid.*

99. *Report of the Commissioner of Indian Affairs for the Year 1863* (Washington: Government Printing Office, 1864), p. 16.

100. Bancroft MS, P-L329, Fol. II, 20.

101. Bancroft MS, P-L23, p. 11.

102. Bancroft MS, P-L329, Fol. II, 20.

103. Letter from John Evans to Samuel G. Colley, November 2, 1863, Indian Letter Book, John Evans Collection.

104. *Report of the Commissioner of Indian Affairs for the Year 1863*, p. 16. See also the report of Evans to Dole, October 14, 1863, in *ibid.*, 124-25.

105. Bancroft MS, P-L329, Fol. II, 19.

106. Report of Evans to Dole, October 30, 1862, in *Report of the Commissioner of Indian Affairs for the Year 1862*, p. 231.

107. Letter from William P. Dole to John Evans, October 11, 1862, Records of the Office of Indian Affairs, Letters Sent, LXIX, 204, National Archives.

108. See the *Report of the Commissioner of Indian Affairs for the Year 1862*, pp. 229-31; Bancroft MS, P-L329, Fol. II, 14.

109. The plan is outlined in Dole's letter to John Evans, June 1, 1863, Records of the Office of Indian Affairs, Letters Sent, LXX, 514, National Archives.

110. Letter from John Evans to William P. Dole, August 24, 1863, John Evans Collection.

111. Letter from John Evans to William P. Dole, July 29, 1863, John Evans Collection. Other reasons were probably the disagreement over the date for the Ute conference and Dole's constant reminders to conserve funds.

112. Letter from John Evans to William P. Dole, October 16, 1863, Indian Letter Book, *ibid.* Members of the Capote and Wiminuche bands also attended but lacked sufficient representation for treaty negotiations. See James Warren Covington, "Federal Relations with the Colorado Utes, 1861-63," *The Colorado Magazine*, XXVIII (October, 1951), 261.

113. Report of John Evans to William P. Dole, October 30, 1862, in *Report of the Commissioner of Indian Affairs for the Year 1862*, p. 231.

114. *Ibid.*

115. Letter from William P. Dole to John Evans, July 28, 1863, Records of the Office of Indian Affairs, Letters Sent, LXXI, 200, National Archives.

116. Bancroft MS, P-L329, Fol. II, 12.

117. Bancroft MS, P-L23, p. 12.

118. Bancroft MS, P-L329, Fol. II, 14.

119. Bancroft MS, P-L23, p. 15.

120. Covington, *The Colorado Magazine*, XXVIII (1951), 261-63.

121. Letter from John Evans to William P. Dole, October 16, 1863, Indian Letter Book, John Evans Collection.

122. *Report of the Commissioner of Indian Affairs for the Year 1863*, p. 17. See also the letter from John Evans to William P. Dole, October 16, 1863, Indian Letter Book, John Evans Collection.

123. Bancroft MS, P-L329, Fol. II, 15-16.

124. *Ibid.*, 16. The Espinosas were later killed by Tom Tobin, apparently in the belief that Evans had advertised in the *Rocky Mountain News* a reward of $2,500 for their capture. Tobin finally collected $1,500, but none of the money came from Evans, who denied having offered the reward. No evidence of the reward offer has yet been found, and Tobin seems to have told contradictory stories of the offer. See Edgar L. Hewett, "Tom Tobin," *The Colorado Magazine*, XXIII (September, 1946), 211; Thomas T. Tobin, "The Capture of the Espinosas," *The Colorado Magazine*, IX (January, 1932), 61-65; *Denver Republican*, January 22, 1884, p. 8.

125. *WRMN*, October 21, 1863, p. 1.

126. Report of John Evans to William P. Dole, October 14, 1863, in *Report of the Commissioner of Indian Affairs for the Year 1863*, pp. 121-27.

127. Letter from John Evans to John M. Chivington, August 26, 1863, Indian Letter Book, John Evans Collection.

128. Report of John Evans to William P. Dole, October 14, 1863, in *Report of the Commissioner of Indian Affairs for the Year 1863*, p. 127.

129. Craig, *Fighting Parson*, pp. 145-46.

130. *WRMN*, January 29, 1863, p. 1.

131. Letter from John Evans to William H. Seward, [September 22, 1863], Indian Letter Book, John Evans Collection.

132. *Ibid.*, October 28, 1863.

133. Letter from John G. Nicolay to William H. Seward, November 6, 1863, State Department Territorial Papers, Colorado Series, Fol. CV, 53, National Archives.

134. Letter from John Evans to William H. Seward, October 28, 1863, Indian Letter Book, John Evans Collection.

135. Letter from John Evans to William H. Seward, August 18, 1862, State Department Territorial Papers, Colorado Series, Fol. LXXX, 40, National Archives.

136. Letter from John Evans to Lafayette Head, [October, 1863,] Indian Letter Book, John Evans Collection.

137. Letter from John Evans to William P. Dole, November 4, 1863, *ibid.*

138. Letter from John Evans to John M. Chivington, November 7, 1863, *ibid*.

139. See the letter of John Evans to Samuel G. Colley, November 7, 1863; and the statement by North in the letter from John Evans to William P. Dole, November 10, 1863; both in *ibid*.

140. Letter from John Evans to John M. Chivington and letter from John Evans to William P. Dole, November 9, 1863, *ibid*.

141. Letter from John Evans to William P. Dole, November 9, 1863, *ibid*.

142. *Ibid*., November 11, 1863.

143. Letter from John Evans to John Lorey, November 14, 1863, *ibid*.

144. Letter from John Evans to John M. Chivington, September 7, 1863, *ibid*.

145. Letter from John Evans to Samuel G. Colley, November 7, 1863, *ibid*.

146. *Daily Commonwealth* [Denver], November 17, 1863, p. 3.

147. Letter from William P. Dole to John Evans, April 9, 1862. Records of the Office of Indian Affairs, Letters Sent, LXVIII, 50, National Archives.

"Murdering Horse-Stealing Indians"

1. Letter from William P. Dole to John Evans, April 9, 1862, Records of the Office of Indian Affairs, Letters Sent, LXVIII, 50, National Archives. The conflicting duties of governor and Indian superintendent are summarized in William N. Neil, "The Territorial Governor as Indian Superintendent in the Trans-Mississippi West," *Mississippi Valley Historical Review*, XLIII (September, 1956), 213-37.

2. Letter from John Evans to William P. Dole, June 15, 1863, in U. S., Department of the Interior, *Report of the Commissioner of Indian Affairs for the Year 1863* (Washington: Government Printing Office, 1864), p. 136; letter from Evans to E. M. Stanton, December 14, 1863, in U. S., Department of the Interior, *Report of the Commissioner of Indian Affairs for the Year 1864* (Washington: Government Printing Office, 1865), pp. 225-26; letter from Evans to Dole in *ibid.*; statements of Robert North, November 10, 1863, and June 15, 1864, in *ibid.*, 217; letter from Evans to Dole, November 9, 1863, in the Indian Letter Book, John Evans Collection.

3. Letter from N. P. Bennett to William P. Dole, January 28, 1864, in *Report of the Commissioner of Indian Affairs for the Year 1864*, p. 24; letter from Dole to John Evans, May 18, 1863, in Records of the Office of Indian Affairs, Letters Sent, LXX, 455-57, National Archives; letter from Charles E. Mix to Evans, August 11, 1864, and letter from Dole to Evans, July 30, 1863, *ibid.*, LXXI, 200, 246.

4. Letter from S. G. Colley to William P. Dole, September 30, 1863, in *Report of the Commissioner of Indian Affairs for the Year 1863*, pp. 134-35.

5. Charles J. Kappler (ed.), *Indian Affairs: Laws and Treaties* (Washington: Government Printing Office, 1904), II, 807-11.

6. Letter from John Evans to William P. Dole, October 14, 1863, *ibid.*, 172; letter from Dole to Evans, October 11, 1862, Records of

the Office of Indian Affairs, Letters Sent, LXIX, 204, National Archives; Evans to Dole, October 30, 1862, in *Report of the Commissioner of Indian Affairs for the Year 1862* (Washington: Government Printing Office, 1863), p. 231. The soundness of Evans' ranching idea is seen in the fact that this principle was a major part of the treaty which he negotiated with the Tabeguache Utes in 1863. The Utes gave relatively little trouble throughout the remainder of the war.

7. Letter from William P. Dole to John Evans, June 1, 1863, in Records of the Office of Indian Affairs, Letters Sent, LXXI, 200, National Archives.

8. Bancroft MS, P-L23, 11; P-L329, Fol. II, 20. Some of the material covered in the previous chapter is reviewed here in order to present a more comprehensive account of the events leading up to the Indian war in 1864.

9. Letter from John Evans to William P. Dole, October 30, 1862, in *Report of the Commissioner of Indian Affairs for the Year 1862*, p. 230; Bancroft MS, P-L329, Fol. II, 11.

10. *WRMN*, June 28, 1862, p. 1. Donald Berthrong has managed to convert this twenty-mile overnight journey into a major campaign that ended on the upper Republican River. Compare the newspaper account cited here with Professor Berthrong's account in *The Southern Cheyennes* (Norman: University of Oklahoma Press, 1963), pp. 157-58.

11. Letter from John Evans to William P. Dole, November 4, 1863, Indian Letter Book, John Evans Collection.

12. Letter from William P. Dole to John Evans, November 21, 1862, Records of the Office of Indian Affairs, Letters Sent, LXIX, 359-61, National Archives.

13. Letter from John Evans to William P. Dole, October 14, 1863, *Report of the Commissioner of Indian Affairs for the Year 1863*, p. 122.

14. Letter from John Evans to Samuel Colley, November 7, 1863, Indian Letter Book, John Evans Collection.

15. Letter from John Evans to John M. Chivington, September 21, 1863, *ibid.*

16. Craig, *Fighting Parson*, pp. 145-46.

17. "An Act to Organize the Militia of Colorado Territory," in Colorado Territory, *General Laws* (1862), sec. 21; see also the telegrams from John Evans to Samuel R. Curtis, June 21, 1864, and from Evans to Edwin M. Stanton, June 14, 1864, Indian Letter Book, John Evans Collection.

18. Letter from John Evans to Samuel R. Curtis, June 16, 1864, and June 21, 1864; telegram from Evans to Edwin M. Stanton, June 14, 1864; letter from Evans to William A. Kelly, June 20, 1864; letter from Evans to Hiram P. Bennet, June 24, 1864; letter from Evans to William P. Dole, August 9, 1864, Indian Letter Book, John Evans Collection.

19. Letter from John Evans to Samuel R. Curtis, April 25, 1864, *ibid.*

20. Letter from John Evans to Brig. Gen. Carleton, June 16, 1864, *ibid.*; and letter from Evans to William P. Dole, October 14, 1864, in *Report of the Commissioner of Indian Affairs for the Year 1864*, pp. 216-24.

21. Hubert Howe Bancroft, *History of Nevada, Colorado, and Wyoming* (San Francisco: History Co., 1890), p. 463. Early in July the total was, according to one source, "not less than 50 . . . killed." See the letter from Rufus K. Frisbee to George A. Frisbee, July 10, 1864, photocopy in the John Evans Collection. Berthrong, *Southern Cheyennes*, p. 206, says fifty whites were killed during the month of August, 1864, on the Platte route alone.

22. See the Letters Received by the Office of Indian Affairs, 1824-81, Upper Arkansas Agency, 1855-64, particularly the letter from William Baker to John A. Kasson, September 7, 1864, and the letter from George K. Otis to William P. Dole, August 31, 1864 (National Archives Microfilm Publication).

23. Letter from John M. Chivington to Samuel R. Curtis, April 29, 1864; *The War of the Rebellion: A Compilation of the Official Records of the Union and Confederate Armies* (Washington: Government Printing Office, 1891), Ser. I, Vol. XXXIV, Part III, 354, cited hereafter as *Rebellion Records*. See also letter from Chivington to C. S. Charlot, June 11, 1864, *ibid.*, Part IV, 318-19; letter from John Evans to William P. Dole, June 15, 1864, Indian Letter Book, John Evans Collection.

24. Letter from John Evans to William P. Dole, June 15, 1864; letter from Evans to Elbridge Gerry, June 10, 1864, Indian Letter Book, John Evans Collection.

25. Letter from John Evans to William P. Dole, June 15, 1864, *ibid.*; letter from J. S. Maynard to C. S. Charlot, June 13, 1864, in *Rebellion Records*, Ser. I, Vol. XXXIV, Part IV, 353-54.

26. Telegram from Samuel R. Curtis to John Evans, June 13, 1864; letter from Evans to William P. Dole, June 15, 1864, Indian Letter Book, John Evans Collection.

293

27. Executive Order, No. 1, June 12, 1864; No. 2, June 12, 1864; and No. 3, June 14, 1864, Executive Record, Book "A", pp. 168-70.

28. Telegram from John Evans to Samuel R. Curtis, June 12, 1864; letter from Evans to William P. Dole, June 15, 1864; telegram from Evans to Edwin M. Stanton, June 14, 1864, Indian Letter Book, John Evans Collection.

29. Telegram from Samuel R. Curtis to John Evans, June 13, 1864, *ibid.*

30. Letter from John Evans to Hiram P. Bennet, June 24, 1864, *ibid.*

31. Letter from John Evans to D. C. Collier, editor of the Central City *Miners' Register*, June 21, 1864, Letter Book No. 1, John Evans Collection.

32. Hall, *History of Colorado*, I, 312; *DRMN*, June 29, 1864, p. 2; August 11, 1864, p. 2; August 16, 1864, p. 2; August 26, 1864, p. 2; answering charges made by the *Mining Journal* [Black Hawk].

33. *DRMN*, August 26, 1864, p. 2.

34. Bancroft MS, P-L23, p. 18.

35. Executive Order No. 4, June 15, 1864, Executive Record, Book "A", p. 170.

36. Letter from John Evans to William P. Dole, June 15, 1864; telegram from Evans to Dole, June 14, 1864; and letter from Evans to Samuel Colley, June 16, 1864, Indian Letter Book, John Evans Collection.

37. Letter from John Evans to William P. Dole, June 15, 1864, *ibid.*

38. Telegram quoted in a letter from John Evans to William P. Dole, October 15, 1864, in *Report of the Commissioner of Indian Affairs for the Year 1864*, p. 218; letter from Charles E. Mix to Evans, June 23, 1864, in *ibid.*, 230.

39. Letter "To the Friendly Indians of the Plains," June 27, 1864, in *ibid.*, 218.

40. Letter from John Evans to Samuel R. Curtis, June 16, 1864, Indian Letter Book, John Evans Collection.

41. Letter "To the Friendly Indians of the Plains," June 27, 1864, in *Report of the Commissioner of Indian Affairs for the Year 1864*, p. 218. That Evans had waited for word from Curtis or the War Department before issuing this proclamation is evident from his letters to Samuel Colley, June 16, 1864, and to Hiram P. Bennet, June 24, 1864, Indian Letter Book, John Evans Collection.

42. Letter from John Evans to Samuel Colley, June 29, 1864, Indian Letter Book, John Evans Collection. Evans had instructed the

agents as early as June 16 to begin feeding and protecting the friendly Indians at the appointed locations. See his letters to Colley, June 16, 1864; to Samuel R. Curtis, June 16, 1864; to Scout Uriah Curtis, June 22, 1864; to Hiram P. Bennet, June 24, 1864; and his proclamation to the presumably friendly Arapahoe Chief Roman Nose, [June 17?], 1864, *ibid.*

43. *Report of the Commissioner of Indian Affairs for the Year 1864*, p. 23. "Friday's Band" of Arapahoes, which went to Camp Collins, seems to have intended to use its compliance to induce the government to establish a separate reservation on the Cache la Poudre. See the letters from Simeon Whiteley to Evans, June 14, 1864, August 30, 1864, and September 13, 1864, in *ibid.*, 235-38. Arapahoe Chief Roman Nose had introduced this demand in the fall of 1863. See the letters from John Evans to William P. Dole, November 9 and 11, 1863, Indian Letter Book, John Evans Collection. In the spring of 1865 all of the band except Friday himself left to join the hostile Indians. Friday entered "the employ of the military authorities." See the letter from Daniel C. Oakes to D. N. Cooley, September 2, 1865, *Report of the Commissioner of Indian Affairs for the Year 1865*, p. 177.

44. Letter from John Evans to Samuel Colley, June 29, 1864, Indian Letter Book, John Evans Collection.

45. Letter from Samuel Colley to John Evans, July 26, 1864, Indian Letter Book, John Evans Collection.

46. Proclamation of August 11, 1864, Executive Record, Book "A", pp. 174-75.

47. Letter from George K. Otis to William P. Dole, August 13, 1864, *Report of the Commissioner of Indian Affairs for the Year 1864*, pp. 254-55.

48. Letter from John Evans to William P. Dole, October 15, 1864, *ibid.*, 218, and *DRMN*, August 10, 1864, p. 2.

49. Letter from John Evans to Charles Autobees, August 26, 1864, Indian Letter Book, John Evans Collection.

50. Executive Record, Book "A", pp. 174-75.

51. *Ibid.*, August 12, 1864, p. 3.

52. Letter from John Evans to William P. Dole, October 15, 1864, *Report of the Commissioner of Indian Affairs for the Year 1864*, p. 219.

53. Executive Record, Book "A", p. 173-74.

54. LeRoy R. Hafen, *The Overland Mail, 1849-1869* (Cleveland: Arthur H. Clark Co., 1926), pp. 260-61.

55. Berthrong, *Southern Cheyennes*, p. 206.

56. Letter from John Evans to John M. Chivington, September 14, 1864; letter from Evans to Samuel Colley, September 19, 1864, Indian Letter Book, John Evans Collection. Letter from Edward Wynkoop to Evans, September 18, 1864, *Report of the Commissioner of Indian Affairs for the Year 1864*, p. 234.

57. See Evans' letter to Agent Samuel Colley, September 19, 1864, in which he said: "I do not deem it advisable to take any steps in the matter until I hear the result of his expedition." Indian Letter Book, John Evans Collection.

58. Testimony of Edward W. Wynkoop, in U.S., Congress, Senate, *Report of the Secretary of War, Communicating, in Compliance with a Resolution of the Senate of February 4, 1867, a Copy of the Evidence Taken at Denver and Fort Lyon, Colorado Territory, by a Military Commission Ordered to Inquire into the Sand Creek Massacre, November, 1864*, 39th Cong., 2nd Sess., 1867, Doc. No. 26, p. 90 (referred to hereafter as *Sand Creek Massacre*).

59. *Ibid.*, 97, 101; and U.S., Congress, Senate, "The Chivington Massacre," *Condition of the Indian Tribes: Report of the Joint Special Committee Appointed under Joint Resolution of March 3, 1865*, 39th Cong., 2nd Sess., 1867, Doc. No. 156, pp. 62-64, 75-77 (referred to hereafter as *Condition of the Indian Tribes*). Compare these statements with the account in Wynkoop's "Unfinished Colorado History" (MS in the library of the State Historical Society of Colorado), p. 33. In the first source Wynkoop gives testimony regarding the conduct of his soldiers at the conference with the Cheyenne and Arapahoe Indians on the Smoky Hill River that is contradicted in his "Unfinished History." According to a study by Gene R. Marlott this was a conscious deviation from the truth. See his "Edward W. Wynkoop: An Investigation of His Role in the Sand Creek Controversy and Other Indian Affairs, 1863-1868," M.A. thesis, University of Denver, 1961. Marlott's study is devoted in great part to an analysis of the reliability of Wynkoop's testimony. Also compare Wynkoop's testimony of January 16, 1865, and June 9, 1865, in *Condition of the Indian Tribes*, pp. 62-64 and 75-77; testimony of March 21, 1865, in *Sand Creek Massacre*, p. 90; and letter to Samuel R. Curtis, October 8, 1864, in *Sand Creek Massacre*, pp. 120-22. In each of these documents, as his testimony was removed further in time from the conversation with Evans before the Camp Weld Conference, Major Wynkoop's testimony became more critical of Evans.

60. Testimony of Edward W. Wynkoop, June 9, 1865, in *Condition of the Indian Tribes*, p. 77; letter from John Evans to Joel Evans, October 30, 1864, David Evans Papers; letter from Evans to

William P. Dole, October 15, 1864, *Report of the Commissioner of Indian Affairs for the Year 1864*, p. 224.

61. The report is published in full in John Evans, *Reply of Governor Evans, of the Territory of Colorado to That Part Referring to Him, of the Report of "The Committee on the Conduct of the War," Headed "Massacre of Cheyenne Indians"* (Denver: n.n., 1865), pp. 1-4, and in *Condition of the Indian Tribes*, pp. 87-90. In spite of Whiteley's statement that it was "correct and complete," a cursory inspection shows that it is not a verbatim transcript of what was said.

62. Evans, *Reply of Governor Evans*, p. 3.

63. *Ibid.*, 2; see also the letter from John Evans to Samuel G. Colley, September 29, 1864, Indian Letter Book, John Evans Collection. The suggestion has been made by Donald G. Berthrong that Evans promoted the Indian war in order to force the tribes to cede the land above the South Platte River. See his *Southern Cheyennes*, pp. 169, 171, 173, 188-89. William E. Unrau took a different approach to the land question, suggesting that Evans wanted to extinguish Indian title to land north of the South Platte by treaty but that hostilities prevented his doing so. See "A Prelude to War," *The Colorado Magazine*, XLI (Fall, 1964), 311-13. Both of these explanations make the land question seem more important than it actually was. Although Evans was concerned about getting the non-signatory Indians to agree to the Treaty of Fort Wise or some similar treaty, there is no evidence in his correspondence or in the published records to indicate that he was overly concerned about extinguishing the Indian titles to land in Colorado.

64. See Whiteley's report of the conference in Evans, *Reply of Governor Evans*, p. 2.

65. *Ibid.*, 2, 4.

66. This was Left Hand's band, mentioned in Evans' letter to William P. Dole, October 15, 1864, *Report of the Commissioner of Indian Affairs for the Year 1864*, p. 219. The four Arapahoe chiefs present at the Camp Weld Council were members of that band. See the report of the council in *ibid.*, 87, and in Evans, *Reply of Governor Evans*, p. 1.

67. Whiteley's report in Evans, *Reply of Governor Evans*, p. 2.

68. Letter from John Evans to William P. Dole, October 15, 1864, *Report of the Commissioner of Indian Affairs for the Year 1864*, p. 222.

69. See Whiteley's report in Evans, *Reply of Governor Evans*, p. 2.

70. Letters from John Evans to Samuel Colley, September 29, 1864; November 10, 1864, Indian Letter Book, John Evans Collection. A telegram from General Curtis to Colonel Chivington, which arrived just after the conference, warned Chivington not to allow Evans to make peace. "No peace," said Curtis, "must be made without my directions." This telegram, dated September 28, 1864, is printed in *Report of the Commissioner of Indian Affairs for the Year 1864*, p. 221. See also Evans' account in *Reply of Governor Evans*, p. 8.

71. Julie S. Lambert said that Smith was known at Fort Lyon as "Lying John." See her "Plain Tales of the Plains," *The Trail*, IX (June, 1916), 17.

72. *Condition of the Indian Tribes*, pp. 95-96. Hall, *Colorado*, I, 329, strongly implies that Colley "sold and traded away" the greater part of each consignment of treaty goods. See also the testimony of John W. Prowers, *Sand Creek Massacre*, p. 107, who reports that Colley had sent goods into the Indian camp at Sand Creek. A similar story is told in William Henry Ryus, *The Second William Penn: A True Account of the Incidents That Happened along the Old Santa Fe Trail in the Sixties* (Kansas City, Mo.: Frank T. Riley Publ. Co., 1913), pp. 49-51. In Ryus' book Colley is referred to as Macauley.

73. Lambert, *The Trail*, IX (1916), 17-18.

74. Letter from D. A. Chever to Samuel Colley, October 18, 1864, Indian Letter Book, John Evans Collection. See also the testimony of John W. Prowers in *Sand Creek Massacre*, p. 107.

75. Letter from John Evans to Samuel Colley, November 10, 1864, Indian Letter Book, John Evans Collection.

76. Letter from Samuel Colley to William P. Dole, January 22, 1862, quoted in Unrau, *The Colorado Magazine*, XLI (1964), 304. Unrau suggests that "the prospect of difficulties (or opportunities) may not have been unrelated to Dole's decision to send cousin Colley to the Upper Arkansas Agency." *Ibid.*, 307.

77. See Smith's testimony in *Condition of the Indian Tribes*, p. 51.

78. See Evans' testimony in *ibid.*, 48, and the testimony of Rev. Oliver O. Willard in *ibid.*, 70. In 1890 Chivington told the *Denver Republican* that only he and Colonel George L. Shoup knew the location of the band that Chivington intended to attack. Quoted in Raymond G. Carey, "Another View of the Sand Creek Affair," *The Denver Westerners Monthly Roundup*, XVI (February, 1960), 14.

79. As will be seen in the next chapter, Colorado voters rejected statehood by a decisive majority on September 13, 1864. See the schedule of election returns in *Congressional Globe*, 39th Cong., 1st Sess., 1866, Part II, 1353.

80. Letter from John Evans to John P. Usher, September 23, 1864, microfilm reel no. 82, Abraham Lincoln Papers, Library of Congress.

81. Letter from John Evans to William H. Seward, October 18, 1864, Indian Letter Book, John Evans Collection.

82. *Ibid.*

83. Letter from John Evans to William H. Seward, December 14, 1864, State Department, Territorial Papers, Colorado Series, Fol. CXVI, 61, National Archives.

84. *Ibid.*, August 18, 1862, Fol. LXXX, 40. There is no record of an answer to Evans' leave request in the fall of 1863 (see his letter to William H. Seward, October 28, 1863, Indian Letter Book, John Evans Collection), but Evans left Denver for Washington on November 17, 1863. *Daily Commonwealth* [Denver], November 17, 1863, p. 3.

85. *DRMN*, November 16, 1864, pp. 2-3.

86. See the several letters from John Evans to Abraham Lincoln, March 6, 1865, and the letters from John Evans to J. M. Ashley, March 14, 1865, microfilm reel no. 93, Abraham Lincoln Papers, Library of Congress. The letters to Ashley are endorsed by Ashley for forwarding to Lincoln.

87. See Ashley's endorsement on the letter recommending the removal of Associate Justice Armour, *ibid.*

88. Letter from Abraham Lincoln to John Evans, March 16, 1864, in Basler (ed.), *Collected Works of Abraham Lincoln*, VIII, 356; and *DRMN*, June 19, 1865, p. 2.

89. Janet Lecompte, "Sand Creek," *The Colorado Magazine*, XLI (Fall, 1964), 327-30.

90. *DRMN*, June 19, 1865, p. 2, and Evans, *Reply of Governor Evans*, p. 15.

91. *DRMN*, July 19, 1865, p. 2; Bancroft MS, P-L329, Fol. V, 35; Bancroft MS, P-L23, p. 19. A copy of John W. Wright's pamphlet, apparently published in January, 1865, and entitled *Chivington Massacre of Cheyenne Indians* (n.p.: Gideon & Pearson Printers, [1865]), is in the Colorado Collection of the Charles Leaming Tutt Library, Colorado College, Colorado Springs.

92. Evans, *Reply of Governor Evans*, p. 15.

93. *Ibid.* The report is in U.S., Congress, Senate, "Massacre of Cheyenne Indians," *Report of the Joint Committee on the Conduct of the War*, 38th Cong., 2nd Sess., 1865, Report No. 142.

94. Letter from John Evans to William H. Seward, August 1, 1865,

State Department, Territorial Papers, Fol. CXXIII, 66, National Archives microfilm.

95. *Condition of the Indian Tribes*, p. 48.

96. Evans, *Reply of Governor Evans*, pp. 2, 15.

97. *Ibid.*, 1.

98. Since this report, published in 1867, was not overly critical of his conduct, Evans considered it a complete exoneration. Bancroft MS, P-L329, Fol. V, 36.

"All Hail the State of Colorado"

1. *Congressional Globe*, 38th Cong., 1st Sess., 1864, Part II, 1228.

2. *Daily Commonwealth* [Denver], March 24, 1864, p. 2.

3. Elmer Ellis, *Henry Moore Teller, Defender of the West* (Caldwell, Ida.: Caxton Printers, Ltd., 1941), p. 67.

4. Hall, *History of Colorado*, I, 311.

5. *Ibid.*, 301.

6. *Ibid.*, 309.

7. See the comment of Congressman James M. Ashley, who drafted the three statehood bills, in *Congressional Globe*, 39th Cong., 1st Sess., 1866, Part III, 2372-73; Ellis, *Henry Moore Teller*, p. 65; James G. Randall and David Donald, *The Civil War and Reconstruction* (2d ed.; Boston: D. C. Heath and Company, 1961), pp. 476, 608-09.

8. *DRMN*, June 29, 1864, p. 2, quoting an editorial in the *Daily Mining Journal* [Black Hawk]; letter from John Evans to D. C. Collier, June 21, 1864, Letter Book No. 1, John Evans Collection.

9. *Daily Miners' Register* [Central City], June 20, 1864, p. 2; June 29, 1864, p. 2; June 30, 1864, p. 2; July 2, 1864, p. 2. See also the letter from John Evans to D. C. Collier, editor of the *Register*, June 21, 1864, Letter Book No. 1, John Evans Collection.

10. *Daily Mining Journal* [Black Hawk], June 27, 1864, quoted in *DRMN*, June 29, 1864, p. 2; *Daily Mining Journal* [Black Hawk], September 7, 1864, p. 2.

11. Letter from John Evans to Ovando J. Hollister and Frank Hall, editors of the *Mining Journal* [Black Hawk], June 7, 1864, Letter Book No. 1, John Evans Collection; see also the letter from Allen A. Bradford to Andrew Johnson, May 22, 1865 (Records of the Department of State, Applications and Recommendations for Office), which repeats these charges.

12. The charge that Evans exaggerated the Indian danger did not become current in Colorado until after the Sand Creek scandal. Some

writers have cited a letter from Nathaniel P. Hill to his wife, June 19, 1864, recently published in "Nathaniel P. Hill Inspects Colorado: Letters Written in 1864," *The Colorado Magazine*, XXXIII (October, 1956), 249. In this letter Hill said: "The Governor is a very fine man, but very timid and he is unfortunately smitten with the belief that they are to have an Indian War. He encourages sending all the reports of Indian troubles to the states, to enable him to get arms and soldiers." Those who take this statement at face value overlook two points. First, Hill was obviously trying to set his wife at ease regarding the Indian danger. Secondly, Hill later told his sister that everyone seemed to expect the Indian War to continue to be serious but that no one thought Denver would be attacked. See his letter of August 1, 1864, in "Nathaniel P. Hill Inspects Colorado: Letters Written in 1864," *The Colorado Magazine*, XXXIV (January, 1957), 25-26. For two recent studies which cite Hill's correspondence to show Evans' alleged near-hysteria, see Janet Lecompte, "Charles Autobees," *The Colorado Magazine*, XXXV (July, 1958), 224; and Stan Hoig, *The Sand Creek Massacre* (Norman: University of Oklahoma Press, 1961), p. 69.

13. Letter from John Evans to D. C. Collier, June 21, 1864, Letter Book No. 1, John Evans Collection.

14. *Ibid.*

15. *DRMN*, August 16, 1864, p. 2, quoting the Black Hawk *Mining Journal*, August 13, 1864.

16. Telegram from John Evans to Samuel R. Curtis, August 11, 1864, with endorsement by George K. Otis, superintendent of the Overland Stage Line, Indian Letter Book, John Evans Collection; Carey, *Denver Westerners Monthly Roundup*, XVI (1960), 8.

17. Letter from Abraham Lincoln to Samuel R. Curtis, September 1, 1864, in Basler (ed.), *Collected Works of Abraham Lincoln*, VII, 530.

18. Letter from John Evans to John P. Usher, September 23, 1864, microfilm reel no. 82, Abraham Lincoln Papers, Library of Congress. Evans said in this letter: "This will go by the first mail for weeks."

19. Ellis, *Henry Moore Teller*, p. 66.

20. *Ibid.*

21. *DRMN*, August 3, 1864, p. 2.

22. Elmer Ellis, "Colorado's First Fight for Statehood, 1865-1868," *The Colorado Magazine*, VIII (January, 1931), 25.

23. Letter from John Evans to John P. Usher, September 23, 1864, microfilm reel no. 82, Abraham Lincoln Papers, Library of Congress.

24. Minute book, Denver Council of the Union League of America, p. 35, State Historical Society of Colorado, Denver.

25. *Ibid.*, 61.

26. *Ibid.*, 77-84.

27. *DRMN*, September 1, 1864, p. 2.

28. See the schedule of election returns in *Congressional Globe*, 39th Cong., 1st Sess., 1866, Part II, 1353.

29. Hall, *History of Colorado*, I, 311.

30. Pencil copy of a letter from Schuyler Colfax to President Andrew Johnson, June 2, 1865, John Evans Collection; and letter from John Evans to John P. Usher, September 23, 1864, microfilm reel no. 82, Abraham Lincoln Papers, Library of Congress.

31. Ellis, *Colorado Magazine*, VIII (1931), 25-26.

32. See his letter to O. J. Hollister and Frank Hall, June 7, 1864, Letter Book No. 1, John Evans Collection; also see *DRMN*, June 29, 1864, p. 2, and November 14, 1864, p. 2.

33. Ellis, *Colorado Magazine*, VIII (1931), 25-26.

34. Letter from John Evans to Joel Evans, October 31, 1864, David Evans Papers.

35. Letter from John Evans to Abraham Lincoln, November 11, 1864, Indian Letter Book, John Evans Collection.

36. Letter from John Evans to William H. Seward, October 18, 1864, Indian Letter Book, John Evans Collection. See also Evans' letters to his brother Joel, October 31, 1864, and November 4, 1864, David Evans Papers; *DRMN*, November 16, 1864, pp. 2-3; *WRMN*, November 23, 1864, p. 1; letter from John Evans to William H. Seward, December 14, 1864, Department of State, Territorial Papers, Colorado Series, Fol. 116, National Archives. Seward later told Evans that he had not received the request for leave. He, therefore, asked Secretary of Interior Usher and Commissioner of Indian Affairs Dole to verify that Evans' presence in the national capital was necessary. Dole replied that, while he did not know beforehand of Evans' proposed trip, the Office of Indian Affairs was making good use of his presence to bring about a settlement of the Indian war. Seward thereupon granted the leave. See the letter from William P. Dole to John P. Usher, December 22, 1864, and the letters from Evans to William H. Seward, December 14, 1864, and January 28, 1865, in *ibid.*, Fols. 116, 118, and 120.

37. *DRMN*, November 14, 1864, p. 2; Hall, *Colorado*, I, 318-19; and Percy S. Fritz, "Mining in Colorado," *Colorado and Its People*, II, 491.

38. Letter from John Evans to John P. Usher, September 23, 1864; from John Evans to Abraham Lincoln, March 6, 1865; and from John Evans to J. M. Ashley, March 14, 1865, Abraham Lincoln Papers, Library of Congress, microfilm reel no. 82.

39. Letters from John Evans to Abraham Lincoln, March 6, 1865, *ibid.*

40. *Congressional Globe*, 39th Cong., 1st Sess., 1866, Part III, 2372-73.

41. Letters from John Evans to Abraham Lincoln, March 6, 1865, Abraham Lincoln Papers, Library of Congress, microfilm reel no. 82.

42. Bancroft MS, P-L329, Fol. V, 37-39; Eugene Parsons, "John Evans, Colorado's Second Governor," *The Mining American*, LXXV (February, 1917), 8; and letter from James M. Ashley to William H. Seward, May 22, 1865, Records of the Department of State, Applications and Recommendations for Office, National Archives.

43. Letter from Abraham Lincoln to John Evans, March 16, 1865, in Basler (ed.), *Collected Works of Abraham Lincoln*, VIII, 356.

44. *DRMN*, January 13, 1865, p. 2, and January 14, 1865, p. 2.

45. Evans, *Reply of Governor Evans*, p. 1.

46. *Ibid.*, 14; and *Congressional Globe*, 39th Cong., 1st Sess., 1866, Part III, 2169.

47. Evans, *Reply of Governor Evans*, p. 14; Bancroft MS, P-L329, Fol. V, 36-37; and *DRMN*, June 19, 1865, p. 2.

48. *Condition of the Indian Tribes*, pp. 5-6. See also Doolittle's extended remarks on this subject in *Congressional Globe*, 39th Cong., 1st Sess., 1866, Part III, 2166.

49. Ellis, *Colorado Magazine*, VIII (1931), 26-27; Ellis, *Henry Moore Teller*, pp. 69-70.

50. Letter from James Harlan to John Evans, May 30, 1865, John Evans Collection.

51. See, for example, the remarks of Senators Doolittle and Lane, April 25, 1866, *Congressional Globe*, 39th Cong., 1st Sess., 1866, Part III, 2165, 2169.

52. Letter from Matthew Simpson to Abraham Lincoln with endorsement by James Harlan [February, 1861], Department of State, Applications and Recommendations for Office, National Archives; letter from John Evans to James Harlan, January 30, 1862, with endorsement by Harlan dated February 6, 1862, *ibid.*

53. Letter from John Evans to Matthew Simpson, December 13, 1864, Matthew Simpson Papers, Library of Congress. Evans stated

that he had spoken to Lincoln about the appointment and that the response seemed favorable.

54. Evans and Harlan, for example, cooperated closely in handling the bishop's investments. See Clark, *Life of Matthew Simpson*, p. 276. They were not, however, on good terms with other prominent Methodist friends of Simpson. See the letter from John M. Chivington to Simpson, March 9, 1865, Matthew Simpson Papers, Library of Congress, which illustrates Harlan's strong dislike of Chivington. The hostility between Evans and Alexander Cummings, the Methodist chosen by Simpson to replace him, is another case in point.

55. Letters from Allen A. Bradford to Andrew Johnson, May 22, 1865, and from J. M. Ashley to William H. Seward, May 22, 1865, Records of the Department of State, Applications and Recommendations for Office; *DRMN*, June 19, 1865, p. 2; letter from John Evans to James M. Ashley, March 14, 1865, microfilm reel no. 93, Abraham Lincoln Papers, Library of Congress.

56. Letter from Matthew Simpson to John Evans, June 28, 1865, John Evans Collection.

57. Letter from James M. Ashley to William H. Seward, May 22, 1865, Records of the Department of State, Applications and Recommendations for Office.

58. Letter from John Evans to William H. Seward, August 1, 1865, John Evans Collection.

59. Letter from Schuyler Colfax to Andrew Johnson, June 2, 1865, pencil copy in *ibid*.

60. Letters from James Harlan to John Evans, May 30, 1865; from Matthew Simpson to John Evans, June 28, 1865, and August 4, 1865, *ibid*.

61. Letter from Matthew Simpson to John Evans, June 28, 1865, *ibid*.

62. *Ibid*., August 4, 1865.

63. *Ibid*.

64. Letter from John Evans to Andrew Johnson, August 1, 1865, *ibid*.

65. Letter from John Evans to William H. Seward, August 1, 1865, *ibid*.

66. Letter from Matthew Simpson to John Evans, August 4, 1865; letter from James Harlan to John Evans, August 12, 1865; *ibid*.

67. Hall, *History of Colorado*, I, 366-67.

68. Ellis, *Henry M. Teller*, p. 69.

69. Hall, *History of Colorado*, I, 367; *Congressional Globe*, 39th Cong., 1st Sess., 1866, Part III, 2140, 2166.

70. See the schedule of Colorado election returns in *Congressional Globe*, 39th Cong., 1st Sess., 1866, Part II, 1353.

71. Ellis, *Henry M. Teller*, pp. 69-70.

72. Hall, *History of Colorado*, I, 290.

73. Ellis, *Henry M. Teller*, pp. 70, 72.

74. *DRMN*, December 18, 1865, p. 1.

75. Letter from Alexander Cummings to William H. Seward, December 22, 1865, State Department Territorial Papers, Colorado Series, National Archives.

76. Hall, *History of Colorado*, I, 378.

77. *Ibid.*, 367.

78. Alexander Cummings, message to the legislature, January 23, 1866, State Department Territorial Papers, Colorado Series, National Archives.

79. Alexander Cummings to William H. Seward, December 23, 1865, *ibid.*, Fols. 136, 138, 140.

80. John Evans, J. B. Chaffee, and G. M. Chilcott, *Admission of Colorado: Memorial of Her Congressional Delegation* (Washington: Gibson & Bros., 1866), p. 3.

81. *Congressional Globe*, 39th Cong., 1st Sess., 1866, Part II, 1357.

82. *Ibid.*, 2136.

83. *Ibid.*, 2033.

84. See, for example, the remarks of Senator Henry Wilson, *ibid.*, 2033-34.

85. Senator William M. Stewart, in *ibid.*, 2140-41.

86. *Ibid.*, 2166.

87. *Ibid.*, 2169-70.

88. *Ibid.*, 2169.

89. *Ibid.*, 1679.

90. *Ibid.*, 1809, 1861.

91. *Ibid.*, 1809.

92. In an interview on March 10, 1886, that was supposed to have been off the record, Evans said: "Andy Johnson was trying to get back the states into the union on what he called 'my policy.'" He offered Evans and Chaffee "our seats in the Senate if we would support his bill, which we refused to do." In spite of his request that he not be named, the newspaper identified Evans as the source of the story. See the *Denver Tribune-Republican*, March 10, 1866, p. 1. See also *DRMN*, June 5, 1866, p. 1, quoting the New York *Tribune*. According to the *Tribune*, the offer was made at the White House by Johnson's secretary. When it was refused, Evans and Chaffee were ushered into the President's office, where Johnson repeated the offer.

The two men refused again. See also *DRMN*, December 26, 1866, p. 1. Walter Lawson Wilder quoted Judge Robert W. Steele as saying in a public speech on January 31, 1907: "John Evans and Jerome B. Chaffee . . . proceeded to Washington, expecting to take their seats in the senate, but they were informed that they would be admitted to the senate upon condition (and I have it from one of the actors) that they would support the president and his policy. This they declined doing, and the president promptly vetoed the bill." See W. L. Wilder, *Robert Wilbur Steele, Defender of Liberty* (Denver: Carson-Harper Co., 1913), p. 92.

93. *Congressional Globe*, 39th Cong., 1st Sess., 1866, Part III, 2609.

94. *Ibid.*

95. *Ibid.*, 2712.

96. *Ibid.*, 2713.

97. *Ibid.*, 39th Cong., 2nd Sess., 1867, Part II, 818-20; Part III, 1928.

98. Letter from John Evans to Joel Evans, March 11, 1867, David Evans Papers.

99. Letter from John Evans to Edward Cooper, May 12, 1866, State Department Territorial Papers, Colorado Series, National Archives; letter from Rufus K. Frisbee to John Evans, February 5, 1866, photocopy in John Evans Collection.

100. Randall and Donald, *Civil War and Reconstruction*, p. 609.

101. Ellis, *Henry M. Teller*, pp. 74-75; *DRMN*, March 13, 1868, p. 2; *Congressional Globe*, 40th Cong., 3rd Sess., 1868, Part IV, 3547-51.

102. Letter from John Evans to Margaret Evans, July 5, 1868, John Evans Collection.

103. *DRMN*, July 21, 1868, p. 1.

"For Denver and my Railroad"

1. See the voluminous correspondence and financial records in the David Evans Papers.

2. The lesson of Oreapolis was still in Evans' mind when he arrived in Denver. His first trip to Colorado City showed the ill-chosen capital of the territory to be a half-deserted collection of tumbledown shacks, far removed from the main routes of trade. He told his wife that it reminded him of "a deserted Nebraska village . . . near the mouth of the Platte River," and said that Denver was "really the only tolerable place of residence in the whole country." See his letter to Margaret Evans, June 15, 1862, John Evans Collection.

3. *DRMN*, May 17, 1862, p. 2.

4. *DRMN*, June 27, 1862, p. 2. For Berthoud's account of his survey see *ibid.*, June 4, 1861, p. 2.

5. *Ibid.*, June 21, 1862, pp. 1, 3. See also his message to the territorial legislature, July 18, 1862, Executive Record, Book "A", p. 60.

6. *DRMN*, July 25, 1862, p. 3.

7. Samuel D. Mock, "Colorado and the Surveys for a Pacific Railroad," *The Colorado Magazine*, XVII (March, 1940), 56.

8. Quoted in *ibid.*

9. U. S., Congress, Senate, *An Act to Aid in the Construction of a Railroad and Telegraph Line from the Missouri River to the Pacific Ocean, and to Secure to the Government the Use of the Same for Postal, Military and Other Purposes*, 37th Cong., 2nd Sess., 1862, Misc. Doc. No. 108, 1-2.

10. *DRMN*, August 16, 1862, p. 2.

11. *Ibid.*, September 18, 1862, pp. 2-4.

12. Quoted in Mock, *Colorado Magazine*, XVII (1940), 57.

13. John Evans' message to the territorial legislature, in Executive Record, Book "A", pp. 137-38.

14. *Daily Commonwealth* [Denver], January 23, 1864, p. 3, and January 26, 1864, p. 2.

15. George L. Anderson, *Kansas West* (San Marino, Calif.: Golden West Books, 1963), 13. See also Evans' message in Executive Record, Book "A", pp. 137-38.

16. Letter from John Evans to John Pierce, February 24, 1866, John Evans Collection.

17. Letter from John Pierce to John Evans, February 25, 1866, *ibid.*

18. See the letters between John Dix and John Evans, February 6, 1866, and February 12, 1866, in *DRMN*, March 7, 1866, p. 2; and the letter from Dix to Evans, March 2, 1866, John Evans Collection.

19. *Ibid.*

20. Anderson, *Kansas West*, pp. 13-15.

21. *DRMN*, June 28, 1866, p. 1.

22. Anderson, *Kansas West*, pp. 13-15.

23. Richard C. Overton, "The Colorado and Southern Railway," *The Colorado Magazine*, XXVI (April, 1949), 86.

24. The Union Pacific board of directors determined to go through Cheyenne in a meeting in New York on November 15, 1866 (*ibid.*). Since the news did not break in Denver until early December, there apparently was no immediate announcement of the plan; Herbert O. Brayer, "History of Colorado-Railroads," *Colorado and Its People*, II, 639. On November 30, John Evans wrote his brother Joel from Chicago: "Telegram just received from my colleague Mr. Chaffee calls me to New York immediately." It seems logical to assume that this was the reason. See the letter in the David Evans Papers.

25. Richard C. Overton, *Gulf to Rockies: The Heritage of the Fort Worth and Denver—Colorado and Southern Railway, 1861-1898* (Austin: University of Texas Press, 1953), p. 12.

26. Samuel D. Mock, "The Financing of Early Colorado Railroads," *The Colorado Magazine*, XVIII (November, 1941), 202.

27. *Ibid.*, 202-03.

28. *Ibid.*, 203.

29. *DRMN*, November 18, 1867, p. 1.

30. *DRMN*, November 19, 1867, pp. 1, 4.

31. *DRMN*, December 3, 1867, p. 1.

32. Mock, "Early Colorado Railroads," *The Colorado Magazine*, XVIII (1941), 204-06.

33. *DRMN*, November 19, 1867, p. 1.

34. Mock, "Early Colorado Railroads," *The Colorado Magazine*, XVIII (1941), 203.

35. *DRMN*, March 17, 1868, p. 4.

36. *DRMN*, March 30, 1868, p. 1.

37. Mock, "Early Colorado Railroads," *The Colorado Magazine*, XVIII (1941), 203. Mock estimates that no more than $150,000 was ever realized from these bonds.

38. *DRMN*, May 5, 1868, p. 4; letter from John Evans in the *Denver Times*, May 3, 1877, p. 2; Mock, "Early Colorado Railroads," *The Colorado Magazine*, XVIII (1941), 204-05.

39. *Ibid.*

40. *Congressional Globe*, 40th Cong., 2nd Sess., 1868, Part IV, 3304.

41. *Ibid.*, Part II, 1759.

42. *Ibid.*, Part I, 4436; letter from John Evans in the *Denver Times*, May 3, 1877, p. 2.

43. *Congressional Globe*, 40th Cong., 2nd Sess., 1868, Part V, 4435-42.

44. *Ibid.*, and letter from John Evans in the *Denver Times*, May 3, 1877, p. 2.

45. *Ibid.*; *Congressional Globe*, 40th Cong., 3rd Sess., 1869, Part II, 1082, 1239-40, 1770; John Pierce, *Report of the Board of Trustees to the Stockholders of the Denver Pacific Railway and Telegraph Company*, broadside, Denver, January 11, 1870; referred to hereafter as *Report of the Board of the Denver Pacific, 1870*. See also the resolution of the Denver Board of Trade, March 20, 1869, which gives Evans full credit for the favorable land grant legislation; quoted in Bancroft MS, P-L329, Fol. I, 1.

46. Letter from John Evans in the *Denver Times*, May 3, 1877, p. 2.

47. *Ibid.*; *Congressional Globe*, 40th Cong., 3rd Sess., 1869, Part II, 1082.

48. Pierce, *Report of the Board of the Denver Pacific, 1870*.

49. Letter from John Evans in the *Denver Times*, May 3, 1877, p. 2.

50. As a step toward securing the agreement with Durant and Dillon, the board had increased the capital stock to $4,000,000 in December, 1868. Arapahoe County owned $500,000 of the stock. See *ibid.*

51. *Ibid.* See also Pierce, *Report of the Board of the Denver Pacific, 1870*, which fails to mention the capital stock arrangement.

52. Letter from John Evans in the *Denver Times*, May 3, 1877, p. 2; *DRMN*, April 1, 1870, p. 2; September 25, 1872, p. 2; May 20, 1877, p. 1.

53. Hall, *History of Colorado*, I, 487.

54. Letter from John Evans in the *Denver Times*, May 3, 1877, p. 2.

55. Anderson, *Kansas West*, p. 25.

56. Samuel D. Mock, "Railroad Development in the Colorado Region to 1880" (unpublished Ph.D. dissertation, University of Nebraska, 1938), p. 134.

57. *Ibid.*; Mock, "Early Colorado Railroads," *The Colorado Magazine*, XVIII (1941), 206; letter from John Evans in the *Denver Times*, May 3, 1877, p. 2.

58. Letter from John Evans in the *Denver Times*, May 3, 1877, p. 2.

59. Pierce, *Report of the Board of the Denver Pacific, 1870.*

60. *Ibid.*

61. Mock, "Railroad Development in the Colorado Region," p. 138, quoting the Golden *Transcript*, August 31, 1870.

62. Pierce, *Report of the Board of the Denver Pacific, 1870.*

63. Hall, *History of Colorado*, I, 487-88.

64. *Third Annual Report of the Officers of the Denver Pacific Railway and Telegraph Company, Made at the Stockholders' Meeting, Held May 8, 1871* (Denver: Woodbury & Walker, 1871), pp. 5-6, 10.

65. *Ibid.*, Mock, "Railroad Development in the Colorado Region," p. 168. Edgar McMechen states that Evans owned a controlling interest in the Boulder Valley Railroad. See his *Life of Governor Evans*, p. 172.

66. Brayer, "History of Colorado Railroads," *Colorado and Its People*, II, 643.

67. Mock, "Early Colorado Railroads," *The Colorado Magazine*, XVIII (1941), 204-08.

68. Palmer later said that Evans and his Denver friends had "very little if anything except the bonds of Arapahoe County" invested in the Denver Pacific. "As near as I can figure out," added Palmer, "Arapahoe County was my real partner." Quoted in Anderson, *Kansas West*, p. 84.

69. *DRMN*, February 20, 1872, p. 1; Bancroft MS, P-L329, Fol. V, 46.

70. *DRMN*, November 21, 1868, p. 2; December 3, 1868, p. 1; Meredith C. Poor, *Denver, South Park & Pacific* (Denver: Rocky Mountain Railroad Club, 1949), p. 97.

71. *DRMN*, November 21, 1868, p. 2; April 1, 1870, p. 1.

72. *DRMN*, June 24, 1870, p. 4.

73. *DRMN*, April 30, 1871, p. 1.

74. Bancroft MS, P-L329, Fol. III, 1.

75. *DRMN*, March 10, 1872, pp. 1-2; Poor, *Denver, South Park & Pacific*, p. 98.

76. *DRMN*, March 21, 1872, p. 2.

77. *DRMN*, October 6, 1872, p. 4; October 9, 1872, p. 2; October 16, 1872, p. 2; October 19, 1872, p. 4; November 6, 1872, p. 4; December 13, 1872, p. 4; January 18, 1873, p. 2; June 14, 1873, p. 4. The Colorado Central ultimately reached Georgetown in 1877. See Brayer, "History of Colorado Railroads," *Colorado and Its People*, II, 646.

78. *DRMN*, October 4, 1872, 4.

79. Poor, *Denver, South Park & Pacific*, p. 115.

80. *Ibid.*, 117-18.

81. *DRMN*, June 20, 1873, p. 4; June 22, 1873, p. 4; July 17, 1873, p. 2.

82. Bancroft MS, P-L329, Fol. III, 1. The correspondence between Evans and Palmer appeared in the *DRMN*, July 17, 1873, p. 2; July 22, 1873, p. 2; July 26, 1873, p. 2.

83. *Republican* [Denver], October 27, 1881, p. 4.

84. Poor, *Denver, South Park & Pacific*, p. 121.

85. These were thirty-year, eight-per-cent bonds. *DRMN*, August 5, 1873, p. 4.

86. Bancroft MS, P-L329, Fol. III, 1-3.

87. Poor, *Denver, South Park & Pacific*, p. 114.

88. Bancroft MS, P-L329, Fol. III, 1. Although he was closely associated with the town company, Evans was not an officer in the wagon road company. See his letter in *DRMN*, March 8, 1876, p. 4.

89. Bancroft MS, P-L329, Fol. III, 1-3; *DRMN*, February 28, 1874, p. 4; *DRMN*, March 4, 1874, p. 4.

90. *DRMN*, June 27, 1874, p. 2.

91. *DRMN*, January 3, 1875, p. 2.

92. *DRMN*, January 3, 1875, p. 2; Poor, *Denver, South Park & Pacific*, pp. 126-31; Bancroft MS, P-L329, Fol. III, 2.

93. Bancroft MS, P-L329, Fol. III, 2; *DRMN*, October 20, 1874, p. 4; December 20, 1874, p. 4; April 24, 1875, p. 4; May 26, 1875, p. 4; letter from John Evans to Margaret Evans, October 31, 1875, John Evans Collection.

94. Letter from John Evans to Margaret Evans, December 6, 1875, John Evans Collection.

95. Letter from John Evans to Margaret Evans, December 28, 1875.

96. Letter from John Evans to Margaret Evans, December 6, 1875, John Evans Collection. See also *ibid.*, February 8, 1876, in which

Evans wrote that "henceforth it would be war between the Rio Grande and K. P.," according to a conversation he had with R. E. Carr of the Kansas Pacific.

97. Overton, *Gulf to Rockies*, pp. 16-17, 20-21.

98. Letter from John Evans to Margaret Evans, February 8, 1876, John Evans Collection.

99. Letters from John Evans to Margaret Evans, February 8, 1876, and February 27, 1876, *ibid.*; *DRMN*, March 4, 1876, p. 2.

100. Letters from John Evans to Margaret Evans, February 8, 1876, February 14, 1876, March 27, 1876, April 2, 1876, May 6, 1876, June 2, 1876, July 9, 1876, John Evans Collection; Poor, *Denver, South Park & Pacific*, p. 134.

101. *DRMN*, April 23, 1876, p. 4; Poor, *Denver, South Park & Pacific*, p. 134.

102. Letter from John Evans to Margaret Evans, August 3, 1876, John Evans Collection.

103. *Ibid.*, December 6, 1875.

104. *Ibid.*, August 4, 1876.

105. *Ibid.*, August 21, 1876.

106. Poor, *Denver, South Park & Pacific*, p. 134; Bancroft MS, P-L329, Fol. III, 2-3.

107. Poor, *Denver, South Park & Pacific*, p. 144.

108. Bancroft MS, P-L329, Fol. III, 2-3.

109. Anderson, *Kansas West*, p. 194.

110. Bancroft MS, P-L329, Fol. III, 3-4; letter from Jay Gould to John Evans, January 8, 1878, John Evans Collection.

111. *DRMN*, November 10, 1878, p. 4; Bancroft MS, P-L329, Fol. III, 3-4.

112. Brayer, "History of Colorado Railroads," *Colorado and Its People*, II, p. 646.

113. Quoted in Poor, *Denver, South Park & Pacific*, pp. 190-91.

114. *Ibid.*; *DRMN*, December 3, 1878, p. 4. The suit was entered in the name of D. M. Edgerton, president of the Kansas Pacific, which had acquired a block of South Park stock in exchange for hauling construction material to Denver. Gould had acquired control of the Kansas Pacific in the spring of 1878. See Poor, *Denver, South Park & Pacific*, pp. 146, 190-99.

115. *DRMN*, December 13, 1878, p. 4.

116. Letter from John Evans to M. D. Thatcher, May 6, 1879, Colorado and Southern Letter Book, John Evans Collection. In this letter Evans referred to previous "cheerful and hopeful" correspondence from Thatcher.

117. The story is told with some detail in Anderson, *Kansas West*, pp. 219-53.

118. *Ibid.*, 199-200.

119. Letters from Jay Gould to John Evans, December 9, 1879 and December 20, 1879, John Evans Collection. See also Nelson Trottman, *History of the Union Pacific: A Financial and Economic Survey* (New York: Ronald Press Co., 1923), pp. 155-64.

120. Poor, *Denver, South Park & Pacific*, pp. 190-99.

121. Anderson, *Kansas West*, pp. 194-200.

122. *DRMN*, May 28, 1879, p. 4; September 30, 1879, p. 8.

123. See the letter from John Evans to Winslow, Lanier & Co., October 24, 1879, Colorado and Southern Letter Book, John Evans Collection; typed copy of Gould's agreement of October 1, 1879, John Evans Collection; letters from Jay Gould to John Evans, October 13, 1879, October 20, 1879, and October 25, 1879, *ibid.*

124. Letters from Jay Gould to John Evans, October 13, 1879, November 4, 1879, November 18, 1879, and December 9, 1879, *ibid.*

125. See the letter from John Evans to Winslow, Lanier & Co., October 24, 1879, Colorado and Southern Letter Book, John Evans Collection. See also the testimony of John Evans given July 12, 1887, in U.S., Congress, Senate, *Report of the Pacific Railway Commission*, 50th Cong., 1st Sess., 1887, Ex. Doc. No. 51, Vol. III, 1856, referred to hereafter as *Pacific Railway Commission*. See also the copy of the agreement executed by Gould, October 1, 1879, John Evans Collection.

126. *Pacific Railway Commission*, III, 1856.

127. Anderson, *Kansas West*, pp. 197-200; letters from Jay Gould to John Evans, October 13, 1879, and October 19, 1879, Colorado and Southern Letter Book, John Evans Collection.

128. Poor, *Denver, South Park & Pacific*, p. 191. Gould himself said that he paid $100,000. See his letter to John Evans, December 20, 1879, John Evans Collection.

129. Byers, *Encyclopedia of Biography of Colorado*, 249.

130. See, for example, *DRMN*, January 22, 1879, p. 4; February 23, 1879, p. 4.

131. *DRMN*, June 1, 1879, p. 6.

132. *DRMN*, December 2, 1879, p. 8. Apparently there was little or no opposition to the measure, although the *News* did say that "some of the South Park officials" were "just a trifle" active in support of the measure. See *DRMN*, December 3, 1879, p. 8.

133. See the letters from William N. Byers to O. J. Hollister, June 15, 1866; to John Evans, May 24, 1866; to John Evans, April 5,

1868; Byers letter books, Western Historical Collections, University of Colorado Library, Boulder.

134. Letter from John Evans to Margaret Evans, September 3, 1876, John Evans Collection.

135. Letter from John Evans to "the Editors of the Newspaper Press of Colorado," June 27, 1881, single-sheet broadside in the John Evans Collection.

136. *Denver Tribune*, September 8, 1881, quoted in *Denver Republican*, November 19, 1881, p. 8; *Denver Republican*, August 29, 1882, p. 8; *DRMN*, November 8, 1881, p. 1.

137. According to Evans "it never came to trial because they went away." Bancroft MS, P-L329, Fol. III, 8-9.

138. See the testimony of John Evans in *Pacific Railway Commission*, III, 1851.

139. Letter from Jay Gould to John Evans, December 20, 1879, John Evans Collection.

140. Letter from John Evans to Jay Gould, November 18, 1879, *ibid*.

141. Note the furious activity reported in the letters from Jay Gould to John Evans, October 25, 1879, November 4, 1879, November 8, 1879, November 18, 1879, and January 3, 1880, *ibid*.

142. Letter from John Evans to Jay Gould, February 6, 1880, *ibid*.

143. See the typed copy of the pooling agreement, dated January 1, 1880, *ibid*.

144. Robert G. Athearn, *Rebel of the Rockies: A History of the Denver and Rio Grande Western Railroad* (New Haven: Yale University Press, 1962), p. 106.

145. See the typed copy of the pooling agreement, dated January 1, 1880, in the John Evans Collection.

146. Letter from Jay Gould to John Evans, July 5, 1880, *ibid*.

147. C. E. Hagie, "Gunnison in Early Days," *The Colorado Magazine*, VIII (July, 1931), 126.

148. Robert G. Athearn states that Palmer deliberately violated the agreement because he felt that Gould's intention to purchase the South Park "would result in Union Pacific control and a circumvention of the agreement." See his *Rebel of the Rockies*, p. 106.

149. Testimony of John Evans, *Pacific Railway Commission*, III, 1852; in Poor, *Denver, South Park & Pacific*, p. 193; Bancroft MS, P-L329, Fol. III, 4.

150. Athearn, *Rebel of the Rockies*, p. 106.

151. Letter from Jay Gould to John Evans, July 5, 1880, John Evans Collection.

152. *Ibid.*; *DRMN*, November 18, 1880, p. 8.

153. Testimony of John Evans, *Pacific Railway Commission*, III, 1853. The South Park board, on August 2, 1880, gave Evans "full power to negotiate for the sale" of the road. Minute Book of the Board of Trustees of the Denver, South Park and Pacific Railway Co., p. 167 (microfilm in Colorado State Archives, Denver).

154. Bancroft MS, P-L329, Fol. III, 4; testimony of John Evans, *Pacific Railway Commission*, III, 1853.

155. The line showed a phenomenal net profit of $996,621 on 162 miles in 1880. See the testimony of Commissioner E. Ellery Anderson and Jay Gould in *Pacific Railway Commission*, I, 572.

156. Bancroft MS, P-L329, Fol. III, 4; and testimony of John Evans, *Pacific Railway Commission*, III, 1853.

157. Bancroft MS, P-L329, Fol. III, 4; and testimony of John Evans, *Pacific Railway Commission*, III, 1853. These negotiations were carried on in New York, but when Evans and Palmer failed to agree on the terms of the sale, Evans returned to Denver.

158. Telegram from Jay Gould to John Evans, November 5, 1880, *Pacific Railway Commission*, III, 1853.

159. Telegram from John Evans to Jay Gould, November 5, 1880, *ibid.*

160. Telegram from Jay Gould to John Evans, November 6, 1880, *ibid.*

161. Telegram from John Evans to Jay Gould, November 8, 1880, *ibid.*

162. Telegram from Jay Gould to John Evans, November 8, 1880, *ibid.* Just what the reference to Ames implied is hard to say. Evans seems to have felt that it meant Gould's negotiations had the blessing of the Union Pacific but that the Union Pacific was not a party to the negotiations. See his testimony of November 11, 1893, in *John Evans* v. *Union Pacific, Denver and Gulf Railway et al.* (Case No. 3001, United States Circuit Court for the District of Colorado; typescript in John Evans Collection); hereafter cited as *John Evans* v. *UPD&G.*

163. Telegram from John Evans to Jay Gould, November 9, 1880, *Pacific Railway Commission*, III, 1854.

164. Telegram from Jay Gould to John Evans, November 9, 1880, *ibid.*

165. Bancroft MS, P-L329, Fol. III, 4.

166. See the undated release from trust for J. S. Brown, photostatic copy in the John Evans Collection.

167. Letter from John Evans to D. H. Moffat, January 16, 1880,

Colorado and Southern Letter Book, John Evans Collection. See also the testimony of Charles Wheeler, former auditor of the Denver and South Park Railroad Construction and Land Company, in *Pacific Railway Commission*, III, 1736. Wheeler stated that Gould held 5,716 shares of South Park stock at the time of the sale and that this did not represent a full quarter-interest, since he "transferred subsequently a portion of that" stock.

168. If Evans had 5,600.25 shares in the trust at the time of the sale, having previously sold one-fourth of his stock to Gould, his original holdings would have been 7,467 shares; similarly, his wife's original holdings would have been 500 shares. If only his own shares were included in the repurchase deal with Gould, Evans held 1,866.75 shares outside the trust in 1880; if his wife's shares were included, the amount would have been 1,991.75. That Evans held stock outside the original trust is conjecture, but two points support it. First, Gould's method of payment, discussed later, is most easily explained by assuming that there were several trusts or that individuals held stock outside the original trust. Evans' letter to Winslow, Lanier & Co., October 24, 1879, clearly indicates that Evans held at least a small amount of stock outside the original trust. See the letter in the Colorado and Southern Letter Book, John Evans Collection.

169. Letter from John Evans to Winslow, Lanier & Co., October 24, 1879, *ibid.*

170. This is based on the fact that Gould paid Evans $14,000 for one-fourth of Evans' stock. See the letter from John Evans to D. H. Moffat, January 16, 1880, *ibid.*

171. See the testimony of Charles Wheeler, *Pacific Railway Commission*, III, 1735-36. Poor (*Denver, South Park & Pacific*, p. 197) arrived at a different total, partly because of counting Gould's Arapahoe County shares twice.

172. See the testimony of John Evans, *Pacific Railway Commission*, III, 1854-55.

173. Testimony of John Evans, *ibid.*, 1853.

174. Minute Book of the Board of Trustees of the Denver, South Park and Pacific Railway Co., meeting of November 22, 1880, p. 215 (microfilm, Colorado State Archives, Denver).

175. Letter from John Evans to Jay Gould, January 7, 1881, Colorado and Southern Letter Book, John Evans Collection.

176. *John Evans* v. *UPD&G.*

177. Bancroft MS, P-L329, Fol. III, 5.

178. Trottman, *History of the Union Pacific*, p. 194; and Poor, *Denver, South Park & Pacific*, p. 198.

179. Overton, *Gulf to Rockies*, p. 233.

180. Letter from Charles Francis Adams to G. M. Dodge, March 26, 1886, quoted in Overton, *Gulf to Rockies*, p. 155.

181. Bernard Axelrod, "Rocky Mountain Customs Port of Entry," *The Colorado Magazine*, XLI (Spring, 1964), 127-28.

182. John Evans, *Third Address on the Crises of Denver before the Denver Chamber of Commerce and Board of Trade* (Denver: n.n., 1886), pp. 3-4, pamphlet in the John Evans Collection; hereafter cited as *Third Address on the Crises of Denver*.

183. The date of organization was apparently January 5, 1881. See the *Confidential Statement, Denver and New Orleans R. R. Co.* (Denver: n.n., 1881), p. 1, pamphlet in the John Evans Collection. Plans were not made public until January 25, 1881, when the articles of incorporation were filed. See the *DRMN*, January 26, 1881, p. 8.

184. *DRMN*, January 26, 1881, p. 8; Overton, *Gulf to Rockies*, p. 51. Overton's book is the only complete and authoritative work on this railroad; corporate history is traced in infinite detail in this well-researched volume.

185. Bancroft MS, P-L329, Fol. III, 5-6.

186. Evans, *Confidential Statement, Denver & New Orleans R.R. Co.*, p. 1; *Statement Regarding the Denver and New Orleans R.R., Its Important Connections, Progress of Construction, Business Prospects, Stock, Bonds, etc., Made May 20th, 1882* (New York: E. Wells Sackett & Rankin, 1882), p. 1.

187. *Speech of Ex-Gov. John Evans, President of the Denver and New Orleans Railroad, to the Stockholders of the Construction Company, Showing the Importance of that Enterprise in Making of Denver the Great Commercial and Manufacturing City of the New West* (Denver: n.n., 1881), p. 6. Referred to hereafter as *Speech of Ex-Gov. John Evans*.

188. Letter from Champion Vaughan to John Evans, July 24, 1881, John Evans Collection.

189. Letter from John Evans to A. B. Sopris, August 30, 1881, Colorado and Southern Letter Book, *ibid*.

190. Bancroft MS, P-L329, Fol. III, 8-9.

191. *Tribune* [Denver], July 17, 1881, p. 4.

192. *Ibid.*, July 19, 1881, pp. 1, 4. In March the *Tribune* had charged Evans with failure to pay proper taxes on his bonds. *Ibid.*, March 22, 1881, p. 8. The real battle on this question was not opened, however, until August, 1881. See *ibid.*, August 10, 1881, pp. 1, 4; August 11, 1881, p. 4; August 13, 1881, p. 4. See also the *Republican* [Denver], August 10, 1881, p. 6.

193. *Tribune* [Denver], July 17, 1881, p. 4; July 19, 1881, p. 1; July 20, 1881, pp. 1, 4; July 21, 1881, p. 4; July 22, 1881, pp. 1, 4; *Republican* [Denver], July 22, 1881, p. 8; July 23, 1881, p. 8; *DRMN*, July 20, 1881, p. 8.

194. *Republican* [Denver], July 26, 1881, p. 4. This charge was to be revived in 1884 in a confused and rambling document by George Morrison to the effect that Evans was guilty of "unmasonic" conduct in selling the South Park's interest in the Morrison Town Co. to Jay Gould. The exact reason for Morrison's accusation is not clear, but Evans was declared "not guilty of the charges." See the copy of Morrison's statement dated November 14, 1884, the report of the investigating committees, and O. A. Whittemore's letter to George Morrison and John Evans of the same date, all of which are in the John Evans Collection.

195. *DRMN*, July 20, 1881, p. 8; *Republican* [Denver], July 23, 1881, pp. 2, 8.

196. Letter from John Evans to "The Editors of the Newspaper Press of Colorado," June 27, 1881, single-sheet broadside in the John Evans Collection.

197. Letter from John Evans to A. B. Sopris, August 30, 1881, Colorado and Southern Letter Book, John Evans Collection.

198. Perhaps the best illustration of this statement is Evans' observation some years later that the *Tribune* editors left town in order to avoid standing trial for libel (Bancroft MS, P-L329, Fol. III, 8-9). To be precise, Evans stated to the Bancroft interviewer that Rothacker and Field were never brought to trial on the grand jury indictment "because they went away." The indictment is printed in the *Republican* [Denver], November 19, 1881, p. 8. Evans' own libel suit against the two was to have been heard in August, 1882. It was continued at that time, and apparently did not come to trial. See the *Republican* [Denver], August 29, 1882, p. 2.

199. *DRMN*, October 26, 1881, p. 4; *Speech of Ex Gov. John Evans*, pp. 6 7.

200. *DRMN*, October 8, 1881, p. 8.

201. *Ibid.*

202. *Ibid.*, October 10, 1881, p. 4.

203. *Republican* [Denver], October 22, 1881, p. 1.

204. *Tribune* [Denver], October 23, 1881, p. 12.

205. *DRMN*, October 23, 1881, p. 5.

206. *Tribune* [Denver], October 23, 1881, p. 12.

207. *Speech of Ex-Gov. John Evans*, p. 7; *DRMN*, October 14, 1881, p. 4; October 29, 1881, p. 4.

208. *DRMN,* October 23, 1881, p. 5.

209. *DRMN,* October 29, 1881, p. 4.

210. *Ibid.,* quoting a recent issue of the *Times.*

211. *Republican* [Denver], November 1, 1881, p. 4.

212. *Ibid.,* October 30, 1881, p. 4.

213. *DRMN,* November 10, 1881, p. 4.

214. *Ibid.,* November 12, 1881, p. 4.

215. *Speech of Ex-Gov. John Evans,* p. 7.

216. *Republican* [Denver], July 19, 1881, p. 5; Bancroft MS, P-L329, Fol. III, 6.

217. *Tribune* [Denver], May 4, 1882, p. 1; *DRMN,* May 4, 1882, p. 6; *Republican* [Denver], May 4, 1882, p. 1.

218. Overton, *Gulf to Rockies,* p. 23.

219. *Ibid.,* p. 84; John Evans, *Memorial Praying for the Passage of Senate Bill No. 1, or Its Counterpart, House Bill No. 19* (Denver: n.n., 1885), p. 7.

220. Bancroft MS, P-L329, Fol. III, 7-8.

221. *Ibid.,* 7.

222. *DRMN,* August 25, 1881, p. 6; Bancroft MS, P-L329, Fol. III, 7. In 1888, Evans told an interviewer that the Denver and New Orleans had been "living on that coal for several years." See *ibid.,* 7.

223. Bancroft MS, P-L329, Fol. III, 6-8; Henry V. Poor, *Manual of the Railroads of the United States for 1883* (New York: H. V. & H. W. Poor, 1883), p. 885; Poor, *Manual of the Railroads of the United States for 1884* (New York: H. V. & H. W. Poor, 1884), p. 860; Poor, *Manual of the Railroads of the United States for 1887* (New York: H. V. & H. W. Poor, 1887), p. 735. Richard Overton, *Gulf to Rockies,* pp. 84-87, states that the loan was made by the Mercantile Trust Company. This is obviously based on a misinterpretation of the Bancroft MS, and a failure to consider the additional data in Poor's *Manual for 1887.*

224. See the sources cited above.

225. Bancroft MS, P-L329, Fol. III, 6-8.

226. Letter from Charles Wheeler, secretary of the Denver Texas and Gulf Railroad, to John Evans, March 28, 1887, John Evans Collection. Wheeler gives John Evans' holdings as $262,072.97 and Sage's as $260,195.99. These figures included the ten per cent annual interest. Evans' original investment was apparently $226,500 and Sage's was $232,975. See Evans' list of names signed to the pooling contract, dated July 6, 1883, in the John Evans Collection. According to this list, Sage still had not signed. The letter from Charles Wheeler to John Evans, March 28, 1887, indicates that Sage later agreed to

the new arrangement. Wheeler explained the difference in interest by saying that the "Trust Notes had widely varied in dates."

227. Bancroft MS, P-L329, Fol. III, 8.

228. Overton, *Gulf to Rockies*, pp. 104-07.

229. *DRMN*, March 14, 1884, p. 6.

230. *Tribune* [Denver], March 21, 1884, p. 6.

231. Poor, *Manual for 1884*, p. 860.

232. Telegram from Winslow, Lanier and Company to John Evans, March 15, 1884, John Evans Collection.

233. Telegram from John Evans to Winslow, Lanier and Company, March 14, 1885, *ibid*.

234. Bancroft MS, P-L329, Fol. III, 9; letter from John Evans to G. M. Dodge, April 5, 1884, John Evans Collection.

235. Overton, *Gulf to Rockies*, p. 114. Overton was apparently not aware of Dodge's agreement with Evans, and for this reason he interpreted Evans' action in leaving the Denver and New Orleans directory as a "no-confidence" vote on the part of the other stockholders.

236. Bancroft MS, P-L329, Fol. III, 9.

237. *DRMN*, October 29, 1884, p. 2; letter from John Evans to Jay Gould, October 28, 1884, Colorado and Southern Letter Book, John Evans Collection; Bancroft MS, P-L329, Fol. III, 9.

238. Letter from John Evans to Jay Gould, October 28, 1884, Colorado and Southern Letter Book, John Evans Collection; and letter from Russell Sage to John Evans, January 22, 1885, *ibid*.

239. *DRMN*, December 20, 1884, p. 2; December 21, 1884, p. 6.

240. Letter from Russell Sage to John Evans, January 22, 1885; letter from Edward D. Adams to William Barth, May 16, 1885; letter from John Evans to Russell Sage, May 27, 1885, Colorado and Southern Letter Book, John Evans Collection.

241. Letter from John Evans to Augustus Kountze, May 28, 1885, *ibid*.; letter from John Evans to Russell Sage, May 27, 1885, *ibid*.

242. Poor, *Manual for 1887*, pp. 735-36; letter from John Evans to Augustus Kountze, May 27, 1885, Colorado and Southern Letter Book, John Evans Collection.

243. *DRMN*, August 19, 1885, p. 8; letter from George Tritch to John Evans, June 23, 1885, John Evans Collection; Overton, *Gulf to Rockies*, pp. 139-40.

244. Overton, *Gulf to Rockies*, p. 140.

245. Letter from Russell Sage to John Evans, December 17, 1885, John Evans Collection.

246. *Ibid*., December 14, 1885.

247. *DRMN*, March 19, 1886, p. 7; Poor, *Manual for 1887*, p. 735.

248. Letter from Charles Wheeler to John Evans, March 28, 1887, John Evans Collection. Overton misconstrued Wheeler's letter to mean that Evans and Sage each held some $750,000 in Denver and New Orleans securities and received only about a third of this amount in exchange. See his *Gulf to Rockies*, p. 140.

249. Poor, *Manual for 1887*, p. 735.

250. Overton, *Gulf to Rockies*, pp. 82-83, 131, 141-46; Bancroft MS, P-L329, Fol. III, 11-12.

251. Overton, *Gulf to Rockies*, pp. 146-48; Bancroft MS, P-L329, Fol. III, 9-11. The interviewer wrote that Strong raised the offer "to two hundred thousand dollars" but the context shows that $2,000,-000 is the correct figure.

252. *DRMN*, February 11, 1887, p. 1; February 25, 1887, p. 4, and April 13, 1887, p. 8; Bancroft MS, P-L329, Fol. III, 11.

253. Poor, *Manual for 1889*, p. 752. This was arranged through the influence of David Moffat, who became president of the Rio Grande in April, 1887. Overton, *Gulf to Rockies*, pp. 161-62.

254. Overton, *Gulf to Rockies*, p. 181.

255. *Ibid.*, 199.

256. *Ibid.*, 200-01; letter from John Evans to G. M. Dodge, August 3, 1888, Letter Book No. 2, John Evans Collection.

257. Letter from John Evans to Morgan Jones, February 4, 1889, Letter Book No. 2, John Evans Collection.

258. Letter from John Evans to G. M. Dodge, January 29, 1890, *ibid.*; Overton, *Gulf to Rockies*, pp. 244-45.

259. Overton, *Gulf to Rockies*, p. 237.

260. *Ibid.*, 257.

261. Letter from John Evans to Sidney Dillon, November 27, 1890, Letter Book No. 2, John Evans Collection.

262. Although the South Park investments were carried on in the name of Gould, and the Denver and New Orleans in Sage's name, Evans refers to them as though they were partners in both investments, and this was undoubtedly the case. See the Bancroft MS, P-L329, Fol. III. There is also evidence of Sage's heavy investment in the South Park in the Minute Book of the Board of Trustees of the Denver, South Park and Pacific Railway Co. meeting of November 22, 1880, p. 215 (microfilm, Colorado State Archives, Denver).

263. Bancroft MS, P-L329, Fol. III, 5; letter from John Evans to Sidney Dillon, November 27, 1890, Letter Book No. 2, John Evans Collection.

264. *Republican* [Denver], August 11, 1868, p. 6.

265. *DRMN*, October 5, 1891, p. 4; *ibid.*, November 20, 1891, p.

4; letter from F. L. Dana to John Evans, February 13, 1891, and August 15, 1891, John Evans Collection; Overton, *Gulf to Rockies*, p. 318.

266. Overton, *Gulf to Rockies*, p. 352.

267. Letter from E. T. Wells to John Evans, September 20, 1891, John Evans Collection.

268. Letter from John Evans to Walter Gresham, January 14, 1892, *ibid.*

269. *DRMN*, March 11, 1892, p. 5.

270. *Ibid.*, March 26, 1892, p. 3; April 5, 1892, p. 4; October 1, 1892, p. 3.

271. *DRMN*, April 5, 1892, pp. 3-5, records his election as president of the Denver and El Paso line; his election to the presidency of the Denver, Salt Lake, and San Francisco is in *DRMN*, July 8, 1893, p. 3; *DRMN*, July 4, 1894, p. 5, reports his election as president of the Denver, Sioux City, Lake Superior, and Chicago Railroad.

272. Overton, *Gulf to Rockies*, pp. 283-84, 288.

273. *Ibid.*, 290-91.

274. *Ibid.*, 306-07.

275. *Ibid.*, 310.

276. *DRMN*, April 11, 1894, p. 3

277. Overton, *Gulf to Rockies*, pp. 273, 284, 297.

278. See his Journal, January 1, 1895-November 16, 1896, pp. 40, 42, 44, 71, John Evans Collection. Numerous entries in this journal show that Evans' financial records were both incomplete and inaccurate. It is quite possible that his stockholdings were listed elsewhere, or not listed at all. See, for example, the entry on page 41, which states that "many charges and debits have never been entered."

279. Letter from John Evans to Margaret Evans, December 28, 1875, John Evans Collection.

"The Personal Interests of John Evans"

1. *Daily Commonwealth* [Denver], January 30, 1864, pp. 2-3; Helen Cannon "First Ladies of Colorado: Josephine Evans Elbert," *The Colorado Magazine*, XXXIX (October, 1962), 265.

2. Cannon, "Josephine Evans Elbert," *The Colorado Magazine*, XXXIX (1962), 265.

3. Matthew Simpson, "I Shall See the Sun Rise in Heaven," *Northwestern Christian Advocate* [Chicago], December 2, 1868, p. 1.

4. Letter from Matthew Simpson to John Evans, June 28, 1865, John Evans Collection.

5. Cannon, "Josephine Evans Elbert," *The Colorado Magazine*, XXXIX (1962), 268.

6. Letter from John Evans to Margaret Evans, July 5, 1868, John Evans Collection.

7. *Ibid.*; Simpson, *Northwestern Christian Advocate* [Chicago], December 2, 1868, p. 1.

8. Letter from John Evans to Margaret Evans, July 5, 1868, John Evans Collection.

9. *Ibid.*

10. McMechen, *Life of Governor Evans*, p. 108.

11. *Ibid.*; *Denver Times*, June 13, 1917, p. 6; McMechen, "A Forest Home in the Mountains of Colorado," *House Beautiful*, XLII (June, 1917), 22-23. The mountain trip in question was the famous excursion of 1868 taken by Schuyler Colfax, former Lieutenant Governor Bross of Illinois, Ovando Hollister, Frank Hall, Colorado Territorial Governor A. C. Hunt, and others. During the trip Colfax, Hollister, and Hall met and wooed the young ladies who were to become their wives. There is some question whether the Evans family was present during the entire journey. Mrs. Daniel Witter, who was there, said: "The last day out, John Evans and party joined us." See her "Pioneer Life," *The Colorado Magazine*, IV (December, 1927), 173. Isa Hunt Stearns, who was also on the trip and twelve years old

at the time, said many years later that the Evans family was present during the entire trip. See Isa Stearns Gregg (ed.), "Reminiscences of Isa Hunt Stearns," *The Colorado Magazine*, XXVI (July, 1949), 189. Mrs. Frank Hall, another member of the party, agreed with Mrs. Stearns on this point. See her reminiscences recorded by LeRoy Hafen in "Seventy Years Ago: Recollections of a Trip through the Colorado Mountains with the Colfax Party in 1868," *The Colorado Magazine*, XV (September, 1938), 164. Samuel Bowles, another member of the party, writing in 1869, mentioned the Evans family as being with the party only on the last day of the trip. See his book, *The Switzerland of America: A Summer Vacation in the Parks and Mountains of Colorado* (Springfield, Mass.: Samuel Bowles & Co., 1869), p. 144.

12. Letter from John Evans to Margaret Evans, July 16, 1876, John Evans Collection.

13. Letter from John Evans to Margaret Evans, December 30, 1875, John Evans Collection.

14. *DRMN*, May 11, 1870, p. 4.

15. *Ibid.*, June 24, 1870, p. 4.

16. *Ibid.*, November 9, 1870, p. 4. Letter from Mary Lincoln to Mrs. Robert Todd Lincoln [December], 1870, quoted in Katherine Helm, *The True Story of Mary, Wife of Lincoln, Containing the Recollections of Mary Lincoln's Sister Emilie (Mrs. Ben Hardin Helm), Extracts from Her War-Time Diary, Numerous Letters and Other Documents Now First Published* (New York: Harper & Bros., 1928), p. 278.

17. Letter from Mary Lincoln to Mrs. Robert Todd Lincoln, [December,] 1870, quoted in Helm, *True Story of Mary, Wife of Lincoln*, p. 278.

18. Letter from Mary Lincoln to Mrs. Robert Todd Lincoln, February 12, 1871, quoted in *ibid*. Although the date is given there as 1870, it is obviously 1871, as Ruth Painter Randall indicates in her *Mary Lincoln: Biography of a Marriage* (Boston: Little, Brown & Co., 1953), p. 511, n. 64.

19. Cannon, "Margaret Gray Evans," *The Colorado Magazine*, XXXIX (1962), 27.

20. *DRMN*, April 1, 1871, p. 1.

21. *Specification of John Evans; Apparatus for Supporting Bed in Steam Ships, &c.* (London: Great Seal Patent Office, 1872), pamphlet in the John Evans Collection.

22. A letter from John Evans to Margaret Evans, June 2, 1876, John Evans Collection, implies that Margaret used the special berth on her 1875 ocean voyage.

23. Letters from Haseltine, Lake and Company to John Evans, November 12, 1871; February 15, 1872; March 13, 1873, *ibid.*

24. *DRMN*, August 4, 1871, p. 1; August 10, 1871, p. 1; December 17, 1871, p. 1.

25. McMechen, *Life of Governor Evans*, pp. 178-79.

26. Allen D. Breck, *William Gray Evans, 1855-1924: Portrait of a Western Executive* (Denver: University of Denver, 1964), p. 36.

27. McMechen, *Life of Governor Evans*, pp. 178-79.

28. *DRMN*, November 7, 1871, p. 1.

29. *DRMN*, December 9, 1871, p. 1.

30. *Denver Post*, July 25, 1909, Sunday supplement, p. 3; *Denver Tribune*, February 4, 1881, p. 8; letter from John Evans to Margaret Evans, July 31, 1876, John Evans Collection.

31. J. H. Ballenger, T. B. Corbett, and W. C. Hoye, *Second Annual City Directory for 1874 of the Inhabitants, Institutions, Incorporated Companies, Manufacturing Establishments, Business, Business Firms, etc., in the City of Denver* (Denver: Ballenger, Hoye & Co., 1874), pp. 107-08; referred to hereafter as *Denver City Directory*. An example of the social affairs during Elbert's administration was the reception of January 8, 1874. See the account in *DRMN*, January 9, 1874, p. 4.

32. Hall, *History of Colorado*, II, 155.

33. Letter from John Evans to Margaret Evans, June 26, 1876, John Evans Collection.

34. *Ibid.*; letter from John Evans to Margaret Evans, November 11, 1876, *ibid.*

35. This is Evans' recollection of the conversation an hour or so after the lunch was over. See his letter to Margaret Evans, June 26, 1876, *ibid.* As it turned out, Elbert did not get the appointment, but he was elected to the state supreme court in 1876. Bancroft MS, P-L21, 11.

36. See the letter from John Evans to Margaret Evans, August 12, 1876, John Evans Collection, in which Evans assured his wife that "there are very many nice people here [in Denver]—more than formerly." His long letter is apparently a reply to Margaret's complaint about their lack of good friends in Denver. See also the letters from John to Margaret, August 12, 1876; September 24, 1876, *ibid.* In an effort to find a congenial home for Margaret, Evans even suggested a return to Evanston, but he plainly was reluctant to do this and she apparently did not press the matter. See the letter from John to Margaret, November 10, 1876, *ibid.* In Margaret's obituary it was

noted that she did not make friends easily, particularly in her later years; *DRMN*, September 8, 1906, p. 7.

37. Letter from John Evans to Margaret Evans, October 1, 1876, John Evans Collection. *DRMN*, April 21, 1877, p. 4.

38. Letter from John Evans to Margaret Evans, August 3, 1876, John Evans Collection.

39. *DRMN*, May 26, 1875, p. 4.

40. *DRMN*, October 20, 1874, p. 4.

41. Letters from John Evans to Margaret Evans, October 22, 1875; October 31, 1875; November 7, 1875; November 11, 1875; March 22, 1876; John Evans Collection.

42. Letter from John Evans to Margaret Evans, March 22, 1876, *ibid.*; Wilbur F. Stone, "Evan E. Evans," *History of Colorado* (4 vols.; Chicago: S. J. Clarke Publ. Co., 1918), II, 8.

43. *DRMN*, December 30, 1875, p. 4.

44. Letter from John Evans to Margaret Evans, March 6, 1876, John Evans Collection.

45. Letter from Margaret Evans to John Evans, March 29, 1876, *ibid.*

46. Letter from Margaret Evans to John Evans, April 5, 1876, *ibid.*

47. Letter from Margaret Evans to John Evans, April 11, 1876, *ibid.*

48. Letters from John Evans to Margaret Evans, April 23, 1876; April 29, 1876, *ibid.*

49. Letter from Margaret Evans to John Evans, May 7, 1876, *ibid.*

50. Letters from John Evans to Margaret Evans, November 7, 1875; December 30, 1875; John Evans Collection.

51. Letter from John Evans to Margaret Evans, June 10, 1876, *ibid.*

52. Letter from John Evans to Margaret Evans, June 16, 1876, *ibid.*

53. Letters from John Evans to Margaret Evans, August 12, 1876; November 3, 1876, *ibid.* See also the letter from William G. Evans to Margaret Evans, September 4, 1876, quoted in Breck, *William Gray Evans*, pp. 40-41.

54. Letter from John Evans to Margaret Evans, September 24, 1876, John Evans Collection.

55. *Ibid.*

56. Letters from John Evans to Margaret Evans, August 21, 1876; November 3, 1876, *ibid.*

57. *DRMN*, April 21, 1877, p. 4; they also wanted to visit Egypt

(see the letter from John Evans to Margaret Evans, August 12, 1876, John Evans Collection), but there is no record of their having done so.

58. *DRMN*, December 31, 1879, p. 8.

59. *Denver Tribune*, February 4, 1881, p. 8.

60. *Denver Republican*, December 13, 1883, p. 5. See also the accounts in *DRMN*, December 13, 1883, p. 3; and *Denver Tribune*, December 13, 1883, p. 8.

61. *DRMN*, October 11, 1878, p. 4; see also the pamphlet, *Evans Memorial Chapel; University of Denver*, which was distributed at the chapel in 1960, after it was moved to the University Park Campus. Although Evans paid construction costs, the furnishings were donated by others. See the letter from John Evans to F. L. Millington, August 7, 1878, John Evans Collection; John Alton Templin, "A History of Methodism in Denver, 1876-1912" (unpublished doctoral dissertation, Iliff School of Theology, Denver, 1956), p. 55.

62. *DRMN*, February 14, 1865, p. 3; letter from John Evans to Mattie Stewart Smith, October 19, 1887, John Evans Collection; Templin, "History of Methodism in Denver," p. 41.

63. McMechen, *Life of Governor Evans*, p. 212. See also Evans' statement in a public speech in October, 1881: "All the old settlers know, that . . . [in times past], I made large donations to all the churches and schools in the state." *Denver Republican*, October 30, 1881, p. 5.

64. Letter from Margaret Evans to John Evans, May 4, 1876, John Evans Collection. Margaret had said much the same thing in a letter of May 3, 1876, *ibid*. As it turned out Evans was unable to attend because of the "critical condition" of his railroad negotiations. See his letter to Margaret, May 6, 1876, *ibid*. For a glimpse of his work at conference sessions, see *DRMN*, July 22, 1871, p. 1; July 23, 1871, p. 1; July 27, 1873, p. 4; August 2, 1874, p. 4; *Denver Tribune*, August 17, 1881, p. 1; and the published minutes of the Colorado Conference sessions from 1870 to 1896 (various titles).

65. Ann W. Hafen and LeRoy R. Hafen, "The Beginnings of Denver University," *The Colorado Magazine*, XXIV (March, 1947), 57-60.

66. *WRMN*, June 11, 1863, p. 2; July 30, 1863, p. 1; March 16, 1864, p. 2.

67. "An Act to Incorporate the Colorado Seminary," Colorado Territory, *General Laws* (1864), sec. 5, p. 209.

68. *Ibid.*; *WRMN*, March 16, 1864, p. 2.

69. Hafen and Hafen, *The Colorado Magazine*, XXIV (1947), 64-66. Isaac Haight Beardsley said that 103 students attended in the

first year. See his *Echoes from Peak and Plain; or Tales of Life, War, Travel and Colorado Methodism* (Cincinnati: Curts & Jennings, 1898), p. 391.

70. Beardsley, *Echoes from Peak and Plain*, pp. 392-93.

71. Hafen and Hafen, *The Colorado Magazine*, XXIV (1947), 62, n. 7, quoting the records of the Landon Abstract Company.

72. *DRMN*, July 23, 1871, p. 1.

73. Quoted in Beardsley, *Echoes from Peak and Plain*, p. 394.

74. Hafen and Hafen, *The Colorado Magazine*, XXIV (1947), 62, n. 7. In 1877, the Conference reported that Evans owned the seminary property outright. See Beardsley, *Echoes from Peak and Plain*, p. 395.

75. Smiley, *History of Denver*, p. 758.

76. Letter from John Evans to Margaret Evans, February 21, 1876, John Evans Collection.

77. *DRMN*, August 2, 1874, p. 4.

78. *Denver Tribune*, October 5, 1880, p. 8.

79. Michael McGiffert, *The Higher Learning in Colorado: An Historical Study, 1860-1940* (Denver: Sage Books, 1964), p. 18.

80. Beardsley, *Echoes from Peak and Plain*, p. 393.

81. *DRMN*, June 11, 1879, p. 4.

82. Smiley, *History of Denver*, p. 759.

83. *DRMN*, September 17, 1879, p. 8.

84. In accepting Evans' gift, the board valued the property at $20,000. This amount apparently did not include the seminary building, since the contribution was listed as "lots." See University of Denver, Minutes of the Board of Trustees, II, 26; Smiley, *History of Denver*, p. 759; Beardsley, *Echoes from Peak and Plain*, p. 396.

85. His contribution may have been higher. On December 16, Evans offered to match all contributions to a $25,000 fund to pay for the new wing and other necessary expenses. See University of Denver, Minutes of the Board of Trustees, II, 27, and *Denver Tribune*, December 17, 1880, p. 4. At the Colorado Conference meeting in 1881, it was announced that the wing had cost $16,000 and that Evans was one of the major contributors. See the *Minutes of the Nineteenth Session of the Colorado Annual Conference, Methodist Episcopal Church, Held at Leadville, Colorado, August 3-7, 1881* (Denver: Whipple & Pierson, 1881), p. 38 (referred to hereafter as *Colorado Conference Minutes*).

86. *Denver Tribune*, October 5, 1880, p. 8.

87. Beardsley, *Echoes from Peak and Plain*, p. 397.

88. Breck, *William Gray Evans*, p. 29.

89. Stone, *History of Colorado*, II, 8.

90. *Denver Republican*, November 4, 1888, p. 10. The school was an American girls' school, operated by a Mrs. Willard. See Bancroft MS, P-L329, Fol. III, 1, and Fol. IV, 2, 10.

91. "Anne Evans," *Who's Who in Colorado* (Boulder: Colorado Press Assoc., 1938), p. 255.

92. McGiffert, *Higher Learning in Colorado*, pp. 131-32.

93. *Ibid.*, 132.

94. *DRMN*, November 6, 1889, p. 4.

95. *DRMN*, June 16, 1889, p. 7; June 18, 1889, p. 4; August 11, 1889, p. 1.

96. Letters from John Evans to Margaret Evans, February 8, 1876, and February 21, 1876, John Evans Collection. In an earlier letter, Evans compared Colorado's anti-Catholic bigotry of 1876 to the Know Nothing movement in Illinois in the 1850's. Most of those who opposed the Catholic position on taxation of religious property in 1876, he said, "would like to tax the Catholics and be exempted themselves." See his letter to Margaret Evans, January 9, 1876, *ibid.* For a brief account of the religious controversies in the convention see Harold H. Dunham, "Colorado's Constitution of 1876," *Dicta*, XXXIV (March-April, 1959), 127-28.

97. *DRMN*, November 7, 1889, p. 4.

98. *DRMN*, January 12, 1891, p. 5.

99. *DRMN*, April 19, 1891, p. 3.

100. *DRMN*, January 1, 1892, p. 20.

101. Robert B. Rhode says that Evans' gifts to Denver University exceeded $150,000. See his "Governor John Evans, Builder of Two Universities" (unpublished Master's thesis, University of Denver, 1952), p. 199. While it is quite likely that his contributions reached this figure, the record simply does not show his total donations. His own financial records are confusing and incomplete. The University has never made an attempt to tabulate his contributions. The major gifts that can be verified are as follows: 1862, $500 (*WRMN*, December 11, 1862, p. 1); 1879, Evans' share in property worth $1,000 (this estimate is based on the fact that the trustees paid that amount for an adjoining lot; see University of Denver, Minutes of the Board of Trustees, II, 13); 1880, $23,000 (*ibid.*, 26); 1880, half of the amount contributed to pay the $16,000 cost of the new wing on the building and other costs (see *ibid.*, 27; *Colorado Conference Minutes, 1881*, 38); 1884, $1,000 (subscription of this amount is recorded in *DRMN*, December 15, 1884, p. 8); 1891, $100,000 (*DRMN*, January 1, 1892, p. 20). These amounts total about $133,000.

102. See, for example, the entries in his cash book for the period

January 1, 1881, to December 31, 1882, pp. 2-3, John Evans Collection. Hardly a week in his cash books fails to show sizable donations to charity.

103. LeRoy R. Hafen, "History of the State Historical Society of Colorado: I. The First Twenty Years," *The Colorado Magazine*, XXX (July, 1953), 166.

104. *Ibid.*, 174.

105. *DRMN*, November 25, 1888, p. 15; November 26, 1888, p. 2; November 21, 1889, p. 2.

106. *DRMN*, October 4, 1887, p. 4; October 5, 1887, p. 4.

107. *DRMN*, November 28, 1894, p. 4; December 21, 1894, p. 4; December 26, 1894, p. 6. See also the draft of a speech prepared by John Evans for delivery at a public meeting on the park question. An introduction by William G. Evans outlines John Evans' park ideas and explains that the speech was never given. The draft is in the John Evans Collection.

108. *DRMN*, November 2, 1887, p. 4; May 3, 1891, p. 14; *Denver Republican*, October 29, 1887, p. 8; February 28, 1888, p. 8; October 21, 1888, p. 7.

109. See the records of the Denver Probate Court, "Inventory of the Real and Personal Estate of John Evans," August 5, 1897, Estate No. 4522.

110. Smiley, *History of Denver*, p. 960.

111. Interview with John Evans II, July 26, 1961.

112. See the entries in his Journal, January 1, 1895-November 16, 1896, John Evans Collection. Beginning July 10, 1895 (p. 28) the entries show a constant effort on the part of Will and Evan to straighten out the accounts.

113. Stone, *History of Colorado*, II, 8.

114. See the Journal, January 1, 1895-November 16, 1896, John Evans Collection, p. 41, in which it is stated that "many charges and debits have never been entered." Other entries, on pages 40, 42, 44, and 71, tell a similar story.

115. See the Letters of Conservatorship, filed in Arapahoe County Court, November 18, 1896, records of the Denver Probate Court, Estate No. 4522. According to John Evans II (interview, July 26, 1961), Evans had invested most of his fortune in the Denver and New Orleans Railroad, and by the time of his death he was "nearly broke." Although his Arapahoe County real estate had an assessed valuation of $265,010 in 1886 (*Denver Tribune-Republican*, October 29, 1886, p. 2), and $403,590 in 1890 (assessed values were 35 per cent to 40 per cent of market values, according to *DRMN*, October

26, 1890, p. 27), his holdings dropped to a fraction of their original worth in the Panic of 1893. An "Inventory of the Real and Personal Estate of John Evans," filed by Margaret Evans, August 15, 1897 (records of the Denver Probate Court, Estate No. 4522), showed that the estate was worth nearly a million dollars, but there were heavy mortgages on the real estate holdings and stocks were "hypothecated." It took several years of careful management to realize the estate's real worth. Until then Mrs. Evans had to "pinch pennies." (Interview with John Evans II, July 26, 1961.) To complicate matters Evans died intestate, and several years of court proceedings were necessary to clear title to the estate.

116. According to a letter from Edgar McMechen to Richard C. Overton, February 27, 1952, Evans was not pleased with Bancroft's proposed biography, which was based on interviews made in Denver in 1889. See Overton's *Gulf to Rockies*, p. 47, n. 50. McMechen is obviously mistaken here, as is shown in a letter from Margaret Evans to John L. Smith, June 10, 1892, John Evans Collection; in this letter Mrs. Evans told Smith that Evans refused to pay for the biography simply because he understood that it was to be published without charge. Said Mrs. Evans: "He has always resisted all demands for money for that purpose though frequently applied to by publishers." The approach used by Bancroft's "solicitors" is detailed in John W. Caughey, *Hubert Howe Bancroft, Historian of the West* (Berkeley: University of California Press, 1946), pp. 313-23.

117. Pp. 445-47. The $1,500 price tag is listed in the Arapahoe County Court records, *James T. White & Co., Plaintiffs* v. *The Estate of John Evans Defendant* (1897), filed in records of the Denver Probate Court, Estate No. 4522.

118. *DRMN*, July 4, 1897, p. 1.

119. See, for example, the *Claim of J. N. Kinney* v. *The Estate of John Evans*, filed January 4, 1897, records of the Denver Probate Court, Estate No. 4522.

120. *DRMN*, July 3, 1897, p. 1.

121. *Ibid.*, July 4, 1897, p. 1.

122. Letter to Margaret Evans from the Denver Fortnightly Club, July 4, 1897, John Evans Collection. The state legislature named the mountain in honor of John Evans in a Joint Resolution approved March 5, 1895. See Colorado, General Assembly, *Senate Journal*, 10th Sess., 1895, Senate Joint Resolution No. 15, pp. 475, 553, 568.

123. *DRMN*, July 5, 1897, p. 1; July 6, 1897, p. 2; July 7, 1897, p. 1.

124. *Ibid.*, July 4, 1897, p. 12.

125. *Ibid.*, July 4, 1890, p. 7.

BIBLIOGRAPHY

Archival Material

LIBRARY COLLECTIONS

Abraham Lincoln Papers, Library of Congress. Microfilm.

Byers, William N. Letter books, Denver Public Library Western History Collection.

David Evans Papers. MSS in the library of the Ohio Historical Society, Columbus.

Draper, Benjamin Poff. "Manuscripts in the Bancroft Library Relating to Colorado." Undated, unpublished MS in the Denver Public Library Western History Collection.

Elbert, Samuel H. "Public Men and Measures."Bancroft MS, P-L 21. MS interview in the Bancroft Library, Berkeley, California.

Evans, John. Bancroft MSS, P-L329 and P-L23. MS interviews in the Bancroft Library, Berkeley, California.

Hall, Frank. MS letters in the library of the State Historical Society of Colorado, Denver.

John Evans Collection. MSS in the library of the State Historical Society of Colorado, Denver.

Lane Papers. William Henry Smith Memorial Library, Indiana Historical Society, Indianapolis.

Matthew Simpson Papers. MSS in the Library of Congress.

Robert Todd Lincoln Collection. Library of Congress. Microfilm.

Wynkoop, Edward W. "Wynkoop's Unfinished Colorado History." Unpublished MS, 1876, in the library of the State Historical Society of Colorado, Denver.

FEDERAL, STATE, AND COUNTY

City and County of Denver. Records of the Denver Probate Court, Estate of John Evans, No. 4522.

Colorado Bureau of Vital Statistics. Death Certificate of Evan E.

Evans, No. 5335.

Colorado Secretary of State. Corporation Records, books B and C. Colorado State Archives, Denver.

Colorado State Canvassing Board. Proceedings, August 19, 1861, to December 1, 1903. Colorado State Archives, Denver.

Colorado Territory. Executive Record, Book A. Colorado State Archives, Denver.

Colorado Territory. Letters of the Secretary of Colorado Territory. Colorado State Archives, Denver.

U.S. Bureau of the Census. Census of 1870. Inhabitants of the City of Denver. Microfilm.

U.S. Department of State. Applications and Recommendations for Office. National Archives.

U.S. Department of State. Territorial Papers, Colorado Series. Microfilm.

U.S. Bureau of Indian Affairs. Records of the Office of Indian Affairs. National Archives. Microfilm.

U.S. War Department. Records of the War Department, United States Army Commands, District of Colorado. National Archives. Microfilm.

Warren County, Ohio. Probate Court Records, Estate of David Evans. County Court House, Lebanon, Ohio.

Government Documents

CONGRESSIONAL DOCUMENTS

U.S. Congress, Senate. *An Act to Aid in the Construction of a Railroad and Telegraph Line from the Missouri River to the Pacific Ocean, and to Secure to the Government the Use of the Same for Postal, Military, and Other Purposes.* 37th Cong., 2nd Sess., 1862. Misc. Doc. No. 108.

U.S. Congress, Senate. "Massacre of Cheyenne Indians," *Report of the Joint Committee on the Conduct of the War.* 38th Cong., 2nd Sess., 1865. Report No. 142.

U.S. Congress, Senate. *Memorial of Doctor John Evans, Praying for the Establishment of a System of Quarantine for the Prevention of the Spread of Cholera.* 39th Cong., 1st Sess., 1866. Misc. Doc. No. 66.

U.S. Congress, Senate. *Memorial to Edwin Snow, M.D.* 39th Cong., 1st Sess., 1866. Misc. Doc. No. 85.

U.S. Congress, Senate. *Report of the Pacific Railway Commission.* 6 vols. 50th Cong., 1st Sess., 1887. Ex. Doc. No. 51.

U.S. Congress, Senate. *Report of the Secretary of War, Communicating, in Compliance with a Resolution of the Senate of February 4, 1867, a Copy of the Evidence Taken at Denver and Fort Lyon, Colorado Territory, by a Military Commission Ordered to Inquire into the Sand Creek Massacre, November, 1864.* 39th Cong., 2nd Sess., 1867. Doc. No. 26.

U.S. Congress, Senate. "The Chivington Massacre," *Condition of the Indian Tribes: Report of the Joint Special Committee Appointed under Joint Resolution of March 3, 1865.* 39th Cong., 2nd Sess., 1867. Doc. No. 156, pp. 26-98.

OTHER FEDERAL DOCUMENTS

Kappler, Charles J. (ed.). *Indian Affairs: Laws and Treaties.* 3 vols. Washington: Government Printing Office, 1904-27.

U.S. Library of Congress. *Index to the Abraham Lincoln Papers.* Washington: Government Printing Office, 1960.

U.S. War Department. *The War of the Rebellion: A Compilation of the Official Records of the Union and Confederate Armies.* 128 vols., 4 series. Washington: Government Printing Office, 1880-1901.

U.S. Department of the Interior. *Report of the Commissioner of Indian Affairs for the Year 1862.* Washington: Government Printing Office, 1863.

U.S. Department of the Interior. *Report of the Commissioner of Indian Affairs for the Year 1863.* Washington: Government Printing Office, 1864.

U.S. Department of the Interior. *Report of the Commissioner of Indian Affairs for the Year 1864.* Washington: Government Printing Office, 1865.

U.S. Department of the Interior. *Report of the Commissioner of Indian Affairs for the Year 1865.* Washington: Government Printing Office, 1866.

STATE DOCUMENTS

Colorado Division of State Archives and Public Records. *Colorado Territorial Officers and Members and Officers of the Legislative Assemblies under Territorial Government.* Denver: Colorado State

Archives, 1959.

Colorado General Assembly. *Senate Journal.* 10th Sess., 1895.

Colorado Territory. *General Laws* (1861).

Colorado Territory. *General Laws* (1862).

Colorado Territory. *General Laws* (1864).

Colorado Territory. *General Laws* (1865).

Evans, John. *Report on the Subject of Hospitals for the Insane, Made to the Commissioners of the Lunatic Asylum of Indiana, June 22, 1845.* Doc. No. 17 in *Documents of the General Assembly of Indiana.* Indianapolis: J. P. Chapman, 1845.

Indiana Board of Trustees of the Central Indiana Hospital for Insane. *Sixty-Seventh Annual Report of the Board of Trustees and Superintendent of the Central Indiana Hospital for Insane at Indianapolis, Indiana, for the Fiscal Year Ending September 30, 1915.* Indianapolis: Wm. B. Burford, 1915.

Indiana Commissioners of the Hospital for the Insane. *Fourth Annual Report of the Commissioners and Superintendent of the Hospital for the Insane to the General Assembly of the State of Indiana,* Doc. No. 1 in *Documents of the General Assembly of Indiana.* Indianapolis: John D. Defrees, 1848.

Indiana Commissioners of the Hospital for the Insane. *Second Annual Report of the Commission and Superintendent of the Hospital for the Insane to the General Assembly of the State of Indiana, October 31, 1846.* Doc. No. 5 in *Documents of the General Assembly of Indiana.* Indianapolis: J. P. Chapman, 1846.

Indiana Commissioners of the Hospital for the Insane. *Third Annual Report of the Commissioners and Superintendent of the Hospital for the Insane to the General Assembly of the State of Indiana.* Doc. No. 2 in *Documents of the General Assembly of Indiana.* Indianapolis: John D. Defrees, 1847.

Indiana Commissioners of the Lunatic Asylum. *Report of the Commissioners of the Lunatic Asylum to the General Assembly.* Doc. No. 16 in *Documents of the General Assembly of Indiana.* Indianapolis: J. P. Chapman, 1845.

Other Primary Sources

MANUSCRIPTS

Colorado Seminary. Minutes of the Proceedings of the Board of

Trustees of Colorado Seminary. Vol. II. University of Denver Archives.

Denver Council of the Union League of America. Minute Book. Library of the State Historical Society of Colorado, Denver.

Denver, South Park and Pacific Railway Company. Minute Book of the Board of Trustees of the Denver, South Park and Pacific Railway Company, October 1, 1872-March 19, 1889. 101 Years of Chicago, Burlington & Quincy Official Minute Books and Records. Microfilm in the Colorado State Archives, Denver.

Northwestern University. Minutes of the Board of Trustees. Northwestern University Archives. Microfilm.

BOOKS AND PAMPHLETS

Annual Report of the Burlington and Missouri River Railroad Co. to the Stockholders. Boston: Press of T. R. Marvin and Son, 1860.

Annual Report of the Directors of the Burlington and Missouri River Railroad Co. to the Stockholders. Boston: Press of T. R. Marvin and Son, 1859.

Basler, Roy P. (ed.). *The Collected Works of Abraham Lincoln.* New Brunswick, N.J.: Rutgers University Press, 1953.

Beardsley, Isaac Haight. *Echoes from Peak and Plain; or Tales of Life, War, Travel and Colorado Methodism.* Cincinnati: Curts and Jennings, 1898.

Bowles, Samuel. *The Switzerland of America: A Summer Vacation in the Parks and Mountains of Colorado.* Springfield, Mass.: Samuel Bowles and Company, 1869.

Confidential Statement, Denver and New Orleans R.R. Co. Denver: n.n., 1881.

Drake, Daniel. *Pioneer Life in Kentucky, 1785-1800.* Edited by Emmett Field Horine. New York: Henry Schuman, 1948.

Evans, John. *Reply of Governor Evans of the Territory of Colorado to That Part Referring to Him, of the Report of "The Committee on the Conduct of the War," Headed "Massacre of Cheyenne Indians."* Denver: n.n., 1865.

————. *Third Address on the Crises of Denver before the Denver Chamber of Commerce and Board of Trade.* Denver: n.n., 1886.

First Report of the President and Directors of the Cedar Rapids and Missouri River Rail Road. Chicago: Beach and Barnard, 1860.

Journal of the Thirty-fifth Session of the Colorado Annual Conference of the Methodist Episcopal Church Held at Colorado Springs, Colorado, August 25 to 30, 1897. Denver: Dove Printer, 1897.

337

Journal of the Thirty-fourth Session of the Colorado Annual Conference of the Methodist Episcopal Church, Held at Leadville, Colorado, August 26 to 31, 1896. Denver: Dove Printer, 1896.

Journal of the Twenty-fifth Session of the Colorado Annual Conference of the Methodist Episcopal Church, Held at Denver, Colorado, July 13 to 18, 1887. Denver: Dove General Book and Job Printer, 1887.

Journal of the Twenty-fourth Session of the Colorado Annual Conference of the Methodist Episcopal Church, Held at Greeley, Colorado, July 15 to 20, 1886. Denver: Dove General Book and Job Printer, 1886.

Journal of the Twenty-ninth Session of the Colorado Annual Conference of the Methodist Episcopal Church, Held at Denver, Colorado, June 10 to 13, 1891. Denver: The Shattuck Printing Company, 1891.

Lanier, James Franklin Doughty. *Sketches of the Life of J. F. D. Lanier.* 2nd ed. N.p.: J. F. D. Lanier, 1877.

Lunt, Cornelia Gray. *Sketches of Childhood and Girlhood: Chicago, 1847-1864.* Evanston, Ill.: Cornelia Gray Lunt, 1925.

Minutes of the Eighth Session of the Colorado Annual Conference, Held at Pueblo, Colorado Territory, June 23, 1870. Pueblo: Chieftain Book and Job Office, 1870.

Minutes of the Fourth Annual Session of the Kansas and Nebraska Conference of the Methodist E. Church Held at Omaha, Nebraska, April 14-18, 1859. Omaha: Robertson and Clark, 1859.

Minutes of the Kansas and Nebraska Annual Conference of the Methodist Episcopal Church, Fifth Session, Held in Leavenworth, K.T., March, 1860. Leavenworth, Kan.: Herald Book and Job Office, 1860.

Minutes of the Nineteenth Session of the Colorado Annual Conference, Methodist Episcopal Church, Held at Leadville, Colorado, August 3-7, 1881. Denver: Whipple and Pierson, 1881.

Minutes of the Seventeenth Session of the Colorado Annual Conference of the Methodist Episcopal Church, Held at Pueblo, Colorado, August 7-11, 1879. Denver: Whipple and Pierson, 1879.

Pierce, Bessie Louise and Joe L. Norris (eds.). *As Others See Chicago: Impressions of Visitors, 1673-1933.* Chicago: University of Illinois Press, 1933.

Pierce, John. *Report of the Board of Trustees to the Stockholders of the Denver Pacific Railway and Telegraph Company.* Denver: n.n., 1870.

Porter, Henry M. *Pencilings of an Early Western Pioneer.* Denver:

World Press, Inc., 1929.

Proceedings of the First Three Republican National Conventions of 1856, 1860 and 1864, Including Proceedings of the Antecedent National Convention Held at Pittsburg, in February, 1856, as Reported by Horace Greeley. Minneapolis: Charles W. Johnson, 1893.

Report of Business Manager and Treasurer of Northwestern University, Fiscal Year 1914-1915. Evanston, Ill.: Northwestern University, 1915.

Report of the Directors of the Burlington and Missouri River Railroad Co. to the Stockholders. Boston: Press of T. R. Marvin and Son, 1858.

Rives, F., and J. Rives. *The Congressional Globe: Containing the Debates and Proceedings of the First Session of the Thirty-ninth Congress.* Washington: Congressional Globe Office, 1866.

——————. *The Congressional Globe: Containing the Debates and Proceedings of the Second Session of the Thirty-ninth Congress.* Washington: Congressional Globe Office, 1867.

——————, and George A. Bailey. *The Congressional Globe: Containing the Debates and Proceedings of the First Session of the Fortieth Congress; Also, Special Session of the Senate.* Washington: Congressional Globe Office, 1867.

——————, and George A. Bailey. *The Congressional Globe: Containing the Debates and Proceedings of the Second Session, Fortieth Congress, Together with an Appendix Comprising the Laws Passed at That Session, and a Supplement Embracing the Proceedings in the Trial of Andrew Johnson.* Washington: Congressional Globe Office, 1868.

——————, and George A. Bailey. *The Congressional Globe: Containing the Debates and Proceedings of the Third Session, Fortieth Congress, Together with an Appendix Comprising the Laws Passed at That Session.* Washington: Congressional Globe Office, 1869.

Rives, John C. *The Congressional Globe: Containing the Debates and Proceedings of the First Session of the Thirty-eighth Congress.* Washington: Congressional Globe Office, 1864.

Root, Frank A., and William E. Connelley. *The Overland Stage to California.* Topeka, Kan.: Root and Connelley, 1901.

Ryus, William H. *The Second William Penn: A True Account of Incidents That Happened along the Old Santa Fe Trail in the Sixties.* Kansas City, Mo.: Frank T. Riley Publishing Company, 1913.

Smith, John Lewis. *Indiana Methodism: A Series of Sketches and*

Incidents Grave and Humorous Concerning Preachers and People of the West, with an Appendix Containing Personal Recollections, Public Addresses and Other Miscellany. Valparaiso, Ind.: n.n., 1892.

Speech of Ex-Gov. John Evans, President of the Denver and New Orleans Railroad, to the Stockholders of the Construction Company, Showing the Importance of that Enterprise in Making of Denver the Great Commercial and Manufacturing City of the New West. Denver: n.n., [1881].

Statement Regarding the Denver and New Orleans R.R., Its Important Connections, Progress of Construction, Business Prospects, Stock, Bonds, etc., Made May 20th, 1882. New York: E. Wells Sackett and Rankin, 1882.

Stern, Philip Van Doren (ed.). *The Life and Writings of Abraham Lincoln.* New York: Random House, 1940.

Third Annual Report of the Officers of the Denver Pacific Railway and Telegraph Company, Made at the Stockholders' Meeting, Held May 8, 1871. Denver: Woodbury and Walker, 1871.

Twenty-first Session of the Colorado Annual Conference of the Methodist Episcopal Church, Held at Denver, July 25-30, 1883. Denver: Whipple and Pierson, 1883.

Twenty-second Session of the Colorado Annual Conference of the Methodist Episcopal Church, Held at Longmont, August 7-10, 1884. Denver: Pierson and Gordon, 1884.

Wyeth, John Allen. *With Sabre and Scalpel: The Autobiography of a Soldier and Surgeon.* New York: Harper and Brothers, 1914.

ARTICLES AND ESSAYS

Ashley, Susan Riley. "Reminiscences of Early Colorado." *The Colorado Magazine*, XIV (March, 1937), 67-76.

Gregg, Isa Stearns (ed.). "Reminiscences of Isa Hunt Stearns." *The Colorado Magazine*, XXVI (July, 1949), 183-93.

Hall, Mrs. Frank. "Seventy Years Ago: Recollections of a Trip through the Colorado Mountains with the Colfax Party in 1868." *The Colorado Magazine*, XV (September, 1938), 161-68.

Hodder, Halie Riley. "Crossing the Plains in War Times." *The Colorado Magazine*, X (July, 1933), 131-37.

Lambert, Julie S. "Plain Tales of the Plains." *The Trail*, IX (June, 1916), 16-24.

"Nathaniel P. Hill Inspects Colorado: Letters Written in 1864." *The Colorado Magazine*, XXXIII (October, 1956), 241-76.

Simonin, Louis L. "Colorado in 1867 as Seen by a Frenchman." Translated by Wilson O. Clough, *The Colorado Magazine*, XIV (March, 1937), 56-63.

Smith, Joseph Emerson. "Personal Recollections of Early Denver." *The Colorado Magazine*, XX (January, 1943), 5-16.

Tobin, Thomas T. "The Capture of the Espinosas." *The Colorado Magazine*, IX (January, 1932), 59-66.

Witter, Mrs. Daniel. "Pioneer Life." *The Colorado Magazine*, IV (December, 1927), 165-74.

Secondary Sources

THESES AND DISSERTATIONS

Angel, Donald E. "A History of the University of Denver, 1880-1900." Unpublished Master's thesis, University of Denver, 1961.

Brandon, Barbara. "The Care of the Insane in Indiana, 1840-1890." Unpublished Master's thesis, University of Chicago, 1938.

Bridenhagen, Clement Francis. "John Evans: Western Railroad Builder." Unpublished Master's thesis, University of Denver, 1951.

Crane, John L. "Doctor John Evans, the Middlewestern Years, 1814-1862." Unpublished Master's thesis, University of Indiana, 1959.

Dunleavy, Jeannette Joan. "Early History of Colorado Seminary and the University of Denver." Unpublished Master's thesis, University of Denver, 1935.

Frazier, James L. "Early Stage Lines in Colorado." Unpublished Master's thesis, University of Denver, 1959.

Knittel, Bernard J. "John Evans: Speaker and Empire Builder." Unpublished doctoral dissertation, University of Denver, 1950.

Marlott, Gene R. "Edward W. Wynkoop: An Investigation of His Role in the Sand Creek Controversy and Other Indian Affairs, 1863-1868." Unpublished Master's thesis, University of Denver, 1961.

Mock, Samuel D. "Railroad Development in the Colorado Region to 1880." Unpublished doctoral dissertation, University of Nebraska, Lincoln, 1938.

Rhode, Robert B. "Governor John Evans, Builder of Two Universities." Unpublished Master's thesis, University of Denver, 1952.

BOOKS AND PAMPHLETS

A Catalogue of the Officers and Students of the Cincinnati College, in Its Medical, Law and Academical Departments for 1836-7. Cincinnati: N. S. Johnson, 1837.

Adams, Silas. *History of the Town of Bowdoinham, 1762-1912.* Fairfield, Me.: Fairfield Publishing Company, 1912.

Anderson, George L. *Kansas West.* San Marino, Calif.: Golden West Books, 1963.

Andreas, A. T. *History of Chicago from the Earliest Period to the Present Time.* 3 vols. Chicago: A. T. Andreas Company, 1884-86.

——————. *History of Cook County Illinois from the Earliest Period to the Present Time.* Chicago: A. T. Andreas, 1884.

——————. *History of the State of Nebraska: Containing a Full Account of Its Growth from an Uninhabited Territory to a Wealthy and Important State; of Its Early Settlements; Its Rapid Increase in Population, and the Marvellous Development of Its Great Natural Resources. Also an Extended Description of Its Counties, Cities, Towns and Villages, Their Advantages, Industries, Manufacturers and Commerce; Biographical Sketches, Portraits of Prominent Men and Early Settlers; Views of Residences and Business Blocks, Cities and Towns.* Chicago: The Western Historical Company, 1882.

Athearn, Robert G. *Rebel of the Rockies: A History of the Denver and Rio Grande Western Railroad.* New Haven: Yale University Press, 1962.

Bancroft, Hubert Howe. *Chronicles of the Builders of the Commonwealth: Historical Character Study.* 8 vols. San Francisco: The History Company, 1891-92.

——————. *History of Nevada, Colorado and Wyoming.* Vol. XXV of *The Works of Hubert Howe Bancroft.* 39 vols. San Francisco: The History Company, 1882-90.

Ballenger and Richards' Eighteenth Annual Denver City Directory, Containing a Complete List of the Inhabitants, Institutions, Incorporated Companies, Manufacturing Establishments, Business, Business Firms, etc., in the City of Denver for 1890. Denver: Ballenger and Richards, 1890.

Ballenger, J. H., T. B. Corbett, and W. C. Hoye. *Second Annual City Directory for 1874 of the Inhabitants, Institutions, Incorporated Companies, Manufacturing Establishments, Business, Business Firms, etc., in the City of Denver.* Denver: Corbett, Hoye and Company, 1874.

342

Beckwith, H. W. *History of Fountain County, Together with Historic Notes on the Wabash Valley, Gleaned from Early Authors, Old Maps, and Manuscripts, Private and Official Correspondence, and Other Authentic, Though, for the Most Part, Out-of-the-Way Sources.* Chicago: H. H. Hill and N. Iddings, 1881.

Bell, John Wesley. *The Development of the Public High School in Chicago.* Chicago: University of Chicago Libraries, 1939.

Berthrong, Donald J. *The Southern Cheyennes.* Norman: University of Oklahoma Press, 1963.

Bonner, Thomas Neville. *Medicine in Chicago, 1850-1950: A Chapter in the Social and Scientific Development of a City.* Madison, Wis.: The American History Research Center, Inc., 1957.

Brayer, Herbert O. *William Blackmore: The Spanish Mexican Land Grants of New Mexico and Colorado, 1863-1878.* 2 vols. Denver: Bradford-Robinson Printing Company, 1949.

Breck, Allen du Pont. *William Gray Evans, 1855-1924: Portrait of a Western Executive.* Vol. IV of *The University of Denver Department of History Series: The West in American History.* Denver: University of Denver, 1964.

Bronson, C. P. *Abstract of Elocution and Music, in Accordance with the Principles of Physiology and the Laws of Life, for the Development of Body and Mind.* Auburn, Ind.: H. Oliphant, 1842.

Buley, Roscoe Carlyle. *The Old Northwest: Pioneer Period, 1815-1850.* 2 vols. Bloomington, Ind.: Indiana University Press, 1951.

Byers, William N. *Encyclopedia of Biography of Colorado: History of Colorado.* Chicago: The Century Publishing and Engraving Company, 1901.

Caughey, John W. *Hubert Howe Bancroft: Historian of the West.* Berkeley: University of California Press, 1946.

Clark, O. S. *Clay Allison of the Washita, First a Cow Man and Then an Extinguisher of Bad Men; Recollections of Colorado, New Mexico and the Texas Panhandle; Reminiscences of a '79er.* N.p.: O. S. Clark, 1922.

Clark, John G. *The Grain Trade in the Old Northwest.* Urbana: University of Illinois Press, 1966.

Clark, Robert D. *The Life of Matthew Simpson.* New York: The Macmillan Company, 1956.

Corbett, Thomas B., and John H. Ballenger. *Corbett and Ballenger's Eleventh Annual Denver City Directory . . . for 1883.* Denver: Corbett and Ballenger Publishers, 1883.

—————. *Corbett and Ballenger's Ninth Annual Denver City*

Directory . . . for 1881. Denver: Rocky Mountain News Printing Co., 1881.

—————. *Corbett and Ballenger's Tenth Annual Denver City Directory . . . for 1882.* Denver: Corbett and Ballenger Publishers, 1882.

—————. *Corbett and Ballenger's Thirteenth Annual Denver City Directory . . . for 1885.* Denver: Corbett and Ballenger Publishers, 1885.

—————. *Corbett and Ballenger's Twelfth Annual Denver City Directory . . . for 1884.* Denver: Corbett and Ballenger Publishers, 1884.

Craig, Reginald S. *The Fighting Parson: The Biography of Colonel John M. Chivington.* Vol. XVII of *Great West and Indian Series.* Los Angeles: Westernlore Press, 1959.

Crooks, George R. *The Life of Bishop Matthew Simpson of the Methodist Episcopal Church.* New York: Harper and Brothers, 1890.

Danforth, Isaac Newton. *Life of Nathan Smith Davis, A.M., M.D., LL.D., 1817-1904.* Chicago: Cleveland Press, 1907.

Davis, Nathan Smith. *History of Medical Education and Institutions in the United States from the First Settlement of the British Colonies in America to the Year 1850; with a Chapter on the Present Condition and Wants of the Profession, and the Means Necessary for Supplying Those Wants, and Elevating the Character and Extending the Usefulness of the Whole Profession.* Chicago: S. C. Griggs and Company, 1851.

Dedicatory Exercises of the New Building of Rush Medical College. Introductory Lecture to the Thirty-fourth Annual Session, October 4, 1876. With an Appendix, Containing a Historical Sketch of the College; Proceedings at the Laying of the Cornerstone, Nov. 20th, 1875, Etc., Etc., Etc. Chicago: C. H. Blakeley and Company, 1876.

Dunn, Jacob P. *Indiana and Indianans.* 2 vols. Chicago: American Historical Society, 1919.

—————. *Greater Indianapolis: The History, the Industries, the Institutions, and the People of a City of Homes.* 2 vols. Chicago: Lewis Publ. Co., 1910.

Dupuy, Charles Meredith, and Herbert Dupuy. *A Genealogical History of the Dupuy Family.* Philadelphia: J. B. Lippincott Company, 1910.

Ellis, Elmer. *Henry Moore Teller: Defender of the West.* Caldwell, Idaho: The Caxton Printers Ltd., 1941.

Evans, John. *Address to the Graduating Class of Rush Medical Col-*

lege on the Nature, Utility, and Obligations of the Medical Profession, Delivered February 7, 1850. Chicago: C. A. Swan, 1850.

—————. *Memorial Praying for the Passage of Senate Bill No. 1, or Its Counterpart, House Bill No. 19*. Denver: n.n., 1885.

—————. *Observations on the Spread of Asiatic Cholera, and Its Communicable Nature*. Chicago: n.n., 1849.

—————. *Oreapolis, Nebraska Territory: Its Institutions, Advantages in Site, etc., etc. Plan of the Co. for Building up the Town, Inducements Offered to Emigrants to Settle There. Bonus for Manufacturers, Tradesmen, etc.* Chicago: Press and Tribune, 1859.

—————, J. B. Chaffee, and G. M. Chilcott. *Admission of Colorado: Memorial of Her Congressional Delegation*. Washington: Gibson and Brothers, 1866.

Evans, John II. *From Stagecoach to Space Age: 100 Years of Banking in the Rocky Mountain West (1860-1960)*. New York: The Newcomen Society, 1960.

Evans Memorial Chapel: University of Denver. [Denver: University of Denver, 1960.]

Fishbein, Morris (ed.). *A History of the American Medical Association, 1847 to 1947*. Philadelphia: W. B. Saunders Company, 1947

Galdston, Iago. *Progress in Medicine: A Critical Review of the Last Hundred Years*. New York: Alfred A. Knopf, 1940.

Grodinsky, Julius. *Jay Gould: His Business Career, 1867-1892*. Philadelphia: University of Pennsylvania Press, 1957.

Hafen, LeRoy R. *Colorado and Its People*. 4 vols. New York: Lewis Historical Publishing Company, 1948.

—————. *The Overland Mail, 1849-1869*. Cleveland: Arthur H. Clark Company, 1926.

—————, and James H. Baker. *History of Colorado*. 5 vols. Denver: Linderman Company, 1927.

Hall, Frank. *History of the State of Colorado: Embracing Accounts of the Pre-historic Races and Their Remains; the Earliest Spanish, French and American Explorations; the Lives of the Primitive Hunters, Trappers and Traders; the Commerce of the Prairies; the First American Settlements Founded; the Original Discoveries of Gold in the Rocky Mountains; the Development of Cities and Towns, with the Various Phases of Industrial and Political Transition, from 1858-1890*. 4 vols. Chicago: Blakeley Printing Company, 1889-95.

Heller, Herbert L. *Indiana Conference of the Methodist Church, 1832-1956*. Greencastle, Ind.: The Historical Society of the Indiana Conference, 1956.

Helm, Katherine. *The True Story of Mary, Wife of Lincoln, Containing the Recollections of Mary Lincoln's Sister Emilie (Mrs. Ben Hardin Helm), Extracts from Her War-Time Diary, Numerous Letters and Other Documents Now First Published.* New York: Harper and Brothers, 1928.

Hinshaw, William Wade. *Encyclopedia of American Quaker Genealogy.* 6 vols. Ann Arbor, Mich.: Edward Roos Brothers, Inc., 1946.

History of Warren County, Ohio, Containing a History of the County; Its Townships, Towns, Schools, Churches, etc.; General and Local Statistics; Portraits of Early Settlers and Prominent Men; History of the Northwest Territory; History of Ohio; Map of Warren County, Constitution of the United States, etc., etc. Chicago: W. H. Beers Co., 1882.

Hoig, Stan. *The Sand Creek Massacre.* Norman: University of Oklahoma Press, 1961.

Hollister, O. J. *Life of Schuyler Colfax.* New York: Funk and Wagnalls, 1886.

Hurd, Harvey B., and Robert D. Sheppard (eds.). *History of Northwestern University and Evanston.* Chicago: Munsell Publishing Company, 1906.

Hyde, James Nevins. *Early Medical Chicago: An Historical Sketch of the First Practitioners of Medicine, with the Present Faculties, and Graduates since their Organization, of the Medical Colleges of Chicago.* Chicago: Fergus Printing Company, 1879.

In Memoriam: Orrington Lunt. N.p.: n.n., n.d.

Jackson, Helen Hunt. *A Century of Dishonor: A Sketch of the United States Government's Dealings with Some of the Indian Tribes.* New York: Harper and Brothers, 1881.

James, Frank Cyril. *The Growth of Chicago Banks.* 2 vols. New York: Harper and Brothers, 1938.

Juettner, Otto. *Daniel Drake and His Followers: Historical and Biographical Sketches.* Cincinnati: Harvey Publishing Company, 1909.

Kennedy, R. P. *Historical Review of Logan County, Ohio.* Cincinnati: S. J. Clarke Publishers, 1903.

McGiffert, Michael. *The Higher Learning in Colorado: An Historical Study, 1860-1940.* Vol. III of *The University of Denver Department of History Series: The West in American History.* Denver: Sage Books, 1964.

McMechen, Edgar C. *The Moffat Tunnel of Colorado: An Epic of Empire.* Denver: Wahlgreen Publishing Company, 1927.

——————. *Life of Governor Evans, Second Territorial Governor of Colorado.* Denver: Wahlgreen Publishing Company, [1924].

Memorial of Cincinnati Monthly Meeting of Friends Concerning Our Deceased Friend, Jason Evans. Cincinnati: A. H. Pugh, 1877.

Minnich, Harvey C. *William Holmes McGuffey and His Readers.* New York: American Book Company, 1926.

Minot, George, and George P. Sanger (eds.). *The Statutes at Large and Treaties of the United States of America, from December 3, 1855 to March 3, 1859, and Proclamations since 1791, Arranged in Chronological Order with References to the Matter of Each Act and to the Subsequent Acts on the Same Subject.* Vol. XI. Boston: Little, Brown and Company, 1863.

Mohr, Philip E. (ed.). *American Medical Directory, 1956.* 19th ed. Chicago: American Medical Directory, 1956.

Mote, Luke Smith. *Early Settlements of Friends in the Miami Valley.* Edited by Willard Heiss. Indianapolis: John Woolman Press, Inc., 1961.

Norwood, William Frederick. *Medical Education in the United States before the Civil War.* Philadelphia: University of Pennsylvania Press, 1944.

O'Neall, John Belton. *The Annals of Newberry, Historical, Biographical, and Anecdotal.* Charleston, S.C.: S. G. Courtenay and Company, 1859.

Overton, Richard C. *Gulf to Rockies: The Heritage of the Fort Worth and Denver-Colorado and Southern Railway, 1861-1898.* Austin: University of Texas Press, 1953.

Parker, Nathan Howe. *The Kansas and Nebraska Handbook for 1857-8, with a New and Accurate Map.* Boston: John P. Jewett and Company, 1857.

Pennewell, Almer M. (ed.). *The Methodist Movement in Northern Illinois.* Sycamore, Ill.: The Sycamore Tribune, 1942.

Perkin, Robert L. *The First Hundred Years: An Informal History of Denver and the Rocky Mountain News.* Garden City, N.Y.: Doubleday and Company, Inc., 1959.

Pierce, Bessie Louise. *From Town to City, 1848-1871.* Vol. II of *A History of Chicago.* 2 vols. New York: Alfred A. Knopf, 1937-40.

Poor, Henry V. *Manual of the Railroads of the United States for 1883.* New York: H. V. and H. W. Poor, 1883.

—————. *Manual of the Railroads of the United States for 1884.* New York: H. V. and H. W. Poor, 1884.

—————. *Manual of the Railroads of the United States for 1887.* New York: H. V. and H. W. Poor, 1887.

—————. *Manual of the Railroads of the United States for 1889.* New York: H. V. and H. W. Poor, 1889.

Poor, Meredith C. *Denver, South Park & Pacific: A History of the Denver, South Park & Pacific Railroad and Allied Narrow Gauge Lines of the Colorado & Southern Railway Company.* Denver: Rocky Mountain Railroad Club, 1949.

Powell, Burt E. *The Movement for Industrial Education and the Establishment of the University, 1840-70.* Vol. I of *Semi-Centennial History of the University of Illinois.* 2 vols. Urbana: University of Illinois, 1918.

Pulse: Rush Medical College. Chicago: Rogers and Wells, 1895.

Randall, James G., and David Donald. *The Civil War and Reconstruction.* 2nd ed. Boston: D. C. Heath and Company, 1961.

Randall, Ruth Painter. *Mary Lincoln; Biography of a Marriage.* Boston: Little, Brown and Company, 1953.

Raum, Green Berry. *History of Illinois Republicanism, Embracing a History of the Republican Party in the State to the Present Time, Together with Its Noted Achievements, as Illustrated by the Careers of Men of Commanding Ability; with Biographies of Its Founders and Supporters Whose Foresight, Statesmanship, Patriotism and Energy Have Contributed to the Development of the Party in State and Nation; Also a Chronological Statement of Important Political Events since 1774.* Chicago: Rollins Publishing Company, 1900.

Renze, Dolores C., et al. *John Evans Collection Newspaper Index, 1862-1897.* Denver: Colorado State Archives, 1951.

Sandburg, Carl. *Abraham Lincoln: The War Years.* 4 vols. Sangamon edition. New York: Charles Scribner's Sons, 1944.

Scott, Walter Dill. *John Evans, 1814-1897: An Appreciation.* Evanston, Ill.: Lester J. Norris, 1939.

Simpson, Matthew. *Cyclopedia of Methodism, Embracing Sketches of Its Rise, Progress, and Present Condition, with Biographical Notices and Numerous Illustrations.* Philadelphia: Evarts and Stewart, 1878.

Smiley, Jerome C. (ed.). *History of Denver, with Outlines of the Earlier History of the Rocky Mountain Country.* Denver: Times-Sun Publishing Company, 1901.

Spring, Agnes Wright. *The First National Bank of Denver: The Formative Years, 1860-1865.* Denver: Bradford-Robinson Printing Company, [1960].

Stone, Wilbur F. *History of Colorado.* 4 vols. Chicago: S. J. Clarke Publishing Company, 1918.

Sugars, W. P. *Tales of a Forgotten Village.* Ypsilanti: University Lithoprinters, Inc., 1953.

Sulgrove, Berry R. *History of Indianapolis and Marion County,*

Indiana. Philadelphia: L. H. Everts and Company, 1884.

Summer, George Leland. *Newberry County South Carolina.* N.p.: George Leland Summer, 1950.

Sweet, William Warren. *Indiana Asbury-DePauw University, 1837-1937: A Hundred Years of Higher Education in the Middle West.* New York: The Abingdon Press, 1937.

Sweitzer, Robert M. *The Sisters of Mercy and Chicago: Diamond Jubilee.* Chicago: Sisters of Mercy, 1921.

Thomas, Allen C., and Richard Henry Thomas. *A History of the Friends in America.* Pennbury Series of Modern Quaker Books. 6th ed. Philadelphia: John E. Winston Company, 1930.

Trottman, Nelson. *History of the Union Pacific: A Financial and Economic Survey.* New York: The Ronald Press Company, 1923.

Wade, Richard C. *The Urban Frontier: The Rise of Western Cities, 1790-1830.* Cambridge, Mass.: Harvard University Press, 1959.

Walters, Raymond. *Historical Sketch of the University of Cincinnati.* Cincinnati: Mountel Press, 1940.

Ward, Estelle Frances. *The Story of Northwestern University.* New York: Dodd, Mead and Company, 1924.

Webb, Constance Bell. *A History of Contagious Disease Care in Chicago before the Great Fire.* Chicago: University of Chicago Press, 1940.

Weeks, Stephen B. *Southern Quakers and Slavery: A Study in Institutional History.* Extra Volume XV in *Johns Hopkins University Studies in Historical and Political Science.* Edited by Herbert B. Adams. Baltimore: Johns Hopkins University Press, 1896.

Wharton, J. E. *History of the City of Denver from the Earliest Settlement to the Present Time, to Which Is Added a Full and Complete Business Directory of the City by D. O. Wilhelm.* Denver: Byers and Dailey, 1866.

Whicker, J. Wesley. *Historical Sketches of the Wabash Valley.* Attica, Ind.: *n.d.,* 1916.

Wilde, Arthur Herbert. *Northwestern University: A History, 1855-1905.* 2 vols. New York: The University Publishing Society, 1905.

Wilder, Walter L. *Robert Wilbur Steele: Defender of Liberty.* Denver: Carson-Harper Company, 1913.

Willard, Frances E. *A Classic Town: The Story of Evanston.* Chicago: Women's Temperance Publishing Association, 1892.

Wright, John W. *Chivington Massacre of Cheyenne Indians.* N.p.: Gideon and Pearson, Printers, [1865].

Young, Andrew W. *History of Wayne County, Indiana, from Its First Settlement to the Present Time, with Numerous Biographical and Family Sketches. Embellished with Upwards of Fifty Portraits of Citizens and Views of Buildings.* Cincinnati: R. Clarke and Company, 1872.

ARTICLES AND ESSAYS

Adams, Evelyn C. "The Growing Concept of Social Responsibility Illustrated by a Study of the State's Care of the Insane in Indiana." *Indiana Magazine of History*, XXXII (March, 1936), 1-22.

"Anne Evans." *Who's Who in Colorado.* Boulder: Colorado Press Association, 1938, 255.

Axelrod, Bernard. "Rocky Mountain Customs Port of Entry." *The Colorado Magazine*, XLI (Spring, 1964), 126-34.

Bassoe, Peter. "The Early History of Neurology and Psychiatry in the Middle West." *Bulletin of the Society of Medical History of Chicago*, III (October, 1923), 175-90.

Blaney, James V. Z. "Dr. Drake and the Rush Medical College." *Illinois Medical and Surgical Journal*, I (December, 1844), 135.

—————. Review of *Address on Insanity and the Establishment of a Lunatic Asylum* by John Evans. *Illinois Medical and Surgical Journal*, I (April, 1844), 30-31.

Brayer, Herbert O. "History of Colorado Railroads." *Colorado and Its People.* Vol. II. Edited by LeRoy R. Hafen. 4 vols. New York: Lewis Historical Publishing Company, 1948. 635-90.

Burgess, Kenneth F. "John Evans and the New West." *Program of Reception in Commemoration of Dr. John Evans, 1814-1897.* Evanston, Ill.: Northwestern University, 1951.

Cannon, Helen. "First Ladies of Colorado: Josephine Evans Elbert." *The Colorado Magazine*, XXXIX (October, 1962), 263-69.

—————. "First Ladies of Colorado: Margaret Gray Evans." *The Colorado Magazine*, XXXIX (January, 1962), 18-28.

Carey, Raymond G. "Another View of the Sand Creek Massacre." *The Denver Westerners Monthly Roundup*, XVI (February, 1960), 4-15.

Carr, Elizabeth F. "Dr. John Evans: The Medical Career of the Founder of Northwestern University." *Quarterly Bulletin of Northwestern University Medical School*, XXV (Summer, 1951), 113-17.

"Catalogue of the Medical Department of the Cincinnati College for 1837-8." *The Western Journal of the Medical and Physical Sciences*, XI (January, February, and March, 1838), 665-70.

"Chicago Medical Society." *The North-Western Medical and Surgical Journal*, III (May, 1850), 88.

Clark, Robert D. "Bishop Matthew Simpson and the Emancipation Proclamation." *Mississippi Valley Historical Review*, XXXV (September, 1948), 263-71.

——————, "The Medical Training of Matthew Simpson, 1830-1833." *Ohio State Archeological and Historical Quarterly*, LXI (October, 1952), 371-79.

Covington, James Warren. "Federal Relations with the Colorado Utes." *The Colorado Magazine*, XXVIII (October, 1951), 257-66.

Davis, Nathan Smith. "History of the Medical Profession from the First Settlement of the British Colonies in America to the Year 1850." *The North-Western Medical and Surgical Journal*, III (November, 1850), 267-88.

——————. "The Cholera and the Influences Which Favor or Retard Its Spread or Diffusion." *The North-Western Medical and Surgical Journal*, II (September, 1849), 482.

Davis, Nathan Smith, III. "Nathan Smith Davis, M.D., A.M., LL.D." *A History of the American Medical Association, 1847 to 1947*. Edited by Morris Fishbein. Philadelphia: W. B. Saunders Company, 1947. 3-16.

Drake, Daniel. "Our Institution." *The Western Journal of the Medical and Physical Sciences*, XI (July, August, and September, 1837), 335-36.

Dunham, Harold H. "Colorado's Constitution of 1876." *Dicta*, XXXIV (March-April, 1959), 121-30.

DuSouchet, F. D. "John Evans." *Dictionary of American Medical Biography*. Edited by Howard A. Kelly and Walter Burrage. New York: D. Appleton and Company, 1928. 390-91.

Edenharter, George F. "History and Notes of the Central Indiana Hospital for the Insane, 1832-1915." *Sixty-seventh Annual Report of the Board of Trustees and Superintendent of the Central Indiana Hospital for Insane at Indianapolis, Indiana for the Fiscal Year Ending September 30, 1915*. Indianapolis: William B. Burford, 1915. 100-166.

Elliot, Frank M. "Evanston Real Estate." *History of Northwestern University and Evanston*. Edited by Harvey B. Hurd and Robert D. Sheppard. Chicago: Munsell Publishing Company, 1906. 295-302.

Ellis, Elmer. "Colorado's First Fight for Statehood." *The Colorado Magazine*, VIII (January, 1931), 23-30.

"Evan E. Evans." *The Trail*, XIV (July, 1921), 30-31.

Evans, John. "American Medical Association." *The Northwestern Medical and Surgical Journal*, II (July, 1849), 160-75.

—————. "American Medical Association." *The North-Western Medical and Surgical Journal,* III (July, 1850), 162-76.

—————. "First Annual Meeting of the American Medical Association." *The North-Western Medical and Surgical Journal,* I (June and July, 1848), 180-82.

—————. "Free Medical Schools." *The North-Western Medical and Surgical Journal,* III (September, 1850), 258-60.

—————. "Illinois General Hospital of the Lake." *The North-Western Medical and Surgical Journal,* III (September, 1850), 263.

—————. "Indiana Hospital for the Insane." *The North-Western Medical and Surgical Journal,* IV (January, 1852), 371-78.

—————. "Notice to Subscribers—Extension of Time." *The North-Western Medical and Surgical Journal,* IV (March, 1852), 471.

—————. "Notice to Subscribers: New Arrangement." *The North-Western Medical and Surgical Journal,* IV (January, 1852), 381.

—————. "Observations on Insanity and Its Treatment in Private Practice." *Illinois and Indiana Medical and Surgical Journal,* I (October, 1846), 289-324.

—————. "Observations on the Use of the Obstetrical Extractor." *The North-Western Medical and Surgical Journal,* IV (May, 1851), 40-46.

—————. Review of D. Humphreys, "Report on Obstetrics." (*Transactions of the American Medical Association,* Philadelphia: T. R. and P. G. Collins, 1852), in *The North-Western Medical and Surgical Journal,* IV (March, 1852), 424-26.

—————. Review of *First Biennial Report of the Trustees of the Illinois State Hospital for the Insane,* in *The North-Western Medical and Surgical Journal,* I (February and March, 1849), 503-04.

—————. Review of *Fourth Annual Report of the Commissioners and Superintendent of the Hospital for the Insane to the General Assembly of the State of Indiana,* in *The North-Western Medical and Surgical Journal,* I (February and March, 1849), 501-02.

—————. "Rush Medical College." *The North-Western Medical and Surgical Journal,* I (February and March, 1849), 548.

—————. "The Cholera." *The North-Western Medical and Surgical Journal,* II (July, 1849), 178-79.

—————. "The Concours." *The North-Western Medical and Surgical Journal,* II (January, 1850), 458-59.

—————. "The Obstetrical Extractor—A Paper Read before the Chicago Medical Society." *The North-Western Medical and Surgical Journal,* III (May, 1850), 53-62.

—————. "Treatment of the Fracture of the Clavicle." *Illinois*

Medical and Surgical Journal, I (December, 1844), 133-43.

————. "Two Cases [of] Uterine Hydatids." *Illinois Medical and Surgical Journal*, II (May, 1845), 17-20.

Evans Realty Remarks (May, 1947), leaflet.

"Free Medical Schools." *The North-Western Medical and Surgical Journal*, II (November, 1849), 365-69.

Fritz, Percy S. "Mining in Colorado." *Colorado and Its People.* Vol. II. Edited by LeRoy R. Hafen, 4 vols. New York: Lewis Historical Publishing Company, 1948. 486-514.

Furnas, Davis. "History of Miami Monthly Meeting, Hicksite— from 1828 to 1903." *Proceedings, Centennial Anniversary Miami Monthly Meeting, Waynesville, Ohio, 10th Month, 16-17, 1903.* Waynesville, Ohio: Press of Miami Gazette, n.d. 43-48.

Gilmore, G. H. "Ghost Towns in Cass County, Nebraska." *Nebraska History Magazine*, XVIII (July-September, 1937), 181-84.

Goodykoontz, Colin B. "The Settlement of Colorado." *History of Colorado.* Vol. II. Edited by LeRoy R. Hafen and James H. Baker. 5 vols. Denver: Linderman Company, 1927. 429-74.

Hafen, Ann W. and LeRoy R. Hafen. "The Beginnings of Denver University." *The Colorado Magazine*, XXIV (March, 1947), 58-66.

Hafen, LeRoy R. "Elbridge Gerry, Colorado Pioneer." *The Colorado Magazine*, XXIX (April, 1952), 137-49.

————. "History of the State Historical Society of Colorado: I. The First Twenty Years." *The Colorado Magazine*, XXX (July, 1953), 161-85.

Hagie, C. E. "Gunnison in Early Days." *The Colorado Magazine*, VIII (July, 1931), 121-29.

Hemenway, Henry Bixby. "Medical History (Regular)." *History of Northwestern University and Evanston.* Edited by Harvey B. Hurd and Robert D. Sheppard. Chicago: Munsell Publishing Company, 1906. 245-54.

Herrick, W. B. "Appointment of Demonstrator of Anatomy in Rush Medical College." *The North-Western Medical and Surgical Journal*, II (January, 1850), 457-58.

————. "The Cholera." *The North-Western Medical and Surgical Journal*, I (December, 1848-January, 1849), 452-53.

Hewett, Edgar L. "Tom Tobin." *The Colorado Magazine*, XXIII (September, 1946), 210-11.

"Hon. Isaac N. Arnold." *The National Magazine*, XV (November, 1891), 62-66.

"Illinois General Hospital." *The North-Western Medical and Surgical Journal*, III (March, 1851), 492-93.

"James Harlan." *Appleton's Cyclopaedia of American Biography*, III, 83-84. New York: D. Appleton and Company, 1888.

James, James Alton. "Northwestern University and the Christian Ideals of Its Founders." *The Methodist Movement in Northern Illinois*. Edited by Almer M. Pennewell. Sycamore, Ill.: The Sycamore Tribune, 1942. 132-45.

"John Evans." *The National Cyclopedia of American Biography*, VI, 445-47. New York: James T. White and Company, 1896.

Lecompte, Janet. "Charles Autobees." *The Colorado Magazine*, XXXV (July, 1958), 219-25.

———. "Sand Creek." *The Colorado Magazine*, XLI (Fall, 1964), 327-30.

Leikind, Morris C. "Quarantine in the United States." *Ciba Symposium*, II (September, 1940), 581-82.

McMechen, Edgar C. "A Forest Home in the Mountains of Colorado." *House Beautiful*, XLII (June, 1917), 22-23.

———. "Ouray Memorial Park Acquired by the State Historical Society." *The Colorado Magazine*, XXII (July, 1945), 159.

McClung, Quantrille D. "Colorado Governors: John Evans—2nd Territorial Governor, 1862-65." *The Colorado Genealogist*, XV (July, 1954), 65-69.

"Marion's Past Masters." *The Booster of Marion Lodge No. 35, F.&A.M.*, XXIII (December, 1947), 1, 5-6.

"Matthew Simpson." *Appleton's Cyclopaedia of American Biography*, V, 538-39. New York: D. Appleton and Company, 1888.

"Medical Department of Cincinnati College." *The Western Journal of the Medical and Physical Sciences*, XI (April, May, and June, 1837), 168.

Mock, Samuel D. "Colorado and the Surveys for a Pacific Railroad." *The Colorado Magazine*, XVII (March, 1940), 54-63.

———. "The Financing of Early Colorado Railroads." *The Colorado Magazine*, XVIII (November, 1941), 201-09.

"The Mountain and the Man: A Tribute to Our First Worshipful Master." *The Booster of Marion Lodge No. 35, F.&A.M.*, XXIII (May-June, 1947), 3-4.

Neil, William N. "The Territorial Governor as Indian Superintendent in the Trans-Mississippi West," *Mississippi Valley Historical Review*, XLIII (September, 1956), 213-37.

Overton, Richard C. "The Colorado and Southern Railway." *The Colorado Magazine*, XXVI (April, 1949), 81-98.

Plummer, John T. "Reminiscences of the History of Richmond." *A Directory of the City of Richmond, Containing Names, Business*

and Residence of the Inhabitants, Together with a Historical Sketch.
Richmond, Ind.: R. O. Dormer and W. R. Holloway, 1857. 9-63.

Pusey, William Allen. "High Lights in the History of Chicago Medicine." *Bulletin of the Society of Medical History of Chicago*, V (May, 1940), 159-207.

Ross, Earle Dudley. "James Harlan." *Dictionary of American Biography*, VIII, 268. Centenary edition. New York: Charles Scribner's Sons, 1946.

Sanford, Albert B. "Organization and Development of Colorado Territory." *History of Colorado.* Vol. II. Edited by LeRoy R. Hafen and James H. Baker. Denver: Linderman Company, 1927. 475-523.

Selby, Paul. "The Editorial Convention of 1856." *Journal of the Illinois State Historical Society*, V (October, 1912), 343-49.

Seybolt, Robert Francis. "Jonathan Baldwin Turner." *Dictionary of American Biography*, XIX, 68. Centenary edition. New York: Charles Scribner's Sons, 1946.

"Since 1851 Men of Vision have Guided Northwestern." *Northwestern University Alumni News*, XXXI (October, 1951), 12.

Smith, H. E. "The Quakers, Their Migration to the Upper Ohio, Their Customs and Discipline." *Ohio Archaeological and Historical Publications*, XXXVII (1928), 35-85.

Smith, Horace G. "Garrett Biblical Institute." *The Methodist Movement in Northern Illinois.* Edited by Almer M. Pennewell. Sycamore, Ill.: The Sycamore Tribune, 1942. 113-31.

Starr, Harris Elwood. "Sarah Tittle Barrett Bolton." *Dictionary of American Biography*, II, 424. Centenary edition. New York: Charles Scribner's Sons, 1946.

Teetor, Henry Dudley. "Hon. John Evans, War Governor of Colorado." *The Magazine of Western History*, IX (April, 1889), 722-25.

Temple, Wayne C. "Lincoln's Fence Rails." *Journal of the Illinois State Historical Society*, XLVII (Spring, 1954), 20-34.

Thomas, Charles S. "Fifty Years of Political History." *History of Colorado.* Vol. III. Edited by LeRoy R. Hafen and James H. Baker. Denver: Linderman Company, 1927. 901-56.

Thomas, John Hardin. "The Academies of Indiana." *Indiana Magazine of History*, X (December, 1914), 331-58.

"To Our Patrons." *The North-Western Medical and Surgical Journal*, I (February and March, 1849), 535.

"To Subscribers." *The North-Western Medical and Surgical Journal*, II (March, 1850), 548.

Unrau, William E. "A Prelude to War." *The Colorado Magazine*, XLI (Fall, 1964), 299-313.

"Walter Bennett Scates." *Appleton's Cyclopaedia of American Biography*, V, 414. New York: D. Appleton and Company, 1888.

Whicker, J. Wesley. "Dr. John Evans." *Indiana Magazine of History*, XIX (September, 1923), 226-40.

White, Carl F. "Lengthened Shadow of a Man." *The Indiana Freemason*, XXIV (May, 1947), 14-15, 30-38.

Willard, James F. "John Evans," *Dictionary of American Biography*, VI, 204. Centenary edition. New York: Charles Scribner's Sons, 1946.

SPEECHES AND INTERVIEWS

Interview of Helen Cannon, July 18, 1961.

Interview of John Evans, II, July 26, 1961.

Yungmeyer, D. W. "John Evans, Chicago's Forgotten Railroad Pioneer." Paper read at the Centennial Observance of Northwestern University, Evanston, Illinois, February 21, 1951.

Newspapers

Chicago Daily News, June, 1890; February, 1891.

Chicago Tribune, October, 1862-July 4, 1897.

Cincinnati Enquirer, March 23, 1958.

Daily Commonwealth [Denver], November, 1863-June, 1864.

Daily Democratic Press [Chicago], November, 1854-January, 1858.

Daily Illinois State Journal [Springfield], May, 1856-May, 1860.

Daily Miners' Register [Central City, Colorado], June, 1864.

Daily Mining Journal [Black Hawk, Colorado], June, 1864-September, 1864.

Daily Rocky Mountain News [Denver], March, 1862-September, 1906.

Denver Republican, January, 1881-August, 1884; January, 1887-December, 1888.

Denver Times, May, 1877; May-June, 1881; June, 1921.

Denver Tribune, January, 1880-June, 1884.

Denver Tribune-Republican, August, 1884-December, 1886.

Evanston [Illinois] *Index*, September, 1872; April, 1887; June, 1890; June, 1894.

Evanston [Illinois] *Press*, July 10, 1897.

Illinois Daily Journal [Springfield], June, 1852.

Miami Gazette [Waynesville, Ohio], May 9, 1885.
Nebraska Herald [Plattsmouth], May 3, 1865.
Northwestern Christian Advocate [Chicago], December, 1868.
Press and Tribune [Chicago], February, 1860.
The Methodist [New York], May 6, 1865.
Weekly Rocky Mountain News [Denver], March, 1862-March, 1869.

Picture Credits

Page 3, Ohio Historical Society Library; 4, Cincinnati *Enquirer*,
March 23, 1958; 7, Bronson, *Abstract of Elocution*, p. 70; 10, Ohio
Historical Society Library; 12, *Curator*, IX (September, 1966), p.
250; 19, Ohio Historical Society Library; 45, Northwestern University
Medical Society Library; 50, *Dedicatory Exercises of the New Build-
ing of Rush Medical College*, p. 32; 57, Chicago Historical Society;
62, John Evans Collection, State Historical Society of Colorado
Library; 67, Chicago *Tribune*, July 4, 1897; 71, State Historical
Society of Colorado Library; 76, Illinois State Historical Society; 83,
Illinois State Historical Society; 89, Northwestern University Archives;
93, John Evans Collection, State Historical Society of Colorado Li-
brary; 98, Northwestern University Archives; 116, State Historical
Society of Colorado Library; 119, Denver Public Library Western
Collection; 128, State Historical Society of Colorado Library; 143,
147, Tutt Library, The Colorado College, Colorado Springs; 148,
State Historical Society of Colorado Library; 178, John Evans Col-
lection, State Historical Society of Colorado Library; 185, 190, State
Historical Society of Colorado Library; 213, *History of the City of
Denver, Arapahoe County, and Colorado* (Chicago: O. L. Baskin and
Co., 1880), p. 27; 217, Denver Public Library Western Collection;
220, *History of the City of Denver*, p. 27; 223, Denver Public Library
Western Collection; 227, *History of the City of Denver*, opp. p. 22.

357

INDEX

370

This book is based on the Ph.D. dissertation by Harry E. Kelsey for the University of Denver, Department of History, in 1965. Design and editing were by the staff of the State Historical Society of Colorado. The text type is Times Roman, and display is Craw Clarendon Book and Century Schoolbook and Expanded Italic. Printing is offset lithography on 70 lb. Warren's Olde Style Antique Wove paper.